_Children with Specific Learning
Difficulties_
A Critical Review of Research

Paula Tansley
John Panckhurst

NFER-NELSON

Published by The NFER-NELSON Publishing Company Ltd,
Darville House, 2 Oxford Road East,
Windsor, Berkshire SL4 1DF

First Published 1981
Reprinted 1982, 1984, 1985, 1986, 1987 (twice), 1988, 1989, 1991
© NFER-NELSON, 1981
ISBN 0-85633-216-X
Code 8070 02 1

Typeset by Unicus Graphics Ltd, Horsham, West Sussex

Printed and bound in Great Britain by
Antony Rowe Ltd, Chippenham, Wilts

Contents

Contents

Contents

Introduction

The problems of children with specific learning difficulties have for many years caused concern to parents and teachers and distress to the children themselves. At the same time there has been a great deal of research into the causes and nature of these difficulties and how they might be overcome or alleviated.

The Department welcomes the publication by the National Foundation for Educational Research of this wide-ranging review of research. The review makes it clear that the problems are complex and that there are no simple and universally effective solutions. As the appendix indicates, the Department has recognized the need for further research directed principally towards improving the skills of teachers in identifying children with specific learning difficulties, in assessing their needs, and in meeting those needs in the classrooms.

However, although there is more to be discovered, there is need, as the Warnock Report expresses it, to 'pay greater attention to what is already known and make a more discriminating approach to children with reading, writing and spelling difficulties'. The Department commends the review to those working in the field of specific learning difficulties and to those engaged in in-service training. A shortened version of the detailed review is planned for separate publication.

Department of Education and Science
Elizabeth House
York Road
London SE1 7PH
April 1980

Acknowledgements

We would like to thank the following people for their help at various stages during the preparation of this review:

Dr H. T. Chasty, Director of Studies, Dyslexia Institute; Mrs B. Hornsby, Director of the Dyslexia Clinic, St Bartholomew's Hospital; Professor T. Miles, Dyslexia Unit, Psychology Department, University of North Wales; and Mrs B. Wattles, Hon. Sec., Cambridge Specific Learning Disabilities Group, for their assistance in giving a sense of perspective to the field of learning difficulties.

Helen Beaglehole, Jenny Stockley and Ola White, for their painstaking reading of references.

Sarah Gerrard, Deputy Librarian, for her invaluable assistance and advice, given cheerfully and unstintingly.

Dr Seamus Hegarty, our Principal Research Officer, for his useful comments and unwavering support.

Hilary Hosier, Christine Negus, Lorna Ormand and Jane Pagett, for their fast and accurate typing under pressure of time.

Chapter 1

Background and Preview

Background to the project

The National Foundation for Educational Research in England and Wales undertook this critical review of research, relating to the *Assessment and Education of Children with Specific Learning Difficulties*, at the invitation of the Department of Education and Science. The review is intended to inform a committee of experts set up to advise the DES on research about, and provision for, children with specific learning difficulties.

The review proposal reads:

> It is proposed to carry out a critical review of research into the problems of assessing and making appropriate educational provision for children with specific learning difficulties. The review will concentrate on research carried out in this country, but will also take account of the major American and Scandinavian contributions to the literature. The review will be an evaluative one and will be written up in a form suitable for publication, although the main purpose of the exercise will be to produce a substantial background paper for the DES ad hoc committee.

It was agreed that the present review would most usefully examine work in three areas:

(i) Definitions and symptoms: clarification of what constitutes specific learning disability; this is seen as essential before intervention can be attempted.

(ii) Remedial methods: to establish what methods, and intervention programmes, have been used successfully with children with specific learning disabilities.

(iii) Incidence: to give information on implications for personnel and resources if the needs of children with specific learning disabilities are to be met.

Our prime concern is with children who exhibit severe difficulties in reading. However, there is evidence that other areas such as spelling, writing, arithmetic and speech may also be involved. Consequently, a short section dealing with these associated problems is included although pressures of time and space have not made it possible to consider them in great detail.

In the early stages of the project, it became evident that the amount of literature available on this topic was large and so it was decided to concentrate primarily on work published since 1968. Equally, it was obvious that research in this area tends to be dominated by American studies. However, we have tried to focus on British research but set against an international backdrop which takes into account work carried out in other countries.

The concern with specific learning difficulties in Britain

The history of specific learning difficulties in Britain can be looked at from two perspectives: private initiatives and state involvement.

Private sector

There have been two separate but related paths of development in the private sector. First, the concern of parents, whose children were not learning to read despite adequate intelligence, freedom from physical or emotional defect and conventional instruction, led to the setting up of voluntary local dyslexia associations. Eight local associations were created between 1965 (the first was formed at Bath) and 1972 when the British Dyslexia Association was formed as a national co-ordinating organization. Local dyslexia associations consist of parents, teachers, psychologists and anyone interested in the problem of dyslexia. The aims of the BDA are to promote understanding of the problem of dyslexia and to support research into all aspects of the problem. Since 1977 it has had formal links with the DES, and regular meetings are held twice yearly to discuss developments. The BDA is also in contact with international organizations concerned with learning disabilities.

Secondly, a number of organizations became involved in offering treatment, teacher training and research. St Bartholomew's Hospital commenced treating dyslexia in the early 1950s and is continuing to do so. The Word Blind Centre, established by the Invalid Children's Aid Association, was opened in 1963 but was forced to close some nine years later due to lack of funds. In 1969 the British Council for the Rehabilitation of the Disabled took a major initiative in setting up a national working party at the request of the Department of Employment to study the problems of dyslexia in adults. The Working Party Report, *People with Dyslexia*, was published in 1974. In 1972 the Council also opened a clinic offering treatment and teacher training.

The Dyslexia Institute, sponsored by the North Surrey Dyslexia Society, was established in 1972. This organization, which now has branches in many parts of the country is privately financed – mainly from fees charged to clients. The services provided by the Institute include:

1. Specialist teaching for dyslexics
2. Educational and psychological assessment
3. Courses for teachers
4. Advisory service for parents and teachers
5. Research

Both private individuals and local education authorities can, and do, refer children and adults for assessment and treatment. The Dyslexia Institute publishes a journal, *Dyslexia Review*, which includes items of topical interest to those in the field (both parents and teachers) and research reports.

Another example of an organization concerned with research and practical help in the area of developmental learning difficulties is the Cambridge Specific Learning Disabilities Group. This multi-disciplinary group was set up in 1975 with the following aims:

1. To set up a research register and provide an information and resources service.
2. To review existing screening methods for detecting specific learning disabilities with a view to improving diagnostic methods.
3. To provide possibilities for practical research and the setting up of a pilot assessment and remedial teaching project.
4. To consider methods of extending knowledge of the incidence and treatment of specific learning disabilities within relevant professional groups, such as the medical and educational.

Courses are regularly held, mainly on workshop lines, and are attended by practising teachers.

There are also a number of private schools catering for dyslexic children both of primary and secondary school age.

Public sector

The Chronically Sick and Disabled Persons Act 1970 includes a section on 'Special educational treatment for children suffering from acute dyslexia', which reads as follows:

27. (1) It shall be the duty of every local education authority to provide the Secretary of State at such times as he may direct with information on the provision made by that local education authority of special educational facilities for children who suffer from acute dyslexia.

(2) The arrangements made by a local education authority for the special educational treatment of children suffering from acute dyslexia shall, so far as it is practicable, provide for the giving of such education in any school maintained or assisted by the local education authority.

(3) In the application of this section to Scotland for any reference to a local education authority there shall be substituted a reference to an education authority within the meaning of section 145 of the Education (Scotland) Act 1962.

In 1971 the Secretary of State for Education and Science asked the Advisory Committee on Handicapped Children for advice on whether any guidance was required by local education authorities on the education of children suffering from dyslexia. A sub-committee was set up, chaired by Prof. Jack Tizard, which produced its report, *Children with Specific Reading Difficulties*, in 1972. The report carefully examined the terms 'dyslexia' and 'specific developmental dyslexia' and concluded that, while it was possible to separate a minority of children with severe reading difficulty (and often spelling, writing and number problems), the term dyslexia, in its various manifestations, was not favoured because of the loose and misleading ways in which it was being used. In its place was proposed 'a more usefully descriptive term', *specific reading difficulties*. The report specifically criticized the term 'acute dyslexia' used in the *Chronically Sick and Disabled Persons Act, 1970* as unhelpful. It made nine recommendations on how children suffering from reading 'backwardness' of all kinds might be helped.

In 1975 the Bullock Report, *A Language for Life*, was published. This included a chapter on children with reading difficulties which, after listing some of the causes of reading failure due to the circumstances of a child's upbringing, limited natural ability, sensory defect, anxiety and loss of confidence, referred to 'a rather smaller group of children who experience difficulty in learning to read that cannot be accounted for by limited ability or by emotional or extraneous factors'. The report was not in favour of using the term 'dyslexic' to describe these children. Instead, preference was expressed for the term 'specific reading retardation' and the conclusion drawn that, given skilled assessment and intensive help and support, most of these pupils would eventually learn to read. The report noted that these children might best be given the intensive treatment they needed in a remedial centre or reading clinic, with the support of an adviser with special responsibility for children experiencing learning difficulties.

In February 1977 HMI wrote to all local education authorities about the facilities provided for children with reading difficulties. Seventy-nine out of the 104 LEAs responding has reading clinics or remedial centres; the other 25 relied instead on peripatetic teachers or provided special classes. Following on from this, HMI and a Medical Adviser visited selected clinics and centres dealing with children with reading difficulties in the summer and autumn of 1977 (Fish, 1977). Clinics were visited in both the independent and maintained sectors and some general conclusions arrived at were as follows:

1. Children with specific learning difficulties do exist, and their needs should be recognized by LEAs.
2. There are few agreed criteria for distinguishing this group of children from others with difficulties caused by other factors.
3. The present criteria are not sufficiently discriminating.
4. The provision of treatment for these children is complicated by the variety of remedial procedures currently used.
5. Although many pupils respond to treatment 'up to a point', there is no agreed length of treatment, nor is there any agreed programme for children who need long-term help.

In May 1978 the Warnock Report, *Special Educational Needs: Report of the Enquiry into the Education of Handicapped Children and Young People*, was published. Among other quite radical recommendations on nomenclature, and categorization of handicap, the report adopted the term 'specific learning difficulties' to cover children with severe and long-term difficulties in reading, writing and spelling. And among the research topics which it considered should receive attention 'as soon as possible' it numbered: *'The assessment and education of children with specific learning difficulties in reading, writing and spelling, and the evaluation of different approaches'.*

Preview

The critical review to follow is in four chapters. In addition there is a short concluding chapter. The four main chapters are on *terminology, aetiology, incidence* and *remediation* respectively. The terminology chapter was considered necessary in order to establish ground rules before attempting to sample and review the mass of material published on children with severe learning difficulties by whatever name. The other three chapters are the areas set down in the research brief.

Terminology

We have arrived at definitions and terms which appear to represent a current consensus. *Specific learning difficulties* is the term which we think should subsume all others, including dyslexia in its various guises. However, the research literature uses the full range of possible terms. Where dyslexia is used in a research paper it will probably be used in this review. There is clearly a problem in comparing one 'dyslexic' group with another; there can be no certainty that the criteria used to select the sample in one study were the same as those used to select the sample in another. There is no guarantee, either, that dyslexia in one study meant the same as dyslexia in another study. Nor is there agreement on the nature of dyslexia. In spite of those problems it was felt that there was a sufficient core of agreement — namely, acceptance of the seriousness and intractability of the learning problems under discussion — to warrant examination of disparate studies, which used different terminology, in the unifying context of specific learning difficulties.

Aetiology

This section examines research in three main areas: *primary or constitutional learning difficulties, secondary correlates* and *reading and non-reading difficulties.* This incorporates the earlier concentration on organic causes of specific learning difficulties, which can be distinguished from associated but secondary correlates, and reflects an increasing emphasis on difficulties associated directly with the reading process. This trend looks to be of more practical relevance in linking theoretical and aetiological considerations with remedial strategies, and represents a hopeful prognosis for future research.

Incidence

Incidence is treated in three ways: *problems of definition and measurement, incidence of specific learning difficulties in Great Britain,* and *incidence of specific learning difficulties world-wide.* Despite the relative scarcity of information, especially in respect of large-scale surveys, it has been possible to identify a clustering of estimates around several levels of incidence. Furthermore, it seems that a 'hard core' of severely retarded readers can be isolated from the general mass of backward readers, although more information from epidemiological studies is needed to reinforce this finding.

Remediation

The remediation section is in four parts: *children with specific learning difficulties: their learning characteristics, efficacy of remedial treatment, assessment and diagnosis* and *remedial methods.* There is some overlap between this chapter and the third chapter, *Aetiology.* Some studies discussed in Chapter 3 are taken up again to illustrate remedial themes. It is in the *Remediation* chapter that the gap between research and remedial practice becomes frustratingly evident. The initiatives which have been made in remedial methods seem mainly to have been built bit by bit by practitioners, on the foundations of theory and practice established by the writers and theorists of 30, 40 and more years ago. Nevertheless there is some work deriving from information-processing, and other work on how children learn, which is opening up new possibilities for early intervention and remedial treatment. It may be that intervention early in the first year of a child's school life coupled with the skills of the practitioners, using well-tried methods and new approaches, will be the way ahead.

Chapter 2

Terminology

Dyslexia and specific learning disability

What is dyslexia?

Critchley (1970) cites two definitions drawn up by the Research Group on Developmental Dyslexia of the World Federation of Neurology in 1968. *Dyslexia* was defined as 'a disorder in children who, despite conventional classroom experience, fail to attain the language skills of reading, writing and spelling commensurate with their intellectual abilities'. *Specific developmental dyslexia* was defined as 'a disorder manifested by difficulty in learning to read despite conventional instruction, adequate intelligence, and socio-cultural opportunity. It is dependent upon fundamental cognitive disabilities which are frequently of constitutional origin.'

Critchley (op. cit.) cites four premises on which the existence of a specific type of developmental dyslexia rest: persistence into adulthood; the peculiar and specific nature of the errors in reading and spelling; the familial incidence of the defect; and the greater incidence in the male sex. These premises had changed, by 1970, from those given six years earlier (Critchley, 1964). Spelling was substituted for writing in the third premise and the fourth – greater incidence in the male sex – was new, having displaced 'frequent association with other symbol defects'. To the 1970 criteria Critchley added: 'the absence of signs of serious brain-damage or of perceptual defects; the absence of significant psychogenesis; the continued failure to read despite conventional techniques of instruction; and the association of normal if not high intelligence'.

Puzzling in Critchley's 1970 additional criteria is 'the absence of ... perceptual defects' since it is often the *presence* of perceptual defects of various kinds which is said to be a characteristic feature of children with hard-core learning problems (Ingram *et al.*, 1970). For example the following four criteria tend to appear in various definitions of *specific learning disability*, the term favoured in the United States and, as far as can be judged, describing the same group of children covered by the 'specific developmental dyslexia' label:

1. failure to learn at an expected rate (e.g. reading or spelling 18 to 24 months behind the average for the age);
2. evidence of average, or better, intelligence;
3. exclusion of mental retardation, emotional disturbance, or demonstrable defects of vision, hearing and motor functions;
4. underlying neurologic disorganization leading to impairment of one or more perceptual processes such as visual and auditory discrimination, and memory (Ohlson, 1978).

It is interesting that Ingram *et al.* (1970) separate out neurologic disorganization from perceptual functioning presumably because perceptual malfunctioning can be observed but neurologic disorganization only inferred in the absence of grosser organic defect.

Disagreement on terminology

It is evident that there is disagreement on terminology. Not only is there no assent internationally on the terms to be used to define children with intractable learning difficulties (Tarnopol and Tarnopol, 1976) but there is difference of opinion within countries both on terminology and on the existence of a clearly identifiable syndrome by which children suffering from severe learning difficulties may be recognized. So it is that in the United Kingdom the use of the term 'dyslexia' is officially discouraged (DES, 1972: Tizard Report; DES, 1975: Bullock Report) and, in its place, 'specific reading difficulties' proposed:

> ... we are highly sceptical of the view that a syndrome of 'developmental dyslexia' with a specific underlying cause and specific symptoms has been identified. Since the term 'dyslexia' has recently been used so very loosely and misleadingly ... we think it would be better to adopt a more usefully descriptive term, 'specific reading difficulties', to describe the problems of the small group of children whose reading (and perhaps writing, spelling and number) abilities are significantly below the standards

which their abilities in other spheres would lead one to expect (Tizard Report).

The Bullock Report (DES, 1975) rejected the term on the grounds that it served little useful purpose other than to draw attention to the fact that the problem of the children it was used to describe — those who experience a difficulty in learning to read that could not be accounted for by limited ability or by emotional or extraneous factors — could be chronic and severe. Further, 'dyslexia' was seen as neither susceptible to precise operational definition nor as indicating any clearly defined course of treatment.

The Warnock Report (1978), while not explicitly rejecting the dyslexia label, concurred with the conclusions of the Tizard Report and opted for a more general descriptive term: *children with specific learning difficulties*. The Report did not appear to confine that term to children with average or better intelligence since, in discussing 'children with moderate learning difficulties' (the preferred term for children at present labelled ESN(M)), it numbered specific learning difficulties among their characteristics. This is an important point to note since it gives a breadth of meaning to the term which does not exclude children of less than average intelligence. At the same time the Report made special mention of one group of children on whose behalf representations had been made by dyslexia associations:

> Although there are no agreed criteria for distinguishing those children with severe and long-term difficulties in reading, writing and spelling from others who may require remedial teaching in these areas, there are nevertheless children whose disabilities are marked but whose general ability is at least average and for whom distinctive arrangements are necessary (Warnock Report, 1978).

The Warnock comment reflects the lack of certainty about the existence of a dyslexia syndrome. Notwithstanding, those who support the use of the term consider that it not only represents an identifiable condition but that the diagnoses 'dyslexia', 'developmental dyslexia' or 'specific developmental dyslexia' can be operationalized (Ingram *et al.*, 1970) and thus point the way to particular remedial approaches. Hornsby and Miles (1979) argue for a distinctive dyslexic group, among whom may be found, with only minor variations (Miles, 1978), the same constitutionally based general pattern of learning difficulties, '... possibly involving some kind of shortcoming in immediate memory'; for these students, it is claimed, a remedial approach, derived from work with dyslexic children and which is 'structured, sequential, cumulative and thorough' has been shown to be the most effective (Hornsby and Miles, op. cit.), Ingram *et al.* (op. cit.) are less confident about aetiology when they say that neither 'specific dyslexia' nor 'specific developmental dyslexia' should be used to imply any particular causation, such as genetic defect or brain damage.

The position taken by Hornsby and Miles seems to depend on the importance, in dyslexia, of the immediate memory deficit: 'If there is a reduced span of immediate memory only certain procedures, such as the ones which we have described, will be effective.' Therefore, the argument runs, children who are helped to overcome their learning difficulties with such a programme have a memory deficit and are by definition, dyslexic. To take the point further, and illustrate the conviction of those who hold this view, Hornsby and Miles (op. cit.), in reporting on the work of three dyslexia centres, say: 'The fact that the programme used at the three centres was specifically designed for dyslexic children makes it somewhat uncomfortable ... for sceptics to admit its effectiveness while at the same time rejecting the dyslexia concept on which it was based.'

It may be, as Tarnopol and Tarnopol (op. cit.) suggest, that differences in terminology reflect divergent opinions about the causes and remediation of learning problems (there is no lack of acceptance of the existence of reading and learning disabilities in intelligent children). Yet there is surprising similarity of view on causes across international boundaries: from their survey of 18 countries Tarnopol and Tarnopol reported almost unanimous agreement on the aetiology of reading disabilities in children of adequate intelligence as most likely to be neurological, with possible secondary emotional effects, and the possibility of a genetic base. But the overall evidence does not appear to support that collective opinion. Ingram *et al.* (op. cit.) cite evidence from the literature which supports their own finding, from a follow-up study of children suffering from 'specific dyslexia', of the 'association between children's reading ability and their visual-perceptual development ... their auditory-perceptual organization ... and the integration of the modalities'. But the evidence for positive neurological signs in 'specific dyslexics' was not forthcoming.

Tizard's rejection of 'specific developmental dyslexia' as a verifiable disorder was on scientific grounds. He considered that the evidence on which it was based was unsatisfactory. Paediatric neurologists were not agreed on its definition or cause and the Education and Child Psychology Division of the British Psychological Society questioned its use as a clinical entity. Further, wide-scale investigations (Margaret Clark in Scotland; the Isle of Wight Study) showed that although all of the dysfunctions claimed for dyslexia were found in children with severe reading difficulties, they were not all present in any one child, and the quite varied combinations of difficulties did not fit easily into specific syndromes. On the other side of the coin, children who displayed features said to be characteristic of 'dyslexia' could read well.

Dyslexia by compromise: the 'variable syndrome'

The 'variable syndrome' might be seen as coping with Tizard's criticism. A variable syndrome is one in which not every sign or symptom of a condition is present yet there is a clustering of signs which makes the diagnosis convincing. Those who derive their insights from clinical practice sometimes assert that they can recognize a case of specific dyslexia 'almost unerringly' by a number of signs and symptoms (Reid, 1969) even when those signs and symptoms differ from one case to another: because the variable syndrome copes with the inconsistencies, the argument might go, therefore the central idea of specific dyslexia can be retained. But the nagging doubt remains. As Reid (op. cit.) says:

> It is difficult to see how, unless certain of the signs are regarded as necessary, and perhaps even if they are so regarded, the identification can ever, on this basis alone, be more than a probabilistic one, with the probability increasing as the number of signs – or the severity of those present – increases.

Perhaps the variable syndrome, then, is the compromise: a constellation of behaviours which alerts the teacher to the likelihood of learning difficulties (if the child is young) or to possible causes of retardation (if the child is older). But need there be a 'syndrome' at all? If there is to be constant argument as to whether the child's behaviours constitute dyslexia or not, are the needs likely to be overlooked while the diagnosis is debated?

Specific learning difficulties

For that reason, *specific learning difficulties* might be seen as the term likely to serve the child's interests best. It does not imply a definite aetiology. By using 'specific' as an adjective it suggests a particular learning problem (not general backwardness) which urgently needs attention; the nature of the attention is not circumscribed by the diagnostic label. It is broad enough, without losing its implication of seriousness, to subsume dyslexia in its various manifestations ('specific', 'developmental' and so on) and the American equivalent, *specific learning disability*. It does not exclude children of less than average intelligence (backward children) who may have learning difficulties just as acute as the child of average intelligence and better. And it copes with children who are retarded.

Backwardness and retardation

It is as well to consider some of the traditional terminology of educational measurement in the context of specific learning difficulties. A concise discussion may be found in Pilliner and Reid (1977). The terms which immediately concern us are *backwardness* and *retardation*. Their use became widespread, in education, and they took on particular meaning, as standardized tests of attainment and intelligence became popular in the 1930s and their use increased through the 1940s and 1950s.

Backwardness was used to describe those who were functioning, in one school subject or another, below the average for their age. A child was regarded as backward if his attainment was below his chronological age by an agreed amount. For example a 10-year-old reading at an eight-year level would be counted backward if the two-year 'gap' between reading age and mental age, as measured by standardized tests, was considered an appropriate criterion of backwardness.

Retardation was used to describe those whose attainment fell seriously short of an expected level based on ability (as measured by an intelligence test). Thus our 10-year-old, who was reading at an eight-year level, would be seen as retarded if his ability was average or higher. In that case he would be both backward and retarded: he would be achieving below the average for his age (backwardness) and he would be underfunctioning in terms of his own intellectual ability (retardation). The extent to which a child is seen as retarded depends on the size of the discrepancy that it has been agreed will be accepted as evidence of academic retardation; that will usually depend on the age of the child.

> Thus, while a discrepancy of 6 months might be considered to be severe in a 7-year old, it would not be considered significant in, say, an 11-year old. It is common practice to adopt a discrepancy

of 2 years or more between ability and attainment for children
9 years and older. The discrepancy tends to reduce proportion-
ately to the drop in age of the children concerned (Walsh, 1978).

The past tense was used deliberately in the earlier part of this discussion. Backwardness and retardation no longer have the precision in
use which their authors intended. Sometimes they are used interchangeably. They are also, to some extent, anachronistic since the
measures from which they derive — standardized tests of intelligence
and attainment — are now regarded with some scepticism as valid and
reliable measures of potential and performance. Nevertheless, since the
terms are used in some of the studies reported it is important that their
conventional meanings be understood. Further, there is some point for
accuracy of communication if retardation is understood to mean
a discrepancy between potential and performance.

The use of a discrepancy model — difference between potential and
achievement — to detect retardation and even 'over-achievement'
(a curiously illogical notion) have come to be seen as naive (Pidgeon
and Yates, 1957). The nature of standardized tests ensures a built-in
error factor (standard error of measurement) which means that a given
score on a test can only be taken as indicating a range in which a
person's true score will lie. A further source of error derives from the
less than perfect correlation between intelligence test scores and attainment test scores: achievement cannot be predicted with certainty from
a score on a test of intelligence.

The correlation between reading age and mental age is typically in
the region of +0.6. This means, when testing a group of children, that
those who are well above average on one measure will not score as
highly on the second measure. Similarly, low scorers on the first
measure will, on the average, score higher on the second: this is the
'regression effect'. As Yule and Rutter (1976) point out, this means
that any measure of underachievement that fails to allow for the effect
of regression to the mean will ensure that some bright children will be
incorrectly dubbed 'underachievers' and some dull children, who are
underachieving, will be missed altogether.

The problem can be overcome when there is a strong correlation
between a predictor variable (say, ability) and a criterion variable (say,
reading comprehension) for a group of children (the regression sample)
similar to those individuals for whom predictions are to be made
(Popham, 1967). In that case expected scores on reading comprehension, and the statistical probability of deviations from those scores, can

be calculated for subsequent individuals with relative precision, using multiple regression techniques (Yule and Rutter, op. cit.; Pilliner and Reid, 1977). Such techniques are not readily available to the teacher.[1] But they are available to researchers and should be used when investigating retardation. The teacher, on the other hand, should be cautiously sceptical in accepting the results of standardized tests as accurate measures of individual ability and achievement.

Specific reading retardation: what is it?

The difference between backwardness and retardation has been discussed. Both concepts, as defined, are unacceptably gross but they enable backwardness and retardation to be distinguished in principle without revealing the nuances of either. There are different forms of backwardness which may be differentiated by aetiology (for example the child whose backwardness is due to Downs' syndrome may have quite different learning needs and strategies from a child whose backwardness is due to cerebral palsy even though the degrees of backwardness may be similar). Retardation too may be considered to take different forms. Clearly, there may be quantitative differences — one child demonstrably more retarded in reading than another — but are there qualitatively different forms of retardation? The question has point if the answer leads to helpful remedial action.

A study of reading retardation

Yule and Rutter (1976) used the 'regression equation between aptitude and intelligence' (Thorndike, 1963) to investigate reading retardation. They set out to examine four questions:

1. Are over- and under-achievement in reading equally distributed in the general population, or is there an excess of underachievers?
2. Are retarded readers different from generally backward readers?
3. Do the two groups have different educational prognoses?
4. Are 'specific reading retardation' and 'dyslexia' synonymous?

In their examination they used data from five studies of total child populations which employed group tests of intelligence and reading, and from three epidemiological studies of the same populations which used individual tests. There were: approximately 1,100 children in each of three age groups, nine, 10 and 11 years on the Isle of Wight (Rutter,

---

[1] The norms of the British Ability Scales (1978) allow for the regression effect.

Tizard and Whitmore, 1970); 2,100 children aged 14 years – the nine-
and 10-year-old children seen above and followed-up to their final year
of schooling (Yule, 1973); and 1,634 10-year-old non-immigrant
children in an inner London borough (Berger, Yule and Rutter, 1975).

(1) An excess of underachievers?

In all eight studies the rate of *severe specific reading retardation*
(underachievement of at least two standard errors below prediction)
was above the predicted level. Theoretically 2.28 per cent of the
population would be expected to be shown up as severe underachievers.
In fact 3.5 per cent of Isle of Wight 10-year-olds, about 4.5 per cent
of Isle of Wight 14-year-olds and 6.0 per cent of London 10-year-olds
showed specific reading retardation. The authors have checked the
figures, and conclude that the observed rates are minimum estimates.

(2) Reading backwardness versus reading retardation

Yule and Rutter defined *backwardness* as 'an attainment on reading
accuracy or reading comprehension on the Neale test which was two
years four months or more below the child's chronological age'; specific
reading retardation as an 'attainment on either reading accuracy or
reading comprehension which was two years four months or more
below the level predicted on the basis of the child's age and short WISC
IQ'. Comparison of backwardness and retardation was made on the
nine- and 10-year-olds on the Isle of Wight. There were 2,300 children
of whom 155 were shown up as backward and 86 as retarded; 76
children fell into both groups (presumably those of around average IQ).
Comparisons were made between the 86 children with specific reading
retardation and the remaining 79 who showed general reading backwardness alone.

The groups were compared on IQ, sex, neurological disorders, motor
and praxic abnormalities and speech and language difficulties. The
retarded group had a mean IQ of 102.5, the backward group of 80;
76.6 per cent of the retarded group were boys but only 54.4 per cent
of the backward group. There were no definite *organic disorders* such
as cerebral palsy in the retarded readers but 11.4 per cent of the backward group had such a condition. *Motor and praxic abnormalities* were
more common among the backward children: three-fifths of the backward readers and one-quarter of the retarded group had 'constructional
difficulties'; clumsiness was twice as common among the backward
group (about 20 per cent affected); motor impersistence was twice as

common among the backward children; and 28 per cent of the backward group compared with 15 per cent of the retarded readers showed errors in right-left differentiation. In both groups there were *speech and language difficulties*: one-third had parents or siblings who were reported to have had reading difficulties; one in 10 had parents or siblings who were delayed in the acquisition of speech; and about a third had themselves been delayed in speech acquisition.

Yule and Rutter concluded that general backwardness was associated with overt neurological disorder and with abnormalities on a wide range of motor, praxic, speech and other developmental functions. It is present in both boys and girls and it is more commonly found in children from large families and in children whose fathers have a job of very low social status.

Specific reading retardation was found to be associated to a marked degree only with abnormalities of speech and language development. It is much more common in boys, and in children from large families, but there is no link with social status. A study by Ingram *et al.* (1970) of 82 children described as being 'dyslexic' or having a 'specific learning disability' came up with broadly comparable conclusions.

It must be noted that the generalized differences are based on group comparisons. There is a strong likelihood that there are children in the backward group who, apart from IQ would have the same kinds of learning difficulties, and therefore the same educational needs as many children in the retarded group.

(3) Educational prognosis

The poor readers, both backward and retarded, were followed up until their final year of compulsory schooling. At age 10 years each group was 33 months below the general population control on the reading measure. At follow-up the children were tested individually on the Neale Analysis of Reading Ability, the Schonell Spelling Test and the Vernon Arithmetic–Mathematics Test (Yule, 1973). The retarded readers had made significantly less progress in reading (six months behind the duller, backward readers) and spelling (eight months behind). In arithmetic both groups were performing below age level but the retarded group had made more progress. Yule and Rutter comment: 'Educators cannot assume ... that bright children with reading difficulties will catch up. Good intelligence in a disabled reader is no talisman against long-lasting reading failure.'

(4) 'Specific reading retardation' or 'dyslexia'?

Yule and Rutter (op. cit.) point out that specific reading retardation carries no implications concerning aetiology, nor does it imply any type of unitary causation. But similarities between the characteristics of children with specific reading retardation (Rutter and Yule, 1973) and those described as having 'dyslexia' raise the possibility of specific reading retardation and dyslexia being the same thing. Speech and language difficulties, and problems in sequencing, are the behaviours most strongly associated with specific reading retardation (Rutter and Yule, op. cit.). However, the same kinds of problem, say Yule and Rutter, are now said to characterize dyslexia (Yule, 1976; Boder, 1971; Miles, 1974). They suggest that the question of a constitutional component in dyslexia is far from being answered. This, of course, runs counter to the definition of 'specific developmental dyslexia' adopted by the World Federation of Neurology (Critchley, 1970) and to the views of some of the 18 countries surveyed by Tarnopol and Tarnopol (1976), who considered a genetic component possible.

Yule and Rutter take an interactionist, multifactorial view of specific reading retardation:

> It is suggested that the developmental impairment in reading retardation may be due to a relative failure in the normal maturation of certain specific functions of the cerebral cortex, or some neurological damage or a lack of suitable environmental stimulation, or a combination of all three. These factors interact with school influences, temperamental features, motivation and family circumstances. In particular, it appears that language impairment (due either to some biological factor or to some environmental privation) renders the child at risk, and whether he actually shows reading retardation will depend on his personality characteristics, the nature of his home environment, and the quality of his schooling (Yule and Rutter, 1976).

This is a catch-all view of reading retardation whereas it is claimed that dyslexia is a unitary condition. However, a dispassionate reading of the literature does not reveal the evidence in support of the unitary concept. Yule and Rutter observe that Naidoo (1972), in an investigation of a highly selected clinic sample widely regarded as dyslexic, could not demonstrate any clustering of the developmental anomalies said to characterize dyslexia.

The Yule and Rutter (op. cit.) conclusion is blunt and unambiguous: 'There has been a complete failure to show that the signs of dyslexia constitute any meaningful pattern. There is no evidence for the validity of a single special syndrome of dyslexia.'

Thus specific reading retardation may be seen to subsume dyslexia. Nevertheless the seriousness – or even the nature – of the learning problems which children described as dyslexic have is not denied. What is denied is that the problems, and their aetiology, can be put in a single neatly labelled package. Yule and Rutter underline the seriousness with which they regard the problem of the retarded reader when they say: 'It is clear from our epidemiological studies that at present if a child is a retarded reader by 10 years of age, one can only be pessimistic about his educational future.'

Summary

In the foregoing discussion a clear distinction has been made between backward readers and retarded readers. What has not been drawn out is that some backward readers may have the same kinds of learning difficulties as retarded readers and may need, and benefit from, the kinds of techniques used with children described as dyslexic. We have not found any research which shows that children of below average intelligence do not have learning problems similar to, and as qualitatively serious as, those of children dubbed dyslexic. We have found no evidence, either, to show that these same children will not benefit from carefully structured remedial help. Cashdan *et al.* (1971) hold that it is not necessarily so 'that children who underfunction in relation to their mental age are somehow more promising or more deserving than those who are simply behind in relation to their chronological age'.

The case has been made for the term *specific learning difficulty*, as a generic term which embraces dyslexia and specific learning disability, but which does not imply a given aetiology or a circumscribed remedial programme. Rather, it retains the notion of seriousness without excluding children on the grounds of intelligence. At the same time the use of 'specific' as an adjective suggests a particular learning problem which urgently needs attention.

Chapter 3

Aetiology

Introduction

This chapter is concerned with studies investigating the possible causes of specific learning difficulties. However, the term 'aetiology' is not so straightforward as it might seem. Some writers are prepared to assert that these difficulties are 'caused' by a particular dysfunction or dysfunctions, the details of which may at present be unclear. Miles (1971) claims that dyslexia is a nosological (based on knowledge of a cause) rather than nosographic (description of disease) entity and states in no uncertain terms: 'I am in no doubt ... that the disabilities are constitutional in origin.' However, other writers are rather more cautious and prefer to talk of 'associated' difficulties, the cause remaining unknown. Very often criteria are selected with the distinction between 'necessary' and 'sufficient' not always made clear and one is frequently left with 'identification by elimination', to use Reid's (1969) term. She gives the following example of this type of practice: 'This child is a very retarded reader of good intelligence. He has had an enlightened home and normal schooling. His vision and hearing are intact, and he has no overt neurological damage. He has no history of emotional upset prior to going to school and starting to learn to read. He wants to learn but has failed. He must be dyslexic.' Although this may be an oversimplification, it does show that this mode of identification is negative not positive and merely places the residual cases in a category called 'idiopathic' in medical terminology, i.e. of unknown origin. Even though this is an acceptable procedure, whereby one can recognize a condition operationally or behaviourally but give no explanation of its aetiology, nevertheless it appears to imply that dyslexia (or specific learning

difficulties) as a condition will only exist if all the other conditions
are present, i.e. it will not occur in a child of poor intelligence, from
a deprived background and inadequate schooling, etc., which is clearly
not the case.

Another important point is that many of the 'causes' advanced are
present in children who learn to read without difficulty. Merritt (1972)
puts it like this: 'In the case of every factor that is supposed to contribute to reading disability we can find a child who should be at risk who
can read perfectly well.' He suggests that certain children may be 'at
risk' on the grounds of a variety of handicaps which impair learning
ability by a chance combination of circumstances in learning situations.
He goes on to say, 'I am sure that teachers would appreciate more help
in trying to understand the learning problems and possible modes of
treatment of these unfortunates, and would prefer less emphasis on
factors they could not conceivably control and which serve, largely, to
justify our own failures.' Tizard (1972) is in agreement with this view
when he states in no uncertain terms, 'We do not believe that the
question of aetiology has any great significance for the educationalist,
though the identification of predisposing factors may well have
importance from the point of future prevention.'

This seems to be an overstatement. Whilst a main purpose of aetiological studies must be to inform remediation, and certainly there has
not been sufficient weight in experimental studies on the practical
implications of the findings for practising teachers, nevertheless a 'cure'
will be all the more effective if it is based on sound aetiological
premises. Reid (1969) emphasizes this point (when she says): 'It might
be ... true to say that educators have not concerned themselves
sufficiently with aetiology, in that they have sometimes put together
for remedial purposes children who were retarded for a variety of
reasons and who perhaps required very different sorts of help.' What is
needed is increased attention to experiments which have a direct
bearing on remedial help, or at least point to ways in which this could
be investigated.

Many writers have been concerned particularly with the constitutional aspects of specific learning difficulties, and there have been many
attempts to classify such difficulties along these lines. Thus Naidoo
(1971) claims that specific developmental dyslexia is both specific and
constitutionally determined and can be considered under the following
headings: genetic, maturational lags, neurological dysfunction and
cerebral dominance. Singleton (1976) gives virtually the same four

categories: genetic, developmental delay, brain damage and defective lateralization, although he stresses that they are not mutually exclusive. Scott (1976) similarly refers to four major hypotheses to account for dyslexia: genetic, developmental delays, organic brain damage and late or ill-established cerebral dominance. Sampson (1975) reviewing 50 years of dyslexia theory, again distinguishes two main lines of inquiry: 'specific' and 'congenital', subsuming genetic, maturational lag, brain damage and dominance problems under the latter term, although she does also refer to language disorders and explanations implicating the senses. Gessert (1976), writing of specific reading difficulties in Britain, identified the same four theories of causality, and Tarnopol and Tarnopol (1976), reviewing the international scene, found that neurological causes were the most frequently cited, followed by genetic factors and in some cases emotional explanations.

Newton *et al.* (1979), in discussing the main theories of the aetiology of dyslexia under the headings, genetic factors, maturational lags, neurological dysfunction and cerebral dominance, say: ' ... They are hardly explanatory in that they do not describe the perceptual and motor difficulties observed in the children, nor the actual process whereby these factors give rise to difficulties in written language.' They themselves summarize six classificatory systems for dyslexia derived from research and clinical work: Eisenberg (1966), Keeney and Keeney (1968), Rabinovitch (1968), Bannatyne (1971), Ingram (1971) and Klasen (1972).

Overall these six systems can be summarized to give eight underlying causes postulated by these authors which appear to possess basic commonality:

1. Brain damage involvement
2. Maturational lag, delay
3. Genetic, constitutional, inherited
4. Neurological organization, brain function
5. Perceptual/motor difficulties
6. Cognitive difficulties
7. Secondary to environment
8. Sensory defects

Newton *et al.* (op. cit.) are concerned to highlight the aspects of aetiology which stress the interaction of developing individual skills with a highly structured written language system and therefore present a flow diagram in which the last two causes mentioned above: secondary to environment, and sensory defects, are excluded as extraneous, and a new factor is added – that of the written language itself as a 'cause' of dyslexia.

Integrated model of aetiology

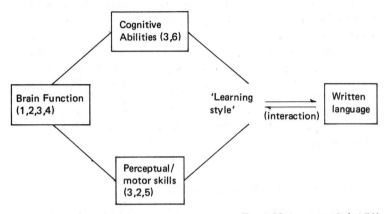

From Newton *et al.* (1979)
Reproduced by kind permission of Learning Development Aids

This model has the advantage of grouping together the four main hypotheses referred to above under Brain Function and separating out the various non-neurological elements into three other groupings. However, the inclusion of genetic causes with cognitive abilities, and of maturational lag and genetic causes with perceptual/motor skills, detracts from their value as separate categories. Furthermore, whilst the interaction of the written language with the other theories is an important aspect of specific reading retardation, it is questionable whether it constitutes a 'cause' of dyslexia in itself.

For the purposes of this review, it has been decided to classify the aetiological findings into three main groups:

1. Primary or constitutional specific learning difficulties, which include the four main hypotheses highlighted by major writers in the field: neurological functions, neurological dysfunctions, maturational lag and genetic factors. This section resembles Newton *et al.*'s category termed 'Brain Function'.

2. Secondary correlates, including perception, cognitive style, attentional, physical, environmental and emotional correlates, together with a short section on drug studies. These are seen to be con-

comitants of specific learning difficulties and to include both Newton's Cognitive Abilities and Perceptual/Motor Skills Categories.

3. Reading and non-reading difficulties. This group is similar to Newton's 'written language' category although it focuses both on language and reading sub-skills associated with specific learning disabilities, and on non-reading disabilities such as spelling, writing, arithmetic and speech in an attempt to circumscribe the field of investigation more precisely.

This seems to overcome some of the shortcomings of the earlier classifications, which concentrated rather heavily on constitutional and neurological aspects, and reflects the increasing concern with difficulties associated directly with the reading process.

1. Primary or constitutional learning difficulties

Neurological functions

Cerebral dominance

Historical aspects

One of the earliest writers on the subject of word-blindness, James Hinshelwood (1917), was one of the first to suggest that there must be separate places in the brain for general visual memory, visual letter memory and visual word memory. However, this early emphasis on structure was gradually replaced by an emphasis on the functional nature of the brain: how information gets from one part of the brain to another.

The most renowned early exponent of this approach was Samuel T. Orton (1925, 1937). He postulated that reversals and mirror images in the writing of children with specific reading disorders were due to the confusion of competing images in the two cerebral hemispheres because of a failure in the establishment of unilateral cerebral dominance. Mirror writing showed that the information must be stored in more than one orientation, and Orton concluded that the functions of the right hemisphere reflected the activities of the left. Normally a child learned to read and write correctly by learning that the left hemisphere images were the correct ones. Either hemisphere could perform perceptive (reception of sensory information) and recognitive (visual association) activities but associative activities (object meaning) had to be performed by the left hemisphere alone. Brain injury affecting the first two activities did not impair behaviour unless it occurred in both hemispheres but injury affecting the associative activities, whilst it made no difference if it occurred in the right hemisphere, produced word blindness if it occurred in the left hemisphere. This dominance failure of the left hemisphere involved inability to suppress the right hemispheric images and led to failure to associate sounds and meaning. Orton called this condition 'strephosymbolia' or 'twisted signs', and listed six clusters of disabled behaviours which could be subsumed under this heading:

1. Developmental alexia — unusual difficulty in learning to read but not other abnormalities, characterized by letter confusion, letter reversals, word confusions and reversals, severe spelling difficulties, and often difficulties in writing.
2. Developmental word deafness — difficulty in recognizing the spoken word, normal hearing but distortion of speech.
3. Developmental agraphia — special difficulty in learning to write.
4. Developmental motor aphasia — slow development and disorder of speech but good understanding of the spoken word.
5. The childhood stuttering — spasms of speech musculature, sometimes accompanied by jerky movements of the body.
6. Developmental apraxia — abnormal clumsiness, with speech and small hand muscles possibly affected, leading to the likelihood of associated speech and writing disorders.

The two hemispheres
   Since Orton's time, a great deal of research has been carried out into the functions of the two hemispheres. In the normal human brain information received by the right hand, right visual field and right ear is relayed to the left hemisphere, whilst information received by the left hand, left visual field and left ear is relayed to the right hemisphere.
   Three methods have generally been used to investigate hemispheric specialization. The first and most commonly used involves relating known or suspected brain damage to observable symptoms. A classic example of this approach is that of Joseph Dejerine (as reported by Hinshelwood, 1917) whose patient had lost the ability to read but could still write and spell even though he could not read back what he himself had written and spelled correctly. After his death, an autopsy was performed and it was discovered that a stroke had destroyed the

left visual cortex and also the connecting bridge between the left and right hemispheres — the corpus callosum. Although the patient could see with his right visual cortex he was unable to read what he saw, due to his inability to relay this information to the left hemisphere, which deals with the meanings associated with words.

A recent study along these lines is Coltheart's description (1979) of what he terms 'deep dyslexia', which is associated with left-hemisphere damage. The symptoms of this disorder are listed as semantic errors (response wrong but semantically related to stimulus, e.g. 'chair' instead of 'table'), visual errors (response resembles the stimulus visually rather than semantically, e.g. 'sandals' instead of 'scandal'), deviational errors (stimulus is a syntactic deviation from the response or vice versa, e.g. 'edition' is the response to 'editor' or 'am' to 'be') and inability to convert letters to sounds (e.g. cannot pronounce nonsense words aloud). Coltheart supports the prevailing view that with deep dyslexics the left hemisphere system used in normal reading is partially damaged or possibly destroyed. Deep dyslexics, to read at all, must be using a reading system located in the right hemisphere. The right hemisphere must comprehend the words and send the information to the left hemisphere via a *semantic* code (since there is some evidence to suggest that the right hemisphere cannot convert letters to sound) which allows the left hemisphere to retrieve the pronunciation, but synonyms may be confused and some information may be lost in transit.

Newton (1970) carried out electroencephalograph studies on 25 dyslexic and 25 normal reading children (aged eight–13). The results showed the presence of lateral dominance and cortical organization in the controls as indicated by greater alpha activity of the non-dominant hemisphere, but no comparable resolution of dominance in the dyslexic group, who showed more activity on the dominant side or no difference at all. Newton quotes her results as supporting the writings of Critchley (1970) and Reitan (1964a) that unresolved dominance is a critical feature of dyslexia.

Several investigations involving surgical disconnection of the corpus callosum — the fibre connecting the right and left hemispheres — have been undertaken to demonstrate the functions of the two hemispheres and the interaction between them. Split-brain experiments with animals have shown that they act independently as if they had two separate brains. Myers (1962) reported that a normal animal trained to do a trick with one paw will also know this trick with the other paw. If, however, a sectioning of the corpus callosum is carried out before the trick is learned by one paw, it has to be learned all over again by the other paw. Trevarthen (1962) found that two simultaneously conflicting memories of visual patterns associated with reward may be retained separately in the two halves of the cerebrum. Gazzaniga and Sperry (1966) found human split-brain patients can show simultaneous learning activity by presenting a visual discrimination task to the left hemisphere first, then the same tasks accompanied by another discrimination task to the right hemisphere.

Related to this kind of research is the field of electrophysiological studies, although few studies have concentrated on lateral asymmetry in dyslexia. Rebert and Wexler (1977) quoted by Beaumont and Rugg (1978) found an asymmetry in the alpha band of the EEG for dyslexics but have not yet published data from a suitable control group. Evidence from visual evoked response studies is rather confusing. Parietal asymmetry was reported by Conners (1970) although he included no control group, and this was also found by Sobotka and May (1977) but equally in both dyslexic and normal subjects. The only study of auditory evoked responses (Cohen, 1977) found no abnormality. The general conclusion must be that there is no evidence from electrophysiological studies of atypical patterns of cerebral lateralization in dyslexics.

Two other methods of investigating hemispheric specialization and cerebral dominance have recently been developed: dichotic listening and visual half-field procedures. These will be reviewed in detail in the section dealing with cerebral dominance and laterality.

Returning to the question of hemispheric specialization, there seems to be overall general agreement as to the specific functions of the two hemispheres although there is far less agreement as to whether dyslexics or poor readers follow the normal pattern of brain organization.

There is a general consensus that the left hemisphere is specialized for language and linguistic processing. Goldberg and Schiffman (1972) state, 'In the patient who has left-hemisphere dominance, language is found in this area in a ratio of 97 per cent to three per cent.' However, this is not true of left-handed persons where the ratio is much lower, although the left hemisphere is still very likely to be dominant for the language function. Kimura's dichotic listening and visual half-field experiments (Kimura, 1971; Kimura and Durnford, 1974), have found a right visual field advantage for verbal material and a left visual field advantage for non-verbal tasks, suggesting left hemisphere specialization for verbal material. Similar experiments in the auditory mode have shown a right ear advantage for verbal material again suggesting left hemisphere specialization for verbal material. An experiment by McKeever and Huling (1970) also found a right visual field advantage for words. Davidoff, Cone and Scully (1978) go so far as to say: 'It is now clear that the time-honoured dichotomy between verbal and non-verbal skills has a real basis in terms of hemispheric specialization. In the majority of right-handed individuals ... analysis puts language-based skills in the left hemisphere and perceptually based skills in the right hemisphere.' Their own study concerns the constancy of this specialization during development, and they conclude that there is an effect of learning to read that is associated with an increasing left hemisphere advantage for linguistic tasks, even for a normally right hemisphere task, but there is a return for boys to the right hemisphere for visual tasks, and for both sexes in auditory tasks. Zangwill (1976) also supports the general assumption for language acquisition and suggests it is in addition specialized for thought processes. Seth (1975) emphasizes that speech function is usually specialized in the left hemisphere although this is not usually stabilized until the age of nine or 10. Use of sodium amytal, which disturbs speech if it enters the hemisphere containing the speech system, has been used to determine the lateralization of the speech system and to demonstrate its location in the left hemisphere in the large majority of cases (Milner, 1974).

Finally it is thought that the left hemisphere is responsible for analytical sequential processing of information (Zaidel, 1977; Bradshaw *et al.*, 1976; Witelson, 1977b) whereas the right hemisphere is responsible for simultaneous holistic processing. Cohen (1973) additionally suggested that the left hemisphere processes serially and the right hemisphere in parallel. Friedman, Guyer-Christie and Tymchuk (1976) believe the left hemisphere may have attentional and executive control in integrating the activities of the different processing systems (Gazzaniga, 1974). They point out that the attentional function of the left hemisphere has received insufficient emphasis in learning disability analyses.

The right hemisphere is specialized for spatial and pictorial perception, and, as stated above, for holistic processing (Farnham-Diggory, 1978). Newton *et al.* (1979) state that global, visio-spatial and artistic skills have pre-eminence in the right hemisphere whereas the left hemisphere is responsible for language, symbolic order, timing judgements and analytic and discrete skills. Dimond and Beaumont (1974) suggest that only a limited role is played by the right hemisphere, but Kershner (1975) is of the opinion that although verbal reasoning is located in the left hemisphere, this does not mean the right hemisphere is of minor importance. He quotes recent research showing that the right hemisphere is the locus for adapting to spatial relations, depth perception, form discrimination, and right–left orientation (Kershner and Jeng, 1972; Kimura, 1971; Milner, 1971) – all skills that are logically related to the reading process. Goldberg and Schiffman (1972) report that right-hemisphere lesions lead to impairment of spatial perception and memory, impairment of visuoconstructive activity, defects in visual perception and memory for non-verbal material, impairment of certain aspects of auditory perception and memory and motor impersistence, suggesting right hemisphere specialization for these activities.

Pizzamiglio (1976) points to evidence that the right hemisphere is responsible for identification of faces (De Renzi and Spinnler, 1966; Hécaen and Angelergues, 1963), sketch completion and identification of overlapping figures (De Renzi and Spinnler, 1966) and perception of spatial exploration (De Renzi, Fagioni and Scotti, 1970), and conconcludes that the role of the right hemisphere may be a visuospatial orientation ability. He further posits that the left hemisphere operates analytically, dealing with verbal features, whereas the right hemisphere functions for gestalt perception (Levy-Agresti and Sperry, 1968; Levy, Trevarthen and Sperry, 1972).

Apart from the specialized functions of the two hemispheres, increasing attention has been paid recently in the literature to the interconnections between them. Farnham-Diggory (1978) draws attention to the fact that reading and writing clearly involves both hemispheres. For example, the serial and language functions are the province of the left hemisphere but the spatial characteristics of words and letters are the province of the right hemisphere. One of the examples she gives of co-ordinated hemispheric interchange is of the informal model of the writing task.

		Hemisphere
Step 1	Choose a word	left
Step 2	Hold its overall sound in mind	left
Step 3	Select a sound particle	left
Step 4	Find a letter pattern in semantic memory	right
Step 5	Write the letters	left for the motor action;

right, for the
configuration
of the letters

Step 6 Test: do I recognize the letter pattern   right
Step 7 Test: word finished   right

Farnham-Diggory (1978)

Reproduced by kind permission of Fontana/Open Books

Leading on from this she suggests that learning disabilities may occur in three different areas:

1. There may be a problem in moving information from one hemisphere to another.
2. There may be a task-specific problem with one of the hemispheres so that it performs inadequately when it takes its turn.
3. There may be a task-specific problem of overall control by the left hemisphere.

Vellutino (1979b) addresses himself to the first area and reports results from a study which he believes to be the first of its kind employing a population of carefully defined disabled readers (Vellutino, Bentley, and Phillips, 1978). Novel symbols (Chinese ideographs) paired with common English words were presented to poor and normal readers in grades 2 and 6. Stimuli were presented randomly to either the left visual field (right hemisphere), right visual field (left hemisphere) or a central fixation point (as a control measure). The hypothesis that poor readers would have more difficulty than normal in visual-verbal learning supported unilaterally by the right hemisphere but would not be differentiated in presentations to the left hemisphere and central fixation point was *not* supported. Vellutino concluded that the transmission deficit explanation of reading disability was not upheld by this study but remains cautious in his approach, recommending further research. Indeed, he quotes a study by Yeni-Komshian, Isenberg and Goldberg (1975), reviewed elsewhere in this book, in which they conjectured that results obtained with normal and poor readers on visual field presentations and dichotic listening tasks might support the attribution of reading disability to either a right hemisphere deficiency or to dysfunction in interhemispheric transmission. Wheeler, Watkins and McLaughlin (1977) report that a number of researches have shown that information decoding is processed in a parallel manner in both hemispheres (Klatzky and Atkinson, 1971) but information encoding is serially processed, which requires information to be processed sequentially from right to left hemispheres.

Kershner (1975) also devotes some attention to the question of whether reading is a bilateral or unilateral act. He points out that although it has been implied that reading involves both the spatial-orientation ability of the right hemisphere and the auditory linguistic ability of the left hemisphere, there is no clear evidence for this assumption. He refers to several studies (Sommers and Taylor, 1972; Witelson and Rabinovitch, 1972; Zurif and Carson, 1970; Leavell and Beck, 1959) which suggested a disturbance in the neurological distribution of language processing in retarded readers but revealed little about how the spatial and auditory-verbal systems interact in processing written language or about the role of the right hemisphere in reading. An experiment by Geffen, Bradshaw and Nettleton (1972) demonstrated that written language can be processed visually either by a rotational left-hemisphere or a spatial right-hemisphere process. Subjects were required to match letters of the alphabet that were similar in name (Aa) or similar physically and in name (AA). The longer reaction time for a name match by the right hemisphere suggests hemispheric interchange of information. An experiment carried out by Kershner and Brown (in preparation) reinforces this conclusion. Good and retarded readers were shown a series of single letters projected tachistoscopically in their centre, right and left visual fields. Whereas poor readers were equal to good readers in centre-field recognition, which projected the letter to both hemispheres simultaneously, retarded readers were significantly inferior when the letters were presented to either the left or right visual half-field. However, as Kershner himself points out, the results could have been due to less efficient processing within the right or left hemisphere by the poor readers.

Whilst many difficulties seem to arise in association with two hemispheres being involved in the reading process and the complexity of their interrelations, nevertheless there seems to be general agreement that the advantages of hemispheric asymmetry outweigh any disadvantages. Kershner reports results of experiments (Noble, 1966, 1968; Corballis and Beale, 1970) that show that animals with bilateral processing (both hemispheres) of visual spatial stimuli cannot differentiate their left from their right sides without obvious external lateral cues, and cannot discriminate mirror images. Whilst this is appropriate to non-symbolic animals whose perceptual world is largely made up of symmetrical data, it is more advantageous for human beings, who have to deal with nonsymmetric symbols to develop visual-spatial asymmetry. He uses his experimental evidence (op. cit.) that readers processed single letters better when they were presented in centre-field rather than to the left or right visual half-field to support this thesis. Seth (1975) points to the obvious advantages of both hands working independently and concludes that strong cerebral dominance is good whereas cerebral ambivalence is less so.

Developmental aspects of hemispheric asymmetry

So far we have considered hemispheric asymmetry as if it were a static condition of brain organization, but some researchers have hypothesized that specialization develops over time. Seth's research (1973, 1975) has shown that in early infancy (up to 20 weeks) the left hand (right hemisphere) is preferred until 28 weeks when the right hand (left hemisphere) takes over.

This anticipates by four weeks the attainment of success by either hand (for example in touching a cube) and by eight weeks a comparable level of achievement by the left hand. According to Seth this right-hand takeover appears to occur on the basis of cross-education (bilateral transfer) rather than direct practice by the right hand itself, suggesting a maturational rather than a learning or social pressure explanation of lateral asymmetry. Leong (1976) also sees cerebral specialization as a maturational process of successive and overlapping neurological and psychological changes. In particular he describes the differentiation of brain function as proceeding from the lateralization of gross and fine motor skills followed by the lateralization of sensori-motor functions to the lateralization of speech and language. Maturational lag refers to a delayed or undifferentiated pattern of functional cerebral development. Leong himself, in a dichotic experiment with dyslexic boys, finds evidence to support this hypothesis. He also describes Luria's (1966a, 1966b, 1970, 1973) model of the two basic forms of integrative activity of the cerebral cortex: simultaneous (primarily spatial) and successive (primarily temporal) activity and suggests that further insight into the mechanisms of reading dysfunction may come from reconciling lateralization and the interchangeable simultaneous-successive syntheses as modes of information-processing. His own experiments with disabled and nondisabled readers involving dichotic listening tests and a factorial-structure analysis of perceptual-cognitive tasks support these theoretical models. As mentioned above,

Davidoff *et al.* (1977) also found developmental changes in hemispheric specialization, particularly for boys who switched temporarily from right- to left-hemispheric dominance on two tasks — recognizing environmental sounds and a visual field task (dot patterns) at about the age of six, returning to right hemispheric control of these tasks at the age of eight. Many other studies have been devoted to the concept of a maturational lag in the development of hemispheric specialization, and these will be reviewed in a separate section.

Witelson (1976) also found sex differences in hemispheric functions. She found that the right hemisphere generally takes control of abstract haptic form recognition in boys by the age of six but does not seem to appear in girls up to the age of 14, the oldest age group tested. This means that girls recognize abstract haptic forms equally with both hemispheres whilst boys recognize them better with their right hemisphere, *except* for dyslexic boys who behave like females who can read on this task. Witelson concludes that dyslexic males have 'Two Right Hemispheres and None Left', the sub-title of her article, i.e. the left hemisphere may be able to do right-hemisphere processing. Dyslexic females, however, seem to behave like normal females on this task, leading to the hypothesis that female dyslexics have a left-hemisphere deficiency alone, whilst dyslexic males have a left hemisphere that is not only deficient in its own skills but is also burdened with extra right-hemisphere skills. This may account for the higher and more severe incidence of dyslexia in males than in females.

Cerebral dominance and laterality

An important concomitant of hemispheric asymmetry is the concept of hemispheric dominance. Up till now we have been discussing the specialized functions of each cerebral hemisphere but it is probable that one hemisphere has overall control for different functions. Farnham-Diggory (1978) describes the current state of knowledge on hemispheric dominance thus:

> We know only five things for sure:
> 1. It is possible for one hemisphere to take control of a simple task that is presented — through the ears, eyes or hands — to both hemispheres at once.
> 2. These dominance effects may change with development.
> 3. The effects may not be the same for males and females.
> 4. They may not be the same for dyslexic and normal children.
> 5. They may shift as a function of learning sets induced by certain forms of school instruction.

Ill-established cerebral dominance has been suggested by many researchers to be associated with reading disability. Klasen (1972) mentions inadequate cerebral dominance as one of the physiopsychological symptoms of dyslexia whilst Bakker (1974) found a less established cerebral dominance amongst dyslexic children. Zangwill (1962) wondered whether there might be two sorts of developmental dyslexia: a type occurring in poorly lateralized individuals and a type occurring in individuals who are fully lateralized. He put forward three explanations for why only some ill-lateralized children have reading problems:

1. Poorly developed laterality and reading-deficit could both be due to the effects of an actual cerebral lesion.
2. Reading-deficit and lack of cerebral asymmetry could both be taken as evidence of a constitutional maturational lag.
3. Children who lack firm lateral preferences also happen to be particularly vulnerable to stress.

A study by Keefe (1976) also suggested that dyslexics could be divided into two groups according to laterality: one group who are weakly lateralized with an apparent deficit in left hemisphere processing, and those who are strongly lateralized with a deficit in the right hemisphere processing.

One of the problems in this area of research is that a confusion exists in the literature over the terms cerebral dominance and lateral preference. Briefly, cerebral dominance refers to which of the two hemispheres of the brain (left or right) has control either of a specific task, or more usually, has overall control. Laterality refers to the awareness within the body of left and right (Gredler, 1977). Generally speaking, lateral preference has been taken to be an indicator of hemispheric dominance, i.e. it is hypothesized that there is a direct but opposite correspondence between brain dominance and lateral preference founded upon the idea that sensory and motor pathways moving between the brain and the peripheral organs are contralateral; that is, the right side of the body is controlled by the left hemisphere and vice versa. Normal brain dominance is associated with consistent lateral preference on the side of the body preferred in motor and perceptual activities, with the left-hemisphere being the usual dominant hemisphere, since more people are right-handed. However, the use of body laterality as an index of neurological status is at least questionable, and this must be borne in mind during the following review of literature concerned with laterality.

The main measures of body laterality that have been investigated in relation to reading disability have been handedness, eyedness and earedness, although footedness is sometimes used in conjunction with the other measures.

One problem to be taken into account is the difficulty of measuring cerebral dominance without being able to specify what combinations of laterality, and in what proportion, should be used, and what measures should be used to ascertain laterality. Various measures, such as statements of preference, or the observation of actual performance or measured relative skill, may be employed but the results may not be consistent and in any case may vary according to the task performed. Much of the evidence is of doubtful value due to low validity or limited information as to the tests used.

Several studies point to connections between mixed or crosslaterality and reading disabilities. Naidoo (1972) found the incidence of left-handedness, left-eyedness, left-footedness, cross-laterality and mixed hand, eye and foot dominance higher in those children attending the Word Blind Centre than in controls, although the difference was not significant. Farr and Leigh (1972) in Tasmania found a significant association between retarded reading and indeterminate eye dominance, and between reading retardation and ambidexterity in a study of 12,000 primary school children. Newton's study (1970) found 84 per cent of her dyslexic group showed mixed laterality compared with only eight per cent of normal readers. Grant (1974) carried out an experiment to discover whether crossed laterality is one of the causes of reading difficulty. An experimental group of 662 children aged 7–10 years with two years' reading retardation was compared with 1,316 primary school age children in an urban area, in tests measuring hand and eye dominance. When joining two horizontally opposed crosses no significant difference between the groups with mixed laterality and the groups with uniform laterality was found. However, the percentage of right-handed children who joined the crosses from right to left among children with reading difficulty was far higher than in the control group. The difference was also marked among children with crossed laterality. Several studies point to an association between reading retardation and poor left-right discrimination (Kinsbourne and Warrington, 1963a; Rutter, Tizard and Whitmore, 1970; Bale, 1974). An investigation by Shearer (1968) of an unselected group found a higher proportion of perfect performance on tests of right/left discrimination among the non-retarded group of readers. In addition he found that there was a higher proportion of mixed handedness and weak hand preference among the retarded group, and in tests of finger localization the retarded group scored well below the nonretarded group. Kaufman, Kalma and Kaufman (1978) also found established hand dominance at a younger age to be significantly related to cognitive, motor and directional variables.

Thomson (1975) administered a questionnaire on laterality to a group of reading retardates and a control group, including questions on handedness, eye preference, foot preference and ear preference. He suggests that the relationships between laterality and reading vary considerably depending upon the index used and the amount of information in each category; and that the significant feature in many cases of reading disability seems to be an individual pattern of inconsistency. He concludes that being mixed-handed, cross-lateral or left-eared gives the best 'predictions' of poor reading, whilst being completely uni-lateral is the best predictor of good reading. He hypothesizes that inconsistent laterality reflects a neurological organization which pre-disposes individuals to perform less well on ordered directional and sequential tasks which are essential in reading.

Wheeler, Watkins and McLaughlin (1977), in a study relating reading retardation and cross-laterality to short-term information-processing tasks, found that the cross-lateral group took significantly longer to process information correctly and their performance significantly deteriorated as the information load was increased from three to five units. The cross-lateral group were also significantly inferior to the controls (who had consistent laterality) on reading age. However, these results should be interpreted with caution as the numbers of children in each group were small ($N = 10$). An investigation by Sawyer and Brown (1977) found that less able boys showing a right preference of eye, hand and foot were superior in reading ability compared with their non-right-preferring counterparts, whilst an opposite trend was reported for more able children. However, this study involved a clinical sample and, following Annett and Turner's findings (1974) that clinical samples tended to result in findings of a relationship between laterality and educational attainments whereas random samples from normal popula-tions did not, the study was repeated in a normal school population (Sawyer, Lord and Brown, 1979). Similar results were obtained although the results for the junior school sample were not significant, leading to the possibility that lateral preference is more clearly established by the secondary school age. The authors conclude that the degree of establishment of right lateral preference is related to reading ability although only for less able children, possibly because more able non-right-preferring children are able to use compensatory techniques.

In a recent review of literature linking left-handedness, cerebral organization and reading disability, Beaumont and Rugg (1978) note that although the general association between left-handedness and reading ability is slight or nonexistent (Benton, 1975; Hardyck *et al.*, 1976), nevertheless there may be an association between less coherently lateralized cerebral systems and reading disability (McBurney and Dunn, 1976). Crossed eye–hand co-ordination was found to be associated with reading difficulty by Dunlop *et al.* (1973) whilst crossed ear–hand dominance was found to have a similar association by Bryden (1970). The authors suggest that the slight relationship found between these factors and dyslexia may be due to a dissociation between auditory and visual language laterality, more likely in left or mixed handers or in those with a typical lateral specialization for eye or ear–hand co-ordination, referring to a study by Hines and Satz (1974) which showed that in normal right handers the results of dichotic listening and divided visual field estimates of language lateralization correlate but in left handers there is a relative dissociation.

Two new avenues of research into laterality measures and hemispheric dominance have been developed in recent years — dichotic listening and visual half-field procedures, which rely on the assumption that hemispheric dominance can be inferred from ear and eye asymmetry. Satz's review (1976) of the literature relating to laterality and reading disability described 19 published and unpublished studies, 15 of which employed at least a dichotic verbal task and four of which employed a visual half-field task. Kimura referred to a study by Taylor (1962) which found a right ear advantage (REA) in both poor readers and good readers who were female (ages seven–11) but no REA in poor readers who were male — suggesting a developmental lag in left hemisphere speech in the latter group. A study by Kimura (1967) involving older boys (ages not specified) reported finding an REA and concluded that the normal developmental lag is simply accentuated in boys with reading problems. Sparrow and Satz (1970) found a similar REA for a specific reading disabled group and for average readers, although an analysis of variance revealed almost four times as many dyslexic children had a left ear advantage. Bryden (1970) revealed a REA for good and poor readers (69 per cent, 58 per cent respectively) whilst Zurif and Carson (1970) reported no REA. Satz, Rardin

spheric speech representation in disabled readers, as measured by the dichotic or VHF asymmetry scores, is only partially supported by the data because, firstly, most studies have reported a significant REA or RVHF in both normal and disabled readers and have not conducted the critical test of asymmetry differences between groups, and secondly, many studies have been marred by procedural artefacts such as ceiling and floor effects.

Beaumont and Rugg (1978), reviewing Satz's study and other studies on the lateralization of auditory language processing by dichotic listening techniques, suggest that although as Satz points out there are many problems of inference involved in such studies and methodological deficiencies inherent in several, it is possible to conclude that in younger dyslexic children at least a normal right ear advantage and normal lateralization of auditory language processing are to be found. A more recent study by Chasty, Turner and Seth (1976) found a significant association between right ear specialization and a rapid rate of progress in reading/language acquisition. However, a later experiment carried out by Chasty (1979) to investigate further this confused area, found that a sample of dyslexics showed a strong left ear advantage and indeed other experiments do not wholeheartedly support this conclusion (Taylor, in Kimura, 1967; Zurif and Carson, 1970; Bakker, 1973; Witelson and Rabinovitch, 1972; Darby, 1974; Thomson, 1976) but the authors feel it to be justified if true pathological samples are studied. They concede that there is less agreement about older children who, they feel, may have undergone changes as a result of having been dyslexic, but even so some studies have found the normal right ear advantage.

Reviewing divided visual field studies of language lateralization, they conclude that with verbal stimuli there is a tendency for the right visual field advantage to be smaller in dyslexics than normals (Kershner, 1977; Marcel *et al.*, 1974; Marcel and Rajan, 1975; McKeever and Van Deventer, 1975). One study (Leavell and Beck, 1959) in fact found a reversed left visual field superiority for digits. Three studies showed a superior right visual performance in dyslexics compared with controls (Olson, 1973; McKeever and Huling, 1970; Yeni-Komshian *et al.*, 1975) although in all three poor readers rather than dyslexics were used, and in one case no controls were used.

Only one study has examined divided visual field and dichotic listening studies, of verbal material, in dyslexic subjects (McKeever and Van Deventer, 1975). No correlation between the two measures was found but dyslexics showed normal dichotic listening performance and reduced visual field asymmetry, this latter finding being attributed to a dysfunction of left hemisphere visual-associative cortex.

Reviewing theoretical formulations of the associations between laterality and dyslexia, Beaumont and Rugg reject the maturational lag in lateralization hypothesis (suggested by Bakker, 1973; Kinsbourne, 1975; and Satz and Sparrow, 1970) on the grounds that there is no direct evidence for the maturation of the lateralization of cerebral language processing (Beaumont, 1978; Kinsbourne, 1976), and that the necessary interaction between the lag and the critical learning experience which would produce a chronic reading disorder has not been specified.

They also reject a second group of hypotheses which suggest a deficit in visual-verbal and therefore inter-hemispheric integration (Vellutino *et al.*, 1973, 1975; Marcel *et al.*, 1974; Marcel and Rajan, 1975). Witelson (1977b) in particular concluded that there was bilateralization of spatial function in dyslexics whereby analytic left-hemisphere functions are interfered with by right hemisphere spatial holistic functions, and Kershner (1975) ascribes dyslexia to a dysfunction of the integration of left and right hemisphere-based systems of linguistic analysis and spatial perception, or more recently (Kershner, 1977), to the inappropriate operation of right hemisphere-based perceptual coding strategies. Rosenthal (1973) suggests dyslexia can stem from both lesions of the right hemisphere, involving perceptual problems in the spatial arrangements of letters, words and sentences, and/or lesions of the left hemisphere which lead to problems in graphic code comprehension.

Beaumont and Rugg themselves suggest that in dyslexics there is a relatively bilateral processing of visual-verbal stimuli, rather than unilateral processing in the left hemisphere which leads not to *interference* in left hemisphere processes by right hemisphere activities (Witelson's view) but a *dissociation* of the two processes normally integrated in the left hemisphere by the bilateralization of one of them, leading to integration problems. They claim that this hypothesis offers a means to combine two types of explanation: interhemispheric integration and intersensory integration.

Vernon (1978), in commenting on Beaumont and Rugg's hypothesis, suggests that it is not so much the auditory linguistic functions of the left hemisphere which are affected in dyslexics but its analytic and sequential functions. She prefers to concentrate on difficulties in the reading process itself and their variation in different dyslexics.

More recently, Chasty (1979) has examined hemispheric specialism for language of dyslexic children. In a comparison of normal and dyslexic children using dichotic listening techniques, dyslexic children, in contrast to the normal children, were found to have a strong left ear advantage, indicating a marked right hemisphere control of language. Although right hemisphere control of language is not always associated with poor language skills, Chasty tentatively proposes that this 'different' development of hemispheric specialism for language 'appears to be the central core of the dyslexic disability'. In particular, the transmission of information in the brain is disrupted by a 'neural interference mechanism' which effectively prevents efficient control over the separate visual, auditory and kinaesthetic skills. Since Chasty does not explain this mechanism and since, on his own admission, the sample used in his experiment has serious shortcomings, this claim must at present remain unsubstantiated.

Newton, Thomson and Richards (1979) also conclude dyslexics have a brain organization, in terms of cortical specificity of function, which has a less clear-cut preponderance for verbal tasks and symbolic ordering in the left hemisphere than the non-dyslexic. This is reflected in a more inconsistent lateralization of function for sensory and motor mechanisms, with possible inconsistencies in perception (sensory) and production (motor) of a serial ordered and directional skill (viz. written language).

Although much of the evidence is conflicting, the weight of opinion at present tends to favour minimizing connections between laterality measures and reading disability, certainly at least at the lower age ranges. Satz (1975) states research has failed to show a relationship between left-handedness or deviant hand–eye preference and specific reading disability (Belmont and Birch, 1965; De Hirsch, Jansky and Langford, 1966; Satz and Friel, 1974, etc.); and further points that induction from these symptoms to the construct of 'faulty dominance' is speculative. As support for his position he cites that knowledge is still lacking on the relationship between handedness and cerebral speech dominance in adults, and that the relationship between handedness and cerebral speech dominance is virtually unknown in children. Satz and Sparrow found in an earlier study (1970) that all early developing aspects of laterality (e.g. manual preference, manual strength and dexterity, visual preference, controlling eye) are not significantly different in normal and retarded readers (aged 12), but late developing aspects of laterality (e.g. lateral awareness, finger differentiation, ear asymmetry and verbal intelligence) did differentiate the groups.

A recent study by Irwin and Newland (1977) compared children's knowledge of left and right with their knowledge of up and down. Poor readers (intelligence controlled) did not differ from normal readers in their ability to tell left from right or up from down. Evidence from investigations by Valtin (1970, 1978-9) based on 100 pairs of dyslexic and normal children also support the hypothesis that left-handedness, left-eyedness and mixed eye-hand dominance show no relationship to dyslexia. Two large-scale investigations involving whole populations found no connection between defective lateralization and retarded reading (Clark, 1970; Rutter *et al.*, 1970). A recent large-scale survey undertaken in California (Hardyck, 1977) of 7,688 children in grades 1-6 found no differences of any kind between left-handed and right-handed children (five tests of ability were given — figure copying, listening, attention, speed and persistence, intelligence using the Lorge-Thorndike and Stanford tests which include measures of reading, spelling and arithmetic). In fact the left-handed children were as likely to be at the upper end of the ability range as at the lower end. Hardyck found Annett and Turner's hypothesis (see below) to be not supported (possibly because the latter's sample was small) and he also found no support for the suggestion that handedness in some children may be related to developmental delay of cognitive functioning. Yule and Rutter (1976), reporting on five studies of total child populations, distinguished between backward readers (those children who, irrespective of their ability, are at the bottom end of a continuum of reading attainment) and specifically retarded readers (those children who are underachieving in relation to their chronological age and their level of general intelligence), and found errors in right-left differentiation to be higher in the backward readers' group (28 per cent) than in the retarded readers (15 per cent). Goldberg and Schiffman (1972), in their attempt to draw together the available information in this field, report that many surveys have failed to support crossed dominance as a consistent link with reading problems. A study of a class of 77 pupils who were tested in reading in the first grade showed that 49 per cent of the students favoured the right hand and right eye; 30 per cent favoured the right hand and left eye; and the remaining 21 per cent exhibited other combinations of hand-eye co-ordination. When tested again in the third grade it was found that students with mixed eye-hand co-

ordination read as well as students with consistent right-sided dominance. They also cite evidence from studies by Whittey and Kopel
(1936), Johnston (1942) and Smith (1950) which showed no correlation between anomalies of lateral dominance and poor reading.
A slightly different approach to laterality has been taken by Annett
(1970), who stresses the distinction between pure left-handers, pure
right-handers and mixed-handers or ambidexters and shows that they
appear to occur in complete population samples in binomial proportions, thus implying that there is no evidence of genetic transmission
of handedness so that neither left-handedness or mixed-handedness is
suggestive of abnormality. Confirming Sparrow and Satz's findings
(1970), Annett shows that consistent left-handers showed a high
average language development, even slightly above that of the consistent right-handers. The mixed-handers showed the poorest verbal
development, which could be seen as consistent with the notion of
a maturational lag in mixed-handed children. Annett also advances
a genetic explanation for lateralization of speech functions, and
suggests that cerebral dominance may be distributed in a binomial
fashion similar to the distribution of handedness.

Kershner (1975) also has information on the distribution of lateral
polymorphism in human populations. Using Annett as one of his
sources, he estimates that 70-90 per cent of human populations are
dextral with left-hemisphere speech representation, that three-eighths
of these are crossed-dominant with respect to eye-preference and that
the remaining 10-30 per cent are left-handed and/or mixed with speech
represented either on the left, the right or bilaterally (Annett, 1972;
Groden, 1969; O'Donnell, 1970). This leads to the formation of four
major groups: right hand–right eye, right hand–left eye, left hand–
left eye, and left hand–right eye, although the usefulness of the latter
two groupings is questionable due to the heterogeneous nature of left-
handers (they tend to be inconsistent with regard to hand, eye and
hemispheric speech lateralization). In fact the incidence of pure left-
sidedness has been found to be no greater than five per cent (Annett,
1972) and this is probably an overestimate since studies have tended
to examine only hand preference, whereas many pure left-handers tend
to possess mixed or right eye preference. Kershner goes on to report
findings from a series of studies carried out by himself and colleagues
(Kershner, 1970, 1971, 1972; Kershner and Jeng, 1972; Kershner and
Brown, in preparation) which showed that crossed ocular-manual
laterality was related to superior special ability, and hypothesizes that

consistent hand and eye preference in comparison may facilitate the acquisition of reading skills. A recent study in this country (Hart and Fagg, 1976), carried out by the National Children's Bureau, discovered that the proportion of left-handed children has increased. A similar survey carried out 12 years ago showed a left-handedness rate of six per cent but the present study revealed 10.4 per cent of 11-year-olds to be left-handed and 5.8 per cent to be ambidextrous. Fewer girls than boys were left-handed (72 girls for every 100 boys). On tests, the right-handed pupils scored better than left-handers on general reading and comprehension, with ambidextrous children scoring somewhere between the two groups. There was no difference in the maths or writing tests. However, teachers, despite contrary evidence, thought left-handers had poorer control of hands, were bad writers and had a slight tendency to poor speech.

Summary

Although the field of laterality and reading disability is a confusing one, a few general points can be made. There seems to be some kind of relationship between some measures of laterality and reading disability. In many clinical situations poor readers present disturbances in laterality. For example Goldberg and Schiffman (1972) report that, of the children they see with reading problems, 65 per cent (not statistically significant) have some disturbance in laterality on evaluation of foot, hand and eye dominance. Thomson (1976) found a clinical sample of dyslexics showed a less well established dominance of hemispheric function. However, findings in clinical situations cannot be generalized to the total population, and in fact large-scale surveys (e.g. Balow, 1963; Clark, 1970; Rutter *et al.*, 1971) have failed to find a similar association, although in this case various aetiologies of reading failure may be present which may make the data not easily comparable to clinical evidence. Satz (1976) stresses this point and argues that more research is needed with normal children of specified ages before extrapolations can be made to clinical groups.

A more important point is that the great majority of children with laterality problems have no reading problems (Singleton, 1976) and that dyslexia is not more frequently present in children who are poorly lateralized (Goldberg and Schiffman, 1972). Since, nevertheless, there seems to be a relationship between reading disability and either ill-established or crossed (or mixed laterality), this had led some researchers to suggest that measures of laterality do not in themselves predict a child's reading performance but, in combination with other disturbances, may be a useful source of information (Anthony, 1968). The variable of IQ also has to be taken into account as it is possible that the laterality variable may only be significant for less able children. A study by Tinker (1965) showed no relationship between laterality and reading disability, but only children whose mean IQ ranged from 126 to 131 were studied. However, two studies which included lower ability children did find a relationship between reading retardation and mixed dominance (Koos, 1964; Trieschman, 1968).

Satz (1976) is at pains to point out the various methodological and conceptual problems in this area. Some of the methodological problems include procedural artefacts, ceiling and floor effects, and failure to isolate specific age effects on tasks so that within- and between-group differences may be masked. Possibly more serious are the conceptual problems. Semmes (1968) states the concept of cerebral dominance '... is little worse than a label, a restatement of the finding that lesions of one hemisphere produce deficits that lesions of the other hemisphere do not', suggesting the concept is virtually useless since it proposes nothing about mechanism. Furthermore the validity of laterality tests as measures of cerebral dominance, as mentioned above, must seriously be questioned. Satz (1976) investigated this problem conducting a Baysean analysis using estimated base rates for left- and right-brain speech in the normal population of right-handed adults and the estimated frequencies for the right- and left-ear asymmetry in the same population. This showed that the probability of left-brain speech given a right-ear advantage was very high but not much higher (p = 0.97) than the probability of left-brain speech given a left-ear advantage (p = 0.90). When subjects are grouped into a predicted right-brain speech group, based on an LEA in a dichotic verbal task, the probability of misclassification is about 90 per cent. However, the population base rates for speech lateralization are strongly asymmetric in favour of the left-hemisphere so one would expect there to be a definite likelihood of left-brain speech, given either an REA or LEA.

In conclusion, then, whilst measures of cerebral dominance and laterality by themselves may be of limited value, they may be of use in combination with other measures, especially those concerned with the transfer of information from one part of the brain to another, in particular the information processing approach.

Information processing

Introduction

One of the most recent and fastest growing areas of research into specific learning disabilities is that of information-processing. Dinnage's review of research relating to specific learning disabilities in *The Handicapped Child* published in 1970 refers to only two studies of impairment in short-term memory (Schubenz and Bohmig, 1964; Schubenz and Buchwald, 1964), and Sampson's review of the literature concerned with dyslexia 1925-75 briefly refers to problems of visual and verbal sequencing and temporal ordering. However, by 1979, Goodacre, in an article entitled 'The state of reading research in the United Kingdom' writes, 'Increasingly the dyslexic is seen as having a deficiency in information-processing, especially in naming or labelling and in memory information storage and capacity, which seems to affect visual and auditory sequencing.'

Most researchers in this area have in mind some kind of schema of the human information-processing system, although they may be carrying out work on only one small part of the stages of processing. Many of the studies are small-scale and relate to very specific aspects of memory or processing, and have little wider applicability. However, there are in particular two detailed accounts of the information-processing approach which are supported by evidence from work carried out by or quoted by the authors.

The first is to be found in Farnham-Diggory's book *Learning Disabilities*, published in 1978. She emphasizes the importance of relating research to theory: 'True information-processing research must permit us to make some inferences about the relationship of the research to a theory ... and it must involve at least an implicit model of stages of processing – that is, the experiment must provide some kind of data about what the subject is doing, inside his head, as he performs the task.' In addition she presents her own schematic flow chart of the human information-processing system.

The first three processes in this schema are concerned with detecting very small aspects of information contained in an object or event. Not all the features of an object or event are picked up at once, and as the information about the features comes in, some of it is retained immediately in the feature buffers – short-term memories for sensory information, of which there are probably several, certainly one each for visual, auditory and tactual information. It is then integrated with other

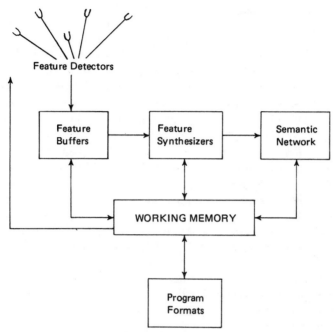

A schematic flow chart of the human information processing system

Farnham-Diggory (1978)

Reproduced by kind permission of Fontana/Open Books

information in the feature synthesizers but this must take place quickly as information fades out of its buffered state very fast. Next the synthesized information must be given meaning, and this is done via the semantic network which provides a collection of ideas or a concept relating to the synthesized information. Complex programmes that repeatedly activate feature detectors and semantic memory are kept in the working memory, from where they can be retrieved when necessary.

These processes all take place at very high speeds. An adult normally registers visual features (i.e. gets them into the buffer) in about 50 msec (50 thousandths of a second). They stay here for about another 200 msec when they are transferred into the synthesizer. The information takes a further 50 msc to be transferred into the working memory so that by 300 msec information has gone through all the initial stages of perceptual processing and has commenced operations involving semantic memory and working memory.

The second account of the information-processing approach to learning disabilities is that advanced by Stanley (1975). However, he restricts himself to a visual information-processing paradigm. There are three stages in this schema: the visual information stores (VIS), short-term memory (STM) and long-term memory (LTM). In the first stage the image (or feature in Diggory's terminology) is retained in a high capacity, short-lived storage sometimes called the icon. This visual information decays rapidly, usually disappearing in less than one second (250 msec according to Diggory). An encoding process transfers a smaller, more manageable amount of this information into the next stage of the memory system, primary memory (Waugh and Norman, 1965) or short-term memory. This is more resistant to decay but of considerably more limited capacity. It is strengthened by rehearsal processes and lasts long enough to provide information for subsequent responding. From short-term memory, information is transferred to long-term memory, a more or less permanent store from which information can be retrieved.

Obviously Stanley is concentrating on *visual* information only, whereas Diggory is concerned with all types of perceptual information. The two schemas can be related in the following way:

Stanley	*Farnham-Diggory*
Visual information store	Feature detectors
Short-term memory	Feature buffers
	Feature synthesizers
Long-term memory	Semantic memory

It is proposed to review the available evidence according to the processes outlined in these two schemas; in particular concentrating on three main areas: the initial stages of perceptual or feature processing, short-term memory and long-term memory. The section on the initial stages will include both visual and auditory processing, and the transfer of information from the primary receptive phase to the secondary synthesizing phase. The section on long-term memory will include deficits in semantic memory and consideration of the retention of information over time. A final section will be concerned with overall deficits in sequencing ability. However, it should be emphasized that the material reviewed does not always fall neatly into these categories and therefore a certain amount of overlapping is inevitable.

Initial stages of perceptual or feature processing

(1) Visual processing

Early studies in this field were devoted to examining the characteristics and duration of the VIS. Research by Averbach and Coriell (1961), and Sperling (1960), found that information was retained in the VIS for up to 200–300 msec. A similar measure of visual persistence was found by Haber and Nathanson (1968) and Haber and Standing (1970).

Stanley has carried out several experiments into the properties of the VIS and transfer of information into the STM. Using a technique developed by Eriksen and Collins (1968), he presented subjects with two-part displays comprising the letters N and O, two halves of a cross and a cross surrounded by a square (Stanley and Hall, 1973). Two measures were obtained: the inter-stimulus interval at which the two parts (presented in succession) were first reported, and the identification of the separated elements (correct on three successive presentations). The subjects were a sample of 33 dyslexics (reading 2.5 years below normal, performance average or better in other subjects, no gross behavioural problems or organic disorders) and 33 'normals'. For normal children to perceive the two parts of the figure they had to be separated by at least 100 msec. For the dyslexic children to perceive separation, the parts had to be separated by 140 msec. Stanley and Hall concluded that dyslexics have 30 to 50 msec-longer separation times than normals or 30–50 per cent longer VIS duration. In the second part of the experiment, identification of the separated elements, the normal group were able to say (or draw) the two parts of the figure if they were separated by at least 180 msec (feature-synthesizing time). The dyslexic children needed almost twice as much time to identify the separated parts correctly: 320 msec.

A similar study (Stanley, 1975) investigated dichoptic and binocular presentations of two halves of a black cross, one half being presented at varying inter-stimulus intervals after the other half. Again dyslexics were found to have thresholds at greater intervals than controls (significant) of the same magnitude as the earlier study.

Stanley has also carried out several experiments comparing the performance of dyslexics and normals in processing various types of information. An early investigation compared dyslexics and normals recalling letter arrays after brief presentation (Stanley and Hall, 1973). Four six-letter displays were presented, one at a time in random order.

The children had to recognize each letter before it was covered by a patterned mask (such as an asterisk). The mask was delayed in 20 msec steps until the latter was recognized correctly. For the normal children, it had to be delayed about 50 msec but for the dyslexics another 15 msec was required for accurate recall. An experiment using digits instead of letters (Stanley, 1976) showed that dyslexics in fact performed at a higher level than controls and had slightly faster reaction times, although this was not significant. However, when the error patterns were examined, dyslexics were found to have consistently confused the digits having curved features, especially 3, 6, 8, 9, (2).

Lastly, an investigation into the visual processing of straight lines in dyslexics and normal children again concluded that dyslexics require longer inter-stimulus intervals than normals to report accurate stimulus presentations, of the order 10 to 15 msec. The experiment had two parts. In the first part, pairs of stimulus lines (white tape on a black background), of the same orientation and spatially overlapping, were projected from separate fields of a three-channel tachistoscope. Subjects had to judge whether one or two lines appeared at each presentation, at orientations from 0 to 90°. In the second part, single straight-line contours were preceded by a homogeneous light mask.

However, Vellutino (1979b) queries Stanley and Hall's interpretations of their findings, suggesting that it is not necessarily the case that poor readers have longer inter-stimulus intervals due to poor trace persistence; it may be due to a more conservative response strategy (attempting to be certain about what they saw) or to the difficulty poor readers generally have in identifying letters. He goes on to quote evidence from studies (Stanley and Malloy, 1975; Stanley, 1976) countering the claim that the visual trace is sustained longer in poor than in normal readers, including some using the forced-choice technique to evaluate trace persistence, rather than the absolute-judgement format employed by Stanley and his colleagues which relies rather heavily on subjective judgement. A study by Arnett (1977) found no significant differences between poor and normal readers on perceptual integration or rate of processing, and a study by Stanley (1976) using the forced-choice technique found that poor readers performed considerably better than normal readers in a task evaluating the rate of processing of individually presented digits from 0 to 9. Other studies by Fisher and Frankfurter (1977), Alwitt (1963) and Morrison, Giordani and Nagy (1977) also cast doubt on the suggestion that trace duration is longer for poor readers than for normal readers. Vellutino concludes that studies *not* supporting the hypothesis that reading disability is due to deficit form perception resulting from dysfunction in initial stage processing outnumber those that do.

Other studies have also investigated the purpose and duration of the VIS or iconic memory stage. Treisman *et al.* (1975) concluded that visual stimuli last for about 120 msec. When two different stimuli are presented within 300 msec of each other, they tend to be seen as one. Sakitt (1976) suggested that the function of iconic memory appears to be to retain images long enough for their information to be extracted and transferred to the next stage of processing.

In a study of iconic memory and reading performance, Riding and Pugh (1977) attempt to relate information-processing to the reading process. They suggest that the reading process may be divided into three stages: (1) registration in visual-sensory memory of the images of the words scanned; (2) analysis in short-term memory of the meaning of the words and sentences; (3) storage of the sense of the sentences in long-term memory. In efficient reading, the image of a word in iconic memory must be retained long enough for its features to be transmitted to the meaning analysis stage. If it fades too quickly, the reader's eyes will remain focused on each word until analysed, causing scanning to be slow and jerky. If it remains too long, it may forward mask the images of the words that follow. In their own study, Riding and Pugh gave 36 nine-year-old children a test of iconic memory and the Neale Analysis of Reading Ability, which yielded scores of reading fluency, accuracy and comprehension. Results indicated that moderate icon-persistence was related to better reading performance than either short or long persistence on all three measures. Long persistence gave marginally better reading performance than short persistence. They suggest that future research could investigate the effect of increasing exposure time of words for short iconic subjects and decreasing exposure time of words for long iconic subjects. In addition the effect of providing a greater contrast between print and background for short duration subjects and less contrast for long duration subjects might be examined.

(2) Auditory processing

Much less work has been carried out with auditory processing. It has been known for some time that learning-disabled children have difficulties processing auditory information but most studies have been either to do with auditory perception or audio-visual integration or auditory memory. However, some work has been done on the initial

stage of registering auditory information. Tallal (in press) experiment-
ally manipulated speech sounds by means of a speech synthesizer. The
wave variation that is processed in registering a single letter takes place
in about 50 msec, but aphasic children needed about 100 msec to hear
it correctly. It follows that children who cannot process auditory
information that fast will mishear, or not be able to discriminate the
whole syllable. Some reading-disabled children showed similar difficulties in auditory discrimination of speech sounds. However, this was
not true of all, which led Tallal to suggest that there may be more than
one cause of disabled reading.

(3) Perceptual masking
     The concept of perceptual masking has already been mentioned
above (Stanley and Hall, 1973; Riding and Pugh, 1977). Kahneman
(1968) reviewed studies showing that forward masking (previously
presented image makes next one less clear) produces greater loss than
backward masking (existing image interfered with by presentation of
a further stimulus). Masking studies enable us to estimate the persistence of iconic memory. In a series of experiments conducted by Ellis
and Miles (1978) 41 dyslexic boys and 41 controls were presented with
arrays of seven digits at exposure times ranging from 50 to 1,200 msec.
Each array of digits was immediately followed by a mask so as to
prevent further processing. The results showed that the mean score for
the number of digits correctly reproduced was lower at all intervals
for dyslexics but became particularly marked at about 150 msec after
presentation, suggesting according to the authors that the source of the
difficulty in dyslexia cannot be early fading of information from the
VIS.
     In the same series of experiments subjects (61 dyslexic children,
22 controls and 26 first-year undergraduates) were presented with a
randomized chess-board with half the cells filled in in a random arrangement. One matrix was shown, and, after a variable inter-stimulus
interval, a second was shown either exactly the same or different in
respect of one cell only. The results showed no differences between the
two groups, suggesting that the rate of decay from the visual code
store and its overall capacity are the same in a dyslexic person as in
anyone else, and evidence suggests that iconic persistence decreases
with age (Pollack *et al.*, 1969; Gummerman and Gray, 1972). In five-
year-olds a letter can be masked at 125 msec, when it is not even fully
registered. In eight- and 10-year-olds, a letter can be masked at 75 msec,

and by the age of 12 or 13 this has been reduced to 50 msec (Liss and Haith, 1970; Welsandt and Meyer, 1974; Welsandt, Zupnick and Meyer, 1973).

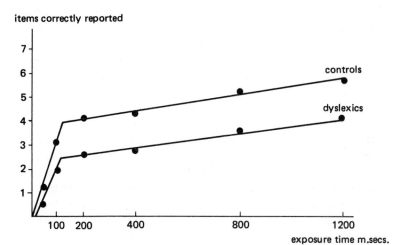

items correctly reported

exposure time m.secs.

The number of digits correctly reported by dyslexic and control children in backward masking experiment

Ellis and Miles (1978)

Reproduced by kind permission of the *Dyslexia Review*

Guthrie (1972) argues that individual variation in iconic memory ability will be reflected in reading performance. Farnham-Diggory and Gregg (1975) analyse the relationship between perceptual masking and reading in greater detail. Normally it takes a picked-up letter about 50 msec to register. If perception is interrupted by a second letter during the 50 msec, the first letter will not be seen. If the two letters are far enough apart spatially there will be no masking no matter what the time parameters are, but if the letters (a) are close together, (b) share similar contours and (c) enter the system erratically, then masking may occur. When dyslexic children read aloud they may say strange words. Although they may be able to tell us the individual letters one by one, they may experience masking during reading if the feature-processing system works slowly. These children may pick up letters from a line of print that is incompatible with their processing rates so that printed features may interfere with previous features.

Test words (exposed for 2 sec)	What the reader said
bracket	'broket'
conceal	'concol'
kerosene	'konsen'
screw	'scree'
alternate	'alfoonite'
definite	'defynit'
estimate	'extermate'
majesty	'marijest'
solution	'slotion'
uncomfortable	'icomfort'

Misreadings by dyslexic children. From Farnham-Diggory (1978).

Reproduced by kind permission of Fontana/Open Books

The authors suggest that remediation for such children might take the form of displaying single letters one at a time on a scope sequentially, at a speed appropriate for each individual child.

(4) Perseveration

Stanley and Hall (1973) found that dyslexics have a greater visual persistence (VIS) than controls. This was displayed in the very earliest stages of processing, the first 50–300 msec. Thomson and Wilsher (1978), in a study where subjects recalled strings of digits presented tachistoscopically in conditions of partial recall using digit matrices with cued rows recalled, found that for dyslexics the peak of correct responses for the 3 × 3 array occurred at 400 msec (better than controls) and might be due to longer duration of VIS as subjects would have a longer time in which to read off the information after 'cueing'. In the 3 × 4 and 3 × 5 arrays the information had been reached and the extra information might have caused interference.

Morrison *et al.* (1977) showed subjects visual stimuli consisting of letters, geometric forms and abstract forms for 150 msec, and then, after delays of varying lengths (0–2,000 msec, unpredictably scrambled), presented an indicator where one of the forms had been. In this way it was possible to:

(i)   estimate the amount of information initially perceived by the subject (0 msec delay)

(ii) trace duration of information in VIS phase (0–300 msec)

(iii) estimate the amount of information encoded and transferred to more permanent storage (300–2,000 msec).

No differences appeared between good and poor readers at early processing stages, but if the indicator was delayed by as much as 300 msec,
the poor reader was in trouble. Whilst this appears to contradict the
earlier mentioned studies, this experiment shows that the perseveration
does not continue indefinitely and that dyslexic children, like normal
children, must *act* on the contents of memory in order to preserve it.

Short-term memory

Short-term memory is thought to be a limited capacity system (four
to seven chunks) of brief duration (about 30 seconds). Active recoding
of information must take place if the amount of information presented
exceeds the upper limit of the individual's short-term memory, or if the
information is to be retained beyond the duration of the short-term
memory and deposited in long-term memory.

A number of studies have found poor readers to be inferior to
normal readers on measures of visual memory. Katz and Wicklund
(1971) found the response latencies for poor readers in a test of rapid
scanning of a probe word embedded in two- and three-word sentences
to be longer than those for normal readers, but a follow-up study (Katz
and Wicklund, 1972) using letters rather than words and a manual
rather than a vocal response as the index of recognition showed no
group differences on response latencies, possibly because both poor and
normal reader groups relied on visual matching rather than naming for
identification. The study by Doehring (1968) comparing dyslexic and
normal readers showed the groups to be differentiated on several tests
of visual memory but comparable on other measures, thus leading to
inconclusive findings. Similarly Lyle and Goyen (1968) found poor
readers to be less accurate than normals in tests involving immediate,
delayed and sequential memory, but not to differ in number of
sequencing or reversal errors. Further studies by Goyen and Lyle
(1971a, 1971b, 1973) and Lyle and Goyen (1975) again generally
found poor readers to be inferior to normal readers on various matching
tests performed under timed conditions, leading them to the conclusion, however, that speed of processing rather than short-term
memory or form discrimination distinguishes poor readers and that
reading disability may be related to a perceptual deficit associated with
maturational lag.

Vellutino (1979b) criticizes these studies on the grounds that it is
a dubious procedure to use children in their first year of reading when
the normal reader has already experienced success and is therefore pre-

disposed to better performance. He also suggests that the disparities between the reader groups may have been due to difficulties in encoding or rehearsal abilities rather than differences in visual processing. To support this hypothesis, he quotes evidence from a number of studies carried out in his own laboratory to ascertain the influence of verbal encoding deficiencies on comparisons of visual memory in poor and normal readers aged nine to 14. In a test involving brief (600 msec) visual presentations of scrambled letters, words of varying length, simple designs and three-digit numerals, poor readers did considerably better in copying words than in pronouncing or spelling the same stimuli. Their performance was comparable to the normal readers on graphic reproduction of both scrambled letters and words, and there were no differences between the groups on memory for simple designs and numerals. However, the poor readers did less well on the items which taxed short-term visual memory (the five-letter items). A second study (Vellutino, Smith, Steger and Kaman, 1975), comparing poor and normal readers at age seven and 11, in general replicated the major findings of the earlier investigation. A rather different study involving the recall of words of varying length printed in Hebrew (Vellutino *et al.*, 1973; Vellutino, Steger, Kaman and DeSetto, 1975) found that poor readers copied the Hebrew words from visual memory as well as the normal readers. Support for Vellutino's hypothesis also comes from a study by Liberman and Shankweiler (1978). Poor and normal readers were compared on an adaptation of Kimura's (1963) test of memory for recurring figures. Poor readers were found to be slightly better than the good readers in memory for nonsense designs, and the two groups were comparable in face recognition. However, poor readers did significantly less well on the recognition of recurring nonsense syllables, leading the authors to the conclusion that 'the good reader had a clear advantage: he could recode the information phonetically and thus hold it more efficiently in short-term memory'.

Long-term memory

(1) Deficits in semantic memory

Many researchers have drawn attention to the fact that although learning-disabled children may have problems with processing visual information, a more serious deficit occurs after the purely visual features of the information have been analysed and when the material has to be named or labelled. Almost any programme in working memory will involve names or verbal labels of some kind. Spring and Capps (1974) investigated whether dyslexics could name familiar pictures, colours and digits as fast as normal children. The children (seven- to 13-year-olds) were shown 25 pictures of common objects, 30 colour patches of familiar colours and 50 randomly sequenced digits, and asked to name the items as fast as they could. Digit naming was tested twice, and naming speeds, i.e. the number of items named per second, were then computed. Naming efficiency was found to increase with age, and normal readers were generally faster than poor readers, especially at naming digits. Spring and Capps also examined the extent to which rehearsal skills affected performance. The children were shown eight cards containing the digits 1 to 8 one at a time, at a one-second rate, which were then placed face down in a row from the subject's left. The child was then shown a new card with one of the digits on it, and he had to point to the card he thought contained the matching digit. In order to determine whether rehearsal was taking place, Spring and Capps recorded the subjects' eye movements. Subjects who scanned the cards from left to right, the order of their appearance, were probably rehearsing the cards in that order and displayed a strong primacy effect. All but one of the good readers were scanners, but only half the poor readers were scanners. The overall performance of the poor readers was worse than the performance of the good readers but the problem lay with the rehearsal (primary) capacities of some of them. (In fact, the deficiencies demonstrated by the poor readers derived from the fact that they were slow to name items and consequently had little time for rehearsal.) Other experiments show a similar primacy defect and rehearsal defect (Swanson, 1977; Torgesen and Goldman, 1977; Bauer, 1977). A study by Denckla and Rudel (1976) investigated rapid 'automatized' naming (RAN) of pictured objects, colours, letters and numbers in dyslexics, other learning-disabled children and normal controls. As in Spring's experiment (1974) the main order of difficulty was as follows: digits were named faster than colours, which in turn were named faster than objects by all subjects. Objects and letters were relatively more difficult for dyslexics to name rapidly, as compared to non-dyslexics and normals. The authors point out that these findings are not compatible with Critchley's (1970) explanation of dyslexia as a form of asymbolia: object and letter-naming are the most powerful predictors at the kindergarten level of which children are likely to fail at reading (Jansky and De Hirsch, 1972). They conclude that a deficit in automatization of verbal responses to visual stimuli correlates specifically with dyslexia. This deficit is not part of a generalized slowing of reaction time since the dyslexics, compared with the non-dyslexic subjects who had more diffuse brain damage, had a higher mean performance IQ.

Studies undertaken by Miles and his colleagues have also investigated verbal labelling. Three experiments were carried out by Done and Miles (1978) to test the performance of dyslexics at tasks where material has to be labelled, compared with tasks where it does not. In the first experiment sequences of digits, pictures and nonsense shapes were presented to subjects in a tachistoscope, each for a period of two seconds. The subjects were required to recall the spatial order in which the items appeared. The dyslexics were found to be differentially weakest at ordering digits, which thus supported the hypothesis that the differences between dyslexic and control subjects would be greatest in the case of the correct ordering of digits (requires verbal labelling) and least in the case of correct ordering of nonsense shapes (does not permit verbal labelling, at least without practice).

The second experiment investigated not only verbal labelling but rehearsal. If rehearsal is prevented from taking place by articulatory suppression (by saying the word 'the' at the rate of once per second for varying intervals) then any advantage arising from the use of names must be lost and the differences between dyslexic and control subjects will diminish or disappear. The results showed that differences between dyslexic and control subjects were minimal in the four conditions of articulatory suppression but significantly different when no articulatory expression was involved.

The third experiment involved learning the names of nonsense shapes. The dyslexics were found to be appreciably weaker than controls in arranging the shapes in correct order with the help of saying their names aloud.

A second series of experiments was conducted by Ellis and Miles (1978), two of which dealt with verbal naming. In the first of these, 21 dyslexics and 21 controls were required to differentiate between (i) pairs of letters (e.g. RR, RM) which could be judged as the 'same' or 'different' on the basis of their visual characteristics and (ii) pairs of letters (e.g. Mm) which could be judged as 'the same' only if they were named. The dyslexics were found to take no more time than the controls in saying 'same' or 'different' in the case of the visually matched pairs but took a significantly longer time when the response involved naming. The other experiment involved a similar procedure using four nonsense shapes instead of letters, and these were varied in the following ways: (i) a rotation through 90°, (ii) an up-down reversal, (iii) a left-right reversal, and (iv) a mutation, i.e. a slight variant. There were no significant differences between the dyslexics and control groups in any of the conditions in the time needed to respond correctly, suggesting that what is sometimes called 'orientation difficulty' (which includes left-right confusion as well as b-d confusion) may in fact be the consequences of a difficulty over naming (b and d show high acoustic confusability). The authors conclude that the deficiency in dyslexia lies not so much in a weakness at picking out visual features but in a deficiency involving the 'name code' pathway which operates in parallel with visual analysis and analysis for meaning. The deficiency is thought to lie in a 'programme of motor instructions' into which the visual features of information are converted and which can afterwards be verbalized or made articulate.

Cohen and Netley (1978) compared children with specific learning disabilities with controls on several tests of information processing and memory. Comparatively large deficits were shown in memory tests using verbal items, with slight deficits shown in memory tests involving visual figures. They concluded that learning-disabled subjects have reading problems associated with the inability to put a serial string of letters together rather than lack the capacity to recognize letter or word patterns.

A study by Vellutino, Steger, De Setto and Phillips (1975) also shows that the inability to recall individual letters may not be associated with poor reading. Subjects selected from the second, fourth and sixth grades were presented with Hebrew letters which they were asked to recall immediately, 24 hours later and six months later. Their performance was compared with that of subjects familiar with Hebrew letters as a control measure. Results showed that retention in the non-Hebrew group was equivalent under all temporal conditions but the performance of both was poorer than the Hebrew groups under the immediate and 24-hour conditions. There was no difference after a six-month delay period. It was concluded that deficient visual memory is an unlikely source of specific reading disability. Various other studies have also pointed to deficiencies in the processing system which stress semantic rather than visual problems. Shankweiler and Liberman (1976) suggest that while they do not rule out the possibility that read words can be held temporarily in some visual form, there is evidence that reading involves storing, indexing and retrieving information by means of a phonetic code and that the reader typically engages in recoding from script to some phonetic form. They cite experimental evidence for phonetic recoding: in a large number of investigations it has been found that when lists of letters or alphabetically written words are presented orthographically to be read and remembered, the confusions in short-term memory are based on phonetic rather than visual similarity (Baddeley, 1966, 1968, 1970; Conrad, 1964, 1972; Hintzman, 1967; Kintsch and Buschke, 1969; Sperling, 1963). It has been inferred from these findings that the stimulus items had been stored in phonetic rather than visual form. In an experiment conducted by Shankweiler and Liberman (1976), where good and poor readers had to recall, immediately and after a delay, phonetically confusable and non-confusable letters, it was found that poor readers were less able to construct and use a phonetic code. The results were similar for confusable letters, but good readers did much better on non-confusable letters. However, a study by Steinheiser and Guthrie (1977) of three groups of readers – disabled readers, same-age normal readers and younger normal readers – found that the disabled and younger groups were slower on physically confusable words rather than dissimilar words, whereas the other readers performed at the same speed for both tasks. The authors concluded that perceptual and decoding processes are learned by normal readers but are a primary source of deficiency in disabled readers.

Perfetti and his colleagues are also of the opinion that children with reading problems have a limited ability to code information phonetically, and may not process semantic information with the same degree of speed and efficiency as normal readers. In a series of experiments (Perfetti and Goldman, 1976; Perfetti and Hogaboam, 1975; Perfetti, Finger and Hogaboam, 1978; Perfetti *et al.*, 1977) they found that poor readers do not process connected text as efficiently as normal readers, although there is no reason to believe that they differ with respect to their ability to extract semantic information. The problem seems to lie in their less efficient coding of linguistic units no smaller than the word or syllable, thus leading to difficulties in using the semantic information that may be coded in these units, particularly under time constraints.

Vernon (1979), in noting the deficiencies of retarded readers, includes the inability to analyse whole-word sounds into phonemes (Savin, 1972; Rozin and Gleitman, 1977), deficiencies in naming (Denckla and Rudel, 1976), vowel sound problems (Vellutino, Harding,

Phillips and Steger, 1975) and the inability to group words together (Perfetti and Goldman, 1976).

(2) Retention and co-ordination of information over time

Miles and Wheeler (1974) suggest that the commonly accepted view of dyslexia as a 'difficulty over orientation' can in fact be seen as part of a new theory they propose: that dyslexia is 'an inability to retain complex information over time'. As evidence they cite that dyslexics can do the first two 'direction' tests in the Terman scale because the 'load' involved is not great. They can also do the Advanced Matrices Test (Raven) because they are able to scan patterns either horizontally or vertically, not necessarily both at once. They also do well at picture completion because it is not complex. However, they have problems spelling long words correctly and reciting arithmetic tables because in these tasks they are required to memorize too great a load of information. This helps to explain why they can read words they cannot spell. This approach helps explain why dyslexics do poorly in the 'digits reversed' task in WISC: earlier information fades before later information can be absorbed. The confusion between b and d is explained by the overload of information required when the child has to decide whether the loop is to the right or the left. Finally, they cite evidence that dyslexics are weak at reading music, which suggests it is the complexity of the material rather than its verbal or non-verbal nature which presents problems (in contrast to the Ellis and Miles study, 1978, mentioned earlier, which concluded that b/d confusion is due to lack of verbal naming ability rather than orientational problems).

Cohen and Netley (1978) also agreed that the inability of the memory to cope with overload is a central feature in many cases of reading/spelling disabilities. In the study by Thomson and Wilsher (1978), performance by dyslexics on the Information Absorption task was significantly poorer than the controls, suggesting dyslexics have a smaller information capacity.

A study by Bruijel (1967) revealed no difference between normals and children with reading difficulties in an experiment which involved either one or two discriminative dimensions. However, an experiment conducted by Van Meel, Vlek and Bruijel (1970), in which the number of discriminant dimensions in a visual discrimination task varied between two and five, did show that children with learning difficulties have relatively more difficulties compared with normals in complex visual discrimination tasks, due to deficiencies in temporal integration.

Farnham-Diggory and Gregg (1975b) investigated two aspects of memory: memory span and memory scanning. In the first task — memory span — letters were presented one-by-one serially in either the visual or the auditory modality. Children were required to say the letters back after four letters had been presented, 10 times in each modality.

When the visual task was presented first, the good readers started at about 80 per cent correct, falling to 65 per cent correct at the end of their 10 trials, due to memory fatigue. After the visual trials they were given the auditory task, and their performance went back up, this time to 90 per cent correct, falling to about 75 per cent correct. Similar results were obtained when good readers were given the auditory task first; they performed at about 80 per cent correct falling to 68 per cent. When they were subsequently given the visual task, they went back up to 90 per cent correct, falling to about 58 per cent correct. The poor readers had a very different pattern of performance. When they began with the visual task, they scored an astonishing 100 per cent correct over the first two trials but fell dramatically down to 50 per cent at the end of the 10 trials. When they subsequently tried the auditory tasks, there was only a slight improvement — to about 68 per cent, where the good readers finished. When the auditory task was presented first, they began at a normal level (80 per cent correct) and finished at 68 per cent correct (the same as for the good readers). But when the visual task began, there was no boost due to changing modality — in fact they began at a lower level, only 50 per cent correct, finishing at 40 per cent correct. This experiment shows how important it is to take into account memory span when attempting to ascertain whether poor readers have good or poor auditory or visual short-term memory capacities.

In the second task — memory scanning — four letters were presented in sequence, and during 40 trials children were asked which letter came first. In the group of good readers the speed at which auditory memory sets were scanned remained about the same as the speed at which visual memory sets were scanned. But poor readers became more efficient at scanning visual elements and less efficient at scanning auditory elements in working memory over trials, thus developing a large discrepancy between auditory and visual memory-scanning speeds. The implications for reading are obvious: the poor reader moves on to the next visual particle before the associated auditory element has been retrieved from memory.

Deficits in sequencing ability

Vernon (1979) refers to problems of sequencing ability and sequential processing in poor readers. There are many examples of dyslexics or poor readers performing at a lower level than normal readers on tests of visual sequential memory (Silver and Hagin, 1970; Hinshelwood — reported by Ingram, 1970; Hartstein, 1971; Stanley, 1975; Nelson and Warrington, 1976; Doehring and Hoshko, 1977; Pollock and Waller, 1978).

Pollock and Waller discuss in detail the sequencing problems of dyslexics, and suggest that a disturbance of sequential organization, both verbal and visual, lies at the root of specific reading difficulties. Nàidoo (1972), in her study of 98 dyslexic boys examined at the ICAA Word Blind Centre from 1967 to 1969, concluded that there was evidence that a sequencing disability may underlie spelling and reading retardation.

Doehring (1976) states that reading disability is highly correlated with visual and verbal tasks that require sequential processing, and, together with a colleague (Doehring and Libman, 1974), spent some years fruitlessly attempting to derive a 'pure' test of sequencing ability. He has since elaborated a hypothesis that reading acquisition is a complex process involving a number of component skills and that there may be a form of reading disability in which a sequencing problem is associated with a specific pattern of reading sub-skills deficit.

Bakker (1970, 1972) has drawn attention to deficits demonstrated by dyslexic children in the perception of serial order, especially the perception and retention of the temporal order for sequences of letters, digits, colours and meaningful figures in various sense modalities. Also to be taken into account is the perception and remembering of the order of letters in words and words in sentences. He refers to a fundamental disturbance in the functioning of language, or, put another way, 'a verbal mediation process placed in a time scheme'.

Vellutino (1979b), however, has advanced some formidable criticisms of Bakker's theory and, whilst conceding that there is some evidence of significant disparities between poor and normal readers on a variety of serial order tasks, especially when the amount of information to be recalled taxes short-term memory (Zurif and Carson, 1970; Bryden, 1972; Senf and Freundl, 1972; Corkin, 1974), disputes the interpretation of the findings. He questions the assumption implicit in the above studies that serial order recall and item recall constitute separate entities in the central nervous system, and suggests that a variety of cognitive functions may be used to store and retrieve representations of both content and sequence. He also draws attention to another implicit assumption in sequential deficit explanations of dyslexia: the relative importance of serial processing to word decoding. This is currently a matter for discussion but it is by no means clear whether word decoding entails serial (left-to-right) processing of its individual letters, or whether indeed sequential processing of individual letters and letter sounds is the necessary means by which words are identified.

Street (1977), exploring the implications of learning shorthand and morse code for dyslexics, points out that despite the phonetic nature of Pitman's shorthand, both symbolic systems involve holding many symbols in an ordered sequence in auditory memory and coping with interference to correct recall caused by the continual superimposition of similar materials.

In a study by Lunzer, Dolan and Wilkinson (1976), one of the minor findings was that short-term memory for the presentation of a visual sequence was a highly significant predictor for success in word recognition. They concluded that significant progress in learning to read depends on the ability to discriminate between different sequential orderings of visual symbols and to retain a memory image of such sequences. A deficit in the ability to retain a sequence of auditory symbols *per se* was not found to be critical for reading. Brewer (1967, 1969) sees the critical process in reading as the 'uncoding or decoding of language symbols placed in a serial or temporal order', and Haith (1971) likewise refers to the inability or lack of strategy displayed by young children with a short-term memory deficit to encode an array of items, presented simultaneously, into a sequential form.

Kinsbourne (1970) on the other hand suggests orientational information is coded in a specific order (vertical–horizontal, top-bottom, left–right) and implies that a deficit of selective attention accounts for these errors made by reading retardates.

The question of orientation and spatial abilities in poor readers with memory deficits has occupied several researchers. Pollock and Waller (1978) draw attention to the difficulties dyslexics face in positioning one object in relation to another. Frith (1971), in a study of 215 London schoolchildren, showed two groups of children letters, numbers and nonsense symbols presented one at a time, to be matched with one of eight symbols on a card. One group of children was unfamiliar with letters (average age 4.3 years), and the other group was familiar with letters (average age 5.10 years). Older children made errors when

familiar letters and numbers were concerned because of a strong preference for a familiar orientation of shape, whereas the pre-school children
had no bias since they were unfamiliar with the stimuli. Another experiment required children aged four to nine to copy symbols (20 letters
and digit pairs) in random order, first in normal, then in mirror-reversed
form. Most errors occurred when the mirror-reversed form of the
stimulus pair had to be copied. The author concludes that dyslexics
may acquire orientation preferences very slowly and will improve with
increased age and prolonged learning.

Stanley (1975) links the deficiency more specifically to memory
problems. In two experiments involving the rotation of wooden blocks
both tactually and using photographs, dyslexics were found to function
at the same level as normals. Stanley suggests that it is the memory for
transformation rather than the ability to transform that is deficit in
dyslexics.

Wheeler, Watkins and McLaughlin (1977) have linked the concept
of memory overload to cross-laterality in poor readers. They took two
groups of 10 children: one group was cross-lateral and significantly
inferior, the other had consistent laterality. Different numbers of units
of information (digits, letters or symbols) were presented simultaneously
by tachistoscope. The cross-lateral group took significantly longer to
process the information correctly, and its performance significantly
deteriorated as the information load was increased from three to five
units. The authors suggest that while information decoding is processed
in a parallel manner in both cerebral hemispheres (Klatzky and
Atkinson, 1971), information *encoding* is processed sequentially from
the right to the left hemisphere. If cerebral dominance is impaired or
ill-established, this manifests itself as a limitation in information-
processing visually in the utilization or capacity of short-term memory —
as shown in this experiment.

Summary
    Several points need to be made at the end of this section on informa-
tion processing.

    First, although a learning disabled child may have problems with
some aspects of information-processing, he is not deficient in all its
aspects. Certain information-processing components fail only sometimes, on certain tasks, not all the time on all tasks. Most of the studies
in this area have concentrated on analysing some processes with which
poor readers have experienced difficulty, but there has been virtually

no attempt to group the subjects according to the combinations of difficulties they may have. Thus we have no clear idea as to whether subjects who are experiencing difficulties in the early stages of information processing are also experiencing difficulties in the later stages. Nor can we be sure whether the subjects who have difficulty in processing visual information also have difficulty in processing auditory or other feature information.

A second important point must be made. At the beginning of this section it was stated that research into information processing is one of the fastest growing areas of research into specific learning difficulties. Yet most of the data obtained are of little practical relevance to the question of remediation. Knowledge that a dyslexic child or poor reader has problems processing visual or auditory material, or is unable to hold more than a limited amount of information in his memory at any one time, has not led to specific suggestions as to how such a child can be helped in the classroom situation, except in very general terms. Miles and Ellis (1980) are aware of this problem, quoting Marcel (1978) who 'has expressed doubts as to whether any information processing model can be of help to the practising teacher except possibly in so far as it suggests "substitute" procedures in the case of the brain damaged'. However, although they concede that existing successful methods 'have evolved as a result of work by gifted individuals who were influenced little or not at all by the findings of experimental psychologists', they nevertheless maintain that 'the value of such research is that it demonstrates the nature of the functional deficiencies shared by all those who are dyslexic'. Some writers have suggested allowing more time for learning the elements of language (Done and Miles, 1978; Ellis and Miles, 1978) or that teaching should be highly structured, with small amounts of work being undertaken at any one time (Thomson and Wilsher, 1978) but it is difficult to see how this approach is different from remedial teaching in general. Farnham-Diggory (1978) suggests technological solutions of the future may teach dyslexic children to read by presenting them not with a line of print (which may cause masking if it is feature-processed too slowly) but with one letter (or orthographic unit) at a time displayed on a scope sequentially, at a speed that is just right for the individual child. Children whose auditory processing is deficient might be given hearing aids that do for speech perception what corrective lenses do for astigmatism. However, in a more practical vein, she recommends the application of protocol analysis to learning disabilities. By sampling, step by step, what an individual has actually been doing in the course of solving a problem, or writing a word, or 'thinking out loud', a suitable remedial strategy can be devised for that particular child.

Finally, in conclusion, it is by no means generally agreed that deficiencies in information-processing are responsible for reading problems. Bale (1974) suggests problems may occur in selecting and integrating perceptual and motor inputs rather than in the actual process of receiving information. Vernon (1975) also believes it is more probable that it is not mere memorization that is defective but problems of integration, especially of verbal functions of the left hemisphere with visuo-spatial functions of the right hemisphere. Clifton-Everest (1974), in two experiments, found no serious defect in the immediate memory of learning disabled children. However, we may end on a more hopeful note by referring to fairly recent attempts to apply the information processing model to the reading process itself. Not only does this help to clarify our understanding of the dynamics of reading but it may also serve to pinpoint the particular stages at which retarded readers are experiencing difficulty. This is discussed more fully in the section on models of reading and reading disabilities. Vellutino (1979b) believes that poor readers experience difficulty on both short- and long-term memory tasks because they lack facility in employing linguistic devices to aid recall, not because of any deficits in memory itself.

Neurological dysfunctions

It has frequently been suggested in the literature concerned with learning disabilities that brain damage or dysfunction of some kind might be wholly or partly responsible for reading difficulties. Although our definition of specific learning difficulties excludes children with gross physical and mental handicap, nevertheless there is a body of opinion which points to the possibility of an underlying neurological disorder. Dinnage (1968) uses the term 'learning disabilities' to refer to 'specific handicaps' which suggest neurological impairments. Newton and Thomson (1975), in their guide for teachers and parents, describe dyslexia as 'neurological in origin'. Kirk's (1967) famous definition attributes learning disorders to 'a possible cerebral dysfunction and/or emotional and behaviour disturbance'.

The extent and location of brain damage has been the subject of many studies. Abrams (1968), for example, distinguishes three types of severe reading disability arising from neurological origins: that arising from a defect in the central nervous system (brain damaged ego), the specific brain injury cases caused by an actual lesion to the occipital-parietal area of the brain (organic remedial) and, finally, children without definite brain damage whose capacity to read is impaired by a disturbed pattern of neurological organization. Gruenberg (quoted in McCarthy and McCarthy, op. cit.) differentiates between children with established neurological impairment (e.g. cerebral palsy, epilepsy); those with a learned impairment (e.g. emotionally and culturally deprived, educationally retarded); and those with suspected but unconfirmed impairment ('soft' neurological signs and specific learning deficits). Rabinovitch *et al.* (1954) suggested that primary lesions to the parietal and parietal-occipital regions of the brain accounted for the primary disability in reading retardation. Studies of adults with dyslexia have pointed to partial occipital damage (Drew, 1956; Casey and Ettlinger, 1960; Kinsbourne and Warrington, 1962).

Some studies have also linked brain damage sustained prior to or during the birth process with reading disability. The well-known study by Kawi and Pasamanick (1959) found that, of 205 children who had reading problems, 16.6 per cent of them had been exposed to two or more complications during birth or immediately thereafter. Only 1.5 per cent of a similar group without reading problems had complications at birth. They postulated 'a continuum of reproductive casualty' extending from miscarriage, still birth and neonatal death, through serious injury such as cerebral palsy and epilepsy, to minor injuring leading to behaviour problems, speech disorders and retarded reading. Gesell *et al.* (1940) also expressed the belief that unrecognized minimal birth injury may later appear in the form of reading difficulty. Newton and Thomson (1975) suggested that dyslexia was sometimes connected with an 'at-risk' birth situation, and Bale (1974), in an unpublished thesis investigating perceptual, motor and language deficits in backward readers, found a greater number of difficulties during pregnancy and birth in the backward readers' group than in the controls, although the association did not reach signifance except in the case of low birth weight. He proposed that 'there exists a group of children with specific reading difficulties of neurological origin as a result of prenatal and perinatal problems'.

However, Naidoo's study (1972) of 98 dyslexic boys examined at the ICAA Word Blind Centre during 1967-1969 found no greater frequency of birth hazards or early illness in dyslexics than controls, so we must conclude that problems associated with pregnancy and birth complications may be linked with reading disability in some instances but the case is by no means proved.

More attention has been paid recently to the 'soft' neurological signs such as exaggerated tendon reflexes, choreiform movements, mild ataxia, clumsiness, and extensor plantar responses. These tend to be implied rather than measured. Goldberg and Schiffman (1972) outline the difficulty in this way:

> The case of the child whose reading problem results from brain damage is possibly the most perplexing of all cases of reading retardation, for his is the most difficult to diagnose. Even if he has minimal brain damage or cerebral dysfunction, the child may appear to be completely normal. A physical examination will frequently show nothing abnormal, and his intelligence may be normal, or even above normal. A sizeable number of children of normal or superior intelligence have reading difficulties because they suffer some degree of brain dysfunction which does not reveal itself in any obvious manner.

They go on to discuss some of the characteristics associated with this kind of brain damage, and include moderate retardation in physical milestones, especially those requiring fine motor control, e.g. handedness, button fastening, physical awkwardness, emotional instability, hyperactivity, and slow development of speech and language.

Critchley (1970) also finds the term 'soft' neurological signs 'unfortunate', and points out that some of these signs 'may elude superficial examination, coming to light only after more searching techniques'. He lists these deficits which may come to light during 'extended' or 'expanded' neurological examinations as (1) disorders of spatial thought; (2) impaired temporal notions; (3) inadequate, inconsistent, or mixed cerebral dominance; (4) defects of speech or of language, other than dyslexia; (5) disorders of mobility; and (6) poor figure-background discrimination. Critchley stresses that these symptoms should be regarded as significant when they occur but not essential to any diagnosis. In any case they will not all occur together in any one dyslexic, and in fact tend to be found in an inverse correlation with the age of the subject, i.e. the younger the subject, the more likely it is that neurological signs will be found, suggesting possible connections with the maturational lag theories.

One of the difficulties encountered here is that of measurement of neurological dysfunction. Farnham-Diggory (1978) quite rightly draws attention to the fact that standard neurological examinations are relatively insensitive except to the most severe forms of brain damage. Diagnosis of minimal brain dysfunction is usually made on the basis of tests, medical history, and clinical examination, but if these are inconclusive we are left with a negative assumption that, in the absence of positive signs of neurological disorder, some kind of underlying neurological dysfunction may be responsible.

The idea that brain damage may be associated with reading disability has not been without its critics. Critchley (1970, 1975), although conceding there may be minor neurological symptoms which are sometimes found in dyslexics, finds the concept of brain damage not fruitful. Crabtree (1976), in his polemic against dyslexia, concludes that brain damaged children learn to read and that in Japan children seem to have little difficulty learning to read (Makita, 1968) whereas the incidence of brain damage is presumably similar. Ross (1977) believes that the inability to sustain selective attention, not brain dysfunction, is responsible for learning disabilities.

Possibly the most promising line of research hypothesizes that neurological dysfunction constitutes one of the many aetiological influences on reading disability, or is the basis of a separately identifiable group of poor readers. Fry, Johnson and Muehl (1970) suggest minimal brain damage may occur coincidentally in dyslexics. Myers and Hamill (1969), in their description of organically based aetiologies of learning disabilities, distinguish three categories as represented by the following drawing:

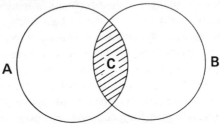

A represents medically diagnosed brain dysfunction
B represents demonstrable educationally defined learning disability
C represents learning disability arising from, and primarily associated with, brain injury.

Reproduced by kind permission of John Wiley and Sons Inc.

Keeney and Keeney (1968) have suggested five basic forms of dyslexia, one of which they described as acquired dyslexia as the result of brain lesions.

Ingram (1968) studied 176 children aged seven years or over, referred for clinical investigation for suspected dyslexia. He divided them into two groups: specifics, who had a specific reading and spelling difficulty only, and generals, who failed in reading, spelling, arithmetic and other learning situations. He found that 68 per cent of the specifics and 35 per cent of the general had *no* significant neurological abnormalities, and concluded that it was possible to classify subjects into clearly definable categories: specific reading handicaps tended to be present where there was no brain abnormality, but where a brain abnormality was present, difficulties were likely to be more general. Yule and Rutter (1976), reporting results from their Isle of Wight and London studies, also divided their poor readers into two groups: backward and retarded readers. Backward readers were two years four months or more below their chronological age in reading accuracy and comprehension, whilst retarded readers were two years four months or more below the level on reading accuracy and comprehension predicted on the basis of the child's age and short WISC IQ. As in Ingram's study, they found more neurological disorder in the generally backward rather than the retarded group. Newton, Thomson and Richards (1979), in their summary of comparative findings from surveys and definitions of dyslexia, found five studies which included brain damage involvement (Rabinovitch, 1968; Eisenberg, 1966; Klasen, 1972; Keeney and Keeney, 1968; Bannatyne, 1971), and concluded that one of eight salient features of dyslexia is 'brain damage, minimal neurological dysfunction', which constitutes a separate category of dyslexic difficulties, although children showing these features were excluded from their current research.

Ingram concludes, and his views are shared by others, that brain damage is not necessarily associated with greater difficulty in learning to read. In his group of generals, 70 per cent without brain damage had severe reading failure compared with 57 per cent with brain damage; and in his group of specifics, 60 per cent without brain damage had reading failure compared with 35 per cent with brain damage. It has also been suggested that children with brain damage may compensate; Hart (1976) believes that if the brain is damaged, a different part will take over or the whole area will shut down. Singleton (1976) also agrees that children can compensate for local damage.

It seems, then, that brain damage or neurological dysfunction is a factor in some types or cases of reading disability. It is difficult to be more precise than that because of the usual difficulties of conflicting or confusing evidence and differing criteria for learning disability. Not the least of the problems stems from terminology. Goldberg and Schiffman (1972) report that tendency to use the label 'brain damage' from 1960 to 1965 which was associated with futility has now been replaced by a host of other terms including minimal chronic brain dysfunction, minimal brain damage, minimal cerebral dysfunction or special education difficulties. They themselves find the term 'minimal cerebral dysfunction' preferable. However, Spreen (1976) dislikes the use of the word 'minimal' and states, 'My own feeling is that the term (minimal brain damage) is quite useless, since there is nothing minimal about brain damage that causes a serious learning disorder.' He suggests the term 'minimal' should be replaced by 'unknown', 'undetermined', 'inferred', or 'dubious'.

Electroencephalographic studies

Some attempt has been made to measure neurological abnormalities through the techniques of electroencephalographic recordings (EEG). A certain amount of evidence points to EEG abnormalities in dyslexics and poor readers. Goldberg *et al.* (1960) compared the EEG tracings of 50 children with severe degrees of reading disability with 50 normal children, and found that the dyslexics registered a higher incidence of abnormalities. Goldberg and Schiffman (1972) report the findings of Dr Taylor Stratten (1953), who studied routine brain wave tracings of 950 patients at Montreal Children's Hospital and found a high percentage of children with reading problems amongst those which were abnormal. Bale (1974), in his review of the literature, quotes studies by Silver and Hagin (1960), Cohn (1961) and Benton and Bird (1963) which support the link between abnormal EEGs and reading disability, but suggests that the validity and reliability of the measures and definitions of reading difficulty may be in doubt. Sklar and Simmons (1972) in an EEG experiment aimed at identifying dyslexic children, compared 12 dyslexics and 13 matched controls in five situations: rest, eyes closed; attentive, eyes open; performing mental arithmetic; reading word lists; and reading text. The programme successfully discriminated between the two groups in all five test situations.

A study by Shields (1973) using a relatively new EEG technique — average evoked response, measuring specific brain responses abstracted from the mass of ongoing electro-chemical activity of the brain (AER) — found that the AERs for learning disabled and normal children are different. Learning-disabled children have longer latencies and larger amplitudes, which indicate both that they need longer to process information and that they focus greater attention on the stimuli than normal. However, it is not clear what the author means by learning disabled.

Hughes (1976) reports evidence for particular kinds of abnormal EEGs and their connections with learning disabilities. A range of incidence for positive spikes in dyslexics has been recorded: Hughes and Park (1968) reported 21 per cent, Knott *et al.* (1965) 30 per cent, Bryant and Friedlander (1965) 35 per cent, and Muehl, Knott and Benton (1965) 55 per cent, but controls often showed spikes too: Stevens *et al.* (1968) and Bryant and Friedlander (op. cit.) found a similar incidence in their control groups. Excessive occipital slowing has also been associated in learning disorders; Hughes and Park (1968) reported a 10 per cent incidence for dyslexics, constituting 27 per cent of those with some kind of abnormality. Hughes concludes that we should be cautious in associating abnormal EEGs with learning disabilities. In the case of positive spikes, he suggests that this may be associated with a behaviour rather than a learning disorder, and that excessive occipital slowing may be linked with visual disabilities. Finally, he proposes that abnormal or positive EEG findings may at times represent the reaction of the brain to stress.

In a later 'state-of-the-art' paper (Hughes, 1978) also reports evidence on various other special features of the EEG which are sometimes associated with dyslexia, such as lack of focused attention (Sheer, 1976), poor alpha synchronization (Martinius and Hoovey, 1972) poorly organized alpha rhythms, and reduced contingent negative variation (CNV) (Dykman *et al.*, 1971). Despite problems of overlapping of groups, the presence of questionable EEG findings in many dyslexics, and the relatively high incidence of 'abnormal' EEG findings in control groups, he feels the results are encouraging enough to justify further investigation especially of pre-school children in order to separate cause and effect. Conners, in a critical review of this paper (Conners, 1978), refers to the 10 papers Hughes cites which give a percentage of abnormality ranging from 27 to 88 per cent, giving a weighted mean of 45 per cent incident of abnormal EEGs. Although four of the studies containing controls show significantly more abnormalities among the dyslexics, the variance between studies is larger than the variance within studies which compare controls and dyslexics. Furthermore the types of abnormality have varied from study to study. Conners concludes, 'Our own interpretation of these studies is that they lend little support to the main conclusion, and in fact can just as easily be interpreted as showing the absence of EEG abnormalities among dyslexics.'

Evidence quoted by Critchley (1970) points to abnormal EEGs in poor readers precipitated by the act of trying to read, suggesting it may be an effect rather than a cause. He quotes studies by Baro (1966) and Oettinger (1964), and Oettinger, Nekonishi and Gill (1967), giving examples from the latter study of a patient with reading problems who developed an autonomic seizure while reading, and another who later developed grand mal while watching television!

Not all the evidence points to an association between EEG findings and reading disability. Ohlson (1978) reports a range from high correlations between the two variables to little or no relationship. He quotes a study by McGrady (1970), who suggests that the problem lies in the subjectivity of readings used. Two readers on two separate sets of EEGs agreed sometimes only 60-70 per cent of the time. Although 29 per cent of children without learning disabilities showed EEG abnormalities, the author concludes that there is a higher chance of this type of abnormality if a child has a learning disorder.

Spreen (1976) finds the EEG findings in the field of learning disabilities to be disappointing. The confused results allow little speculation about causes, and, as Hughes (1976) implies, an abnormal EEG may in fact be a predictor of successful remediation, perhaps the result of the brain's reaction to stress in general. Most results suggest that EEG findings are the result of a deficit in focused arousal (see Shields, above). Finally, Farnham-Diggory (1978) quotes a study by Owen *et al.* (1971) which showed that 11 of their learning-disabled children showed mildly abnormal EEG records but so did 17 children in the various normal groups. However, she is optimistic that recent technological improvements in the recording and analysis of electrical activity of the brain may lead to more reliable findings.

In conclusion, it must be said that there are many shortcomings in studies of EEGs. Definitions of learning disability are none too clear, criteria for abnormality are not very specific, findings are confusing and not generalizable and in any case there is a wide range of patterns in normal children. Little distinction is made between whether abnormal EEG recordings are the cause or the effect of reading problems, and the exact connection between reading disorders and brain wave patterns is not known. We must pin our hopes on the increasing sophistication of our measures and the more precise delineation of our subject area if we intend substantially to increase our knowledge in this field of inquiry.

Maturational lag

During the discussion on hemispheric asymmetry and cerebral dominance, the concept of maturational development was mentioned. There seems to be a fair amount of evidence in the literature that not all functions of the brain develop simultaneously and that learning-disabled children in particular may suffer from delays in the development of specific areas or functions. Lowenberg (1979) cites evidence that the temporal-parietal areas of the brain are the last to develop (Dekaban, 1970; Luria, 1973), and concludes from her own study of 34 pairs of children aged eight to 10 that the experimental group (who were of normal intelligence and physically normal but had retarded reading ages and EEG recordings, reflecting abnormalities in the temporal or temporo-parietal areas) were immature in a number of ways. Vernon quotes Jensen (1973), who has produced evidence that young children do not develop the ability of conceptual learning until a later age, and hypothesizes that certain types of conceptual learning may have failed to develop in dyslexic children through some lag or deficit in maturation. Yule and Rutter (1976) state that one of the factors in specific reading retardation may be due to a relative failure in the normal maturation of certain specific functions of the cerebral context, although they do not describe what exact functions they mean.

More general support for the concept of a maturational lag in development in poor readers comes from Ingram *et al.* (1970). Gulliford (1969), in a post-conference review on the topic of the 'neuropsychology of learning disorders', reports that it has been suggested that maturation during the period of reading skill development produces a shift in emphasis from the occipital area dealing with visual sequencing to the temporal area dealing with auditory processing, whilst other researchers highlight the role of the parietal lobe with regard to reading.

However, by far the most eminent and controversial exponents of the maturational lag hypothesis are Paul Satz and colleagues. Briefly, Satz and Sparrow (1970) suggest that a lag in the maturation of the whole left hemisphere underlies specific developmental dyslexia. They put forward five hypotheses for which they quote supporting evidence:

Hypothesis 1: Younger children with reading disability (seven to eight) tend to show a higher incidence of sensorimotor (visual-motor) complications than older children with reading disability (nine–12) (Benton, 1962; Ball and Owens, 1968; de Hirsch *et al.*, 1966).

Hypothesis 2: A relationship between mixed or ambiguous handedness and reading disability exists, primarily at earlier age levels (five to seven) (Harris, 1957; Coleman and Deutsch, 1964; Belmont and Birch, 1965; Naidoo, 1961).

Hypothesis 3: Younger children with reading disability (ages seven to eight) would also show a higher incidence of *sensorimotor* complications in right–left discrimination and finger differentiation whereas older disabled readers (nine–12) would tend to show more *conceptual* impairment on similar tests (Piaget, 1926; Benton and Swanson, 1955; Belmont and Birch, 1963; Kinsbourne and Warrington, 1963; Boone and Prescott, 1968, Reed, 1967; Sparrow, 1968).

Hypothesis 4: Older children with reading disability (nine–12) would show more impairment on conceptual tasks related to language than younger children (Reed, 1967; Belmont and Birch, 1966; Adams, 1968; Blank and Bridger, 1966).

Hypothesis 5: The pattern of Gerstmann-like symptoms will be observed more often in older (nine–12) than in younger (seven to nine) children with reading disability (Sparrow, 1968).

In summary, experimental investigations of nine to 12-year-old normal and retarded readers showed no significant differences between the two groups in all early developing aspects of laterality (e.g. manual preference, manual strength and dexterity, visual preference controlling eye) but did differentiate the groups in later developing aspects of laterality (e.g. lateral awareness, finger differentiation, ear asymmetry and verbal intelligence). However, whilst these theoretical formulations offer a frame of reference in which to conceptualize some of the scattered findings about dyslexia and deficits in measures of lateralization, the authors themselves are at pains to point out some of their shortcomings. These include lack of direct evidence, the question as to whether the concept of a maturational lag can be evaluated behaviourally, and the (additional) possibility of genetic determinants.

Satz has had to face many criticisms of his theories. Vellutino (1979a), attacks Satz's theory that perceptual problems are more characteristic of poor readers at lower age levels whereas linguistic defects are more characteristic of older poor readers, on the grounds that children can contend with linguistic analysis from the start. He cites a study by Vellutino, Pruzek, Stegek and Meshoulam (1973) where the use of novel visual stimuli (recall of Hebrew words) revealed no differences between poor and normal readers. Satz countered Vellutino's attack by quoting recent evidence from Benton (1975), Satz and Van Nostrand (1973) and Fletcher and Satz (1978) for developmental performance changes within disabled readers, showing that the contribution of sensorimotor-perceptual skills becomes less important as reading becomes more dependent on higher-order linguistic strategies. Vernon (1971) points out that, whilst there is evidence that many of the deficiencies associated with dyslexia, such as weak lateralization (Naidoo, 1961; Harris, 1957), poor left–right discrimination (Cohen and Glass, 1968), reversals in reading and writing, deficiencies of visual perception (Benton, 1962; Nielson and Ringe, 1969) and auditory discrimination, improve with age, on the other hand it is not certain if all defects characteristic of dyslexia are similar to those of younger normal children. In fact, many characteristics such as bizarre writing and spelling and distorted Bender test reproductions, more closely resemble the products of adult patients with parietal lobe injuries. Many dyslexics still display at 11–15 symptoms associated with younger dyslexic children (De Hirsch *et al.*, 1966; Doehring, 1968) and some never do overcome all their difficulties, particularly in spelling. Silver and Hagin (1964), in a follow-up study of 24 children, found that at 19 years of age, they still showed a marked reading disability, and De Hirsch *et al.* (1966) reported that about half of their older cases had become fairly adequate readers but were mostly poor at spelling. This finding is supported by Rawson's study (1968) which showed that 20 dyslexic children, after special individual teaching, were still retarded to some extent in reading (35 per cent by half a year or more) and to a large extent in spelling (90 per cent). Vernon concludes that a fundamental lag may be associated with general immaturity of personality (De Hirsch *et al.*, 1966), poor motivation or emotional stress and possibly related to a permanent dysfunction in the cerebral cortex which persists throughout life but may be alleviated by suitable remedial treatment.

Rourke (1976) has provided a useful analysis of the relative merits of two theoretical explanations of reading disability: the 'developmental lag' model as espoused by Satz and Van Nostrand (1973), De Hirsch *et al.* (1966) and the 'deficit' model as espoused by Doehring (1968), Reed (1968) and Reitan (1964b) which suggests some sort of cerebral dysfunction underlying the acquisition of age-appropriate skills. Although the deficit model is similar to the 'developmental lag' approach in that it predicts a less than age-appropriate level of reading performance during the early years at school, it differs in having no necessary expectation that the children thus affected will ever catch up in these respects.

Rourke reviews seven developmental lag-deficit paradigms of which types 1, 2 and 3 would tend to support the 'developmental lag' view, types 5, 6 and 7 would lend support to a 'deficit' position, and type 4 could be used to support either position. Rourke concludes that in general the developmental lag position is tenable in the case of fairly simple, early emerging abilities but the lack of adequate 'ceilings' and 'floors' for the tests can lead to spurious support for this view. Rourke's own studies provide some evidence that some retarded readers may exhibit advances but there is no reason to predict that they will ever catch up or approximate the performance of their normal reading age-mates. Yule and Rutter (1976), in their Isle of Wight studies, found during a four- to five-year follow-up study that retarded readers made significantly less progress on reading accuracy and spelling although they had made more progress on arithmetic but were still below their age level. They concluded that it cannot be assumed that children with reading difficulties will catch up.

Trites and Fiedorowicz (1976) have reviewed follow-up studies of children with reading disabilities, and have classified the reports into two types — those which conclude a favourable outcome in adulthood (for example Robinson and Smith, 1962; Rawson, 1968; Balow and Blomquist, 1965, although the first two studies were of high IQ subjects and the last study followed up only nine out of 32 subjects) and those which show a persistence of reading disability over time (Silver and Hagin, 1964, 1966; Yule, 1973; Yule *et al.*, 1974; Koppitz, 1971). The authors' own study of three groups — boys with primary reading disability, girls with primary reading disability and· boys with reading disability presumably secondary to neurological diseases — found an improvement in reading, spelling and arithmetic for all three groups, but in fact the discrepancy between grade placement and the actual level of achievement actually increased as the subjects grew older. An increase in the gap between good and poor readers over time was also found by Owen *et al.* (1971) and in the findings of the NCDS study, mentioned in the Bullock report (1975).

Spreen (1976), in a brief review of follow-up studies, reports that 'findings for children identified at an early age are somewhat contradictory and occasionally hopeful, but that findings on children identified at a later age are fairly grim'.

Overall, then, the position seems to be that whilst the concept of maturational lag is an attractive one and usefully explains some of the puzzling features of retarded readers, the evidence is both confusing and conflicting and no firm conclusions can be drawn. There seems to be a possibility that older retarded readers may resemble younger normal readers in some ways (Guthrie, 1973; Money, 1962, 1966; Bender, 1957; De Hirsch *et al*., 1966) suggesting a developmental lag, but a more important consideration must be the long-term prognosis for these disabled readers. Gredler (1977) is concerned that the use of the term 'immature' should be avoided, as it tends to absolve school personnel of any responsibility to help the child. The weight of the findings tends to suggest that although retarded readers may make progress, sometimes quite dramatically over a short period of time, they stand little chance of equalling the performance of their classmates in the long run. While this is the case, the concept of maturational lag must remain in doubt.

Genetic factors

Throughout the literature concerned with the neurological aspects of reading disability, there are references to the role of genetic inheritance. Critchley (1970), for example, sees developmental dyslexia as a 'specific constitutional genetically determined defect lying within the middle zone of a spectrum of non-specific reading disorders', and explains the presence of 'soft' neurological signs as examples of the occasional 'impurity' of the syndrome. Goldberg and Schiffman (1972) outline the main areas for reading disability as a genetic problem, where evidence has been established, as follows:

1. Pedigree or family history.
2. The presence of learning disabilities in monozygotic and dizygotic twins.
3. The likelihood that a genetically determined reading disability will persist through a lifetime.
4. The determination of biochemical and chromosomal abnormalities.

A large number of studies have found an increased incidence of reading difficulties in the family history of poor readers. Critchley lists examples dating from the beginning of the century up to 1950. Plate

(1909) found poor readers among three generations as did Rønne (1936) and also Marshall and Ferguson (1939). Norrie (1939) found familial tendencies in 'practically all' of her cases; Kågén (1943) mentioned hereditary properties in 30 per cent; and one of the most well-known studies, by Hallgren (1950), found 88 per cent of his sample had 'affected relatives'.

In a recent analysis of Hallgren's work, Owen (1978) challenges his final conclusions. Although, using the techniques of Mendelian analysis, he concluded that specific dyslexia with a high degree of probability followed a dominant mode of inheritance, he was unable to produce an unambiguous definition which could distinguish a homogeneous group of dyslexic children. Furthermore, cultural transmission of patterns of learning and behaviour may be as important as genetic explanations for the succession of learning disorders over two or three generations of the same family. Owen's own study (Owen *et al.*, 1971) of 76 matched sets of Educationally Handicapped pupils (EH) and Successful Academic pupils (SA) each with an appropriate matched sibling of the same sex, found that the performance of the EH siblings was significantly lower in both reading and spelling when compared with the SA controls. In addition it was discovered that fathers of SA children had the highest reading scores, followed by mothers of SA children. Fathers of EH children were next, with mothers of EH children having the lowest scores. A neurological examination of the children showed some neurological immaturities to be common to both EH and their siblings, such as were apparent on auditory tapped patterns and on right-left discrimination. Possible prenatal, neonatal or postnatal insults were not significantly more frequent in the EH population. Owen, writing in 1978 (op. cit.), claims that familial genetic patterns of development are suggested by the evidence from her 1971 study, both in respect of their particular pattern of intellectual development and their similar neurological immaturities. She concludes: 'The writer would theorise that multifactorial genetic predisposition is the source of at least one type of learning disability', although she admits that familial incidence will never provide the required information regarding the genetic contribution to dyslexia, and recommends other approaches such as mapping human genes.

Both McClearn (1978) and Childs, Finucci and Preston (1978) echo Owen's allusions to the problems associated with specific reading disability as a phenotype for genetic study. McClearn emphasizes the importance of a multiple-factor model which incorporates environmental and genetic factors, and enables us to distinguish individuals whose condition is due to polygenic, single-gene, or environmental conditions. Childs, Finucci and Preston stress the value of approaches which will rescue definable subtypes from the undifferentiated mass, and be of therapeutic value. In particular, they mention the discipline of epidemiology which can elucidate both genetic and environmental factors necessary for the expression of phenotypes, and investigate the transmission of antipathy to learning.

Returning to other studies showing family histories of reading difficulties Naidoo's (1972) study found this to be more frequent especially amongst her spelling retardates, whilst Ingram (1968) reported a family history of reading difficulties in 40 per cent of his specifics and 25 per cent of his generals. Yule and Rutter (1976) found a greater incidence of family histories of reading difficulties in both their backward and retarded readers, amounting to three times the incidence found in their controls. Silver (1971), in a study of 556 individuals with neurological learning disabilities, found 29.6 per cent had a positive family history of a similar learning disorder, although siblings without a history of prenatal, perinatal and postnatal difficulties also had learning disabilities, pointing to the importance of environmental factors. Doehring (1968) reported that 40 per cent of his backward readers had parents who experienced difficulty in learning to read compared with 10 per cent of normal controls. A rather different approach was taken by Conners (1970) who investigated the link between EEGs and familial reading disabilities. The study of one particular family showed that the brain wave responses of the mother with no reading problem was normal, but all five members with reading problems (father, two girls and two boys) had the same general brain wave abnormality in left parietal response. However, De Hirsch *et al.* (1966) found no significant correlations between reading achievement and any familiar characteristics.

Whilst there is obviously an increased incidence of a family history of poor readers amongst children with reading disabilities, this does not necessarily imply a genetic causation. Many researchers have pointed to the influence of the environment and concluded that it is extremely difficult to disentangle the two. Yule and Rutter (1976) believe there is mounting evidence for the concept of social transmission in that a family history of reading retardation is much commoner in large families, and that reading attainment is regionably variable and varies with the interest of the parents (Davie, Butler and Goldstein, 1972).

Singleton (1976) and Bale (1974) support the notion that poor attitudes to reading may be the determining factor.

Studies of twins possibly provide more convincing evidence of a
genetic transmission of reading disability. Hermann (1959) reported
that in three studies of monozygotic and dizygotic twins, all 12 pairs
of uniovular (monozygotic) twins showed identical disability, whereas
in the dizygotic twins there was only 33 per cent concordance.
Although this is pretty conclusive evidence of a genetic link, it is well
to remember, as Singleton (1976) points out, that only a small number
of cases were involved and that twins are likely to have a greater
incidence of prenatal and perinatal complications.

The third hypothesis put forward by Goldberg and Schiffman — that
a genetically determined reading disability will persist through a lifetime — also receives some support from the literature. Although there
is little evidence from follow-up studies over a large number of years,
some studies (Rawson, 1968; Silver and Hagin, 1964, 1966; Yule, 1973,
Yule *et al.*, 1974) show a persistence of reading disability into adulthood. This hypothesis is, of course, in direct contradiction to the
theory of maturational lag.

As far as biochemical and chromosomal abnormalities are concerned,
the evidence is slight. Two aspects of biochemical functioning in dyslexics have recently been investigated. In a study by Park, Bieber and
Zeller (1975), it was found that the degradation rates of three sub-
strates of monoamine oxidase (MAO), an enzyme used for the regulation of amine metabolism, were consistently increased for dyslexics
over controls, but it is not clear whether these changes are important
in the aetiology of dyslexia, or relate to some effect of the disorder.
A second study, by Park and Schneider (1975) showed that dyslexics
had significantly higher thyroxine levels than controls, which confirms
an earlier study by Hughes and Park (1968) who found higher thyroid
(PBI) values in dyslexics with abnormal EEGs compared to those with
normal records. Despite some experimental limitations Hughes (1976)
suggests these studies can possibly fit together in a unifying hypothesis
which proposes 'that dyslexics with high thyroxine levels may tend to
have hypermetabolic rates, which may be related to high levels of
aminergic compounds, like epinephrine and norepinephrine'. Information concerning chromosomal abnormalities is inconclusive. In a discussion on the genetics of reading disability Childs (1964) indicated
that chromosomal abnormalities were not present in these cases, but
Grenn and Perlman (1971) found that there were alterations in chromo-

somal constitution within a population of children attending a learning disability clinic.

A recent study by Pizzamiglio (1976) into the biological correlates of three cognitive dimensions — field dependence-independence, space rotation and space visualization — concluded that there is a possible genetic basis for all three cognitive dimensions, although the influence of the environment cannot be discounted. A little research has been carried out into the possible role of endocrine factors in the aetiology of learning difficulties. Park (1959) found 20 per cent of backward readers showed symptoms of hypothyroidism — slowing down of the metabolic rate resulting in slowness in speech and movement and retardation in cognitive activity, whilst Smith and Carrigan (1959) suggested severe reading difficulty could be caused by abnormal synaptic transmission, or by failure to achieve adequate reverberatory activity of neural systems.

One of the arguments sometimes put forward in favour of a genetic role in reading disability is the higher ratio of males affected. Critchley (1970) reviews the sex-incidence reported in studies from 1927 to 1968 and could only find one study where no sex difference was shown (Jastak, 1934). The average rate for the remaining studies was about four males to one female. Other researchers have found a lower ratio: Goodacre (1971) quotes the ILTA survey finding of 21 per cent male poor readers compared with 10 per cent girls. Similar statistics are quoted by Money (1962), Bentzen (1963), Clark (1970) and Davie *et al.* (1972). Rutter *et al.* (1970) found a ratio of 3.3 : 1 boys to girls, whilst Naidoo (1972) found a somewhat higher rate: 5 to 1. These differences may be partly explained by the higher proportion of boys referred to clinics than girls; studies of non-clinic populations tend to show a lower ratio. It is certainly clear that reading disability is more of a problem for boys than girls, but it is a matter of dispute as to whether this has a genetic causation. Goodacre (1968) points out that studies comparing the performance of boys and girls tend to use the *mean* performance of the two groups. When the *spread* in the achievement scores of boys and girls is examined, the boys' scores tend to cover a wider range than the girls, i.e. there are more very good as well as very poor readers amongst the boys, whereas the girls' scores are grouped together. Due to this the girls' superiority is more marked at the lower level. She quotes Haggard's study (1957) which showed a superiority in reading ability in favour of boys, but the sample comprised gifted children from professional families. Goodacre concludes that 'social and cultural forces as well as physiological differences are important causal factors'.

There seems to be evidence that boys and girls differ in maturational development (Taylor, 1969; Buffery and Gray, 1972), with girls generally developing earlier (Critchley, 1970; Bakker *et al.*, 1976) than boys. Some studies have found that more boys show delayed speech development (Ingram and Reid, 1956; Davie *et al.*, 1972) whilst superior auditory ability in girls is reported (Thackray, 1965; Kellmer Pringle *et al.*, 1966). Bannantyne (1966) and Critchley (1964) found boys have superior visual spatial ability but lower verbal ability, whilst Moseley (1974) showed that spelling and the ability to visualize were closely related in boys but not in girls. Both Witelson (1976, 1977) and Davidoff (1978) reported hemispheric dominance differences between boys and girls, suggesting that lateralization of language functions in the dominant hemisphere occurs at an earlier age in girls than in boys. However, the higher incidence of boys performing poorly at reading is not necessarily attributable to a genetic origin. Vernon (1957, 1971) thought it might be associated with more general developmental differences between the sexes, and in addition suggested that the preponderance of boys was due to non-reading boys creating more trouble at school than girls, who are more docile and conforming – qualities well suited to reading. Kagan (1964) believed reading was not congruent with the masculine role. Vernon further postulated that parents might take reading inability in a boy more seriously than in a girl, and lastly, that boys with reading problems often had emotional disorders. These latter two arguments could explain why the ratio of boys to girls referred to clinics is higher. Goldberg and Schiffman (1972) emphasize a variety of factors to explain the greater number of boys suffering from reading disabilities. They state: 'It is well recognised that males exceed females in reading disabilities by a frequency that varies from 3 : 1 to 10 : 1. The greater male incidence can be explained by the following possibilities:

(1) Greater female maturity at the age of six.

(2) Greater incidence of cerebral trauma accompanying retinal and cerebral haemorrhages.

(3) Greater motivation of females in the learning situation.

(4) Secondary emotional conflict in the male associated with (1)–(3) above.'

Other environmental factors have been adduced to explain why boys have greater difficulty learning to read. Moseley (1972) found that boys were more interested in the approval of classmates than in pleasing the teacher, whilst McNeil (1964) suggested that women teachers possibly use methods less suitable for boys. In an experiment carried out with children in their first year of schooling under neutral conditions of programmed learning, the boys in his sample had a higher reading achievement than the girls at the end of the year but in the next class, when they were taught by women teachers, they failed to maintain the same progress. Finally, Kelmer Pringle *et al.* (1966) believed that boys might be less interested in reading than girls because the reading schemes tended to be 'home-oriented' whereas their interests were in the 'world around'.

In conclusion, some convincing evidence on the role of genetic inheritance in reading disability comes from twin studies, and to a lesser extent from family histories of poor readers. It also seems clear that there are maturational differences between boys and girls. However, the extent to which these factors are attributable to a genetic origin is by no means clear, especially when environmental influences are taken into account. The recent symposium dealing with the definition and aetiology of dyslexia considered the question of its hereditary aspects (Childs, Finucci and Preston, 1978; McClearn, 1978; Owen, 1978). There was general consensus that available findings, although suggestive, were not conclusive and that the field of genetic correlates of reading disability suffered from a lack of clarity in defining and measuring its behavioural parameters.

2. Secondary correlates

Perception

Introduction

Perception is, of course, intimately connected with the reading process, and many researchers have been concerned to show that deficits in perception and perceptual processes may underlie specific learning difficulties. Perception, the process whereby sensory impressions are transmitted to and understood in the brain, may be broken down into auditory perception; visual perception; integration of the senses; spatial and form perception; and perception and movement (visual-motor perception and auditory motor perception). Defects may occur in any or several of these categories, possibly leading to difficulties in learning to read, but by our definition (see page 259) do not include physical defects such as poor sight or hearing. Several researchers have stressed that perception is not the ability to see or hear accurately, but the interpretation of sensory information by the brain (Goldberg and Schiffman, 1972; Owen *et al.*, 1971). This is possibly the point Vernon (1957) is making when she emphasizes that defects in visual perceptual development have been overstressed and that it is more important to consider the failure of the disabled reader in analysing, abstraction and generalization, all of which can be termed cognitive difficulties.

Perceptual deficits in general

Evidence has been quoted in many studies to support the claim that perceptual deficit is associated with reading or learning difficulties. Steinheiser and Guthrie (1977) examined the response latencies in word matching and sentence completion tasks for three groups of readers (disabled readers, same-age normal readers and younger normal readers), and concluded that perceptual and decoding processes are learned by normal readers, but are a primary source of deficiency in disabled readers. Trieschman (1968) found that poor readers (boys aged seven to nine) made many more perceptual errors than normal readers, and Whipple and Kodman (1969) quote results showing that the perceptual level abilities of children retarded in reading are distinctly inferior to those of the normal reader with the same IQ. Frederiksen (1978) identified five perceptual and cognitive skills related to reading proficiency, and as a result of a letter identification task concluded that low ability readers are slower at scanning a perceptual array, and slower in identifying letters when they do not occur in a predictable sequence. Kirk (1968), quoting research findings on the relationship of the IPTA to reading disabilities, refers to a study by Kass (1966) which found a correlation between difficulties in learning to read and a test of perceptual speed. However, Valtin (1978-1979) quotes evidence that dyslexics are actually faster on Thurstone's test of perceptual speed, a finding supported by Kemmler (1967) and Machemer (1973). Other studies by Ragland (1964), Macleod (1965), Hirshoren (1969) and Macione (1969) all consistently found that reading disabilities were associated with deficits at the automatic level, whereas dyslexics showed one superior ability at the representational level — the ability to interpret pictures.

Other tests of perceptual development include the Bender-Gestalt and the Frostig Tests. These tests have been consistently associated with poorer performance by retarded readers. Bean (1967) found a significant difference in performance on the Bender with retarded and normal readers, and Connor (1966) found poor readers make more errors on the Bender-Gestalt but due to sampling procedures recommended extreme caution in predicting or diagnosing poor reading performance on the basis of this test. Although the Frostig test discriminates between good and poor readers in measures of visual perception, there is, as Goldberg and Shiffman (1972) point out, no evidence that perceptual training helps reading after the age of six, and suggest it is better to concentrate on the deficit: reading disability. In fact Olson and Johnson (1970) claimed that the Frostig test was the least predictive test of reading ability, and suggested that, in order to read, a child must be at a perceptual level beyond that measured by the Frostig test, and indeed Nielson and Ringe (1969) found no difference between nine- to 10-year-old remedial readers and normal readers on the test.

Other writers have suggested that reading retardation is not associated with perceptual deficit but may be linked to difficulties of a different kind. Allington *et al.* (1976) tested the hypothesis that a perceptual deficit is not involved in reading disability. They presented 24 subjects with high frequency, low discriminability words in four tasks and found the hypothesis not proved, suggesting instead that the difficulty lies in making verbal associations with the visual image. These findings are supported by a study carried out by Ellis and Miles (1978) which revealed that dyslexics were not different from controls in matching sequences visually, but were significantly different in their ability to name pairs of letters. Done and Miles (1978), in another series of experiments, showed that tasks which involve verbal labelling are more difficult for dyslexics. Critchley (1970) reports various early experiments (Schilder, 1944; Fildes, 1921) demonstrating that dyslexics, whilst dealing easily with non-verbal tasks, have much greater difficulty with word matching and naming. Cashdan (1970) investigated the effects of instructing nine-year-olds on an auditory-visual test and concluded that although such tests are not performed as well by backward readers, the difficulties lie more in their willingness to attend, plan and label rather than their failure in perceptual ability. McGrady and Olson (1970) gave 99 children (two groups of eight-year-olds, two groups of nine-year-olds — one learning disabled group and one control in each case) 13 automated tests representing various combinations of auditory and visual intra- and intersensory conditions. They found that the learning disabled groups, especially the eight-year-olds, made significantly more errors on *verbal* psychosensory functions, regardless of the sensory conditions, suggesting the children in the study were failing in school primarily because of verbal difficulties, not because of perceptual problems. Lyle (1969) also drew attention to a verbal learning factor, and concluded that a test in which production of letters in sequences was required involved more verbal rehearsal than perceptual memory.

Apart from deficits associated with verbalizing ability, deficiencies in cognitive linguistic strategies rather than visual discrimination have been cited (Gupta, Ceci and Slater, 1978) whilst shortcomings in memory processes have also been implicated (Morrison *et al.*, 1977; Stanley, 1975). Finally, Wedell (1977) feels that perceptual deficiency is likely to be a contributory but not a determining cause of reading retardation.

Perception and maturational lag

Some writers suggest that certain perceptual abilities may be subject to maturational delay in poor readers. Wedell (op. cit.) claims, in common with many investigators, that perceptual variables in reading may be more important in the earlier stages of learning to read, whilst at the later stages other skills involving decoding and extrapolation become more crucial. Evidence suggests (Reynell, 1970; Goldberg and Schiffman, 1972; Fletcher and Satz, 1979) that the developmental sequence of intellectual functions proceeds from the sensori-motor phase, through language and speech development, with the maximum development of perceptual ability occurring at approximately three-and-a-half to six years of age, to a linguistic phase in older children (nine plus). Benton (1962) asserts that impaired form perception, visuomotor skill or directional sense may affect younger children but disappear with age. Whipple and Kodman (op. cit.) found that the perceptual ability of their 10-year-old sample was similar to the perceptual ability level of the normal six- to eight-year-olds used in a study by Gibson and Gibson (1955). Gibson showed that the number of errors in a task involving perception of graphic symbols similar to letters decreased during the ages four to eight. Thompson (1979) claims that students who have had perceptually based learning problems with an emotional overlay in the early grades no longer have perceptual deficits when tested again in early adolescence but still have the emotional overlay with deficits in one or more of the basic skills — reading, spelling, writing, arithmetic or language. He suggests that learning problems in adolescence are no longer caused by developmental lags but are the result of them — due to gaps in knowledge resulting in emotional overlay related to the degree of frustration in the individual's past experience. Newton and Thomson (1975) believe that dyslexia involves individual differences in the development of visual and auditory perception, whilst Vernon (1957) has suggested that some perceptual functions may be affected by maturational delay in cases of reading backwardness.

Auditory perception

As with other forms of perception, auditory perception can be distinguished from both sensations and cognition, occupying an intermediary position between the two. According to Goldberg and Schiffman (1972), 'Auditory perception involves alerting, attention, discrimination, processing, retrieving, sequencing of spoken language, and motor expression of speech.' Specific learning difficulties can be associated with shortcomings in any of these processes and may take a variety of forms. Henry (1975) lists the main symptoms of auditory perceptual difficulties as (i) inability to synthesize sequences of words, (ii) confusion with short vowel sounds, (iii) poor phonic knowledge or lack of phonic rules, and (iv) inability to analyse words into natural auditory units.

The main areas of interest to researchers have been auditory discrimination, auditory memory, blending and auditory sequencing. Auditory discrimination, which may be defined as the capacity to distinguish between phonemes, has frequently been linked with poor reading ability. Goetzinger *et al.* (1960), Wepman (1960, 1962), De Hirsch *et al.* (1966), Silver (1968), Clark (1970) and Valtin (1972, 1973) all found auditory discrimination to be poorer in backward readers, whilst Moseley (1972), Nelson (1974) and Lanyon (1974) show the same association with poor spelling. Bruininks (1968), Hendry (1969) and McNinch and Richmond (1972) all found auditory discrimination to be significantly correlated with reading ability, and Cotterell (1972) and Goldberg and Schiffman (1972) point to a link between poor auditory discrimination and poor reading. However, some experimenters have offered opposite conclusions. Silver and Hagin (1967) found no significant differences between their reading disability group and normals on tests of auditory discrimination, and Naidoo (1972) likewise revealed no significant differences between the auditory discrimination scores of reading and spelling retardates or between dyslexics and controls, although there were differences with short vowel sounds. A large scale study by Dykstra (1966) using seven measures of auditory discrimination found correlations between reading achievement and auditory discrimination to be uniformly low and that the test of intelligence predicted reading achievement better than all the tests of discrimination combined. Finally Vellutino (1979b) questions the use of measures that require relative judgements of same and different which he believes may yield spurious impressions of auditory discrimination in young children, quoting studies by Shankweiler and Liberman (1972) and Kamil and Rudegeair (1972) in support.

Poor auditory memory was found to be associated with reading retardation by Hendry (1969), Tansley (1967), McNinch, Palmatier and Richmond (1972) and Bruininks (1968), whilst McKeever and Van Deventer (1975) concluded that right-handed chronic dyslexics possess clear auditory memory deficits for verbal material. Newton *et al.* (1979), in their validity studies of the Aston index, found poor auditory memory and sound blending to be significantly associated with poor reading. Bruininks (1968), Hendry (1969) and McNinch and Richmond (1972) also found poor auditory blending to be significantly associated with problems in reading.

More attention has been paid recently, however, to poor auditory sequencing — the recall of sounds in the proper time sequence. Both Cotterell (1972) and Goldberg and Schiffman (1972) believe it may be related to reading difficulties, whilst Richie and Athen (1976) explored the ability of children (20 with reading disabilities and 20 with adequate reading skills) to retain serially auditory stimuli. The results of six tests supported the hypothesis that children with reading disabilities could be expected to perform at a significantly poorer level on tests requiring auditory retention on both verbal and non-verbal stimuli. Isom (1969) states in his study of children's referral for reading retardation, 'Almost all poor readers were deficient in the ability to process sequentially presented material, particularly via the auditory as opposed to the visual channel.' However, evidence from Kass (1966) and Macione (1969), quoted by Kirk (1968), found no differences between disabled and non-disabled readers in auditory sequential memory tests.

Two further measures of auditory perception have been investigated: auditory closure and rhythmicity. Pumfrey and Naylor (1978) showed deficits among poor readers in auditory closure, findings which are supported by Kass (1966). Tansley (1967) showed that those with particular difficulty in reading were often lacking in rhythmicity, but Hendry

(1969) found no relationship between Stambak's rhythm test and poor reading ability. More recently Wisbey (1977) has revived interest in this area, and suggests learning-disabled children would benefit from musical remediation, including tone and rhythm.

Wisbey also draws attention to two other important aspects of auditory perception – auditory acuity and auditory maturity. Whilst in general we are not concerned with auditory acuity, Wisbey suggests that a decline in this function starts in early childhood (about six) and that even very slight hearing losses, such as those caused by catarrh, sinusitis, enlarged adenoids and tonsillitis may drastically affect the acquisition of literacy skills. There is, however, evidence to contradict Wisbey's claims: Johnson (1957) found no convincing evidence that auditory acuity and reading achievement are closely linked, whilst Goldberg and Schiffman (1972) suggest that auditory perceptual maturity may not be attained until the age of seven, thus possibly explaining some of the difficulties encountered by beginning readers: in any case, the majority of children suffering from these minor ailments learn to read perfectly adequately.

It seems, then, that auditory perception remains a topic of continuing interest among researchers in specific reading disabilities. Goodacre (1979) reports that current research in the auditory modality tends to be facing problems to do with the validity of measuring instruments and the relationship of perceptual abilities to intelligence (Pumfrey and Naylor, 1978). Although much of the evidence is confusing and in some cases contradictory, there does seem to be an association between poor reading and auditory perceptual difficulties in *some* cases. Perhaps it is most useful to view these particular problems as Tallal (1976) does, as characteristic of a subgroup of children with reading disabilities rather than associated with all cases of reading disorders.

Vision and visual perception

Vision

Goodacre (1979) writes: 'Vision and eye movements have, after a period of nearly 40 years, once again appeared in the literature as topics of investigation.'

In general, there seems to be no definite evidence of any relationship between peripheral visual ability and reading problems. Goldberg and Schiffman (1972) go so far as to say, 'There is no agreement at all among researchers as to the connection of any eye disorder with the ability to read, or even with scholastic achievement in other areas.' They quote a joint organizational statement published by the American Academy of Pediatrics and American Academy of Ophthalmology which similarly concludes: 'There is no peripheral eye defect which produces dyslexia and associated learning disabilities.' They point out that children with learning disabilities have the same incidence of ocular abnormalities as children reading at grade level, and suggest a multi-disciplinary and individually based approach to remediation. Further support comes from Flax (1968), who believes that not only peripheral visual defects but in addition directional confusion and eye dominance are not related to dyslexia, which is usually due to a combination of visual *and* auditory perception difficulties. Critchley (1970) reviews the evidence on visual defects and concludes that developmental dyslexia is not the product of muscle-imbalance or imperfect binocular fusion (Gruber, 1962) or various other defects such as heterophoris, fusion anomalies, field restriction and hypermetropia. Rubino and Minden (1971) tested 23 children with reading disability for nasal and temporal fields in both eyes. Both peripheral and central visual field limits were found to be in the expected range. Recent evidence comes from Rankin and Barber (1978). Interestingly, Sampson (1975) quotes Douglas *et al.* (1968) as finding that short sight actually promotes good reading. However, Fisher (1976) maintains that peripheral vision is important as a pre-screening technique, and that dyslexics are deficient in the basic pattern analysing functions that occur during reading.

Ocular control and eye movements have become topics of revived interest recently. Bouma and Legein (1977) suggest eye control might be a possible deficit in poor readers. Deficits in ocular-motor function are mentioned as a component in some reading disorders by Leisman and Schwartz (1976). They suggest that saccades (movements of the eyes from one fixation point to another) of short duration and high velocity do not allow enough time for effective transmission, with consequential effects on visual processing. This could lead to lack of fluency, segmentation, skipping of words, sentences or paragraphs, and transpositions. A rather similar point is made by Stanley (1975), who hypothesizes that many of the confusions experienced by dyslexics may result from eye-movements feeding new information into the visual system before the old information is processed or masked; therefore abnormal eye movements could be due to the system trying to correct by searching for information that produces less interference.

Other studies have found evidence of abnormal eye movements in poor readers or dyslexics. Leton (1962), Nodine and Lang (1971), Getman *et al.* (1964) and Festinger *et al.* (1972) all found reading errors to be associated with faulty eye movements. Naidoo's (1972) spelling retardates showed a nystagmoid eye movement, and Lesevre's (1964) dyslexics showed more ocular instability, a slower oculomotor reaction-time and a greater number of short pauses than controls. Pavlidis (1978), in an important contribution on erratic eye movements in dyslexics, reviews the literature concerned with several specific abnormalities in eye movements. Dyslexics have been found to have longer saccadic latencies (Dossetor and Papaioannou, 1975; Lesevre, 1964; Pavlidis, 1978; Pavlidis and Robinson, 1978) than normal readers, although no study has compared saccadic latency between poor readers and dyslexics. It has also been shown that dyslexics have an excessive number of fixations (Gruber, 1962; Zangwill and Blakemore, 1972; Ciuffreda *et al.*, 1976; Pirozzolo and Rayner, 1978; Pavlidis, 1978). In addition, dyslexics make many more regressions (movements from right to left), as reported by Ciuffreda *et al.*, 1976; Halpire, reported in Critchley, 1970; Pavlidis, 1978. These regressions vary in size and sometimes appear in clusters of two or more, and often are bigger than the proceeding forward saccade. Finally, a study by Pavlidis (1978) showed that 12-year-old dyslexics had an average perceptual span (size of area from which reader is able to perceive and organize information during a fixation) smaller than that of a first-grade student. Pavlidis concludes that dyslexics exhibit erratic eye movements, but due to the paucity of information feels unable to attribute this to 'a disfunctioning oculomotor control system or to difficulties in information processing systems, or to both, or to "faulty" feedback between the two systems'. He suggests that the dyslexics' bizarre spellings and erratic EMs during reading may be due to their inability to proceed sequentially, a hypothesis which he himself tested in a study comparing dyslexics with matched normal readers on a sequential tracking test (Pavlidis, 1978b). Normal readers were significantly better at tracking moving lights than dyslexics.

Although there seems to be plenty of evidence that dyslexics exhibit abnormal eye movements (there is little evidence comparing the EMs of normal and poor readers with dyslexics), the general opinion at present appears to be that these are the result not the cause of reading problems (Critchley, 1970; Vernon, 1971; Simon and Ward, 1978). Festinger *et al.* (1972) suggests that the dyslexics' abnormal eye movements may usually be seen as an outcome of the disorder rather than a cause but that eye movement disorders may be the cause of reading problems for a subgroup of dyslexic children. Goldberg and Schiffman (1972) examined the eye movements of 50 dyslexic children compared with an adequate number of normal controls, and concluded that improper eye movements seem to be caused by poor comprehension rather than the reverse. They state: 'This evidence suggests that it is the ability to understand which determines the fluidity of the reading and that ocular mobility simply denotes the degree of fluidity.' Obviously, more research is needed in this area before the exact relationship between faulty eye movements and poor reading can be ascertained.

Visual perception

The perceptual aspects of vision have attracted a good deal of attention amongst researchers in the field of reading disorders. Many studies stress that there is a disturbance of the visual perceptual process in disabled readers. Early work by Fildes (1921) found weaknesses in visual discrimination and memory to be characteristic of non-readers, and more recent work points to similar difficulties (Gredler, 1969; Lovell, 1964; Gibson, 1966; Flax, 1968). Crosby (1968) considers visual or tactile imperception to be an important variable, whilst Richardson (1974) identifies six phenomena often associated with dyslexia as being possibly attributable to the lack of a visual Cartesian frame of reference. Other researchers have pointed out specific visual perception deficits, such as deficits in visual memory, visual sequencing and visual closure. Pumfrey and Naylor (1978) found deficits among poor readers in visual sequential memory, whilst Kass (1966) showed a relationship between learning to read and performance on tests of closure and visual memory. Rizzo (1939) reported disabled readers to be inferior to normal readers in visual sequential memory tasks. Thomson and Newton (1979) found significant correlations between both symbolic and pictorial visual sequential memory scores and poor readers and dyslexics. Goldberg and Schiffman (1972) investigated three visual aspects of reading – visual memory, visual sequencing and visual perception. Findings indicated that visual sequential ability and visual memory are significantly correlated with several measures of reading, and the authors suggest that reading disability may result from lack of co-ordination among these three different visual functions required for reading.

Despite these findings there is considerable controversy concerning the role of visual perception in reading. Naidoo (1972) found no differences between her specific and retarded readers in visual retention, and Valtin (1978-1979) claimed that dyslexic failure is not connected with a disturbance in visual perception. Benton (1962) believed that serial-order ability may be a more important variable than visual perception in the reading ability of young children, and Wiener *et al.* (1970) made a similar statement. It has been suggested that visual perceptual difficulties may be due to immaturity (Vernon, 1957; Benton, 1962; Wisby, 1977; Fletcher and Satz, 1979) and that this deficiency may therefore be the result rather than the cause of reading disability (Vernon, 1957; Benton, 1962; Critchley, 1970). Kessler (1970) is not too happy with the maturational explanation − 'The explanation as to why a given child should have the perceptual deficit is vaguely given as a function left behind in successive waves of maturation' − and suggests that cognitive development may influence perceptual development. Doehring (1968) rejects the theory that immaturity of gestalt functioning on perceptual tests is important, but most of his perceptual measures were of perceptual *speed* only. Gredler (1977) feels that the controversy over visual perception may be in part due to the belief that a factor must have an all or none influence, whereas cognitive variables as well as perceptual and personality variables may be involved in severe reading disability. Singleton (1976) also believes that visual perceptual difficulties may be characteristic of a proportion of dyslexics but that only a small proportion of dyslexics show these difficulties alone.

In conclusion it seems that, whilst visual perception is an important variable in reading retardation, it is probably associated, like difficulties in auditory perception, with only a proportion of children with reading problems.

Integration of the senses

Whilst individual perceptual abilities are important, many researchers have drawn attention to the importance of intersensory integration and co-ordination, and the possibility of a deficit in this area in the reading disabled. The majority of the studies have been concerned with auditory-visual integration. Early research by Birch (1962) found that retarded readers were less able to translate visual into auditory patterns than controls, an experiment that was repeated and confirmed by Blank and Bridger (1966), and an experiment by Birch and Belmont

(1964) showed that backward readers perform less well than normals at an intersensory task. Katz and Deutsch (1963) showed they had difficulty in shifting their attention between light and sounds, whilst Kass (1966) found defects in visual and auditory integration. Flax (1968) attributed dyslexia to a combination of visual and auditory perceptual difficulties, whilst Lovell and Gorton (1968) found that 13 per cent of the variance in their backward readers could be accounted for by their inability to associate sound and symbol. McNinch and Richmond (1972) found auditory-visual integration to be associated with reading ability, whilst Gehring (1966) claims that auditory-visual relationship disturbance is a ubiquitous feature of dyslexia which causes difficulty in establishing symbol-sound relationships necessary for the ability to read, write and spell.

Cashdan (1970) gave two groups of nine-year-old good and poor readers an auditory-visual task and found that the good readers performed better. Ford (1967) found auditory-visual integration to be a significant aspect of reading ability, and Blau, Schwalb, Zanger and Blau (1969) drew attention to a defect in the association of sound with symbol in dyslexics. More recently, Nelson (1974) and Zurif and Carson (1970) linked defective intersensory integration with poor reading and spelling, and Doehring and Hoshko (1977) suggested there was a group of backward readers who were deficient in auditory-visual association. On the other hand, a few studies such as the one by Bruininks (1968) found auditory-visual integration not significant in reading achievement. A study by Vande Voort and Senf (1973) compared 16 retarded readers and 16 normal readers on four matching tasks: (1) visual-spatial/visual-spatial; (2) visual-temporal/visual-temporal; (3) auditory-temporal/auditory-temporal; (4) auditory-temporal/visual-spatial. Results showed that the groups differed in tasks (1) and (3) but not in the others, suggesting that the hypothesis that auditory-visual integration is a critical skill lacking in reading disabled children is not supported. The authors suggested that memory and/or perceptual deficits may explain poor reading performance. Vellutino (1979b) goes so far as to say, 'Having reviewed most of the important studies of the past ten to fifteen years, I can say with some degree of assurance that there is no conclusive evidence to support the intersensory deficit explanation of reading disability.' In particular he criticizes many studies such as the Birch and Belmont one (op. cit.), for their failure to control adequately for intrasensory deficits, and suggests, in preference, a verbal encoding deficit explanation for which he finds some support from Blank and her associates who concluded that poor readers' difficulties in intersensory matching and temporal ordering tasks were due to their limited ability to employ a verbal coding system (Blank and Bridger, 1966; Blank, Weider and Bridger, 1968). Wedell (1977) felt visual and auditory perception were not important in the later stages of reading when other skills such as decoding and extrapolation become more important, and this suggestion echoes results quoted by Kahn and Birch (1968) who found a significant correlation between auditory-visual integration and reading up to the age of 12. There was also a suggestion (Reilly, 1971) that auditory-visual integration develops earlier in girls than boys. Furthermore IQ may affect auditory-visual integration; Kahn (1965) and Ford (1967) found the auditory-visual integration association with poor reading disappeared when IQ was held constant.

Crosby (1968) drew attention to deficits in other intersensory combinations which may affect dyslexics, including visual imperception with or without tactile imperception, dysgraphia and motor disability. Several writers point to visual-motor deficits underlying reading disability. Poor visual motor ability was found to be associated with difficulties in spelling and arithmetic by Koppitz (1964), Rosner and Simon (1971) and Rosner (1973), whilst Bender scores (essentially a visual-motor test) were found to be predictive of reading achievement by Goins (1958), Smith and Keogh (1962) and De Hirsch *et al.* (1966). Haworth (1970) found a sample of boys who were all two to three years below expected grade level to be consistently below age expectations on a test of visual-motor performance, and Owen *et al.* (1971) found their sample of learning-disabled children and their siblings to be below average on two tests in perceptual-motor functioning. However, Vellutino (1979b) has cast some doubts on the relationship between reading ability and visual-motor deficits. Reviewing the evidence which he finds to be conflicting, he suggests that visual-motor tests may be measuring some aspect of problem-solving rather than perceptual functioning, and that differing experiences in visual-motor activities may affect children's performance both on such tests and in reading itself.

Finally, the relative importance of auditory or visual sequencing in reading has been investigated. Doehring (1968) thought visual sequencing to be more important, while Isom (1969) and Bannatyne (1966) saw auditory sequencing as paramount. Sabatino and Hayden (1970), Tansley (1967), Vernon (1957), McKeever and Van Deventer (1975) and Levine (1976) all implicated deficiencies in both auditory and visual sequential processing (see also sections on auditory perception and visual perception).

Spatial ability (and form perception)

The evidence on the link between spatial ability and learning difficulties tends to be contradictory, with many studies showing that problems in spatial orientation and discrimination underlie reading problems, whilst other studies show that dyslexics do not have a disturbed spatial ability and may even have a predisposition to spatial skills.

Confirmation of an association between some related aspects of poor spatial ability and reading problems comes from Monroe (1932), Weschler and Hagin (1964), Leader (1968), Silver and Hagin (1960) and Cohn (1961). Hermann (1959) put forward a theory that specific reading disability was due to a hereditary defect in spatial orientation. Poor spatial orientation has also been mentioned by Kinsbourne and Warrington (1966), Lovell and Gorton (1968), Kinsbourne (1970), Fitzhugh and Fitzhugh (1966), and Vernon (1957). Seymour and Porpodas (1978) carried out four experiments with normal and dyslexic subjects, and concluded that dyslexia is associated with a deficiency in the quasi-spatial coding of arrays of elements, which relates particularly to the property of directional polarization. Directional difficulties are also mentioned by Hermann (1959), Gehring (1966), Shankweiler (1964) and Jastak and Jastak (1965). It would seem that deficiencies in left–right discrimination occur more frequently in dyslexics than normal readers but estimates of the extent and nature of this measure vary. To some degree it appears to depend on age (Belmont and Birch, 1963; Shearer, 1968) and intelligence (Benton, 1959), although this latter finding is disputed by Belmont and Birch (1965). Vernon (1971) suggests that there may be an association between directional confusion and errors and reversals in sequential ordering; in fact they may constitute two aspects of the same disability. Miles and Ellis (1980), however, argue that implicit verbalization is needed in many directional tasks and that any directional mistake by a dyslexic may be the result of inadequate labelling. Vellutino (1979b) is also at pains to show that there is little empirical evidence for spatial or directional confusion to be associated with reading disability, and likewise implicates naming and labelling problems. In support of this contention he reports the results of two studies carried out in his laboratory (Vellutino *et al.*,

1973; Vellutino, Steger, Kaman and DeSetto, 1975). In both studies poor readers (aged seven to 12 years) performed as well as normal readers in immediate visual recall of Hebrew words presented tachistoscopically, making no more errors in orienting and sequencing the letters in the words and in scanning the material from left to right. Poor form perception has been associated with reading problems by Monroe (1932), Benton (1962) and Gehring (1966), and, finally, deficiencies in visual-spatial discrimination have been pointed out by Ingram (1971).

However, Valtin (1978–1979) and Jorm (1978) found dyslexics did not have disturbed spatial ability. Kaufman and Biren (1976/1977) investigated the hypothesis that perception of spatial relations is related to reading ability after the age of seven. Results showed no correlation between the percentage of spatial errors and the child's reading grade, although it was thought a correlation might exist between spatial errors and poor spelling and handwriting. Stanley (1975) administered two tests involving photographs and wooden replicas of blocks whose locations and angular rotations were randomly ordered. There was no difference between the ability of dyslexics and normals to identify the different form, and Stanley suggests that it may be the memory for transformation rather than the ability to transform that is deficient in dyslexics. However, Vernon (1971) quotes evidence from Crosby (1968) that dyslexics show deficiencies in the reproduction of complex forms, from Clements and Peters (1962) that they have difficulty in perceiving the relationships between parts and wholes and from Zangwill (1960), Critchley (1970) and Miles (1961), all showing problems of a similar nature. She concludes that dyslexics suffer from an impaired capacity to reconstruct figures in which the spatial dimensions and the relation of the parts to the whole have to be correctly copied. Finally, Yule and Rutter (1976) suggest that visuo-spatial difficulties are a red herring and are not characteristic of the general population of retarded readers.

Two recent approaches have proposed a different arrangement of spatial skills in dyslexics. Witelson (1977) hypothesizes that there is a representation of spatial data in both hemispheres in dyslexics (confirmed in her own study of 85 boys with learning difficulties and 165 control subjects) which could lead to overloading the left hemisphere and thus interfering with its 'native' (i.e. language functions). This study has yet to be replicated. Newton *et al.* (1979) propose that the dyslexic has a brain organization which has a less clear-cut preponderance for verbal tasks and symbolic ordering in the left hemisphere than the non-dyslexic. They suggest that this gives rise to individual differences in cognition, including a predisposition in dyslexics towards 'spatial' thinking abilities including artistic design and graphicability. As evidence, they quote Bannatyne's (1971) findings that dyslexic children score highly on spatial ability, which are supported by Rugel (1974) for disabled readers. Their own experiments showed that dyslexics scored higher on the Object Assembly and Picture Completion subtests of the WISC, and, by categorizing each subject's subtest scores according to the clusters proposed by Bannatyne (1971), they were able to show that the dyslexic group scored significantly higher than the control group on spatial ability. However, it is difficult to equate these findings with their own description of observable behavioural symptoms of dyslexia, such as persistent reversal and disordering of letters, syllables and words, mirror-imaging of letters and words and problems of direction which tend to be related to spatial problems.

Summary

Although at present perceptual problems seem to occupy a less central position in the literature on specific learning difficulties than in the past, they constitute a continuing area of concern. Attention has shifted slightly from measures of perceptual discrimination to an emphasis on memory and sequencing aspects of perception, and the importance of intersensory integration. Auditory, visual and spatial perceptual processes remain a primary emphasis with a recent renewal of interest in auditory and visual acuity, together with related topics. The association between sound and symbol has received a fresh impetus with a new emphasis on the role of verbal labelling. The hypothesis that perceptual abilities are subject to maturational development and may be of more importance in the early stages of learning to read and of less importance in the later stages remains topical, whilst it is also suggested that perceptual problems may be the result, not the cause, of reading difficulties.

Finally, it is thought that perceptual difficulties may be associated with reading disability in some cases, but not all, and that perceptual deficits may be a contributory but not a determining cause of reading problems.

Cognitive style

In the sections on hemispheric function and asymmetry, it was suggested by many writers that reading-disabled children are either deficient in some respects or at least different from normal children in their brain organization. This has led some researchers to point out that such children may actually have a different style of cognitive functioning.

Edwards (1968) points out in a very general way that account should be taken of individual differences in learning styles and remediation planned accordingly. Stott (1971, 1978) is critical of the 'hypothetical deficit' explanation of learning disabilities, and suggests that poor performance could be analysed in terms of wrong use or non-use of a child's neural equipment. He has himself drawn up a guide to identify faulty learning styles comprising seven items for preliminary screening and 15 for in-depth analysis. However, it is probable that educational handicaps due to socio-economic disadvantage, such as Stott concentrates on, would yield to remedial treatment more readily than constitutional handicaps. Thomas (1973), in a study of the acquisition of cognitive functions, stresses the importance of developing standards of inference. He describes a method of estimating the standard (D) adopted by an individual in a recognition-learning situation. In 33 families attending a dyslexia clinic, a much higher proportion of the children than their parents or a comparison group of normal young adult students, had abnormally high or low D values.

Newton *et al.* (1979) claim, 'The results from the experimental studies suggest that many of the difficulties described as dyslexia fit into a model of learning.' They go on to describe the particular kind of brain organization characterizing dyslexics (op. cit.) which includes a predisposition towards 'spatial' thinking abilities combined with poor performance at skills such as sequencing, blending sounds, associating sound and arbitrary symbol, etc. This total 'predisposition' in terms of cognition and perception may be described as a 'learning style'. The skills mentioned above are exactly those required for reading, spelling and writing; thus the dyslexic child has a learning style which is not compatible with our written language system. Gupta, Ceci and Slater (1978), investigating visual discrimination in good and poor readers, concluded that differences found between the two groups were almost certainly caused by differences in cognitive linguistic strategies rather than in visual discrimination abilities. Friedman, Guyer-Christie and Tymchuk (1976) attempt to link cognitive style with hemispheric functioning. Reviewing the literature on cognitive style, they select Witkin *et al.*'s (1962) 'field articulation' construct as being of particular importance for understanding learning disabilities. According to Witkin, field-independent people show a high degree of field articulation and are generally analytic in their approach to cognitive tasks whereas field-dependent or field-sensitive people tend to respond to the total field and use a more global and perhaps less verbal information-processing style. In their own experiment Guyer and Friedman (1975) suggested that field-sensitivity can be associated with 'incomplete dominance' of left hemisphere systems on cognitive behaviour, and found that 63 per cent of their LD group were field-sensitive as compared with 37 per cent of the normal controls, a finding supported by Valtin (1972, 1973). In addition, using three measures of left hemisphere functioning – field articulation, verbal long-term recognition memory, and verbal closure – it was possible to classify correctly 82 per cent of the boys as good or poor readers.

Van Meel, Vlek and Bruijel (1970) also propose that children with reading difficulties may have a particular 'style' of cognitive functioning which can be summarized as a 'foreshortening of temporal perspective', i.e. preference for or pressure towards those cognitive operations that, given a certain task, would do the job in the shortest possible time. This would entail solutions detrimental to other aspects of task accomplishment such as task relevance, elaboration and precision. The authors suggest that their concept is similar to Shapiro's (1965) 'neurotic style' and Kagan's 'conceptual impulsivity' (Kagan, Pearson and Welsh, 1966). An experiment was carried out to test the hypothesis that children with reading difficulties have insufficient capacity for temporal integration of information, so, if compared with normal children, they would do equally well in discrimination tasks where only a few dimensions have to be searched, but would have more difficulties in tasks in which a larger number of dimensions have to be checked. Bruijel (1967) found that an experiment involving one or two discriminative dimensions revealed no difference between normals and children with reading difficulty whereas an experiment conducted involving two to five discriminant dimensions in a visual discrimination task (Van Meel *et al.*, op. cit.) showed that children with learning disability have more difficulties in complex discrimination tasks due, the authors believe, to deficiencies in temporal integration.

A study by Wallbrown, Huelsman, Blaha and Wallbrown (1975) was also concerned with integration. As part of an attempt to investigate the presupposition that individuals who are reading disabled should demonstrate a common pattern of cognitive anomalies which is distinguishable from normals, they tested three cognitive structure hypotheses derived from the work of Myklebust, Bannochie and Killen (1971). They found strong support for two hypotheses: that the overall ability arrangement of the reading disabled group consisted of four orthogonal primary factors which were not organized according to any identifiable scheme, whereas the factor structure for normals consisted of three factors: g, v:ed (verbal-education), and k:m (spatial perceptual) hierarchically arranged; and that the reading disabled showed a less effective ability integration (small proportion of WISC subtests variance attributable to g factor) compared with normals (strong g factor). A third hypothesis concerned with ability organization was not supported.

Meichenbaum (1976) proposed a new method determining learning difficulties: the cognitive-functional approach. He rejected the two general research strategies commonly in use: the comparative populations approach (which involves comparing the performance of learning-disabled children with a 'normal' control group on a comprehensive battery of tests, and thus inferring the nature of the deficit from the differential nature of the performance) and the specific deficits analysis (whereby the investigator hypothesizes a particular type of deficit and attempts to assess this through a battery of tests), and instead suggests conducting a psychological analysis of the cognitive requirements of tasks on which the learning disabled child's performance has been found to be inadequate. This can lead to the identification of inappropriate cognitive strategies and thus appropriate remedial treatment.

Attentional correlates

Some writers, whilst discussing models of cognitive processes, have referred to the role of attentional factors. Levine (1976) proposes a hypothetical model based on attentional and cognitive factors and their interaction. Forty-eight males with a mean IQ of 112 were divided into three groups according to reading ability: normal readers, primary readers and secondary readers (as proposed by Rabinovitch). The subjects were required to pair and put in serial order auditory and visual stimulus digits whilst their heart rates were recorded. Heart-rate deceleration occurred only in normal readers, 'suggesting that a regulatory mechanism controls the physiological parameters of attention and produces an optimal level that facilitates cognitive processing'. The absence of heart-rate deceleration in deficient readers suggests a defective attentional mechanism. Secondary readers were also found to show over-attention during the stimulus period which is thought to prevent early initiation of cognitive processing. A study by Sroufe, Sonies, West and Wright (1973) examined heart-rate deceleration of learning-disabled children and concluded that there is a relationship between learning disability and aspects of attention, and that the drug Ritalin (which was given to approximately half of the experimental group) modified a child's ability to attend. Klees and Leburn (1972) investigated the figurative and operative processes of thought of 40 dyslexic children, and found delays in both types of processes and concluded that dyslexic children rely on the concrete characteristics of objects more than normal children, and follow transformations of them only with certain delay.

Various studies have suggested that learning-disabled children are distractable, unable to pay attention, or prone to focus on irrelevant aspects of the situation. Dykman *et al.* (1970, 1971) linked organically based deficiencies in attention with poorer performance, slower reaction time and decreased physiological reactivity of learning-disabled children. They concluded, confirming Luria's (1961) hypothesis, that hyperactive children are over-attentive to the environment and hyperactive children are under-attentive to the environment. Bryan and Wheeler (1972) and Bryan (1974) found learning-disabled children spent more time in non-task-oriented behaviours than in task-oriented behaviours, and that their attentional behaviour was not dependent upon the subject or content area, as it was with the control group. The attentional hypothesis was also supported by Kinsbourne (1967) and Kinsbourne and Corbin (in preparation). Wedell (1968), discussing Katz and Deutsch (1963), found that some children who are poor at reading may have difficulty in switching their attention from sight to hearing and vice versa, and Hutt and Hutt (1964) linked hyperactive behaviour with a short attention span.

However, these findings must be interpreted with caution as it is possible that they may depend upon the investigator's concept of distractibility and the resulting measures employed. As Tarver and Hallahan (1974) found, learning-disabled children are not more highly distractible by extraneous colour cues or flashing lights but they do seem deficient in their ability to focus their attention on tasks involving embeddedness.

So far we have been talking as if attention was a single entity, but

Berlyne (1970) and Ross (1976) among others point out that it is possible to distinguish between arousal, attentiveness and degree of concentration, and prefer to use the term 'selective attention' to describe the capacity to select among the various visual, auditory, tactual and kinaesthetic impulses and to attend to one or a limited number at a time. Even the term 'selective attention' can be broken down into attention in learning, attention in remembering, and attention in performance. Examples of studies identifying a deficit in selective attention amongst retarded readers are those by Vande Voort, Senf and Benton (1972) and various dichotic listening experiments, for example Broadbent and Gregory (1964), Satz, Rardin and Ross (1971).

Douglas (1976) prefers to use the term 'sustained' attention because of an accompanying deficit labelled 'impulse control' and finds much support from various doctoral theses (Sykes, 1969; Sykes, Douglas and Morgenstern, 1973; Cohen, 1970; Parry, 1973; Peters, 1976) for an attentional-impulsivity deficit in hyperactive children and in addition that stimulant drugs exert a major effect on this deficit.

It has been suggested in the literature that attention may be a developmental phenomenon, i.e. that it is an ability that improves in the course of a child's development. Rourke (1974) reported that the attentional deficit is more characteristic of younger children with learning disabilities, and decreases at puberty. In Douglas' study (1972) of hyperactive children, behaviour of older hyperactives was less disrupting, and they engaged in more purposive behaviour not related to classroom activity. Further evidence comes from two studies by Rourke and Czudner (1972) which showed that clinic children in the young group displayed rather gross difficulties with attention, but the older clinic group's performance did not differ from that of their normal controls. Pick, Christy and Frankel (1972) compared the performance of second-graders and sixth-graders on a task which required the child to indicate whether two objects were the same or different, and concluded that the ability to focus visual attention exclusively on relevant information improves with age.

Follow-up studies provide some support for the hypothesis that learning disabilities can be seen as a developmental lag in selective attention. Weiss, Minde, Werry, Douglas and Nemeth (1971) found that hyperactivity decreased with age. An experiment by Rourke, Orr and Ridgley (1974) found performance on the Grooved Pegboard Test was associated with reading ability for retarded readers at the younger age levels, but not later on.

The literature on attentional deficits, whilst it points consistently in the direction of a link between attentional deficits and learning disability, is of limited value. First, as Ross (1976) stresses, attention remains an inferred construct – it has not been made observable. Many of the measures used, such as detection of significant stimuli, hyperactivity and dichotic listening performance, result in questionable estimates of the hypothesized concept (attention). Secondly, most of the studies have been carried out with either hyperactive or learning-disabled children and not with specifically retarded readers. Whilst hyperactivity has been suggested as a concomitant variable of specific learning difficulty, it is by no means a universal or even common symptom. Finally, it might be more profitable to consider poor attention to be part of a more general syndrome of faulty learning or cognitive style.

Physical correlates

Impairment in motor ability or co-ordination has frequently been linked with specific learning difficulties. Many studies have implicated poor motor performance as at least an associated factor in reading disability. Brenner *et al.* (1967) reported clumsiness in movement and gait, and poor control of fine motor abilities in a sample of children of average intelligence who were poor at spelling, arithmetic and writing. Bannantyne and Wichiarajote (1969) found that scores on spelling clustered with total body balance and balance on one foot. Rabinovitch (1968) showed that reading retardates were awkward and clumsy, whilst Lucas *et al.* (1965) found poor general muscular co-ordination to be associated with hyperactivity and reading disability. The Isle of Wight study (Rutter *et al.*, 1970) provides evidence from a large-scale sample that specifically retarded readers were significantly poorer than controls in motor co-ordination and constructional ability, and demonstrated delayed motor development. Naidoo (1972), Lovell and Gorton (1968), Klasen (1972), Salmon (1978) and Clark (1970) all report various motor impairments to be linked with reading problems, and Newton *et al.* (1979) point to an inconsistent lateralization of motor functions in dyslexics.

There is, however, a small amount of contrary evidence. Trussell (1969) concluded that motor skills are specific and not associated with reading, and Allen (1971) asserted there was no connection between motor ability and other abilities but over half the children in her sample who were motor impaired were also backward readers. Stephens *et al.* (1967) looked at eye/hand preferences of first-grade children and concluded there was no relationship between these variables and performance on visual-motor tests.

A certain amount of research has been carried out on the relationship between self- and body-concept and reading disabilities. Davies (1974), who views motor development as the foundation of all future intellectual development, believes that total awareness of physical self in space is composed of three elements: body image (subjective experience of one's own body), body concept (pupil's 'knowledge' of his own body), and body schema (unconscious awareness derived from tactile and haptic sensations).

Witkin *et al.* (1962, 1965, 1967), Hermann (1959), Rozenberger (1970) and Tansley (1967) all associated a poor body-concept with difficulties in learning to read. Hermann and Norrie (1958) put forward the idea that there might be a kind of Gerstmann syndrome involving some disorder of the body scheme. De Hirsch *et al.* (1966) suggested that a poor body concept pointed to a low level of integration, indicating a severe maturational lag.

Chasey (1972), in a review of the literature regarding self-concept, body image and personality, found the results to have been inconclusive. Although positive relationships between training programmes and improvement in these aspects were reported, correlations were low and controls were often not used. Chasey carried out his own experiment with 30 children who had minimal brain injury with resultant learning disabilities and found no significant differences after seven weeks of physical development training in self-concept or body image. A recent study by Hunt and MacAuslan (1979) into eurythmy and reading disabilities indicated that four measures – rhythm, co-ordination, personal direction and 3D forms in spaces – were performed less efficiently by reading retarded children.

Environmental correlates

Although environmental factors are not generally regarded as primary agents in the aetiology of specific learning difficulties, nevertheless it is important to consider them as components which exert a variable influence on reading, writing and spelling disorders.

Some writers, such as Crabtree (1976) and Stott, 1971, 1978) go so far as to suggest that dyslexia and related difficulties may be largely explained by environmental factors including inappropriate teaching methods and faulty learning styles. Most writers, however, confine themselves to suggestions that some environmental variables may affect reading achievement in a negative way. Vernon (1971), in her book *Reading and its Difficulties*, devotes a chapter to the effect of motivational and emotional factors on learning to read, prefacing her remarks with the comment: 'Difficulties in learning to read are often associated with children's social background. However, we are concerned here not so much with social factors as such, as with their relationship to cognitive and motivational differences in children which appear to affect their reading achievement.' In particular, she is concerned with conditions in the social environment, motivation − both in the home and school environment, and emotional maladjustment.

Chief among the conditions of the social environment that affect reading achievement is that of socio-economic class. Eisenberg's (1966) study showed reading retardation to be highest in the ordinary schools in the Metropolitan area (where socio-economic status was lowest) and lowest in the independent schools (where socio-economic status was highest). In Britain, Kellmer Pringle *et al.* (1966) found that poor readers formed 7.1 per cent of those with parents in occupational classes I and II (Registrar General's classification), 19 per cent in class III and 27 per cent in classes IV and V. Douglas (1964) found significant differences between upper-middle, lower-middle, upper-working- and lower-working-class eight-year-old children in word recognition and sentence completion. Goodacre (1967), however, found the mean test score of infant school children in lower-working-class areas was significantly lower than that of all other children but there was no significant difference between children in middle-class city schools and those in upper-working-class schools, although a written sentence completion test for this age group might not be very reliable. A variable which is often linked with social class is that of intelligence. Vernon says: 'There is little doubt that the average intelligence of the lower social classes is less than that of the higher.' Although she does not discuss the reasons for this she does, however, review the evidence (Morris, 1959; Douglas, 1964; Lovell and Woolsey, 1964) on the association, and concludes that lower social class is associated with backwardness in reading independently of intelligence.

Pumfrey and Naylor (1978) highlighted the importance of social deprivation on the reading attainments of poor readers, and in particular mentioned the socially and economically deprived areas of our industrial conurbations, whilst Vernon (1965, 1969) investigated deprivation experienced by boys living in other cultures − Jamaican, African, Canadian, Indian and Eskimo − and found a general correspondence between the total number of adverse conditions and inferiority of performance on intelligence and other tests. Goldberg and Schiffman (1972) drew attention to ethnic and socio-economic background and Harris (1976), reviewing ten years of progress in remedial reading, referred to the sociological factors in reading difficulties and immigrant children.

Moving on to the influence of the home environment, there is of course plenty of evidence, as Goldberg and Schiffman (1972) pointed out, that family crises such as death, divorce, alcoholism, mental illness, etc., will affect the child's ability to learn. The National Child Development survey (Davie *et al.*, 1972) showed that the chances of a social class V child being a non-reader were 15 times greater than those of a social class I child. There has also been a stress on the influence of maternal factors, ranging from birth injury to maternal employment. Kawi and Pasamanick (1959) found that 16 per cent of children with reading retardation had gestational complications compared with 1.5 per cent of controls. More recently, Bale (1974) found, in a sample of 82 boys who were all at least two years below the appropriate reading age on the Schonell test of Reading Ability, that there was a greater number of difficulties of pregnancy and during birth in the backward readers and a significant difference in the case of low birth weight. Other studies have pointed to the importance of maternal attitudes to the environment (Hess, 1968) and maternal employment (Wright, 1974) in reading readiness and performance. Recently studies (Yule and Rutter, 1976; and Valtin, 1970) have found specific reading difficulties to be commoner in children from large families. Apart from the physical attributes of the home, there has been an emphasis on parental interest and attitudes. Fraser (1959) obtained a correlation of 0.66 between parental encouragement and school achievement, a higher correlation than with any other aspect of home life. However, teacher estimates, on which the figures were based, may have been affected by the teachers' observations of the children's school behaviour, leading to a tendency to overestimate the attributes of middle-class homes and underestimate those of working-class homes. Other studies, by Douglas (1964), Kellmer Pringle *et al.* (1966), Valtin (1970) and Davie *et al.* (1972), also found an association between parental interest and school achievement, including reading. A study by Owen *et al.* (1971) investigated parental attitudes to a variety of topics. Their subjects were 76 educationally handicapped children who had siblings of the same sex, matched to normal controls of the same age and socioeconomic background, with siblings of the same age and sex as the siblings of the learning-disabled children. It was found that parents of learning-disabled children perceived their affected child as anxious and difficult and were more negative than the parents of normal children about their child's schooling. Both mothers and fathers tended to withhold affection if the child was disorganized or lacked impulse control. Interestingly, they found no evidence that the parents of the learning-disabled children pressed their children academically more than normal children.

Linked to the factor of parental interest is that of motivation, both at home and at school. A number of writers have stressed the importance of motivation in school achievement, including Wedell (1977), Stott (1971, 1978), Ackerman (1979), and Gulliford (1969). Lane (1974), Abrams (1970) and Valtin (1972, 1973) all found low motivation to be associated with learning disabilities. It is generally thought that reading achievement is increased by strong achievement motivation, as found by Zimmerman and Allebrand (1965). However, other studies such as the one by Kent and Davis (1957) show that children of demanding parents do have greater verbal reasoning ability but that this does not necessarily affect reading.

Once the child has entered school, a different set of variables may add to his difficulties. Both the effect of teachers' expectations (Beez, 1968), not necessarily accurate in the case of children likely to face learning difficulties (Hart and Fagg, 1976; Goodacre, 1968), and poor teaching may help prevent him achieving his initial educational goals of reading, writing and arithmetic. Vernon (1971) writes: 'It has been established by Morris (1966) beyond a peradventure that reading achievement is related to the skill of the teacher; and that children taught by untrained, inexperienced and unskilful teachers tend to be especially backward in reading.' In this connection she discusses the evidence into the relative efficacy of formal and informal methods, which she finds to be variable. Anderson, Byron and Dixon (1956) found the average age of learning to read was lower in a school using formal methods, but in a school using more informal methods the children soon caught up once they had learned to read. Kellmer Pringle and Reeves (1968) found no differences between children who had received a traditional formal education and those who had learned in a progressive situation. Lovell (1963) tested over 1,300 children in 11 matched pairs of schools and found no significant difference in average reading achievement between the children in the two types of schools, although the amount of backwardness was greater in the schools using formal methods. Thorndike (1973) carried out a reading survey in 15 countries and found that the reading level in three developing countries was far below that of the developed countries, suggesting that the 'schooling' does make a difference to reading achievement.

Not all writers in the field are of the opinion that environmental factors are as influential as has been suggested. Vellutino (1979b), while reporting evidence from a number of studies showing a consistent relationship between socioeconomic disadvantage and inferior language and cognitive development, believes that most critical differences in the experience of disadvantaged children occur in the school setting and can be remedied by individual remediation, citing his own work in this context (Vellutino and Connolly, 1971). Hagger (1970) believed that specific learning disabilities are due to organic rather than environmental factors, and both Klasen (1972) and Naidoo (1972) found no significant correlations between dyslexia and socio-economic and cultural factors. Newton *et al.* (1979) conclude in their summary of comparative findings from surveys and definitions of dyslexia that environmental variables are secondary to the main problem, which is seen as a difference in underlying brain organization.

Summary

It is difficult to be precise about the influence of the environment on the reading disabled. Whilst it is obvious that environmental factors are associated with poor reading, at the same time many good readers face identical problems with no detrimental effects. It is also hard to determine whether such factors are the cause or the consequence (where relevant) of reading disorders. In conclusion, it is probably safest to regard environmental variables as secondary or aggravating conditions, except in a minority of cases where they may assume greater importance.

Emotional correlates

Similarly it has been shown that various emotional disorders are more prevalent in reading disabled children than the norm. Thus Ohlson (1978) cites studies by Chansky (1958), Boise (1955), Berkowitz and Rothman (1955) and Tamkin (1960) all of which report significant correlation between emotional disturbances and reading retardation, although Connolly (1971) believes that few writers have attempted to validate their opinions. Vernon (1971) quotes Chazan (cited by Sampson, 1966) and Silverman, Fite and Mosher (1959) who found that poor readers showed more signs of emotional maladjustment than good readers. Gulliford (1969) and Crabtree (1976) also point to emotional factors as a source of failure, whilst Goldberg and Schiffman (1972) quote Bryant and Patterson as pointing out that emotional difficulties are almost universal among reading disability cases, a view which is shared by Cox (1970).

Other writers have singled out specific emotional problems associated with poor reading. Thus Abrams (1970) refers to 'neurotic factors' and Merritt (1972) to 'reading neurosis'. Rosenthal (1973) carried out an experiment to measure the self-esteem of dyslexic boys and concluded that children with dyslexia esteem themselves less than do normal or asthmatic controls, but that those from families who had been given information about dyslexia had higher esteem than those from families who had been given no information. Eaves (1978) investigated the relationship between reading disability in intelligent children and poor social adjustment. Results showed a significant relationship between reading retardation in intelligent children and over-reaction, but this was not correlated with the total adjustment scores. Eaves felt the results to be inconclusive, and attributed the lack of positive findings to a misconception by teachers of whether poor readers were intelligent, leading to a poorly selected sample. Manzo (1977) puts forward a more controversial view when he proposes that dyslexia could be a form of psychological defence known in psychiatric literature as Hysteria Conversion or Conversion Reaction Syndrome (CRS), whereby the adolescent dyslexic's inability to read is an expression of underlying anxiety. Ravenette (1979) is also concerned with the relationship between external and internal reactions to the situation, and suggests that dyslexics and the people concerned with them may see the situation in ways which are detrimental to a 'cure', i.e. they may not want to learn to read for a variety of underlying reasons.

Many studies have drawn attention to the increased incidence of anxiety and depression in certain backward readers. Silverman, Fite and Mosher (1959) found them to occur in about two-thirds of their emotionally maladjusted cases, whilst Mussen (1965) considered that the ability to learn to read was adversely affected by anxiety, especially in more difficult and abstract tasks. Valtin (1972, 1973) reported higher anxiety levels in dyslexics, and Van Meel, Vlek and Bruijel (1970) believed that their proposed unitary cognitive style found in children with learning difficulties was based, among other things, on the prevalence of anxiety and insecurity feelings. The Bullock report

(1975) drew attention to evidence that boys retarded in reading are more than twice as likely to show anxiety or lack of concentration, and three times as likely to experience irrational fears and anxieties. Aggression has also been found to occur in emotionally maladjusted backward readers by Douglas (1968), Stewart (1950) and Spache (1957) although it has also been suggested by Upson (1968) that backward readers may in some cases actually suppress their aggressive impulses.

Vernon (1971) attributes these emotional problems to a large extent to parental relationships. She quotes extensive evidence from Crane (cited by Bond and Tinker, 1957), Fabian (1955), Ingram and Reid (1956), Silverman, Fite and Mosher (1959) linking reading backwardness with maladjusted or disturbed parents. Other studies, by Ravenette (1968) and Mann (1957), point to over-ambitious parents creating an unbearable pressure on the child.

Kellmer Pringle (1965) showed that parental deprivation, i.e. the partial or complete separation of the child from the parents in early childhood, was associated with retarded reading achievement and maladjustment. Vernon (op. cit.) concludes:

> These studies of interaction between parents and children suggest that in certain cases reading backwardness may be associated with a primary emotional disorder arising from disorganization of the relationship between the child and his parents. It would appear that the child may react to parental inadequacy by failure to learn to read, either as a form of aggression or resistance against dominating, demanding or over-protective parents; or as an expression of dependence or an appeal for help when one or both parents are missing or are rejecting, unaffectionate or merely passive and inadequate.

Summary

Summarizing the evidence on emotional problems and reading backwardness, it seems that the relationship is not on the whole a causative one. Gates (1968), estimated that, in 75 per cent of cases of severe reading disability exhibiting maladjustment, in only a quarter of these cases was maladjustment the cause of reading disability. Malmquist (1958) reported that 23 per cent of poor readers in his sample exhibited 'nervous symptoms' which could have contributed to the reading disability. Whilst emotional disorders may be a predisposing or contributory factor in some cases of reading disability, in general emotional problems arise *because* of feelings of frustration and anxiety associated with the inability to learn to read. Critchley (1970) warns against the attribution of dyslexic problems to environmental or psychogenic causes, which may result in overlooking the specific deficit which then remains unremedied.

Drug studies: what they show
It may be helpful at this stage to digress a little to consider the role of drug therapy in learning disabilities. It must be stressed that behavioural improvement and learning improvement are two very different things. Studies have reported that the use of stimulant drugs improves concentration and selective attention (Conners, 1976; Douglas, 1976), helps reduce hyperactivity (Douglas, 1976) and improves behaviour (Stewart, 1971; Comly, 1971; Sprague and Sleator, 1976). Their use also leads to more controlled motor behaviour (Epstein *et al.*, 1968; Knights and Hinton, 1969) but does not enhance memory (Aman and Sprague, 1974).

A relatively new area of research concerns the use of 'intellectual' drugs (Dimond, 1976), i.e. substances which induce a real and genuine change in intellectual performance that can be assessed in measurable terms. Stewart, writing in 1971, asserts, 'There is no information on whether the drugs (stimulant) affect specific learning problems,' but by 1976 Dimond was writing, 'Research to date indicates that drugs can be used to improve selected intellectual functions of the brain.' An experiment by Sprague and Sleator (1976) indicated that accuracy of performance in a picture recognition task could be significantly influenced by the use of methylphenidate; and further, use of this drug significantly increased attention to the task. Dimond (1976) reports an experiment to investigate the effect of the drug Piracetam (UCB 6215)2 Pyrrolidone acetamide, which has been shown to facilitate transfer of information from one side of the brain to the other in animals (Guirgea, 1971, 1973). Sixteen students from University College, Cardiff, were given tests of verbal learning at intervals in conjunction with daily doses of the drug. Results showed an improvement in the powers of verbal memory but not learning of other types. There was also evidence to suggest that the brain was 'super connected' by the drug, by virtue of the action on the corpus callosum. However, Conners (1970) remains sceptical about the conclusions drawn in this study, questioning whether the improvement which occurs in response to drug treatment in fact derives from some general alerting or arousing effect, and suggests (Conners, 1972) that the studies showing improvements on tests of visual and auditory perception, discrimination and learning are largely attributable to attentional factors rather than specific improvements in those functions.

Nevertheless, there is some evidence that certain drugs such as caffeine, methylphenidate and pemoline (Conners, 1975) produce greater evoked responses in left parietal areas, and that marijuana (Harshman *et al.*, 1974) improves certain aspects of visuo-spatial function in the right hemisphere, but produces deterioration in verbal and analytic capacities.

In conclusion, drug therapy seems to be an interesting new area in the diagnosis and treatment of learning disabilities, particularly with regard to its possible effects on specific deficits in intellectual function. However, the field is as yet relatively uncharted and the question as to whether the effects observed are due to behavioural or neurological changes is speculative. A further shortcoming is that most of the experiments were conducted with either normal or learning-disabled children or adults, with a consequent scarcity of information on the implications of these findings for retarded readers and spellers.

3. Reading and non-reading difficulties

Reading difficulties

The field of specific learning difficulties has been mainly concerned with reading disabilities. There is some dispute as to whether there are in fact two fields: reading and learning disabilities, a position held, for example, by Lerner (1971, 1975) who believes that the learning disabilities specialist is concerned with *intrinsic* (central processing) difficulties relating to reading, whereas the reading specialist is concerned with *extrinsic* problems (environmental). However, on the whole, most writers have treated the concept of 'reading' as central. Dinnage (1970), in writing about learning disabilities, says: 'On both sides of the Atlantic, and in European countries also, the main focus of interest is reading backwardness.' We shall first consider problems associated with the act of reading itself, and then go on to examine associated disabilities such as spelling, mathematics, writing and speech, in an attempt to determine whether a specific learning difficulty is essentially a reading disorder, or whether it may be part of a general disability of which reading retardation is merely a part or symptom (as suggested by Vernon, 1971).

Reading as a developmental process

It has long been thought that reading is a hierarchical and developmental process. As far back as 1917, Hinshelwood described three stages in learning to read. The first stage concerned storing the individual letters of the alphabet in the visual memory and the spelling of words in the auditory memory. In the second stage the individual was able to read words by spelling them out letter by letter, whilst the third stage consisted of the gradual acquirement and storage of the visual memories of words. When this stage was accomplished the individual could read, not by analysing each word into its individual letters but by recognizing each word as a separate picture. It is interesting to note that a very recent thesis describing dyslexia as a 'lexical encoding deficiency' (Miles and Ellis, 1980) has strong similarities with Hinshelwood's first stage in learning to read. Hinshelwood writes: 'The first stage in the old method is to store up in the visual memory the individual letters of the alphabet. When we have stored (them) ... we can recall them into consciousness at will ... It is by comparison with these permanent visual images of the letters and words stored in this cerebral centre that we are able to recognise the printed letters and words on the page of the book.' Miles and Ellis outline one of the central features of their model as follows: 'Each individual can be thought of as equipped with an internal lexicon or dictionary which provides standards against which incoming stimuli can be matched. The energy charges which stimulate the receptors (eyes, ears, etc.) are assumed to be represented in the nervous sytem in the form of engrams or traces, and lexical encoding is the name of the process by which "codes" (that is, representations of relevant features of these traces) are matched to entries in the lexicon.' McClelland and Jackson (1978) also believe that the ability to access stored representations of letters, words and/or phrases distinguishes good and poor readers.

Vernon (1977, 1979) suggests it may be more useful to classify dyslexics and other retarded readers not according to clusters of deficiencies but according to particular reading difficulties. She outlines the successive skills essential in learning to read and suggests that as age increases, different types of failure will occur (see Rourke, 1976). The successive skills involved in learning to read are: differentiation and identification of single letter shapes; grapheme–phoneme association; learning complex irregular associations, especially compounded by matching spatial order to temporal order; and grouping single words together into meaningful phrases. Various writers have shown that poor readers may have problems with one or several of these levels of complexity. Thomson (1978) suggests readers of English use three cue systems simultaneously: graphophonic; syntactic; and semantic. Their use relies on the redundancy in language of individual letters, patterns of letters, and words. In an experiment with 40 children (20 dyslexics and 20 controls), from whom samples of oral reading were obtained, he found that dyslexics made more errors at the graphic and phonemic level (the lower level of psycholinguistic taxonomy) than the controls, whereas the control group made more errors at the bound morpheme, phrase and sentence level. Both groups made similar errors at the syntactical and semantic levels.

However, Scheerer-Neumann (1978a) reported the results of two experiments with reading-disabled children which showed the inability of poor readers to make use of the higher order structure of words, and Guthrie (1973) concluded, in an experiment involving criterion-referenced tests of phoneme–grapheme association skills, that the disabled reader was likely to have a profile in which one or two of the simple skills are likely to have a high level of strength (80+ per cent), whereas all the more complex skills in the hierarchy will have a low level of development.

Delay in language development

Some writers have suggested that language development in retarded readers may be delayed. Indeed, in Guthrie's experiment (reported above) which involved three groups of subjects: disabled readers, young normal readers matched on reading level and IQ with the disabled readers, and a group of 'old' normals matched with the disabled group on chronological age and IQ, the disabled readers at nine years of age manifested a group profile that was virtually indistinguishable from that of young normal readers. Support for the suggestion of delayed language development (in retarded readers) also comes from Fry, Johnson and Muehl (1970), Klasen (1972) and Yule and Rutter (1976). In addition, Fletcher and Satz (1979) believe linguistic deficiencies to be more characteristic of older readers, and quote evidence from Benton (1975), Satz and Van Nostrand (1973) and Fletcher and Satz (1978) in support. However, this theory is seriously questioned by Vellutino (1979a) who argues that the perceptual differentiation of graphic features of letters and words does not necessarily precede linguistic analysis of these items; in fact, children contend with these from the outset.

There is a fair amount of evidence in the literature that language dysfunctions or deficiencies are often present in retarded readers. Singleton (1976), after reviewing studies concerned with grouping dyslexics according to the difficulties they present, concludes that the majority of dyslexics show language dysfunctions, and Nelson (1974) found language retardation in her spelling and reading retardates. Language deficiencies are also mentioned by Rabinovitch *et al.* (1954), Cohn (1961), Benton (1959) and Rawson (1968). However, Martin (1955) and Silver (1968) found no support for the view that language ability was highly related to reading ability.

A new approach to the association between language disorders and reading retardation comes from Newton *et al.* (1979). They suggest that the nature of our written language (which is arbitrary, alphabetic and combinational) requires certain particular skills in the young child in which dyslexics are particularly lacking. They state: 'This interaction between written language and child learner may thus be fraught with difficulties, and many of the clinical observations made on the dyslexic can be explained in terms of a "mismatch" between the intrinsic skills of the child, and the task demands of the written language system.' This is an interesting theory and appears to provide a neat explanation of the reading-disabled child's difficulty as well as suggesting a reason why the incidence of specific learning difficulties is low in some countries (e.g. China and Japan) where the orthography is very different. However, many aspects of this model are open to question, and some of the evidence presented is not substantiated elsewhere (for example, most of the evidence suggests dyslexics are poor in spatial ability whereas Newton *et al.* believe they have a 'predisposition' to spatial thinking abilities), so for the time being we must await further experimental evidence. The Aston Index, which has been produced as a diagnostic instrument to be used with such children, is reviewed elsewhere (Chapter 5).

Deficits in specific reading skills

Recently the trend has been to investigate particular aspects of the reading process in depth to determine in which skills poor readers are lacking.

LOWER LEVEL READING SKILLS: GRAPHEMIC AND PHONEMIC FACTORS

Many studies have been carried out into the lower level skills involved in reading, especially at the graphemic/phonemic level. Kolers (1975) described an experiment involving 22 poor readers and 15 good readers who were given a test of recognition memory for sentences. Both groups of children performed about equally on tests involving language use and grammar, but the poor readers were markedly retarded in aspects of the graphemic analysis (pattern analysing) of the texts. Doehring and Hoshko (1977) distinguished three groups of retarded readers, one of which was deficient in phonic analysis, blending and sequential perception. Vernon (1979) stresses that learning to read involves differentiating and identifying graphemes and associating these with the appropriate phonemes, and quotes work by Gleitman and Rozin (1977) in evidence.

Several studies have been concerned with the inability of poor readers to analyse whole word sounds into phonemes (phoneme segmentation). Savin (1972) states that children who fail to learn to read cannot perceive phonemes in a syllable, and Shankweiler and Liberman (1976) also believe that difficulties of phoneme segmentation may be related to early reading difficulties. In a study by Liberman *et al.* (1974) it was found that at each age test words were more readily segmented into syllables than phonemes, and, in a recent pilot study, a connection was discovered between the reading achievement of the children who had taken part in this experiment and their performance in it. Half the children in the lowest third of the class in reading achievement had previously failed the phoneme segmentation test, whilst there were no failures among the children who scored in the top third in reading ability. Confirmation that poor readers are unable to segment words into phonemes also comes from Hitch and Baddeley (1977) and Rozin and Gleitman (1977).

There has been much discussion as to whether the performance of poor readers is related to the unit of processing used, i.e. letter, word or sentence. Evidence has been presented above that reading-disabled children experience difficulty in breaking words down into their component parts. A recent study by Jorm (1978), comparing dyslexics and normal readers, found that good readers used grapheme–phoneme correspondence rules whereas dyslexics used whole-word reading strategies. In a series of experiments, dyslexics performed poorly whether words, syllables or phonemes were used as the reading unit, leading the author to conclude that dyslexics have a general deficit in the ability to analyse higher order linguistic units into lower order units, and vice versa, attributing this deficiency to a short-term memory disorder (revealed in a factor analysis of the tests used). Walton (1975) also investigated the strategies used in word identification, and suggested that a distinction can be made between skilled readers and developing readers in the 'mediating strategies' used. He stressed that the whole word approach involves learning 50,000 different symbolic representations instead of the 26 alphabetic symbols. Drawing on evidence from Farnham-Diggory (1972) that six-year-olds can hold up to five chunks of information in the short-term memory, he suggested, as does Jorm above, that short-term memory deficits in poor readers make it difficult for them to decode multi-syllable words if relying on the alphabetic script. Walton introduces the concept of 'letter clusters': groups of letters which have a blended phonemic relationship, representing one chunk of information in short-term memory. He believes that letter clustering is an important strategy for developing readers, and represents a significant intermediate stage between the limitations of the alphabet and the whole word approach. There is some evidence (Walton, 1975) that children who have not reached a reading age of eight on the Holborn test are less likely to have developed clustering strategies than those beyond this stage.

Two other studies have drawn attention to the less efficient use of strategies by poor readers. McLesky (1977) described a study designed to investigate the ability of reading-disabled children to generalize on a specific learning set task on the assumption that the ability to generalize is a vital aspect of the processes of learning and reading. It was found that the reading-disabled children used less efficient strategies for problem solving than the normal group. Blank and Bridger (1966), in an experiment testing verbal labelling, found that backward readers failed to adopt strategies that would help them.

Scheerer-Neuman (1978a) is concerned with the reading of single words, although she points out that the assumption of whole-word patterns or shapes as the basic unit is refuted by experiments showing that orthographically legal non-words or redundant letter strings are perceived almost as well as real words (Gibson, 1970; Baron, 1975). She supports the 'unitization' hypothesis put forward by Gibson (1970), which points out that a chunking process is involved in reading whereby the number of functional units in redundant as opposed to unrelated letter strings is reduced. Poor readers might not have acquired an appropriate strategy and are therefore forced to proceed on a letter-by-letter basis which includes omissions, inversions, etc. Two experiments showed that reading-disabled children do not utilize intraword redundancy to the same extent as skilled readers, and that they do not profit as much from syllable grouping.

Remaining at the single word level, other studies have investigated the effect of the familiarity and confusability of single words on the poor reader. Frederiksen (1978) reports that the visual familiarity and integrity of multi-letter units is essential to the process of word recognition, and found poor readers to be adversely affected by reducing the visual familiarity of words. A similar difficulty arises when the words are physically confusable, i.e. they present more demands on both the memory and decoding processes; Steinheiser and Guthrie (1977) found that disabled and younger readers were slower on physically confusable words than dissimilar words. Shankweiler and Liberman (1972) found that beginning readers more often misread vowels than consonants, possibly due to the fact that they are phonetically confusable. Another finding was that medial and final segments of words are more often misread than the initial ones. However, in a later experiment (1976) they found that poor readers performed as well as good readers on phonetically confusable letters, although good readers did much better on non-confusable letters. Difficulty with vowel sounding was also mentioned by Vellutino, Harding, Phillips and Steger (1975). Asso and Wyke (1971) carried out an experiment involving four tasks: matching, copying, naming and dictation of ten spatially confusable letters — b, d, p, q, n, u, m, w, h, y — and ten letters likely to be confused with the experimental letters — a, c, e, f, g, j, l, o, s, t. They found that copying was easier than matching, which in turn was easier than naming. There was no significant difference between naming and dictation. Although this experiment was not conducted with reading-disabled children, it does point to the importance of naming or labelling, at which poor readers have been found to be deficient. In experiments which have already been reviewed in detail (see section on information-processing) Done and Miles (1978) concluded that tasks which involve verbal labelling are more difficult for dyslexics. Ellis and Miles (1978) also found dyslexics to be deficient at naming letters, and Blank and Bridger (1966) report that good readers were better at verbal labelling. Lastly, Denckla and Rudel (1976) point to a deficiency in naming in retarded readers. In a series of investigations, dyslexic and normal readers were compared on rapid automatic naming tasks and were found to differ on both error and latency measures. Dyslexics made more naming errors, especially with low frequency words and were slower to respond, especially to letter naming. The authors suggest dyslexia may be caused by some anomaly in visual–verbal association, which may result in deficient verbal retrieval. It has also been suggested

and pseudowords derived from the words by changing a single vowel, poor and good readers appeared to differ in both the accuracy and efficiency with which they decoded English spelling patterns. Another study by Scheerer-Neumann (1978) showed that poor readers were even better than good readers in reporting the left–right sequence using letter sequences ordered by chance. However, good readers showed better results when letter sequences were used which could be segmented into chunks. Thus, if the phonetic coding process operates on syllables (pul-me-rat), the order of the letters within the syllable is already fixed, but if recoding is done letter by letter (p-u-l-m-e-r-a-t), it is far more difficult to keep the right order. It seems, therefore, that poor readers have internalized the left–right scanning process but fail because of their defective segmentation strategy.

Shankweiler and Liberman (1976) suggest that reading involves storing, indexing and retrieving information by means of a phonetic code, and that the reader typically engages in recoding from script to some phonetic form. As evidence for phonetic recoding (i.e. that stimulus items are stored in phonetic rather than visual form), they cite that confusions in short-term memory arising when lists of letters or alphabetically written words are presented orthographically to be read and remembered are based on phonetic rather than visual similarity (Baddeley, 1966, 1968, 1970; Conrad, 1964, 1972); Hintzman, 1967; Kintsch and Buschke, 1969; Sperling, 1963). Two experiments carried out by the authors, involving recall of visually and auditorally presented phonetically confusable and non-confusable letters, seem to support their theories, although it must be questioned whether these tasks are in fact testing the ability to determine and use a phonetic representation. Farnham-Diggory and Gregg's experiment (1975) already described in the section on information-processing, also suggests that normal readers are more inclined to code stimulus letters auditorily in both visual and auditory presentations but that poor readers use a visual code to store visually presented letters which according to some authors (Conrad, 1965; Baddeley, 1966) is not as well suited to short-term storage as the auditory system. Evidence that poor readers have problems with decoding also comes from Steinheiser and Guthrie (1977), Walton (1975) and Jorm (1978) — Jorm found word imagery and frequency to be associated with decoding problems but not word length. Blackwell (1976) suggests that language deficits, in particular the encoding or decoding of linguistic signals, may underlie some aspects of mathematics disorders, and may take the form of lexical, verbal or graphical disabilities. Perfetti and Lesgold (1978) report that poor readers encode verbally more slowly than fast readers and consequently find comprehension more difficult. Seymour and Porpodas (1978) express the view that dyslexics may suffer from a deficiency in a system for coding of symbols which is critical for the development of procedures for direct visual access to the lexicon. In a series of four experiments they found dyslexics demonstrated a deficiency in the quasi-spatial coding of arrays of elements.

Vellutino (1979b), in a careful and thorough review of the evidence for various theories of the aetiology of dyslexia, in particular the visual deficit theory, the intersensory deficit theory and the serial order deficit theory, concludes that the heart of the problem lies with a deficit 'in one or more aspects of verbal processing'. He writes, 'Poor readers are not as proficient as normal readers in coding information verbally and, further, that this deficiency in verbal coding accounts, to a large extent, for the differences observed between poor and normal readers on a broad variety of basic process measures.' In particular, he believes that success in learning to read depends first upon linguistic ability in general, under which he includes the ability rapidly to retrieve words representing given concepts (the naming function, adequate command of syntax, and proficiency in coding information phonetically); and secondly upon the ability to make one's knowledge of language explicit, i.e. the individual's conscious knowledge of and sensitivity to the internal structure of language.

In a similar vein, Miles and Ellis (1980) believe that dyslexics suffer from a constitutionally caused lexical encoding deficiency (see above for description) which explains their difficulties with both reading (see Ellis and Miles, 1978 for slowness of lexical encoding in dyslexics; Done and Miles, 1978 for slowness of assimilation of verbal material) and a variety of other measures, such as directional confusion, mirror images, handedness, intelligence, arithmetical tables, and concrete representation. Of particular interest is the section on directional confusion. According to Ellis and Miles, this occurs when there is some kind of weakness in the activation of entries in the internal 'lexicon' so that words which fluctuate in their referents (i.e. right and left may change depending on which way you are facing) are more likely to cause difficulty than those which do not (e.g. up/down). They also make reference to cross-cultural differences in literacy skills, suggesting that this lexical encoding deficiency would not show in countries where there is an exact symbol-phoneme association, such as Japan, thus accounting for their much lower incidence rate of dyslexia.

Shankweiler and Liberman (1976) make a related point when referring to the contact between the spoken and written language. They state: 'All writing systems make contact at some point with the spoken language. Some, like Chinese and Japanese logographs, tie in at the level of words, others at the level of the syllable. Some, the alphabets, link their primary symbols to distinctive aspects of the sound structure of the language. In the case of English, there is good reason to believe that script makes contact with the primary language system at more than one level.' This added complexity of the interrelations between speech and written language again could help to account for differing incidence rates of reading disability across the globe. Downing (1973) analyses spoken languages around the world and concludes they are coded in three common ways: phoneme codes, syllable codes and morpheme codes. English is more complex, particularly as far as phoneme codes are concerned, to the extent that Ellis (1845) found 2,000 different ways of printing or writing English phonemes. Downing's somewhat controversial answer is to simplify the initial stages of learning to read by using only one form for each letter (i.e. lower-case), using only one written code sign for each phoneme, abolishing all multiple letter spellings and removing all irregularities of spatial order. These changes have been incorporated into the i.t.a. and Wurld Inglish Spelling (WIS) systems. Downing claims that the probability of failure is greater in traditional orthography than i.t.a., and that there is abundant research evidence that a child transfers his skills from an earlier simplified system to a complex code (Downing and Latham, 1969; Modiano, 1968). However, other writers (e.g. Gessert, 1976) report that in the weakest ten per cent of pupils there is no significant difference in attainment between a group using i.t.a. and a control group using traditional orthography.

SYNTACTIC FACTORS

Although Vellutino (1979b) refers to syntax as one of the three components of language (the other two being semantics and phonology), there have been relatively few studies examining the performance of poor readers in this respect. The findings of a number of studies (Strickland, 1962; Loban, 1963; Menyuk, 1963, 1964; Hunt, 1964, 1965; O'Donnell, Griffin and Norris, 1967; Chomsky, 1969, 1972) showing that syntactic development is gradual during early and middle childhood and continues through adolescence, have obvious implications for understanding reading difficulties, especially when it is borne in mind that there are large individual differences in the ages at which certain syntactic patterns appear in given children.

Evidence from several studies indicates that syntactic functioning and reading may be correlated. An important investigation by Fry, Johnson and Muehl (1970) found that normal readers were characterized by larger speaking vocabularies and greater fluency than poor readers. Reader groups produced structurally different sentences, with normal readers showing greater flexibility and complexity in syntactic usage. Furthermore there were differences in the content of sentences produced, with poor readers tending to employ sentences of the existence type more often, rather than the more detailed and creative stories preferred by the normal readers. These findings, showing less sophisticated and more descriptive linguistic constructions by poor readers, are consistent with the results of studies by Loban (1963), Chomsky (1972) and Goldman (1976).

Other studies indicate a link between reading achievement and knowledge of English morphology. Occurrence of bound morphemes (inflexions) in the language is governed by syntactic rules and Brittan (1970), using a modified form of Berko's (1958) test of morphological usage with first and second graders, concluded that children who have not mastered the morphophonological rules of their language may be characterized by a linguistic retardation which could be expected to hamper their progress in reading. In a similar study, Wiig, Semel and Crouse (1973) found four-year-old 'high' risk children and nine-year-old poor readers to give fewer correct responses on Berko's (1958) test. Of particular interest were the findings that the individual patterns of difficulty among the poor readers were unpredictable and idiosyncratic, whereas they tended to be predictable in the normal readers. Further evidence comes from Vogel (1974) who found the hypothesis that dyslexic children with reading difficulties are deficient in oral syntax to be confirmed in an experiment with 20 dyslexic and 20 normal second graders. In another experiment (Vogel, 1976), she found dyslexics to be inferior in morphological ability, and to have particular difficulty with the more complex items in the tests used, i.e. plurals were more difficult than vowel changes.

Some investigations have concerned the ability of readers to employ syntax to decode the written language. In a series of experiments carried out by Wiener, Cromer and their colleagues, poor readers were found to have a tendency towards inefficient use of language in both word identification and reading comprehension. A preliminary investigation (Cromer and Wiener, 1966) showed that poor readers made more syntactic errors than normal readers. In a second study (Oaken, Wiener and Cromer, 1971), it was found that learning to identify words in a given passage did not substantially affect comprehension of that passage amongst poor readers, due probably to difficulties in processing syntactic information. Lastly, in an experiment by Steiner, Wiener and Cromer (1971), in which the effect of comprehension training on word identification was assessed, it was discovered that prior organization of contextual information did not significantly reduce word identification errors in poor readers, thus strengthening the authors' belief that poor readers do not utilize syntactic information to organize words into larger units but tend to treat them as unrelated units.

Finally, Holmes, Marshall and Newcombe (1971) investigated the variable of syntactic class as a determinant of word retrieval in normal and dyslexic subjects. Sixty words (20 concrete nouns, 20 adjectives and 20 verbs) were divided into five frequency ranges. Overall results indicated that the order of difficulty in syntactic class (verb → noun) and over the frequency ranges (infrequent → frequent) was the same in both dyslexics and normal subjects, but that increased length resulted in greater difficulty for dyslexics. In addition, thresholds for adjectives, which for normal subjects are intermediate between nouns and verbs, were indistinguishable from verbs for dyslexics.

It seems clear that for some children reading disability may be correlated with poor knowledge of or inefficient use of syntax. However, evidence to date is sparse, and is correlational rather than causal. It may be that unsuccessful experiences in reading underlie poor readers' problems with processing syntactic information, although some of the strongest evidence for relating reading disability to deficiencies in syntax comes from studies with children aged seven and below who have had limited experience in reading. However, at least one study (Perfetti *et al.*, 1977) has provided contrary results. In this experiment the authors found that poor readers use contextual information as effectively as normal readers to facilitate the identification of single words. It appears, then, that further information is needed in this area before the exact relationship between reading ability and syntactical knowledge and usage can be determined.

HIGHER LEVEL READING SKILLS: SEMANTIC FACTORS

Less attention has been paid to reading difficulties at the semantic level, probably because of the comparative severity of lower level difficulties, although Wiig and Semel (1976) have identified these areas of difficulty:

1. Semantic units (words and concepts)
2. Semantic classes (associations between related words and concepts)
3. Semantic relations (logical relations between words and concepts)
4. Semantic systems (verbal problems)
5. Semantic transformations (redefinitions of words and concepts)
6. Semantic implications (cause-effect relationships)

McClelland and Jackson (1978) assert that the ability to access semantic information is related to reading achievement, and Frederiksen (1978) suggests that higher level skills such as understanding and comprehension are dependent on the lower level skills of perception and decoding in the sense that the reader who decodes quickly and automatically can concentrate resources on textual understanding. However, he also points out that educational and cultural factors may affect readers in such a way that those who differ in perceptual and decoding skills also differ in the higher-level comprehension skills. Coltheart (1979), in a paper describing deep dyslexia, which is associated with left-hemisphere damage, lists semantic errors amongst the observable symptoms. Thus subjects may say 'chair' instead of 'table', giving a response which is wrong but semantically related to the stimulus. Confirming Holmes, Marshall and Newcombe's work (op. cit.), he finds that deep dyslexics can read nouns best, followed by adjectives, verbs, and lastly function words (articles, prepositions, conjunctions, etc.). Other errors include deviational errors, i.e. the stimulus is a syntactic deviation from the response or vice versa, e.g. responding 'edition' to 'editor', 'am' to 'be'. In contrast to many other writers, Coltheart believes that the defects displayed are not at the early stages of the reading process − input defects − but at the later stages − output defects. The subject may be able to understand printed words, e.g. he may read one function word as another but understands it is a function word, even if he cannot pronounce it correctly. However, we must bear in mind that this study relates to brain-damaged dyslexics and its conclusions may not be directly applicable to the retarded readers identified in this review.

Language disorders as a sub-group

The frequency of language disorders among reading-disabled children has led some writers to assert that language disability may be associated with a particular type of reading disorder, or that reading disorders may be grouped according to the type of linguistic deficiency displayed. Thus Ingram and Reid (1956) distinguished three types of disorder: primary difficulty in sounding printed letters, inability to construct words from letters correctly sounded and difficulty in comprehension, with the first being the most common. In a later study (Ingram, 1968; Ingram, Mason and Blackburn, 1970) two groups of retarded readers were distinguished: 'specifics', who among other symptoms made more primitive errors of audio-phonic origin, e.g. errors involving confusions of letters or audio-phonic synthesis; and 'generals', who made fewer primitive errors in reading. Boder (1970) distinguished three atypical patterns of spelling and reading, one or other of which she claims to be found in all severely retarded readers who fulfil the standard diagnostic criteria for developmental dyslexia, and none of which is found among normal readers and spellers. The three groups are:

Group 1 — Dysphonetic — displaying a primary deficit in letter-sound integration and the ability to develop phonetic skills. This group responds to whole words and is unable to decipher words not in its sight vocabulary.

Group 2 — Dyseidetic — characterized by a primary deficit in the ability to perceive whole words as gestalts. This group reads phonetically, and its misspellings are phonetic, e.g. 'lisn' for 'listen', 'sos' for 'sauce'.

Group 3 — Both dysphonetic and dyseidetic — deficient in developmental phonetic skills and in perceiving whole words as gestalts. Without help, this group will remain non-readers.

In a similar vein, Nelson and Warrington (1976) distinguish two groups of 'dyslexic' children: those who are retarded in both reading and spelling, and those who show a spelling-only retardation. In an earlier study (Nelson and Warrington, 1974) in which the first ten errors made by children on the Schonell test were analysed, the former group made a higher proportion of phonetically inaccurate errors than the spelling-only retardates, who made significantly fewer phonetically inaccurate errors, but had particular difficulty with graphemically inaccurate errors.

Doehring and Hoshko (1977) also identify a group who are deficient in phonic analysis, blending and sequential perception. In a factor analysis by the Q technique they identified three groups, the other two of which are: one group deficient in comprehension skills, and one group deficient in auditory-visual association. Mattis *et al.* (1975) studied 82 dyslexics, aged from eight to 18, and concluded that they could be broken down in the following way: language disorder syndrome (38 per cent), articulatory and graphomotor discoordination syndrome (37 per cent), visuo-spatial perceptual disorder (16 per cent), 9 per cent undetermined. Collins (1975) refers to two different types of dyslexia, 'visual' and 'auditory'. The 'visual' type involves not interpreting accurately what is seen; typical symptoms are poor recall of sequence, confusion of letters and mirror imaging. The 'auditory' type, who are few in number, display an inability to distinguish the separate sounds of the spoken language, cannot distinguish vowel and consonant sounds and are unable to associate specific sounds with printed symbols. However, she does not present any evidence for these assumptions and they must therefore remain in doubt.

Finally, both Doehring (1976) and Vernon (1979) focus on the subskills involved in learning to read, and postulate that different forms of reading deficiency may be associated with different patterns of deficiency in the component skills. Doehring outlines the separate skills involved as processing letters, letter patterns or syllables, words and syntactically-semantically related groups of words. In a series of tests devised to reflect the acquisition of these skills given to 150 children with reading problems and 150 normals, no sets of characteristic profiles in children with reading problems emerged, although there was some indication of a specific pattern of letter and word-reading deficit on a group selected by Trites and Fiedorowicz (1976). He concludes that it is possible that there is a form of reading disability in which a sequencing problem is associated with a specific pattern of reading subskill deficit. Vernon (1977, 1978, 1979) identified the skills involved in learning to read as: the differentiation and identification of graphemes, the association of these with appropriate phonemes, the learning of irregularities, and the ability to group single words together into meaningful phrases. She quotes evidence from Gleitman and Rozin (1977), Savin (1972), Kintsch (1977), Bakker (1972), Spring (1976) and Perfetti and Goldman (1976) to support various aspects of this theory but does not attempt to link deficits in any of these skills with particular groups of retarded readers, suggesting instead that different types of failure will occur at different ages as readers progress through the successive skills associated with learning to read.

In commenting on the studies relating to the identification of sub-groups, various points must be made. First, it is by no means certain that the sub-groups isolated are in fact discrete and homogeneous forms. Applebee (1971) observed that if homogeneous sub-groups of disabled readers exist, then the profile obtained by considering all disabled readers together (by averaging across the sub-groups) is not likely to apply to any sub-group at all, and may well be difficult to distinguish from the profile of normal readers. It may be better to examine differences within groups of disabled readers rather than comparing them as a group with normal readers and thus ignoring the range of differences amongst them. Elkins (1978) examined Applebee's conjecture using a taxonomic approach and showed that a sample of poor readers may be capable of subdivision into groups which are more homogeneous than the entire sample, although he is aware of the limitations of the study. Evidence for different variations of sub-groups is conflicting and it is not clear whether individuals who are included in one group are also eligible for others. It seems that language deficits are associated with reading problems in a proportion of the reading disabled but these may be linked to other problems, such as visual perception or ill-established cerebral dominance in a random and inconsistent way. Furthermore, the nature of these deficits may change both with age and increasing ability to read. Secondly, in many instances, assertions about patterns of deficiencies are made on the basis of tests whose validity is questionable, and even the clusters identified, such as in Naidoo's (1972) study, may not be meaningful. Thirdly, the assignment of retarded readers to sub-groups may be unhelpful in terms of remediation. Although on the surface it seems reasonable to treat individuals according to the pattern of symptoms they present, this assumes that they fall neatly into one or other particular sub-group. Since this is not often the case, it may be better to treat them according to the specific reading difficulties they present rather than a hypothetical cluster of deficiencies they are supposed to have.

Models of reading and reading disability

In the last section it was mentioned that there has been a trend away from determining the deficiencies poor readers share and an increasing interest in the link between reading disabilities and the component parts of the reading process itself. The development of models of reading and reading disability has been part of this trend.

Although there has been a proliferation of models of reading and reading disability (Geyer, 1972, counted 48 partial or comprehensive models of reading), they have generally fallen into three main groups: function models, sub-skills models and a process-oriented approach.

The function model of the reading process asserts that reading is the sum of various cognitive functions such as perception, memory, visual and auditory discrimination, and verbal association, and that deficits in one or more of these areas 'lead to' poor reading. An early example of this type of approach is to be found in Doehring's (1968) study where he attempted to associate one form of reading deficit with a particular pattern of relative strengths and weaknesses on over 100 measures of perceptual, motor, cognitive, and verbal abilities. The findings indicated that the patterns of deficit encompassed a wide range of visual and verbal skills but could not support the reading disability model proposed. Most of the research on dyslexia is based on this model. Groups of dyslexic children and normal readers are compared in these functions and the poor performance of retarded readers is interpreted as a deficit which hinders normal reading. Valtin (1978-9) criticizes these models on the basis that it is not directly inferable that the deficits which are identified actually cause poor reading. She also criticizes the matched pairs method of research on the grounds that if the children are matched for IQ, the poor readers tend to have an IQ above the mean for their population, whereas those who represent the good readers tend to have IQs below the mean for their population. Thus if we define poor readers as having reading test scores more than one standard deviation below the mean, their IQ is around 95, whereas the IQ of average or good readers is around 110–115. Thus the average IQ of matched groups, around 105, results in 'better' readers amongst the dyslexics and 'poorer' readers amongst the children with normal reading achievement. She also draws attention to the fact that subjects selected are often chosen on the basis of a single IQ but dyslexics tend to be weak on verbal IQ and strong on performance IQ, whereas good readers are fairly balanced on both. In a study carried out in 1978 (Valtin, 1978) she found that when either the full-scale IQ or performance IQ were chosen as IQ criterion, the number of dyslexic children was about 30 per cent higher than it was using the verbal IQ, as fewer children with low spelling and reading abilities reached a verbal IQ above 90. This study was a replication of an earlier study by Reed (1970), who suggested that the 'deficits' of poor readers are artefacts of the matched pair design. A final point concerns the use of the functional model as a theoretical basis for remedial treatment. Most of the evidence (see section on remediation) suggests that attempts to provide training in the areas of deficit improve performance on the deficit but have little effect on reading ability. Valtin concludes that the factors measured are irrelevant to the reading process. Guthrie (1973) reports the use of this type of model (which he terms the 'assembly' model) by Bateman (1966), Strang (1969) and Katz and Deutsch (1963). In his own study of disabled readers, 'young' normal readers and 'old' normal readers, he found little support for the assembly model but some support for the sub-skills model (which he terms the 'system' model).

The sub-skills model claims that reading ability involves a number of component skills such as the identification of letters, letter patterns and words and the relation of these to the appropriate phonemes and syntactic and semantic associations. Deficiencies in any or several of the skills may be associated with one or several of the different forms of reading disability. In Guthrie's (op. cit.) experiment involving phoneme–grapheme association skills, he found that the strength of sub-skills in disabled readers and normals with the same reading age was virtually identical but both groups were inferior to the normals matched on age. Intercorrelations among sub-skills were highly positive for normal readers but largely insignificant for the disabled readers, thus providing support for the sub-skills model. A longitudinal study (Guthrie and Siefert, 1977) demonstrated that the acquisition of letter-sound-correspondence rules was similar for good and poor readers and depended on the complexity of the rules. The particular tasks involved (including short vowel words, long vowel words, consonant vowel combinations and nonsense words) formed a hierarchy of difficulty and revealed specific strengths and weaknesses of poor readers in word identification, and might therefore be useful for diagnostic and remedial purposes. However, Doehring (1976) reports an investigation to determine the acquisition of various sub-skills in a large sample of children with reading problems compared with a normal group. He could find no characteristic profiles in children with reading problems, although there was a possibility that a form of reading disability could be identified which is associated with a specific pattern of reading sub-skills deficit. Vernon (1979) is also an exponent of this model although she points out that the successive skills essential in learning to read may be associated with different types of failure as age and expertise increase.

The last group of reading disability models sees reading essentially as a process and attempts to discover the particular processes in which poor readers are deficient. Most studies are concerned with the transformation of visual information into a semantic system. La Berge and Samuel's work (1974) is an example of this approach which described reading in terms of an information processing model. According to this model visual information is transformed through a series of processing stages involving visual, phonological and episodic memory systems until it is finally comprehended in the semantic system. Accuracy and automization at each stage of the process can be measured, and it is thought that attention is necessary at the accuracy level of each stage but not at the automatic level. The degree to which operations involved in the reading process have become automatic is also mentioned by Scheerer-Neumann (1977, 1978). She has outlined a model of reading limited to the reading of single words, in which three operations take place sequentially during the process of word identification: visual feature analysis and segmentation of the visual material into chunks; phonetic recoding; and semantic decoding. She points out, however, that other factors have to be taken into account apart from the one mentioned above: the degree to which these operations are developed and the speed of the processes. Doehring (1976) too suggests a reading disability model involving sequential processing of visual and verbal tasks, but has been unable to derive a 'pure' test of sequencing ability (Doehring and Libman, 1974). However, he has since criticized this model on several grounds: first, that such a simple model is not very plausible; secondly, that artificiality was possibly introduced by the selective criteria for defining reading disability, which can lead to an unwarranted assumption of homogeneity within the sample of disabled readers. Lastly, a single criterion of reading retardation was used – the accuracy of orally read single words – whereas there is little basis for believing that reading is a unitary process.

Riding and Pugh (1977) analyse the reading process in terms of memory. They state that the reading process may be divided into three stages: registration in visual-sensory memory of the images of the words scanned; analysis in short-term memory of the meaning of the words and sentences; and storage of the sense of the sentences in long-term memory. The evidence on memory processes in poor readers is reviewed in the section on information-processing, and need not concern us here except in so far as it permits models of information-processing to be applied to reading. McClelland and Jackson (1978) also imply an information-processing model when they list the factors upon which individual differences in reading depend. These include: the general speed and efficiency of processing visual information; the capacity of the short-term verbal memory, the efficiency of processes that translate information from visual to verbal storage models, and the ability to access stored representations of the letters, words and/or phrases in the display. In conclusion, they state that individual differences in the speed and efficiency of memory access are an important determinant of individual differences in reading in so far as accessing semantic, syntactic and lexical information is concerned. Evidence that poor readers experience difficulty at the stage of transferring visual information into verbal forms is also provided by Ellis and Miles (1978) and Fletcher and Satz (1979).

A rather different approach to reading and reading disabilities is taken by Davies (1973). She distinguishes two main approaches to reading instruction: the traditional instructional approach, and the psycholinguistic approach, as exemplified by Smith (1971, 1973). She has little time for the traditional approach, which she regards as providing descriptive and prescriptive rather than explanatory answers. However, the psycholinguistic approach provides an explanatory model of the reading process which is 'at the same time more precisely defined and more comprehensive than any model which has evolved within the traditional framework'. In particular, Smith's model asserts that the unit of processing can be a letter, word or meaning, depending on the reader and the task, and that feature analysis provides the means of processing, i.e. there are sets of distinctive features for letters, words or meanings which are available to the reader in his search for information.

Finally, Weiner and Cromer's (1967) detailed analysis of reading and reading difficulty, although it predates most of the material reviewed here, has some important comments to make which still remain valid. In particular, they describe six models of reading difficulty by relating the variables associated with reading (antecedents) to the variables associated with reading difficulties (consequents). Briefly, the models are described as follows:

Model 1: A class with a single member, having a single cause, e.g. Delacato's (1959) attribution of reading difficulty to a lack of cerebral cortical dominance.

Model 2: A class with a single member, having multiple factors constituting the radical cause, e.g. Rabinovitch (1959).

Model 3 :   A class with several members, all members having the
            same single cause, no examples in the literature.
Model 4 :   A class with several members, each having single or
            multiple causes that are not necessarily unique to that
            member, e.g. Strang (1964), Bryant (1963).
Model 5 :   A class with several members, each member having a
            single, unique cause, e.g. De Hirsch (1963), Kinsbourne
            and Warrington (1963).
Model 6 :   Like model 5, but includes the notion of an ordinal series
            and implies that if any member of the sequence were
            missing, further evolution would not be expected.

Weiner and Cromer believe model 5 to be the most acceptable form
for explaining reading difficulty, and themselves see reading as a two-
step process involving first identification and then comprehension and
their antecedents.

The development of reading and reading disability models can provide a useful framework within which the pattern of deficiencies associated with reading disability can be analysed. However, these models are
all too often implicit, and the assumptions on which they are based not
made clear. The function type of model, whilst largely used in studies
of dyslexia, is currently viewed with a certain amount of disfavour,
both deriving from its methodological shortcomings and its inapplica-
bility to remedial methods. Both the sub-skills and process approaches
seem more promising, especially in so far as they relate to specific
aspects of reading which are amenable to remediation. But there seems
to be little evidence of studies that have investigated the efficacy of
remedial methods in this area; most studies have been concerned with
the identification of deficiencies and the construction of theory. Perhaps
the solution lies in integrating the latter two models and examining the
possibility of developing remedial methods to treat the deficiencies
thus brought to light.

Not just reading? Non-reading difficulties

This review is concerned primarily with children who have severe
reading difficulties. However, many children who exhibit problems in
this field also demonstrate disabilities in spelling, writing and number,
and it is part of our brief to consider these areas. The association
between speech disorders and reading disabilities will also be examined.

Spelling

There is plenty of evidence that children with severe reading difficulties are also unable to spell adequately (Naidoo, 1972; Yule and
Rutter, 1976; Owen *et al.*, 1971; Newton *et al.*, 1979; Nelson, 1974).
Many children who spell and read badly also have a family history of
similar difficulties (Naidoo, 1972; Ingram, 1968; Klasen, 1972; Owen
et al., 1971). Furthermore there is an indication that the spelling
disability may actually be more severe than reading disability and that
the disability may in fact increase with age (Rutter *et al.*, 1970; Owen
et al., 1971; Vernon, 1971). Tarnopol and Tarnopol (1976a), reviewing
reports on learning difficulties from 16 countries, conclude that reading
is generally thought to be easier than spelling, except in the case of
Uruguay, where 26 per cent of the learning disabled spelled better than
they read.

Many writers make reference to the 'bizarre' spellings associated
with severe reading retardation (Newton *et al.*, 1979; Miles, 1974;
Critchley, 1970; Pollock, 1975). Vernon (1971) describes the 'wild
confusion' of the writing and spelling of dyslexic children, and refers
to samples of these obtained by Miles (1961), Hermann (1959) and
Crosby (1968). Newton *et al.* (1979) describe the spelling errors made
by dyslexics as 'random and inconsistent' and draw attention to their
persistent reversal and disordering of letters, syllables, words and word
order and the phenomenon of mirror-writing, all of which persist long
after the normal age. Miles (1971), Vernon (1971), Critchley (1970),
Frith (1971), Clark (1971) and many others all provide confirmation
of these typical spelling patterns.

Some writers have attempted to investigate in greater depth the
specific kinds of spelling errors exhibited by the reading and spelling
retarded, in particular errors of phonemic/graphemic origin and errors
associated with cognitive and perceptual variables. J. S. Miles (1973)
found two kinds of spelling errors: phonemographic (homophones, near
homophones and phonemographics) and non-phonemographic (trans-
position of adjacent vowel/consonant symbols). Nelson and Warrington
(1974, 1976) investigated phonetic accuracy in the spelling errors of
two groups of children: a group retarded in both reading and spelling,
and a group retarded in spelling only. The reading plus spelling retardates made a higher proportion of phonetically inaccurate errors whereas
the spelling-only retardates made significantly fewer phonetically
inaccurate spelling errors. When both groups were matched for spelling
level (not chronological age), the spelling-only retardates behaved more

like their normally spelling peers in the phonetical aspects of the spelling task, but had particular difficulty with graphemically inaccurate errors. Goyen and Martin (1977), however, believe that phonetic and non-phonetic spelling errors do not constitute independent categories. Their study of 93 boys aged 13-14 from a state secondary school in Sydney revealed three factors to be associated with spelling ability: verbal – intellectual (accounting for 43 per cent of the variance), writing speed (seven per cent) and carefulness (five per cent). They suggest that spelling difficulty is a function of word frequency rather than orthography or grapheme-phoneme regularity (Brown, 1970; Lester, 1964) and that spelling instruction should take account of this.

Moseley (1974) on the other hand believes that spelling is not normally related to verbal reasoning (except in the cases of Boshes and Myklebust's study of 1964 where the neurologically abnormal group showed this) and that possibly verbal intelligence can circumvent spelling difficulty. Although he agrees that word frequency and word length are important causes of spelling difficulty (most errors occur in the middle of the longest words), he is more concerned with visual and auditory abilities and their relationship to spelling problems. He refers to work by Naidoo (1972) and Moseley (1972) showing that poor auditory discrimination is associated with poor spelling, but it is possibly more of a handicap to reading than spelling. He draws attention to the visual errors made by poor spellers including confusion between letters of similar shape, mistakes in left-to-right sequencing and a weak visual memory for letter-clusters and whole words. He also quotes evidence (Beard, 1965; Moseley, 1972) that spelling and the ability to visualize is closely related in boys, but girls depend more on auditory and language fluency skills. Tarnopol and Tarnopol (1976a) reported on the types of spelling errors recorded in different countries, and confirmed that the auditory abilities of the learning disabled tend to be better than their visual perceptual abilities.

Day and Wedell (1972) investigated visual and auditory memory factors in relation to spelling. A sample of 140 children aged eight to 10 were divided into three groups: a VMS group who scored higher on the visual than the auditory memory test, a RSR group who scored higher on the auditory than the visual memory test, and a C group whose scores did not show a preference for auditory or visual memory. No significant differences were found in the groups' spelling scores although there were differences in the proportions of certain error types. Group VMS tended to avoid letter insertions and 'one for two' doubling omissions and inversions of adjacent letters whereas group RSR avoided syllabic confusions. Gulliford (1969) takes a slightly different approach and indicates the points at which the spelling process can break down, thus giving rise to different kinds of spelling errors: faulty pronunciation in speech, weakness in auditory discrimination, inadequate phonic knowledge, errors in visual recall, sequencing and orientation difficulties.

Several writers in the field have gone so far as to divide reading and reading and spelling retardates into distinct groups. Ingram (1968) divided his sample of 82 children into 'specifics' who exhibited a specific reading and spelling difficulty only and 'generals' who failed in reading, spelling, arithmetic and other learning situations. He showed that these groups were different with respect to brain damage, family history of difficulties and reading errors. Naidoo (1972) divided her 98 subjects into reading retardates (two or more years retarded in reading) and spelling retardates (two or more years behind in spelling, reading quotient below 80 but not as severe as the reading retardates) and was able to show various differences between them such as handedness, laterality and WISC performance. However, the division of her sample into these groups has been seriously questioned (e.g. by Newton *et al.*, 1979) on the grounds of lack of rationale. Lastly, Nelson and Warrington (1974, 1976) divided their children into two groups: one group retarded in reading and spelling and one group retarded in spelling only. As with Naidoo the spelling-only retardates were a smaller group and were thought to be representative of a less frequent disability than reading and spelling retardates. They found that the spelling-only retardates suffered from sequential problems, problems of handling units in a linear sequence, and showed no significant difference between mean verbal and performance IQ, whereas the reading and spelling retardates had delayed speech and language development and a poorer verbal than performance IQ on the WISC.

Generally, a severe spelling disorder is thought to be part of a wider problem, although the exact nature of this is a matter of dispute. Some writers believe it is constitutionally determined (Naidoo, 1972; Critchley, 1970). Others attribute it to difficulties in sequencing (Gulliford, 1969; Vernon, 1971). Nelson (1974) suggests it may be part of a more generalized language retardation, whilst Rabinovitch (1968) points to an underlying symbolization deficit. Miles and Wheeler (1974) attribute it to 'an inability to retain complex information over time' which causes long words to be spelled incorrectly because the memory load is too great, but more recently Miles and Ellis (1980) suggest a lexical encoding deficiency may underlie reading and spelling problems. Lastly, in a similar vein, Seymour and Porpodas (1978) conducted four experiments with dyslexics and concluded that dyslexia is associated with a deficiency in the coding of arrays of elements such as letters and words which relate particularly to the property of directional polarization. This affects attentional discipline and leads to the laying down in the permanent memory of structurally unstable representations of spelling (or other ordered series).

Writing

Many psychologists and educationalists working with children with severe reading difficulties have noticed that they are frequently accompanied by handwriting irregularities. Owen *et al.*'s study (1971) showed that the learning-disabled children (two grades behind their normal controls in reading and about a grade and a half behind them in spelling) had irregular handwriting which weaved above and below the line, showed heavy or variable pencil pressure, poor letter formation and letter reversals. Ingram (1971) also found reversing or otherwise confusing the direction of letters, and letter and syllable order, to be associated with reading difficulties. Other writing problems included the inability to find the written equivalents for individual syllables or words and a marked tendency to omit small words of only syntactical significance. Critchley (1970) mentioned dyslexics as demonstrating overall untidiness, illegibility, malformed letters, omissions or repetitions of words and letters, odd punctuation and misspellings and unorthodox ways of joining up adjacent letters. He states: 'Disordered handwriting associated with developmental dyslexia has been noted from the earliest days of this century,' and quotes evidence from Lecours (1966) of addition, deletion, substitution and inversion among the errors in the handwriting of dyslexics, and from Hermann and Voldby (1946) of the tendency of dyslexics to employ too few letters, either by telescoping words together or by omission. Waller refers to malformed letters, tension speed, size of letters, hesitations and alterations, all found in the poor handwriting of dyslexics, which he attributes to poor motor control.

Benson (1970) investigated graphic orientation disorders of left-handed children, and claims that mirror-writing and inverted writing are to be found almost exclusively in left-handed children, and are not part of dyslexia. However, there seems to be little evidence to support this. Frith (1971), on the other hand, suggests mirror-reversals may be associated with a memory deficit. Vellutino (1979b), reviewing the field, writes, 'The literature dealing with mirror writing is meagre and no controlled studies evaluating this phenomenon could be found.' He describes three theories of mirror writing, the visual-deficit hypothesis, the 'motor' hypothesis (Erlenmeyer, 1879) and the idea of a 'writing centre' contralateral to the dominant hand which leads to mirror writing when neither hemisphere is dominant. Dismissing these through lack of evidence, Vellutino instead suggests that the appearance of reversed writing is a predictable consequence of natural tendencies toward response generalization, during the early period of uncertainty concerning the visual-motor patterns and strategies of execution necessary for accurate formation of letters and words. This is quite normal and is subsequently altered as a result of satisfactory experience in reading. However, children who have severe difficulty in letter and word decoding will incorporate few reliable cues in programming for accuracy in spatial orientation. There is a certain amount of evidence that the type of writing taught may affect performance, especially in reading-disabled children. A study by Early *et al.* (1976) found that teaching cursive writing seems to help with problems of letter reversals and transpositions and may in some cases lead to a higher reading and spelling achievement.

Whilst there seem to be indications that handwriting irregularities often occur in children with reading disorders, there is little systematic evidence. Most reports are of clinical samples, and in most cases they are simply mentioned by practitioners as commonly occurring symptoms, without experimental confirmation. We cannot be sure to what extent poor handwriting is associated with severe reading difficulties or to what extent it is associated with reading backwardness or general academic retardation. Further, we cannot be sure of the cause of poor handwriting (which has rarely been mentioned) and therefore to what extent it is incidental to our main concern. It seems unlikely that it is of crucial importance in the aetiology or diagnosis of specific learning difficulties, although improvement of handwriting may help to improve some spelling and reading problems.

Arithmetic

There is a fair amount of evidence that arithmetic skills are impaired in retarded readers, although the exact significance of this is not clear. They frequently perform at a below average level on the arithmetic sub-test of the WISC and in fact Newton *et al.* (1979) present the results of 11 studies which support this finding. Confirmation also comes from Valtin (1978-9), Rutter and his colleagues (Rutter, Graham and Birch, 1966; Rutter, Yule *et al.*, 1966; Rutter, 1967) and Rabinovitch (1968). However, Critchley (1970) and Vernon (1971) find the evidence inconclusive.

There has been some attempt to distinguish different types of arithmetical difficulty. Luria (1966) lists four types, classified according to Farnham-Diggory (1978) as: disorders of logic, defects in planning, perseveration of procedures that are no longer appropriate, and the inability to perform simple calculations. In more general terms Cawley (1973) lists the basic areas of mathematical understanding whilst Dunlap and House (1976) describe a procedure for the diagnosis and treatment of children's mathematical difficulties. Gulliford (1969) refers to Galperin's (1957) scheme for studying difficulties in arithmetic whilst Lansdown (1978) outlines six causes of mathematical difficulty: emotional factors, socio-economic factors, poor teaching, cognitive factors, sex differences (i.e. boys are superior in arithmetic ability possibly because of better spatial ability) and dyscalculia.

This last concept — dyscalculia — is of particular interest. Farnham-Diggory (1978) defines this as 'an inability to perform the operations of arithmetic' but does not describe it in any detail, although she does conclude that 'some forms of arithmetic disability, like some forms of reading disability, may have a basis in brain dysfunctions' and that there may be a syndrome called developmental dyscalculia, a special difficulty with numbers not due to poor teachers or generally low IQ. In addition she makes the surprising claim that arithmetic disability is seldom seen apart from reading disability, although she only cites one case study to support this statement.

Kosc (1974) is more informative. He defines developmental dyscalculia as a disorder of the maturation of mathematical abilities which has its origins in a genetic or congenital disorder in a specific area of the brain. He presents a classification of developmental dyscalculia describing verbal, practognostic, lexical, graphical, ideognostical and operational developmental dyscalculia. An investigation into the mathematical ability of normal children (11-year-olds) in Bratislava found that six per cent of the children can justifiably be expected to have symptoms of developmental dyscalculia, as defined in this study.

Some of the classifications listed by Kosc are taken up by Blackwell (1976) as part of her attempt to show that mathematics disorders are related to language dysfunctions. Four such aspects are described: vocabulary is associated with mathematics disorders (can be broken down into performance, lexical, verbal, graphical, ideognostic); influence of language deficits on calculating ability (overt mathematics behaviour involves receptive or expressive language or the encoding or decoding of linguistic signals); possible aetiologies of mathematics disorders, and remediation of language-related mathematics difficulties. McLeod and Crump (1978) also point to the importance of verbal ability in mathematics. Their study involving 43 children with learning difficulties in mathematics indicated that verbal ability plays a stronger role in learning disabilities in mathematics than previously hypothesized in the literature. Myklebust and Johnson (1962) placed dyscalculia sixth on their list of the 11 common features of their sample of 200 dyslexics, but Lansdown (1978) believes the term to be of doubtful value. He, in fact, refers to children with a 'specific mathematical difficulty' whose mathematics is significantly poorer than might be predicted from their measured intelligence. Such children do less well on performance than verbal tasks (Kinsbourne and Warrington, 1973; Rourke and Finlayson, in press).

It seems, then, that some poor readers are also below average in arithmetical ability, although the precise nature of this association is not clear. It could be part of a broader learning difficulty, as suggested by Valtin (1978-9) and Farnham-Diggory (1978) or it could be attributable to some underlying dysfunction such as defective symbolization (Rabinovitch, 1968), a deficit in lexical encoding (Miles and Ellis, 1980) or cognitive and spatial difficulties (Lansdown, 1978) or a brain dysfunction (Farnham-Diggory, 1978). There is insufficient evidence as to whether poor arithmetical performance is associated with specific learning difficulties rather than general backwardness (in reading) and not enough information as to the particular kinds of arithmetic failure which might be linked with reading disabilities. A promising area of research would appear to be the investigation of verbal or language-based deficits in mathematical abilities and the possible association of these with reading disorders.

Speech

It is common to find mention in the literature of speech problems or delayed speech development in reading-retarded children. Klasen (1972) refers to speech impediments as one of the co-symptoms of dyslexia, and Ingram *et al.* (1970) reported that their subjects had a 50 per cent incidence of a history of deviant speech development but a proportion of the sample were referred from a speech clinic. However, Ingram and Reid (1956) found a similar proportion in a sample from the Department of Child Psychiatry. Owen *et al.* (1971) found that 47 per cent of the learning disabled and 22 per cent of their siblings had been referred for speech therapy, compared with 18 per cent of the normal controls. Cohn (1961) showed that speech articulation was impaired in a sample of dyslexics, and Crookes and Greene (1963) reported speech defects in their 12 clinic cases of children aged five to 15. In a follow-up study of NCDS children with marked speech defects at seven years, Sheridan and Peckham (1978) found these children still to be backward in reading and other scholastic achievements at age 16. Large-scale studies such as those by Clark (1971) and Rutter and his colleagues (Rutter, Graham and Birch, 1966; Rutter, Yule *et al.*, 1966; Rutter, 1967) also provide confirmation of speech problems amongst retarded readers. Calnan and Richardson (1977) found speech problems in a random sub-sample of children in the NCDS study to be related to reading attainment, general ability and syntactic maturity.

Some writers have linked speech difficulties with laterality problems in poor readers. Thus Naidoo (1961) and Kucera, Matejcek and Long-meier (1963) indicated an association between delayed speech development and imperfect lateralization, whilst Bryden (1970) found that boys with speech and motor function oppositely lateralized have a higher proportion of poor readers than those with an uncrossed pattern. However, Zurif and Carson (1970) concluded there was no clear relationship between bilateral organization of speech and poor reading.

Levy (1978) draws attention to the importance of speech recoding for lexical access. Whereas speech recoding is not necessary for lexical access to single words or short passages, she presents evidence to show that it is a useful aid to memory during a comprehension task when detail is necessary, and as such may be a useful strategy for beginning and poor readers.

Slow or retarded speech development has been found to be associated with reading disability in many studies. Miles (1974) includes 'a history of clumsiness, late walking or late talking' in his descriptive 'signs' of dyslexia, and Warrington (1967) found a history of slow speech development in about half the cases of children referred to clinics for reading difficulties whose performance IQ markedly exceeded their verbal IQ. Lyle (1970) found early speech delays related to the perceptuo-motor deficiencies and the capacity for verbal learning in a sample of backward readers. Bowley (1970) in a study of 1,452 pupils, found late talking to be related to a number of factors including retardation in reading, which he attributed to minimal cerebral dysfunctions. Lastly, Nelson (1974) reports that her spelling and reading retardation group tended to present histories of delayed speech development.

The way in which speech is related to reading has attracted some attention in the literature. Straus *et al.* (1971) investigated the transformation of speech into reading and writing and showed that some characteristics of speech such as the existence of an interpersonal relationship between the speaker and listener, and the temporal quality of speech which assists understanding, are not present in the written language and may present the dyslexic with special difficulty. Shankweiler and Liberman (1976) did not find correct serial order to be important but pointed to additional abilities to speech that are necessary during reading such as efficient short-term memory and the knowledge of speech segments represented by strings of letters, for example phonemes and syllables. Poor readers may suffer from a lack of awareness of the necessity to single out phonemes in reading (done automatically in speech) and consequently make mistakes in the medial and final sections of written but not spoken words. Furthermore, poor readers find vowels difficult to read because of the lack of emphasis placed on them in reading and because they are phonetically confusable. In an experiment, good readers performed much better than poor readers in a test involving non-confusable letters.

Finally, there has been a limited amount of research into differences in speech between good and poor readers. Fry, Johnson and Muehl (1970), using a normal school population, found that average readers had a larger speaking vocabulary, were more fluent, used more predicate as opposed to subject modifiers and used less of the enumeration type sentence than poor readers. Owen *et al.* (1971) reported that the speech problems in their learning-disabled children included articulation errors, expressive language difficulties, and receptive deficits. Lastly, Valtin (1978-9), in a vocabulary test, found that dyslexics gave a larger percentage of descriptive and a lower percentage of categorical definitions.

In conclusion there seems to be some hard evidence that speech problems and especially delayed speech development are associated with reading disability. However, it is not clear whether these problems are specific or are part of a more general deficit (there has been little investigation of this aspect) or part of a more general maturational lag. It is also not certain whether speech defects are characteristic only of certain types of retarded readers and whether they are related to particular types of difficulties in learning to read.

Summary

Although our overall concern is with children who have not learned to read despite conventional instruction, it seems clear that such children frequently find difficulty with spelling, writing and arithmetic and may have associated speech disorders. Rabinovitch (1968) writes: 'The dyslexic child's achievement test protocol indicates greatest impairment in spelling, somewhat less impairment in reading, and even less impairment in arithmetic. All three areas, however, are involved, and this is expected, in view of the fact that all three involve symbolization.' This statement draws attention to two points. The first is that impairment in these related areas is not always equal, with some dispute as to whether spelling or reading is the most affected, with writing and arithmetic seen as less important and more weakly related to reading problems. The relationship between speech disorders and reading disability, though evident in many cases, is less clearly delineated. The second point is whether there is a more general or underlying syndrome which unites and accounts for these various findings, or whether the defect is specific and limited to reading. If so, is there only one type of reading disability which is of a specific kind or are there several specific reading disabilities which may or may not be related to impairments in spelling, writing, arithmetic and speech? These points are taken up in other sections.

Summary of chapter

There is a tendency in books concerned with the aetiology of specific learning difficulties to describe the various theories which have been or are currently in vogue in the field (see, for example, Keeney and Keeney, 1968; Ohlson, 1978; Vellutino, 1979b). In this review we have tried to avoid this approach, and to concentrate instead on areas where research into the causes of specific learning difficulties is ongoing in an attempt to show what research is being done and the main trends which seem to be emerging. It is our contention that to assert a definite aetiology for reading difficulties is neither tenable nor fruitful at this point in time. We have therefore favoured the use of the term *specific learning difficulties* in order to avoid some of the restrictions imposed by narrower terms (such as specific or developmental dyslexia, specific learning disability and so on), whilst retaining the connotation of an intractible learning problem, not only in reading but including associated difficulties in writing, spelling and mathematics, requiring urgent attention.

The aetiological findings were divided into three main groups: primary or constitutional learning difficulties; secondary correlates; and reading and non-reading difficulties, although there is a certain amount of overlap between and within the categories. Under the first heading: primary or constitutional difficulties, the various concomitants of neurological functions and dysfunctions and genetic factors were discussed, together with a short section on the concept of maturational lag. Recent work in this area has focused on the specialized functions of the two hemispheres of the brain, in particular using the comparatively recently developed methods of dichotic listening and visual half-field procedures, in order to determine whether poor readers differ in any fundamental way from normal readers in hemispheric function. Increasing attention has also been paid to the interconnections between the two hemispheres and the question of overall cerebral dominance which is thought by some to be related to reading performance. Another development in this field has been the growth of interest in the information-processing approach to reading disabilities. In this section, evidence relating to deficits in initial feature processing, short-term memory and long-term memory, taking into account both visual and auditory information, was considered insofar as it is correlated with poor reading. The idea that brain damage might underlie reading problems has been somewhat eclipsed in favour of an emphasis on 'soft' neurological signs in the literature, together with an attempt to measure neurological abnormalities through the techniques of electroencephalographic recordings (EEG).

The suggestion that learning-disabled children may suffer from delays in the development of specific areas or functions of the brain was examined in the section on maturational lag, and lastly, studies into the genetic factors associated with reading disabilities were reviewed, including information relating to family histories, twin studies, and biochemical and chromosomal abnormalities.

The section on secondary correlates dealt with a number of areas in which poor readers typically exhibit deficits which are thought to be correlated with poor reading rather than to be causative factors in themselves. Some of these, such as physical, environmental and emotional correlates, are associated with poor reading in a generalized way, whereas perception, cognitive style and attentional factors are more specifically related to problems faced by children during the actual process of reading. The evidence on perceptual correlates was sub-divided into auditory perception, vision and visual perception, integration of the senses, spatial and form perception. Lastly, there was a short section on the use of drugs with children with learning disabilities.

The final section concerns reading and non-reading difficulties. The suggestion that reading problems may be associated with either a delay or deficit in language functions was considered, together with the possibility that language disorders may be associated with a particular type of reading disorder which may characterize a sub-group of poor readers. A recent trend in the literature has been to investigate possible deficits in specific reading skills, which have been divided here into four groups: graphemic and phonemic factors, coding deficiencies, syntactic factors and semantic factors. Of special interest has been the development of interest in coding and labelling (or naming) deficiencies in poor readers. Lastly, under the heading of reading difficulties, models of reading and reading disability were analysed in three main groups: function models, sub-skills models and process-oriented models.

Our definition of children with specific learning difficulties states that such children have an intractable learning problem in one or more of reading, writing, spelling and mathematics, and consequently the final section of the aetiology chapter includes consideration, albeit briefly of disabilities in spelling, writing, number and speech and their association with reading disorders. Spelling difficulties merit special attention due to their severity, which in some cases exceeds those of reading, although slow or retarded speech development has also been found to be frequently associated with reading disability.

Chapter 4

Incidence

Introduction

Despite the enormous proliferation of descriptive and experimental studies concerned with the aetiology and remediation of specific learning difficulties, there have been surprisingly few studies concerned with the size of the problem.[1] Most investigators have concentrated on small-scale studies, often of a comparative nature, in an attempt to provide evidence of what the poor reader, compared with the normal reader, finds difficult about learning to read, and the ways in which he can best be helped. Relatively few investigations have attempted to discover what proportion of the population is involved and most of these have been beset with problems of definition and measurement, so that the overall picture is one of confusion, with wildly differing estimates, depending largely on differing types of definition for identifying the children involved.

There is even some dispute about the term 'incidence'. On the whole 'incidence' and 'prevalence' are used interchangeably to indicate the rate of occurrence of reading (and linked) difficulties. The term 'frequency' is sometimes used, although this has the additional statistical connotation of the ratio of the actual to the number of possible occurrences of an event, which has rarely been within the scope of the studies presently under review. The expression 'epidemio-

---

[1] However, a project to determine the incidence (prevalence and characteristics) of children with specific learning difficulties in the school population of a defined LEA has recently been funded by the DES (Dobbins and Pritchard). See appendix for details.

logy' has also been employed, although this is more properly a medical term implying both definition and distribution of a particular condition. Gaddes (1976) examines the usage of this term which in recent years has been extended to cover behavioural syndromes, especially those which may include an organic component such as learning disabilities, and concludes that out of the nine functions of an epidemiological study that can be identified according to Gruneberg (Stevens and Heber, 1965), less than half are transferable to group studies of academic failure, thus limiting its suitability.

Yule and Rutter (1976), however, strongly support the need for epidemiological investigations of total child populations, believing that only in this way can the biases arising from highly selected groups of children, such as those referred to particular clinics, be avoided. In evidence, they cite the generally held view that left handedness is more common among retarded readers, based largely on clinic findings, whereas four independent studies of total populations – Belmont and Birch (1965) in Aberdeen; Malmquist (1958) in Sweden; Clark (1970) in Dunbartonshire; and Rutter, Tizard, and Whitmore (1970) on the Isle of Wight – are unanimous in failing to find any excess of left handers among the poor readers.

It would seem that epidemiological studies or total child population studies are the most informative for estimating the incidence of specific learning difficulties, but even these are not without their drawbacks. Chief amongst these must be their heavy reliance on particular regional areas such as the Isle of Wight or Dunbartonshire, which are not necessarily representative of the country as a whole. Yule and Rutter (1976) attempt to overcome this shortcoming by comparing a sample of children from an inner London borough with their original Isle of Wight population, although even this sample is subject to criticism of the same kind. In conclusion, it appears that in the present situation, we must take into account both epidemiological and smaller-scale studies in the attempt to arrive at an overall incidence rate for specific leaning difficulties, whilst bearing in mind their relative merits and limitations. Additional aspects of these problems are the subject of the next section.

Problems of definition and measurement

Some of the problems of definition have been dealt with in the chapter on terminology. We are concerned here with definitions that give rise to differing estimates of incidence, and in particular with the statistical procedures employed in assessing backwardness and retardation in reading. Pilliner and Reid (1977) describe two main methods of assessing backwardness and three main methods of assessing retardation.

Backwardness is generally taken to mean 'falling short of an age criterion by some specified amount', i.e. a backward child is below the average for his age. This can be assessed in two main ways. Firstly as a simple difference between the chronological and reading age by using a test of reading ability which has been standardized to record the various levels of reading ability in terms of reading age (RA), or as a ratio of reading to chronological age — reading quotient: $RQ = 100 \, (RA/CA)$. Although the quotient method is possibly slightly more informative than the simple difference method and is more frequently used, it does result in a variation from one chronological age to another in the proportion of children designated arbitrarily as backward, i.e. for children at the upper limit of backwardness, the gap between chronological and reading ages is larger for the older children compared with the younger so that a ten-year-old child with a reading age of eight years is backward by 24 months whereas a 14-year-old with a reading age of 11:2 is backward by nearly 34 months although both have the same reading quotient of 80. Secondly, using a standardized reading score (SRS) which overcomes some of these difficulties. According to this method, the raw scores on a reading test of all children of a fixed age in the reference group are ranked, the ranks expressed as percentiles, which are then converted into standardized scores which are 'normally distributed' about a mean, usually of 100, with a standard deviation, usually of 15. Thus age is incorporated into the standardization, so that the older the child, the higher must be his raw score to earn him a standardized score of 100.

Gaddes (op. cit.) severely criticizes the use of the 'two-year-retarded cut-off method' which he claims is 'probably the most common definition in North America of severe reading retardation'. In order to review the validity of this method, he compared three commonly used tests of reading ability: the Wide Range Achievement Test (WRAT), which measures single word recognition, the Canadian Tests of Basic Skills, which measure reading comprehension among other skills, and two sub-tests from the Gates Basic Reading Tests, measuring comprehension and what the authors call General Significance. Results tabulated from the WRAT showed a developmental pattern of increasing recognition of reading problems with age and greater complexity. If two years are subtracted from the average reading level of six-year-olds on this test, less than one per cent of the population is considered retarded, but at age seven, two per cent would be allocated to this classification, and so on until the age of 19 when 25 per cent would be thus categorized. Both of the other tests showed the same developmental pattern with minor variations leading Gaddes to the conclusion that 'using a fixed academic retardation lag at all school ages to define educationally impaired children is illogical and scientifically untenable'. Ullman (1969) makes a similar point when he suggests that the usual definition of dyslexia using 'years below normal grade for age' operates in an irregular manner and gives a picture of disability which is difficult to distinguish from normal variation in ability, leading to the prevalence of reading disorders to appear larger as the years of schooling increase. He proposes that other measures, such as reading achievement scores of one standard deviation below the mental score on a common scale as put forward by Malmquist (1960), give a more conservative and possibly more significant estimate of the prevalence of reading disability.

Retardation is used to describe children whose attainment falls short of their capacity, assessed by a test of mental ability. This can be measured in three main ways. Firstly, as a simple difference between the child's mental age and reading age or as a ratio of reading age and mental age, which has been called the 'achievement quotient' (AQ): $AQ = 100 \ (RA/MA)$. Secondly, using standardized scores in both reading (SRS) and intelligence (SIS) and calculating the simple difference between them $(SIS - SRS)$ to give a measure of retardation. A shortcoming of this method is the implicit assumption that reading and intelligence correlate perfectly, which is of course an ideal rather than an actual correspondence. Thirdly, as the difference between actual and predicted standardized reading scores. This procedure establishes the relationship which empirically exists between standardized scores in intelligence and reading in a reference group of children and uses intelligence to *predict* reading. However, this method does lead to a tendency for more intelligent children to obtain higher scores on the reading test than children less intelligent so that brighter children will need to demonstrate a larger discrepancy $(SIS - SRS)$ than duller children to qualify for selection. If the lowest five per cent is used for selection purposes, then the very bright child (SIS 140) must have a difference in excess of 23 before he qualifies, whereas for the very dull child (SIS 70) the difference need only exceed nine to be included.

The procedures outlined above have many drawbacks. Each will pick out different but overlapping sets of children. As with all measurements using tests of ability or achievement they are subject to errors arising from imperfect reliability and uncertain validity which may lead to the incorrect selection of children for inappropriate reasons. Furthermore these methods are largely normative, i.e. they take the present average performance as the reference point, thus assuming that this is satisfactory. This means that children other than those who are experiencing severe difficulty in learning to read may also be underachieving and could be helped to improve their reading ability.

There have been two slightly different attempts to define and measure backward and retarded readers. The first of these is Myklebust's (1967) Learning Quotient which attempts to relate learning potential and achievement. A child's 'expectancy age' (the average of his mental age, his chronological age, and his grade age) is divided into an age score for a particular type of learning, and a quotient is produced which will indicate whether the child is performing above or below average for his age and learning potential. Thus in reading, a child's Learning Quotient = Reading Age/Expectancy Age.

Using this measure Myklebust and Boshes (1969) carried out a study of 2,767 third and fourth graders, selecting an LQ of 90 as the pass-fail criterion for choosing the underachievers. This selection produced 410 underachievers (or about 15 per cent of the studied sample) and included measures of verbal and non-verbal intelligence, reading, arithmetic, spelling and written language. Gaddes (op. cit.), whilst acknowledging the thoroughness and ambitious scope of the study, criticizes the inability of the authors to summarize their findings in general conclusions.

The second of these is the Isle of Wight study (Rutter, Tizard and Whitmore, 1970) which Gaddes calls 'the only genuine epidemiological study of handicapped children in the English-speaking world'. This has been extensively discussed in Chapter 2 but requires some further analysis here. Yule and Rutter (1976) stress the statistical pitfalls of ratios, such as Myklebust's Learning Quotient, which fail to allow for the statistical effects of regression and therefore result in a group of underachievers in whom bright children are over-represented and dull children are under-represented, although it must be said that Myklebust's chosen IQs are in the mid-IQ range where IQ and reading show similar measures. In their own study, they employ a prediction technique which involves knowing the correlation between a predictor variable (such as an intelligence test score) and a criterion variable (such as a standardized reading score), and calculating the expected value of reading for any particular level of the predictor variable. Thus one can determine whether the child scores above, at, or below this predicted value and what the statistical probability is of any deviation from the expected value. Thus the empirically determined relationship between intelligence and achievement can be used to define severe degrees of underachievement in reading whilst avoiding errors associated with the regression effect. Two groups of children were selected from the total population of nine- and ten-year-olds (which amounted to 2,300 children) for special study. These were: 'backward readers' defined by 'an attainment on reading accuracy or reading comprehension on the Neale Test which was two years four months or more below the child's chronological age'; and 'retarded readers' defined by 'an attainment on either reading accuracy or reading comprehension which was two years four months or more below the level predicted on the basis of the child's age and short WISC IQ', using multiple regression equations. These definitions yielded 155 backward readers and 86 retarded readers but there was a considerable overlap between the two groups, with no less than 76 children in common. Approximately four per cent of the population were found to be specifically reading retarded. The reader is referred to Chapter 2 for details of the differences between backward and retarded readers.

Some of Yule and Rutter's findings are of particular relevance when considering the belief held by many, including Tizard (1972), that there is a continuum spanning the whole range of reading abilities with no definite cut-off between the mass of backward readers and those demonstrating more severe or specific reading difficulties. Those who hold this opinion see specific reading disability as 'the fag end of a normal distribution of reading ability'. However, the weight of recent opinion tends to favour the existence of a hump of poor readers in the tail end of the distribution who are qualitatively different from the majority of poor readers. Reid (1977) says that 'these are not just children towards the lower end of a distribution of attainment: they are children who, in the words of Clark, "lack independent reading skill" ', whilst Sampson (1975) also refers to the humping of reading disability cases at the bottom of the distribution. Spreen (1976) adding his support to this viewpoint, suggests that this population of pathological cases will be normally distributed so that even though the majority of these cases are at the very severe end of the distribution, the full distribution ranges well into what would be called normal intellectual functioning. Most of these writers adduce Yule and Rutter's study (op.

cit.) in support of their views. In this study, the authors report an 'excess of under-achievers' at the low end of the distribution and that extreme degrees of specific reading retardation *do* occur at a rate above that expected if the distribution of over- and underachievement was entirely normal. The distribution of differences between the actual and predicted levels of reading produced a noticeably prolonged 'tail' of severe underachievers. Normally one would expect to find the proportion of children falling below the two standard errors of prediction cut-off in the tail to be of the order of 2.28 per cent. In fact about 3.5 per cent of Isle of Wight ten-year-olds, 4.5 Isle of Wight 14-year-olds and six per cent of London ten-year-olds showed specific reading retardation. These findings provide important evidence for the existence of a group of specifically retarded readers but the study needs to be replicated using a greater variety of social backgrounds to discover the extent to which these rates are minimum estimates, as claimed by the authors.

Bearing these considerations and limitations in mind, we must turn our attention to the actual figures quoted for the incidence of specific learning difficulties, first in this country, and secondly abroad. It must be stressed that many of the figures are not comparable, due to differences in definition, in standards of backwardness and retardation used, in variations of age coverage and in the population's size and type. In particular, there are generally two types of evidence; that from studies concerning the incidence or prevalence of specific reading and associated difficulties such as dyslexia, specific reading retardation, reading disability etc., and studies concerned with identifying poor readers in school populations or community surveys.

Incidence of specific learning difficulties in Great Britain

In this country there are generally two types of figures available: those collected by or for the Ministry of Education or Department of Education and Science (DES) and those quoted by individual studies. During the years 1946–60, a number of local authorities carried out surveys to ascertain reading standards and the incidence of backwardness. Although their findings are difficult to compare due to different criteria of reading ability, ambiguous usage of the terms 'retardation' and 'backwardness', variety in sampling methods and in the age and sex of the testees, and diversity in the norms and standardization of the tests, nevertheless some general conclusions could be made. Standards were found to vary in different parts of England and Wales and were generally better in urban rather than rural districts. Despite the fact that reading ability, on average, had improved, there was a sizeable proportion of children with reading difficulties at different age and intelligence levels in all areas. In 1948 the Ministry of Education examined two age-groups (10+ and 11+) and found that the proportion of backward readers in English and Welsh schools was larger than the estimated ten per cent before the war, but total illiteracy among school leavers was less serious than had often been stated. In 1950 a Ministry of Education survey of reading standards reported 30 per cent of school leavers could be classed as 'backward readers', 'semi-literate' (i.e. had a reading ability between seven and eight years) or 'illiterate' (i.e. had a reading ability of less than seven years). This latter group amounted to four per cent. By 1956 reading standards had improved so that only 25 per cent of children now fell into the three lowest reading categories. The 1961 survey of reading standards in the fourth year of secondary modern schools showed a further improvement: only 20 per cent of secondary modern school leavers now constituted the lowest three reading categories. The reading ability of 11- and 15-year-olds was investigated by the DES in 1964 and provided an account of changing standards monitored by previous surveys. An overall improvement was noted but the lowest ten per cent continued to form a core of virtually illiterate children at age 11. Despite Critchley's (1970) comment that 'Unquestionably official figures from the United Kingdom are wholly unconvincing', these figures provide a useful background to nationwide reading standards.

Their findings can be supplemented by other (large-scale) surveys. Ingram (1971) reports a study by MacMeekan (1939) which found that 9.1 per cent of $7\frac{1}{2}$-$10\frac{1}{2}$-year-olds in Edinburgh had reading quotients less than 85 per cent of their IQs. The NZCER incidence survey (Walsh, 1978) refers to a study of 15,000 children by Schonell (1942) showing that 4-5 per cent of children fell into the category termed 'specific backwardness', i.e. 'ability in a subject – at least one and a half years below their other educational attainments, and at the same time below their level of general intelligence'. Wiseman (1964) reported a study into reading backwardness in the final year of secondary schools in the greater Manchester area for the year 1951. Backwardness, defined as a standard score of 85 or below varied considerably in secondary modern schools from ten to 38 per cent, and in all-age schools up to 75 per cent. By 1957 these figures had changed to 14 per cent and 28 per cent respectively. During the same period the percentage of backward, semi-literate and illiterate 14-year-olds decreased from 31 per cent to 26 per cent. Kellmer Pringle *et al.* (1966) found that 11.2 per cent of boys and 5.9 per cent of girls were still using their first reading book, and that around 20 per cent of children were leaving the infant stage with poor reading attainments. Morris' study (1959) in the county of Kent gave similar results, and in a follow-up study (1966) found 25 per cent of the children to be retarded in reading by one year, and 16 per cent to be having serious difficulties. The Inner London Education Authority conducted a survey of the reading attainment in eight-year-olds in 1968 (reported by Little *et al.*, 1972) which found around 25 per cent with a reading quotient less than 85, although it must be borne in mind that the population of Inner London is atypical of the country as a whole with a marked over-representation of the lower income groups. The Bullock report (1975) found that 13 per cent of secondary schools replying to their questionnaire judged that at least a quarter of their pupils aged 12 required 'special provision' on account of reading and language difficulties, and that in ten per cent of the schools the same number of pupils were in a similar situation at age 14.

More recently two large-scale surveys have investigated reading problems over particular year groups and studied in depth the characteristics of retarded readers (Clark, 1970; Rutter *et al.*, 1970). Using a criterion of a reading quotient of 85 or less, 15.3 per cent of seven-year-olds in Dunbartonshire were identified (Clark, 1970). At age nine, all children from this group with an IQ of over 90 on either the verbal, performance or full scales of the WISC were retested and 6.3 per cent were found to be backward in reading but only 1.2 per cent by more than two years. At age ten half of these were still two years behind, whilst half were now three years behind. However, it should be borne in mind that only children regarded as 'at risk' at the age of seven were followed up. Rutter, Tizard and Whitmore (1970) reported a study of nine- and ten-year-olds on the Isle of Wight. They found 3.7 per cent to be severely retarded in reading (see criterion in previous section) and 6.6 per cent to be backward in reading, with considerable overlap between the two categories.

Two other kinds of variables need to be taken into account when considering the incidence of specific learning difficulties in Great Britain. Socio-economic factors have already been mentioned in the aetiology chapter but they need to be considered here because of the way in which they directly affect incidence figures. The following studies are quoted as examples of this. The National Child Development study (Davie *et al.*, 1972) showed that 48 per cent of the children from social class V were poor readers at seven — compared with eight per cent in social class I. The Educational Priority study (Halsey, 1972) which was undertaken in three inter-city areas and a fourth area comprising two small economically depressed mining towns showed that the proportions of children scoring 80 or less on an NFER sentence completion test were 19 per cent, 35.8 per cent, 21.7 per cent and 17.7 per cent. Further evidence comes from the ILEA survey reported above, and from Rutter *et al.*'s (1970) study where they state 'that inner city children still have an unduly high rate of reading problems even after the effects of intelligence have been parcelled out'.

Again, sex differences in the incidence of specific learning difficulties have also been reviewed in some detail in Chapter 3. In almost all cases, boys with severe reading difficulties outnumber girls but there is a clear difference between the figures for clinic samples and those for the general population. Most studies report a ratio of about four or five boys to one girl in clinic samples (see, for example, Gessert (1976), in a review of specific learning difficulties in Great Britain) but only about three to one in less selective samples. Thus Rutter *et al.* (1970) reports the sex ratio of 3.3 boys to one girl for reading retardation but only 1.3 to one for reading backwardness. This finding illustrates two important points. First, that the sex ratio is affected by the samples used, and second, that it is affected by the types of definition employed.

Reviewing the incidence of reading difficulties in Great Britain as a whole, several conclusions can be drawn. To begin with, there is a very wide variation in the figures quoted, ranging from one per cent to 75 per cent! However, within this overall range, there is a tendency for estimates to cluster, in particular around three levels. The highest level runs from about 20 per cent upwards, as found, for example, in the Ministry of Education surveys, Kellmer Pringle *et al.* (1966), Morris (1959) and Little *et al.* (1972). This appears to be a very general classification of reading backwardness and more precise and more recent studies have given lower figures of between five per cent and 15 per cent, depending on the exact criterion used. Thus Clark's study (1970) showed 15 per cent of seven-year-olds had a reading quotient of 85 or less, but when intelligence was taken into account (i.e. only the backward readers of average intelligence were retested at age nine) this was reduced to 6.3 per cent backward in reading, with only 1.2 per cent by more than two years. The DES survey (1964) found ten per cent of children to be virtually illiterate at age ten whilst Rutter *et al.* (1970) reported 6.6 per cent to be backward in reading whereas 3.7 per cent were severely retarded in reading. This latter figure is more representative of the lowest group of estimates which tend to cluster around two to five per cent. This brings us to the second conclusion: that there seems to be a 'hard core' group of children with severe and specific reading difficulties but whose problems are not necessarily identical and whose difficulties may also be shared by a larger group of backward readers in some respects. Apart from Rutter's severely retarded group, Clark's readers backward by more than two years seem to fall into this category (1.2 per cent). Bannatyne (1971) estimated that two per cent of the school population of average or above intelligence experience abnormal difficulties in learning to read, whilst Naidoo (1973) suggests the same figure for 'children and adults who suffer from a difficulty in learning to read, write and spell, although well able to learn in other spheres'. Confirmation of these broad clusters also comes from international estimates to be reviewed in the next section.

Thirdly, socio-economic and regional variables, and sex differences affect the incidence figures in fairly predictable ways. That is to say, the prevalence of specific learning difficulties will be higher in economically and socially deprived areas and in clinic populations, and that both these variables tend to be associated with a higher sex ratio for boys than is found in the general population.

Incidence of specific learning difficulties world-wide

USA and Canada

As with Great Britain, a great variety of prevalence figures have been quoted by various workers in the field. Some cover a very wide range such as those quoted by Klasen (1972) who showed that estimates of dyslexia in the western world vary between two to 25 per cent of the population. Rubin and Balow (1971) estimated an incidence of 24–41 per cent and Eisenberg (1966) quoted 28 per cent of sixth graders who were reading two or more years below grade level. Silver and Hagin (1960) likewise suggest a variation of between five and 25 per cent. Most of the studies, however, report a more conservative figure, many clustering, as in British studies, around the five to 15 per cent level. For example, Bender (1957) believed that between five and 15 per cent of all school children were unable to acquire language-skills as rapidly as most children with comparable intelligence and schooling. Myklebust and Boshes' (1969) study of 2,767 third and fourth graders found 15 per cent of underachievers, and both Rabinovitch (1968) and Keeney and Keeney (1968) suggest a figure of around ten per cent, although only approximately one third (or three per cent) of these are thought to be dyslexic. Wissink (1972) asked 100 'leaders' in the learning disability field (of which 39 responded) for their estimates of the incidence of learning difficulties in a school population. Half estimated the incidence to be five per cent or less, although almost a third thought that it was 15 per cent or higher. Bryant and McLoughlin (1972), reviewing 21 comprehensive surveys of school populations aimed at establishing incidence figures, concluded that the incidence of learning disabilities ranged from three to 28 per cent, half being above 13 per cent. In Canada the Commission on Emotional and Learning Disorders in Children (CELDIC) (1970) reported that between ten and 16 per cent of school-age children in Canada were believed to be in need of specific diagnostic and remedial help, whereas figures for 1966 showed that less than two per cent of children were actually enrolled in special classes. However, this covers a much broader range of disabilities than we are presently concerned with.

Some studies have given considerably lower incidence rates. Kirk (1972) quoted by Walsh (1978) suggested that 'the best guess is that from one to three per cent at least, and possibly seven per cent at the most of the school population require special remedial education'. Silverman and Metz (1973) surveyed a sample of 2,000 local public schools that were representative of 81,000 schools in the United States enrolling 300 or more pupils. Results indicated that in primary schools 3.1 per cent of the children required special instruction for specific learning difficulties and 1.9 per cent were actually receiving it, and that in secondary schools 1.8 per cent required special instruction and 1.0 per cent were actually receiving it, giving an overall incidence rate of approximately 2.5 per cent. Since this survey was conducted on behalf of the National Centre for Educational Statistics (a branch of the US Office of Education), it must be considered the official count, and in fact is reflected in the Congress 'rule of thumb' concerning learning disabilities, i.e. the States are permitted to designate 12 per cent of all children aged five to 17 as handicapped and of these they are permitted to designate one-sixth (two per cent) as learning disabled by any diagnostic means they choose.

One last study deserves a mention as it gives an indication of the age distribution of a sample of learning-disabled children. The study, by

Owen *et al.* (1971) of children in the school district of the State of California who had been designated as needing remedial educational help (two per cent of the school population) were screened for those having the same-sex sibling. This gave the following range of incidence figures according to age: four per cent were six-year-olds, ten per cent were seven-year-olds, 67 per cent were eight to 11-year-olds, and 18 per cent were 12–16-year-olds. Farnham-Diggory (1978), reporting on this study, claims this is a typical distribution and can be explained in this way: young children may be slow without being learning-disabled, and therefore teachers will find it difficult to identify learning-disabled children until the middle elementary grades. Older children with these handicaps generally move into work that does not strain their reading and writing abilities.

Overall, then, it would seem that a similar picture obtains with regard to incidence figures in the USA and Canada as in Britain. Possibly, there is a greater range of figures quoted, but this may be due to different conceptions of specific learning disabilities. At the same time there are fewer official statistics but more surveys of school populations. As with Britain, there seems to be a cut-off point some-where around the two to five per cent level, between a 'hard core' group of specifically learning-disabled children and a more general group of backward readers.

Europe and Scandinavia

Figures for Europe and Scandinavia are more difficult to obtain, probably because of language barriers. Tarnopol and Tarnopol (1966) report an incidence range of from one per cent in China to 33 per cent in Venezuela in replies to a survey questionnaire received from 16 countries, with a median of eight per cent. The relevant question was, 'In your country, approximately what percentage of non-retarded school children have reading disabilities?' However, they stress that there is no international concept of reading disability, nor any common sets of tests used. In fact most respondents defined 'reading disability' as existing when a child read significantly below either his age or grade level. Contributors to their survey give the following incidence rates:

Denmark (Jansen *et al.*) – Prevalence (percentage in age group) of five per cent; incidence (percentage in total school year) of 15–20 per cent of pupils who are reading retarded.

Belgium (Klees) — 48 per cent of children find it difficult to reach the final year of primary school without repeating one, two or three years (this does not include children in special classes).

Austria (Kowarik) — 1956 study in Vienna found four per cent severe dyslexics, 18 per cent mild dyslexics.

Norway (Vik) — 11 per cent of all first and second graders have the need for remedial reading instruction. Of these, probably about five per cent are intelligent but encounter reading problems.

Germany (Klasen) — five per cent are in need of special programmes for reading-writing weakness (Leserechtschreib-schwäche).

Finland (Syvälahti) — about ten per cent of children in normal elementary classes are in need of special reading instruction.

A review of incidence figures for the same areas by Walsh (1979) showed a similar pattern, adding information on Sweden where Malmquist (1961) found four to eight per cent of the whole population could be included in a category of children with 'special reading disabilities', and on the Netherlands where 6.4 per cent of boys and 2.6 per cent of girls are transferred from elementary to special education schools through having specific learning difficulties (Central Bureau voor de Statistiek, 1974).

Australia and New Zealand

Australia

Walsh (1978) reports that Haggar cited the figure of seven to eight per cent of intelligent children with serious reading disabilities whilst Walsh (1976) identified five per cent as having primary reading retardation or dyslexia in a suburban school population of 482 eight-year-old children. A survey of the reading attainment of 31,000 children entering Victorian secondary schools in 1968 (Educational Department of Victoria, 1971) showed that 14.7 per cent of these children were three or more years retarded in reading whilst a further 16 per cent were retarded by between one-and-a-half and three years.

New Zealand

Lusty (1938), in a study of 366 pupils in a cross-section of Christchurch schools, found that 12.7 per cent of pupils showed specific disabilities, comprising 8.9 per cent in arithmetic, 3.4 per cent in reading (half of these were backward in spelling also) and 0.4 per cent in spelling only. Walsh's incidence survey (1978) of specific learning difficulties in Form I pupils in primary and intermediate schools, used the definition: 'Children with specific learning difficulties are those of adequate intelligence who have unexplained difficulties in acquiring the basic skills of communication, specifically reading, spelling and mathematics.' The following incidence was found: reading vocabulary 7.1 per cent, reading comprehension 5.3 per cent, mathematics 6.8 per cent.

Japan and China

Finally, Japan and China deserve mention due to their considerably lower rates of incidence compared with all the countries surveyed above. The study on which most information about the incidence of SLD in Japan is based is that carried out by Makita (1968). In this survey of 9,195 school children, the incidence of reading disabilities of any type was found to be 0.98 per cent. Similarly in China Butler (in Tarnopol and Tarnopol, 1966) reports that recent research suggests that it is doubtful that specific reading disabilities exist among Chinese pupils, although the Tarnopols quote a figure of one per cent. These figures show a very low incidence rate and must suggest a closer examination of the orthography of western countries to determine whether the clue to the problem of reading difficulties lies there, but they should, however, be viewed with caution as it is very difficult to compare tests used, definitions employed and schooling procedures across such disparate boundaries.

Summary of chapter

The overall picture of regarding the incidence rates for specific learning difficulties is one of confusion, both in the definitions and forms of measurement used and in the estimates arrived at. In particular the distinction between general reading backwardness and reading difficulties of a more specific kind is not often made, with a consequent blurring and overlap between the two categories. Another difficulty arises in the attempt to compare incidence figures derived from very different sources — official statistics, epidemiological or total child population studies, and individual or clinic samples. Thirdly, socio-economic and regional variables, together with age and sex differences, all affect the estimates in complex ways. Despite all these limitations, however, some general conclusions can be drawn.

There is a tendency for estimates to cluster around three levels: the highest level, running from about 20 per cent upwards, which is a very general category of which reading difficulty is one aspect, a middle group clustering around five to 15 per cent, depending on the precise criterion used, but including both backward and retarded readers, and a 'hard core' group of children with severe and specific reading and associated difficulties, comprising about two to five per cent. This is borne out by both British and world-wide studies, with the exception of China and Japan, whose very different writing systems put them in a separate category. Secondly there is a preponderance of boys with specific reading difficulties, in the order of the ratio three to one for total child populations and four or five to one for clinic samples. There is also a higher prevalence rate for urban and economically deprived areas.

As far as incidence according to age is concerned, it is very difficult to come to a precise conclusion. Although Farnham-Diggory (1978) suggests a 'typical' age distribution of: four per cent of six-year-olds, ten per cent of seven-year-olds, 67 per cent of eight to 11-year-olds, and 18 per cent of 12-16-year-olds, the overall incidence figures are by no means so unequivocal. On the whole, there is a fairly even spread of incidence over the entire range of school-age children, with perhaps slightly different emphasis at the different ages. There is a tendency for studies of secondary school pupils to be aimed at determining more general reading backwardness, thus arriving at estimates ranging between 10-30 per cent. Most studies have concentrated on the age range eight to 11, and there is considerable variation in the incidence figures given for this age group, from three to 28 per cent, but with a greater stress on the distinction between severely retarded readers and generally backward readers, giving the usual clusters of from two to five per cent of retarded readers and between five to 25 per cent for the rest. There are necessarily fewer studies of the lower age range (five to seven) as these children are still at the beginning age of learning to read and it is difficult to be sure of their relative success or failure. On the whole, the incidence for this group tends to range from four to 15 per cent, depending on the definitions and criteria used. The question to be asked, of course, is to what extent does the incidence of specific learning difficulties increase or decrease with age. There is very little firm evidence on this, but what there is (Trites and Fiedorowitz, 1976) suggests that reading and spelling problems tend to persist beyond the primary school and into adulthood, although their severity may be less and the relative importance of skills in these areas diminished in later years.

A final point concerns the percentage of those identified who are actually receiving help. Evidence is very sparse on this question, but it appears that many of the children identified are either receiving no help or receiving help that is not specifically suited to their needs. In the United States Silverman and Metz (1973) as reported above, using a sample of 2,000 local public schools that were representative of 81,000 schools in the US enrolling 300 or more pupils, found that 3.1 per cent of primary school children could benefit from special instruction for Specific Learning Disabilities, but only 1.9 per cent were receiving it. In the secondary schools it was estimated that 1.8 per cent of the children could benefit from such instruction but only 1.0 per cent were actually receiving special teaching. It must be borne in mind, however, that these figures may include cases of cultural deprivation. In Australia, Hagger (1976) reports that remediation of specific learning disabilities is inadequate. There are approximately 70 Remedial Centres which he estimates cope with about 1 in 10 of the specifically learning disabled children in need of help. There are also trained remedial teachers who attempt to deal with the problem in hospital or school settings, but again Hagger points to the paucity of provision – about one trained teacher to 10,000 children in school.

In Britain, information on this topic is again limited. Rutter *et al.* (1970), in their report of the Isle of Wight Study, comment: 'Many children who needed special educational treatment were not receiving it. During the 28 months after the survey, largely in the absence of special help, the children made very poor progress. To what extent these educational problems are remediable is uncertain but there seems little doubt that given adequate treatment rather better progress than this should be possible.'

The main reasons for this lack of help were given as: lack of availability of special educational treatment, and failure to use available services. There was no trained remedial teacher in any of the ordinary schools, and progress classes to help children experiencing difficulties had been established in only eight of the junior schools. There was widely differing provision for remedial teaching in the secondary schools but in a form which Rutter and his colleagues believe to be ineffective for very poor readers. As a result of this survey the LEA did appoint one remedial teacher but only a very slightly better rate of progress resulted, leading the author to speculate on how best to teach reading to children with severe problems in learning to read.

The only other report providing information was the nation-wide survey carried out by the Department of Education and Science in 1977 (Fish, 1979) when all local authorities were asked for information about the facilities they provided for children with reading difficulties. Seventy-nine of the 104 LEAs replying stated that they provided reading centres, clinics or remedial centres, amounting to 76 per cent of the total. Most of the remaining 25 authorities depended largely on peripatetic teaching services although a few had neither centres nor peripatetic services but concentrated within schools as a matter of policy. Fish stated: 'It was not possible as a result of this small factual enquiry to draw any conclusions about the extent and appropriateness of provision and the relative merits of centres or peripatetic services. The survey did suggest that local education authorities were aware of the needs of children with reading difficulties and were trying in different ways to meet them.' This survey concentrated on the extent of provision for children with reading difficulties rather than the actual numbers receiving help, and, like the studies mentioned above, did not distinguish between provision for backward readers and provision for poor readers with difficulties of a more specific kind. It would seem, therefore, that more information is required not only of the incidence of specific learning difficulties, but of the extent of suitable remediation provided, which is an essential concomitant.

Summary chart of the incidence of specific learning difficulties

Source and date	Definition and nature of sample	Incidence
BRITAIN		
Ministry of Education, 1950	School leavers classed as 'backward', 'semi-literate' or 'illiterate'	30%
Ministry of Education, 1956	School leavers classed as 'backward', 'semi-literate' or 'illiterate'	25%
Newsom, 1961	School leavers classed as 'backward', 'semi-literate' or 'illiterate'	20%
DES, 1964	Reading ability of 11- and 15-year-olds	Lowest 10% formed a hard core of virtually illiterate children at age 11
Wiseman, 1964	Reading backwardness (standard score of 85 or below) Greater Manchester area in 1951	Secondary modern schools – 10–38%. All-age schools – up to 75%
	Same sample in 1957	Secondary modern schools 14%. All-age schools – 28%
Kellmer Pringle et al., 1966	Still using first reading book	11.2% boys 5.9% girls
	Children leaving the infant stage with poor reading attainments	20%
Morris, 1966	Retarded in reading by 1 year	25%
Little et al., 1972	Survey of reading attainment in 8-year-olds in the ILEA. Reading quotient less than 85	25%
Bullock Report, 1975	Pupils requiring special provision 'on account of reading and language difficulties'	Aged 12: −13% Aged 14: −10%
Clark, 1970	Reading quotient of 85 or less at 7 years of age in Dunbartonshire	15.3%
	Average IQ (over 90) but backward in reading at age 9 years	6.3%
	Average IQ (over 90) but backward in reading by more than 2 years at age 9	1.2%
Rutter, Tizard and Whitmore, 1970	All 9- and 10-year-old children on the Isle of Wight: backward in reading severely retarded in reading	6.6% 3.7%

Source and date	Definition and nature of sample	Incidence
USA and CANADA		
Klasen, 1972	World wide estimates of dyslexia	2–25%
Eisenberg, 1966	Sixth graders (age 11) reading two or more years below grade level. Large metropolitan city	28%
Silver and Hagin, 1960	Incidence of dyslexia	5–25%
Bender, 1957	School children unable to acquire language skills as rapidly as most children with comparable intelligence and schooling	5–15%
Myklebust and Boshes, 1969	2,767 third and fourth graders who were 'underachieving'	15%
Rabinovitch, 1968	Children handicapped by reading incompetence before they reach the seventh grade.	10%
	Percentage of this group who present the syndrome of dyslexia estimated to be between one quarter and one third	3%
Keeney and Keeney, 1968	Handicapped in reading at the seventh grade	10%
	dyslexic	3%
Wissink, 1972	Estimates of 39 'leaders' in the learning disability field of the incidence of learning difficulties in a school population	
	Half estimated	5% or less
	One-third estimated	15% or higher
Bryant and McLoughlin, 1972	Review of 21 comprehensive surveys of school populations aimed at establishing incidence figures	5–28%, half being above 13%
Commission on emotional and learning disorders in children (CELDIC), 1970	School-age children in Canada believed to be in need of specific diagnostic and remedial help	10–16%
Kirk, 1972	Percentage of school population requiring special remedial education	1–3% at least
		7% at most
Silverman and Metz, 1973	2,000 local public schools representative of 81,000 schools in the United States enrolling 300 or more pupils. Requiring special instruction for specific learning difficulties:	
	Primary schools	3.1%
	Secondary schools	1.8%

Source and date	Definition and nature of sample	Incidence
Owen *et al.*, 1971	Children in the school district of the State of California designated as needing remedial educational help with the same sex sibling: 6-year-olds 7-year-olds 8–11-year-olds 12–16-year-olds	2% which gives following age range: 4% 10% 67% 18%

EUROPE and SCANDINAVIA

DENMARK

Jansen *et al.*, 1976	Percentage in age group of pupils who are reading retarded	5%
	Percentage in total school year who are reading retarded	15–20%

BELGIUM

Klees, 1976	Percentage of children who find it difficult to reach the final year of primary school without repeating one, two or three years (not including children in special classes)	48%

AUSTRIA

Kowarik, 1976	1956 study in Vienna severe dyslexics mild dyslexics	 4% 18%

NORWAY

Vik, 1976	First and second graders needing remedial reading instruction	11%
	Percentage of these who are intelligent but encounter reading problems	5%
Stangvik, 1978	Dyslexics	3–5%

GERMANY

Klasen, 1976	In need of special programmes for reading-writing weakness (Leserecht-schreibschwäche)	5%

FINLAND

Syvälahti, 1976	Children in normal elementary classes in need of special reading instruction	10%

SWEDEN

Malmquist, 1958	Children in the total population with 'special reading disabilities'	4–8%

Source and date	Definition and nature of sample	Incidence
NETHERLANDS		
Central Bureau voor de Statistiek, 1974	Percentage of children transferred from elementary to special education schools through having specific learning difficulties	6.4% boys 2.6% girls
AUSTRALIA		
Hagger, 1976	Intelligent children with reading disabilities	7–8%
Walsh, 1976	Primary reading retardation or dyslexia in a suburban school population of 482 8 year old children	5%
Education Department of Victoria, 1968	Reading attainment of 31,000 children entering Victorian Secondary Schools in 1968	
	Three or more years retarded	14.7%
	Retarded between 1½ and 3 years	16%
NEW ZEALAND		
Lusty, 1938	366 pupils in a cross-section of Christchurch schools.	
	Specific disabilities	12.7%
	of these: arithmetic	8.9%
	reading	3.4%
	spelling only	0.4%
Walsh (unpublished)	Specific learning difficulties in Form 1 pupils in primary and intermediate schools.	
	Reading vocabulary	7.1%
	Reading comprehension	5.3%
	Mathematics	6.8%
JAPAN		
Makita, 1968	Incidence of reading disabilities of any type in 9,195 schoolchildren	0.98%
CHINA		
Tarnopol, 1976	Reading disabilities	1%

Chapter 5

Remediation

1. Children with specific learning difficulties:
their learning characteristics

In earlier sections it has been argued that *specific learning difficulties* subsumes such terms as dyslexia, specific learning disability and specific reading retardation. It is justifiable, therefore, to consider under the general heading, specific learning difficulties, the learning characteristics of children said to fall into one or other of the above categories. The first criterion for inclusion in the broad category, regardless of the particular label, is the severity of the learning problem: all writers agree on the existence of hard-core problems apparently resistant to normal teaching methods. This section will look at specific learning difficulties at three levels. First at the generic level of overall categorization; secondly at sub-types; and thirdly at learning characteristics and behavioural characteristics. Some of the material presented in Chapter 3 will be referred to in this chapter. Its use though, will be related where possible to reading in particular and the teacher's task.

Categorization

Newton *et al.* (1979), in discussing the main theories of the aetiology of dyslexia under the headings *genetic factors, maturational lags, neurological dysfunction* and *cerebral dominance*, say: '... They are hardly explanatory in that they do not describe the perceptual and motor difficulties observed in the children, nor the actual process whereby these factors give rise to difficulties in written language.' This is an apposite comment as it illustrates the gap which exists between attempts to devise coherent theories which account for learning difficulties, on one hand, and the problems of describing explicit learning and behavioural characteristics of affected children, and devising appropriate learning, teaching and remedial strategies for them on the other.

Tizard leaves no doubt as to where educational effort should be put:

> There is general agreement among teachers, psychologists and neurologists — whatever their views on aetiology — that the best way of dealing with specific reading difficulties is through appropriate remedial education. It is of course always necessary, as part of the remedial process, to make an assessment of a pupil's reading skills and an examination of the functions that underlie them — visual and auditory perception, association processes, language development and visuomotor skills such as handwriting; but we do not believe that the question of aetiology has any great significance for the educationist, though the identification of predisposing factors may well have importance from the point of future prevention (DES, 1972).

In spite of Tizard's comment, the great interest shown in aetiology justifies an examination of systematic attempts to develop meaningful and useful theories which try to relate causes and characteristics.

Newton *et al.* (1979) summarize six classificatory systems for dyslexia derived from research and clinical work: Eisenberg (1966), Keeney and Keeney (1968), Rabinovitch (1968), Bannatyne (1971), Ingram (1971) and Klasen (1972). In general these systems, while attempting to categorize specific learning difficulties, do not necessarily help the teacher understand the particular child or devise appropriate learning and teaching strategies to help him. All systems describe perceptual/motor difficulties as being characteristic of children who are 'dyslexic'.

Two of the systems are of particular interest: Rabinovitch's because it suggests three categories of reading retardation which support the Yule and Rutter (1976) formulation discussed earlier; and Bannatyne's because it attempts a sophisticated differentiation of different learning and behavioural characteristics for forms of dyslexia with supposed different aetiologies. Rabinovitch suggests three categories of reading retardation all with a significant discrepancy between potential and reading achievement. *Primary reading retardation* reflects a disturbed pattern of neurological organization, with no apparent brain damage, and includes the most severe cases of retardation in reading (writing and spelling also) who have great difficulty in dealing with letters and symbols. *Brain injury with reading retardation* includes those in whom the capacity to acquire language skills is impaired by brain damage with clear-cut neurological impairment and known cause (perinatal toxicity, birth trauma or anoxia, post-natal causes). *Secondary reading retardation* can be put down to a variety of exogenous factors such as anxiety, socio-economic factors, emotional upset and missed opportunities. The primary reading retardation group are Yule and Rutter's specific reading retardates. Rabinovitch's categories are broad enough to provide a beginning frame of reference for a teacher thinking about remedial reading problems without assuming detailed prescriptions for teaching.

It would be difficult to argue that children in any one of Rabinovitch's categories had greater claims for remedial attention than those in another. What could be argued is that, because remedial approaches are likely to be effective to the extent that they are responsive to learner characteristics, differential diagnosis should lead to the most appropriate remedial approach for the individual. At the same time, the categories are probably neither discrete enough nor explicit enough for programmes to be based on them.

Bannatyne (1971) attempts a more ambitious classification: there are, he says, four types of dyslexia. One which arises from primary emotional causes, one from minimal neurological dysfunction, one from social, cultural or educational deprivation and the fourth from genetic factors. It is the second and the fourth which concerns us, particularly as they represent the hard-core group of retarded readers. *Those with minimal neurological dysfunction* (MND) are described as having visuo-spatial disorders, auditory perceptual problems, integrational disorders, conceptualizing and thought disorders and motor, tactile and kinaesthetic disorders. This is a familiar package. *Genetic dyslexia* is interesting for the explicitness with which the major learning characteristics are described (not all need to be present):

1. Often poor auditory discrimination of vowels.
2. Inadequate phoneme-grapheme sequencing memory (for matching).
3. Poor sound blending and auditory closure on experience.
4. Mildly deficient speech development.
5. Maturational lag in most language functions.
6. Reasonably efficient visuo-spatial ability.
7. Unlateralized gaze when reading.
8. Mirror imaging and writing of letters (hemispheric in origin?).

9. Directional configuration in constancy also causing mirror imaging of letters.
10. Difficulty in associating verbal labels to directional concepts but no visuo-spatial disorientation of any kind.
11. Residual spelling disability.
12. Poor self-concept.

How, one asks, does such categorization work for the teacher? Does the presence of an appropriate number of symptoms confirm the diagnosis of genetic dyslexia? If it does, is a particular remedial strategy therefore implied? Or does the experienced practitioner work from the symptoms? Perhaps when it is possible to diagnose genetic dyslexia by chromosome analysis, or in some other technical way, it may be feasible to *anticipate* particular learning problems and prevent their arising. In the meantime the most effective way of helping children with specific learning difficulties may be, as Tizard suggests, to work from a careful analysis of learning characteristics and behaviours rather than from a diagnosis which derives, to a large extent, from the very symptoms on which remedial treatment is to be based.

The discussion so far has been on the relevance of categorization for remedial action.

Identifiable sub-groups?

Naidoo (1971) reviews research on characteristics of children with 'specific reading difficulties'. The following were shown in various studies: history of late speech development, defects of articulation, disorders of language, difficulties in retaining and reproducing a sequence of sounds, poor sound discrimination, difficulties in the discrimination of shapes varying in orientation, constructional apraxia, visuomotor impairment, difficulties in the integration of auditory, visual and tactile sensory patterns and right/left confusion. But did these characteristics come in groups?

She cites research (Kinsbourne and Warrington, 1963; Ingram, 1964; and Johnson and Myklebust, 1967) which identifies two broad dyslexic sub-groups, one characterized by auditory-linguistic deficiencies, the other by visuo-spatial and motor co-ordination problems. Ingram (op. cit.) identifies a third group with both 'audiophonic' and visuo-spatial disorders. Naidoo holds the attempt to identify sub-groups to be theoretically sound although her own research did not confirm the ready identification of separate groups.

In that study Naidoo (1972) followed up, with assessment testing and clinical interviewing, 98 eight- to 13-year-old boys referred for severe retardation in reading and/or spelling to the Word Blind Centre, in London. Some of the boys had a family history of reading and spelling difficulties, and some appeared to have neurological dysfunction. Among the cases with a history of familial disabilities could be differentiated those with auditory-linguistic deficiencies and those with poor visuo-spatial ability. This finding seemed to support the studies mentioned above but Naidoo added an important rider: a variety of contributory factors could be diagnosed in most cases, but clearly defined sub-groups could not be established by means of statistical cluster analysis (Vernon, 1971). The authenticity of presenting symptoms, and the seriousness of disablement, were thus confirmed, but the comfort of a readily recognizable 'dyslexic syndrome', with clear sub-categories, remained elusive.

Newton *et al.* (1979) summarize the results of three surveys: Ingram (1968), Naidoo (1972) and Klasen (1972). The Naidoo study has been referred to above. Ingram's study was of 176 dyslexic children aged seven years and over, and Klasen's of 500 individuals of between six years of age and 18 years 11 months. There was some agreement on aetiology (slow development in early milestones and family histories of reading and spelling difficulties) but no confirmation of a single syndrome of specific dyslexia. Naidoo and Klasen found agreement that general characteristics of the groups included laterality inconsistency, sound blending difficulties, motor difficulties and perceptual difficulties. It is not clear how comparable the three groups were.

As a counter to the writers and theorists who postulate the existence of verifiable sub-groups with discrete characteristics, Yule and Rutter (1976) assert that much of the confusion in the literature on reading retardation comes from the tendency for investigators to examine highly selected groups of children. They report, for example, that Vernon (1971) claims a more frequent occurrence of left or mixed handedness among retarded readers than among the general population, but four independent studies of total populations (Belmont and Birch, 1965, in Aberdeen; Malmquist, 1958, in Sweden; Clark, 1970, in Dunbartonshire; and Rutter, Tizard and Whitmore, 1970, on the Isle of Wight) are reported as unanimous in finding no excess of left handers among the poor readers.

Yule and Rutter (op. cit.) report a study by Kinsbourne and Warrington (1963) which showed visuo-spatial difficulties commonly accompanying reading difficulty. A later study (Warrington, 1967), of a more representative group of children, showed such difficulties to be quite uncommon among retarded readers. These findings were confirmed in a recent study (Walsh, 1978). The study, part of a wider research project on children with learning difficulties, was designed to test the validity of claims that abilities such as *visual-motor co-ordination*, *laterality* and *auditory discrimination* 'have exceptional influence on children's attainment in the basic subjects and, in particular, on reading'. Of 215 eight-and-a-half-year-olds in 15 urban schools 14 subjects of better than average intelligence (WISC Verbal IQ: 107.6; WISC Performance IQ: 116.6), but 'dismally low' in reading, spelling and mathematics were identified; their achievements in reading and spelling were, on the average, two and a half years behind expectancy (Daniels and Diack Graded Spelling Test; Burt Word Recognition Test; New Zealand Council for Educational Research Progressive Achievement Tests of Reading).

Auditory discrimination was assessed with Wepman's Test, laterality with a psychologist's battery (school psychologists did the testing) and motor co-ordination with the Bender Visual Motor Gestalt. The subjects showed a greater incidence of reversals in spelling but there was no significant difference between groups in auditory discrimination, motor co-ordination or handedness. The researcher commented: 'Since almost as many good achievers shared the same deficits in auditory discrimination, laterality and so on as did poor achievers, it seems very unlikely that these factors by themselves could be ... the causes of the learning difficulties being experienced.'

Learning and behavioural characteristics

The teacher looks for specific clues for remedial intervention. What does the research tell her? Rutter *et al.* (1970) say:

> It has been shown that reading retardation is associated with developmental problems in speech, language, perception and motor co-ordination. It may be that special account of these factors will have to be taken in devising methods of teaching reading suitable for this hard core of children with very severe difficulties.

Rutter *et al.* also point to the motivational problems which reading retarded children may have as a result of repeated failure. These may be the first to overcome if success in reading is to be achieved. Vernon

(1971) identifies four principal psychological processes, including motivation, whose defective functioning could affect reading. *Visual perception* involves the ability to discriminate simple shapes and patterns and to analyse words into their constituent elements — recognizable letters; good visual memory is necessary for this. *Auditory-linguistic perception* entails recognizing and remembering words and phrases and, most important, their analysis into recognizable sounds (phonemes). *Intellectual processes* include the conceptual reasoning needed to understand the symbolic nature of written language and the relationship between its auditory and visual components: 'The dyslexic child's basic incapacity lies in associating the appropriate phoneme sequences to printed letter sequences, and synthesising them correctly to form word sounds.' Vernon emphasizes the importance of *motivation*. If the child is not motivated to learn initially or has not experienced the pleasure of achievement and 'effectance' (White, 1959) which mastery brings, learning to read may be an insurmountable hurdle. Nicholls (1976) argues that concern for children's motivation may be the single most important factor in getting them moving.

Rutter *et al.* talk of the poor concentration shown by children retarded in reading and the substantial overlap between reading retardation and 'anti-social disorder'. Restlessness, mischief-making and poor relationships with other children are said to be likely. Some studies (Becker *et al.*, 1967; Carnine *et al.*, 1969) show the value of social reinforcement techniques in eliminating behaviour that interferes with learning. Farnham-Diggory (1978) notes that learning-disabled children have troubled school adjustment.

> Their families have been affected by the stress of dealing with them, but since other members of their families — siblings and one or more parents — have also shown signs of similar difficulties, it would be unrealistic to attribute family problems to the learning disabled child alone (Farnham-Diggory, op. cit.).

Sampson (1976) notes that 'features and characteristics of dyslexic children are detailed in lavish variety by those who have observed them, but the writers' special interests often distort the picture'. Her summary of the 'usual description' of dyslexic children includes the observation that they are 'acceptably motivated'. This would appear to run counter to Rutter *et al.* but she corrects that impression with the observation that behaviourally their 'refractory response to remediation' (Bakker, 1970) is perhaps the outstanding mark of 'true' dyslexics from the teacher's point of view. If failure diminishes motivation — the research would suggest that it does (Nicholls, in press) — it is logical that children with specific learning difficulties should not be highly motivated.

Some research evidence

Visual perception

Visual perception has long been considered an important element in learning to read. Orton, an early theorist (Farnham-Diggory, 1978) saw visual functions as threefold: *visual perceptive, visual recognitive* and *visual associative*. Of these, visual associative was seen as the most important as it could be assumed only by the left cortical hemisphere. Damage to that hemisphere caused 'word blindness': and a whole range of problems in learning to read, write and spell, as well as in the acquisition of spoken language and in fine motor co-ordination. Remedial methods following Orton's theory emphasized association difficulties and gave practice in linking kinaesthetic, auditory and visual information (Gillingham and Stillman, 1956).

A study by Trieschman (1966) showed that a group of reading retarded boys aged seven to eight years 11 months, when asked to match letter-like symbols correctly under two conditions (stimulus present; stimulus exposed and then removed), showed poorer perceptual ability than normal reading controls. That there was no difference for the retarded readers in either condition suggests that there was a real perceptual problem rather than a visual memory problem.

A study by Whipple (1965), following up an earlier study by Gibson and Gibson (1965), compared visual perception learning (scribble patterns) of fourth and fifth grade retarded readers with that of normal readers. The retarded readers showed much poorer 'perceptual learning abilities' than the controls. Gredler (1978) reports Whipple as emphasizing the importance of developing learning skills which deal specifically with perceptual tasks. Whipple appears to be arguing the case for helping the learner to develop independent learning strategies: 'learning how to learn'.

Gupta *et al.* (1978) cite two studies which do not support visual discrimination deficiencies as a causative factor, as such, in reading retardation. They suggest that deficiencies in word and letter discrimination are 'almost certainly' caused by differences in cognitive linguistic strategies rather than by differences in visual discrimination abilities. This would seem to be regarding the learner as the important element rather than the task: process not product. Gredler (1978) appears to be adopting a similar tack when he suggests that rather than emphasizing perceptual errors 'out of proportion to their importance', care must be taken to assess carefully the learning approach — the cognitive strategies — of the learning disabled child.

Memory

Memory, both short- and long-term, is considered important in learning to read and a vital element in specific learning difficulties. Hornsby and Miles (1979) see 'some kind of shortcoming in immediate memory' as an important feature of dyslexia. Is this, in fact, a perceptual associative problem?

Farnham-Diggory (1978) cites a study (Morrison *et al.*, 1977) with 12-year-old boys, nine good readers and nine poor readers (two or more years below grade level), involving retention in memory of letters, geometric forms and abstract forms. The study showed that 'dyslexic' children hold images for a shorter time in the memory than normal readers. Farnham-Diggory says: 'The act of remembering is not a passive operation. There must be programmes for remembering and they will involve attention, rehearsal, or other kinds of information management.'

Farnham-Diggory and Gregg (1975) examined the short-term memory functioning of fifth grade normal and dyslexic children in *memory span* (letters presented one by one both visually and aurally) and *memory scanning*. In the memory span experiment four letters were presented in series and the child asked to repeat them; there were ten trials with visual presentation and ten with aural. In the memory scanning experiment four letters were presented, both aurally and visually, and the child asked such questions as 'Which letter came first?' The speed of correct answers was measured. In both visual and auditory memory span dyslexic children showed high levels of memory fatigue after very good initial scores in visual memory. In memory scanning, good readers maintained their facility to scan in both auditory and visual modes over time. Poor readers dropped off markedly in auditory scanning efficiency while becoming more and more efficient in visual scanning.

Riding and Pugh (1977) assessed the iconic memory of 36 nine-and-a-half-year-old children (18 boys, 18 girls) from an urban middle school against reading fluency, accuracy and comprehension (Neale Analysis of Reading Ability). The reading process was seen as having three stages: the iconic stage when the image of the word is fixed; the analysis stage when the word is processed in short-term memory; and the storage stage when the sense of the word must be retained long enough in iconic memory for its features to be transmitted to the analysis stage. Results indicated that moderate iconic persistence was related to better performance than either short or long persistence in all three measures of reading. Fluency can be affected for the long iconic scanner whose reading is slowed down; accuracy can be affected for the slow scanner when 'forward masking' may occur or for the fast scanner when fast fading can take place. Iconic memory effects could be important for reading retarded children in various ways.

A three-part investigation of reading comprehension, word attack skills and word recognition from 'unilateral tachistoscopic presentation' of familiar and unfamiliar words was carried out with 30 children — 10 normal, 10 backward and 10 dyslexic attending a dyslexic clinic (Newbold, 1978). The dyslexic children began to answer wrongly faster than the other groups, suggesting that associations had been triggered but inaccurately remembered (Farnham-Diggory, 1978; Hornsby and Miles, 1979); they made a greater number of errors in word recognition, including difficulty with double vowel sounds, diphthongs and short vowels, substitutions of letters and mispronunciations; and they required longer to recognize both unfamiliar and familiar words. Overall they could not identify words at a rate necessary for successful reading. Problems with the retention of visual images, the need for auditory reinforcement and difficulty with handling material presented visually were postulated. The results of this study would appear to bolster Orton's theories (op. cit.).

Auditory perception

Westwood (1972), in a review paper, confirms the importance of auditory skills — auditory acuity, auditory discrimination, short-term auditory memory and the ability to blend sounds — and discusses the phenomenon 'learned inattention' as a contributory factor to auditory discrimination problems.

Cashdan (1970) took two groups of nine-year-olds, good and poor readers, matched for age, socio-economic status, sex and non-verbal intelligence, and subdivided them into two further groups. Each group was given an auditory-visual test but two groups were given an 'instructed' version, and two groups an 'uninstructed' version. The good readers scored better overall but the instructed retarded readers did better than the uninstructed group. Cashdan concluded that the problems of the poor readers lie not in lack of ability but in poor attending and planning behaviours. He postulates that the gap could be closed completely with deliberate training.

Cognitive style and cognitive strategies

Are there other, or complementary, ways of looking at learning problems? Cognitive style (Witkin *et al.*, 1962; Kagan and Moss, 1970) may be a powerful concomitant of learning effectiveness.

Galt (1973) investigated problem-solving strategies in three groups of reflective and impulsive children ranging in age from six years seven months to 10 years nine months. Impulsive children asked fewer mature questions than reflective children and made more errors in a 20-questions game. Cognitive style, of which impulsivity/reflection is a dimension, is undoubtedly a relevant variable when considering the learning characteristics of retarded readers.

Kalash (1972) studied first-grade children in New York City and classified them as to preferred learning modality and conceptual tempo (cognitive style). Children with a visual modality preference had higher reading readiness scores than children with an auditory modality preference. Children who were reflective scored higher in reading readiness than those who were impulsive. Most importantly, it was determined that reflective children had higher readiness scores than impulsive children, whether they had an auditory or visual modality preference.

Gredler (1978) argues the case for the 'adequate diagnosis of a child's cognitive strategies' rather than simply using the term 'learning disability'. He agrees with Stott (1971) that behavioural handicaps to learning should be looked at rather than psychometric and/or perceptual variables. He also considers it possible that Vernon (1957) could be correct in suggesting that the cognitive and perceptual difficulties of reading retarded children could be due to developmental immaturity. At the same time many retarded readers have unproductive learning strategies yet show minimum deficits in auditory and visual perceptual performance.

Lansdown and Davis (1972) suggest 'cognitive confusion and lack of system' to be an important characteristic of reading disability. They also call on Vernon (1957) for this insight and would get support for it from Clay (1977a) who argues for the study and strengthening of children's learning strategies.

Stott (1978) develops a case for regarding learning problems as due to faulty learning habits rather than to underlying pathology. In support of his case he cites the work of Larsen and Hammill (1975), who reviewed 60 studies which correlated attainment in reading and arithmetic with the four most recognized perceptual 'deficits' — visual discrimination, spatial relations, visual memory and auditory-visual integration. Stott observes that none of them produced a correlation as high as +0.35. We should, he says, think in terms of non-use or poor use of capabilities rather than of disabilities or deficits. Learning difficulties can more plausibly be attributed to faulty learning habits than to cerebral anomaly, e.g. 'poor skills of attention and reflection'. 'Poor short-term memory' may be the result of learned avoidance because of past experience rather than a basic deficit. 'Short attention span' may reflect lack of interest and therefore be a symptom rather than a cause — 'a symptom of our failure to motivate children rather than of an intrinsic inability to attend'. He cites studies which show that when boys can be made to attend as well as girls, sex differences favouring girls disappear. 'It looks in sum as if disability-producing deficits have become an academic myth' (Stott, op. cit.).

Summary

The sum of the discussion this far would suggest that what is needed is not labelling (perceptual problems, hyperactivity, short attention span . . .) but a description of how the child copes with learning. Thus the teacher would work progressively towards an understanding of a child's learning characteristics and temperamental make-up, develop an appropriate teaching–learning strategy and move from there.

2. Efficacy of remedial treatment

Reviews of research

Assessing the success of remedial teaching is not simple. There are so many variables to consider. Traditional studies took a sample of children who had been given remedial teaching — usually in a remedial centre of some kind — followed them up and assessed their progress in the short- and long-term on standardized tests of attainment. The results were usually disappointing. A review of British research up to the mid-1960s (Chazan, 1967), on the effects of remedial teaching on reading, concluded that most research studies showed substantial short-term gains as a result of remedial teaching but that controlled longer-term studies showed little or no difference between those children who had received remedial treatment and those who had not. The studies tended not to take within-group differences into account, the remedial methods employed were often not differentiated, qualitative assessment (as distinct from assessment on standardized tests) was not used, and the effects of subsequent educational treatment were not considered.

Carroll's (1972) evaluation of the effects of the remedial teaching of reading summarized the main studies of the preceding 25 years. He took as benchmarks papers by Burt and Lewis (1946), Curr and Gourlay (1953), a book by Collins (1961) and a paper by Cashdan *et al.* (1971). The research he examined was in five areas: short-term effects; long-term effects; influence on attitudes (to reading and school) and adjustment; relationship between length of treatment and improvement in reading level; and the effects of counselling as a remedial technique. The general conclusion from most of the studies reported was that remedial teaching improved social adjustment and attitude to reading and 'produced gains in reading ability which were significantly more than . . . would have been achieved had the children not been treated' (Carroll, op. cit.). The level of significance was not given.

Curr and Gourlay's (1953) paper was an important one as it raised important methodological issues. It included criticism of work done to that time on the grounds that studies ignored, or overlooked, three important sources of error or distortion: the influence of practice effects on post-treatment test scores; the possibility of improvements being due to familiarity with the materials of evaluation gained during remedial teaching; and the effects of regression. Other writers (Thorndike, 1963; Yule and Rutter, 1976; Pilliner and Reid, 1977) support the regression argument. Curr and Gourlay had themselves carried out a study, involving remedial teaching with four groups of 32 eight-year-olds (matched experimental and control), which was described by Collins (1961) as 'the only well-designed study' using control groups which he could find. Collins had reviewed British and American research thoroughly.

Collins (1961) carried out a carefully designed study with 60 children, 30 boys and 30 girls, drawn from ten schools and randomly assigned to three treatment groups: one group attending a remedial centre; one treated at school by peripatetic teachers; and the third receiving ordinary schooling. The children were of average IQ, had a mean chronological age of nine years eight months, and were three years retarded in

reading. They were regarded as specifically retarded without environmental, social, physical or health reasons for their retardation. They
were, as far as can be judged, comparable with Yule and Rutter's (op.
cit.) specifically retarded group. The children attended twice weekly for
75 hours of remedial work over six months: mainly in reading but with
some work in arithmetic for one group and some work in spelling in
both remedial groups. There was an immediate assessment of achievement at the end of treatment and two follow-ups at one-year intervals.
Although there were significant immediate gains for the treatment
groups — especially in word attack — with no differences accounted for
by sex or place of treatment, there were no significant differences
between treatment and control groups a year and two years later.
Collins concluded that the results of remedial education were not
permanent. The results were based on groups but, when the groups
were broken down, patterns of individual differences emerged. Some
children improved considerably whatever teaching they received but
others failed to profit even from remedial teaching. Vernon (1971)
considered that the failures were probably 'dyslexic'.

Collins (op. cit.) had some powerful criticisms to make of research:

> It appears that the claim that remedial treatment is desirable and
> beneficial is based upon studies in which mechanical teaching has
> predominated and which are weak statistically. There is also an
> inexcusable lack of objective follow-up of cases to assess the
> permanence of treatment. Finally, failures are seldom referred to,
> although it is clear that failure occurs (Collins, 1961, p. 37).

and further:

> Research since 1956 had done nothing to justify remedial educa-
> tion as an ancillary service. ... Any attempt to disguise the paucity
> and superficiality of the great majority of the studies in remedial
> education is a disservice to the needs of handicapped children in
> particular, and to the prestige of educational research in general.

A study which was more encouraging than that of Collins, and later
ones, was carried out by Lytton (1967). He followed up, one to two
years after remedial treatment, two groups of children, one teacher-
selected and the other test-selected. Some children had maintained
gains made in treatment, particularly those of higher intelligence and
those who remained in primary school after treatment. Did that mean
that younger children, and those who had support in the school,
benefited more? Perhaps the question was answered in part by a study

by Shearer (1967) discussed by Carroll. In that study the reading attainment of those who had been given remedial teaching three and a half years before was significantly higher than that of pupils who had not been helped, particularly those who were given remedial help in their secondary schools.

Cashdan *et al.* (1971) studied the records of 1,200 retarded readers who were given remedial teaching for one or two short sessions a week, by an outside teacher, for 11 months. The children were nine years old, on the average, at the beginning of the treatment period, and had a mean reading age of six years. Their mean gain in reading age was 21 months. Carroll noted that 'irrespective of their measured intelligence and despite the help given, some children had considerable difficulty in learning to read'. Here was acknowledgement that evaluation of remedial reading involved more than reporting mean gains. It also involved looking at individual variations in response. The children who did not respond could well be those described by Yule and Rutter as having 'specific reading retardation'; they could also include those with 'dyslexia'; and could almost certainly be said to have 'specific learning difficulties'.

Carroll (op. cit.) concluded his review by saying: first, that more refined diagnostic and selection techniques, and more specific reading programmes designed to meet individual needs were needed; secondly, that remedial treatment should continue into the child's classroom; and thirdly, that remedial teachers should not lose heart from the unencouraging results of research into the success of remedial teaching. These points will be taken up in a later section.

Carroll's paper was published at a time when change was abroad. Psychological and child guidance services were developing rapidly during the 1960s and attitudes to assessment were in the melting pot. Whereas the emphasis to that time had been on assessing reading retardation on the traditional discrepancy/deficit model, using standardized tests of intelligence and attainment, methods were changing. Psychologists were no longer content with a quantitative, normative approach whereby achievement was assessed in terms of IQs, mental ages, reading ages, percentile ranks and standard scores. They were becoming increasingly concerned with qualitative assessment, with what children could do with the learning strategies they used, with the nature of their reading difficulties and with motivation and interests. Assessment was focusing increasingly on the learning *process* rather than on the *products* of learning. As well there was an upsurge of interest in individual differences. Dyslexia associations were springing up as parents began to demand recognition of, and remedial teaching for, the learning difficulties experienced by their children.

Some recent studies

Vernon (1971) reports a number of studies which showed that the degree of improvement resulting from remedial teaching depended partly on age (Chansky, 1963; Goldberg, 1968). The older the child the more ingrained the retardation was likely to be. Cotterell (1970a) and Naidoo (1970), one an experienced remedial practitioner, the other a psychologist, observe that younger children make better progress than older ones.

Yule and Rutter (1976) found that retarded readers followed up over a four to five year period actually lost ground in reading and spelling to a group of backward readers. Both groups were 33 months behind the general population in reading at the age of ten years. But at the end of the follow-up period the retarded readers had fallen six months behind the duller, backward readers in reading accuracy (Neale Analysis of Reading Ability) and eight months behind in spelling. The reading retarded children made more progress in arithmetic and mathematics. Yule and Rutter comment: 'Educators cannot assume any longer that bright children with reading difficulties will catch up. Good intelligence in a disabled reader is no talisman against long-lasting reading failure.'

Richardson and Brown (1978) identified 105 children in three schools who were nine months or more retarded in reading. No ages were given. Children were randomly assigned to one of three treatment groups: *withdrawal* for 40 minutes daily with a remedial teacher in a remedial centre; *parental education counselling* on how to help their children; *combined withdrawal and parental discussion group* on child development. There was also a control group. The programme ran for a year but there was a total of eight counselling sessions for any one group. The results showed that all groups gained in reading, and retardation was strikingly reduced. There were no significant differences between groups. The children with specific reading retardation turned up again as hard-core problems who did not respond to any of the treatments.

Research with groups of severely retarded children

Studies reviewed in earlier sections have not given much cause for optimism. Definitive remedial approaches have not been turned up. Some work with children with acknowledged hard-core learning difficulties will now be examined.

Naidoo (1972) summarized the characteristics of a sample of boys described as having 'specific dyslexia'. These boys were selected from 271 examined at the Word Blind Centre in London between January 1967 and March 1969. The study was not designed to assess the efficacy of remedial teaching but rather to attempt to define and describe specific dyslexia. However, a long-term follow-up study of some of the boys examined by Naidoo (1972) is to be undertaken by Zangwill at the University of Cambridge during 1980 and 1981. The aim is to ascertain if, and to what extent, they have shown improvement in communication skills over the past ten or 12 years, in particular in reading and spelling, and whether any of their particular disabilities have persisted into maturity.

Trites and Fiedorowicz (1976) followed up a group of 21 boys diagnosed during elementary school as having specific reading disability, and compared their achievement with ten girls with specific reading disability and ten boys with reading disability secondary to overt neurological damage. Specific reading disability was diagnosed if 'in addition to the lag in reading (there was) a family history of reading disability, no evidence of gross or focal brain damage, average intelligence or greater, and no evidence of severe emotional disturbance'. The groups were aged 11.6, 8.9 and 11.5 years on initial assessment and were 2.6 years older when re-assessed. All groups improved in reading, spelling and arithmetic grades but the gap between them and their normally achieving classmates widened in spite of remedial help (unspecified) in all cases. Nevertheless all groups gained 'independence' in reading. The authors concluded that for children with specific reading disabilities deficits persist and increase relative to age and grade placement.

Topping (1977) evaluated the long-term effects of remedial teaching in a psychological service teaching unit. Slow learning children tended to make faster progress in the unit than children with specific learning difficulties but the latter increased rates of progress on transfer back to schools. It was hypothesized that they did so because of increased neurological organization and maturity. Gottesman (1978) assessed the reading attainment of 43 children five to seven years after they had been referred to a medical out-patient clinic for developmentally disabled children at ages seven to 14. At follow-up the group showed very little progress (four months per year). Those who had been taught in ordinary schools made more progress than those in special classes or schools.

Hornsby and Miles (1979) examined the records of three dyslexia centres in England in order to assess their success rates with 'dyslexic' students: those who have reading and spelling problems in spite of 'no lack of intelligence and no lack of opportunity' and for whom 'the source of the problem is believed to be constitutional in origin, possibly involving some kind of shortcoming in immediate memory'. The programmes in the centres were regarded as basically the same, being *structured, sequential, cumulative* and *thorough* (see p. 24), and included a range of language skills in addition to remedial reading.

This study did not employ control groups but used each subject as his or her own control by comparing rate of gain before remedial teaching with rate of gain during remedial teaching. For example a child reading at six years one month on entry, at the age of eight years three months would have gained 13 months of reading age in 39 months of schooling (the difference between five years and six years one month, and eight years three months respectively). The rate of gain in that case would be 0.33. Reading and spelling rates of gain were calculated in the same way. Tests of reading and spelling had been given in all centres: in most cases the Neale Analysis of Reading Ability, the Schonell R1 Word Recognition Test and the Schonell S1 Spelling Test.

An IQ of 95 or above and a spelling age of not less than 80 per cent of chronological age were the criteria by which children were included in the study. 113 children were studied. Of the 87 children whose sex was given in the records 68 were boys: the authors took this as indicating a genuinely dyslexic sample. Ages of children were not given. At selection no child had achieved a spelling rate of better than 0.8 since that was the selection criterion. Five children, however, had achieved a rate of 1.0 in reading (that is they were reading up to chronological age) and a further 12 had a pre-teaching reading gain of 0.8 or 0.9 and were therefore not very retarded.

Overall results were reported optimistically. The children in the sample were taught for an average of 16.8 months during which time the mean reading gain was 33.5 months and the mean spelling gain 27.49 months at gain rates, presumably, of 2.0 and 1.6 respectively. The range of gains is remarkable at six to 99 months for reading and six to 74 months for spelling. Such ranges hint at the great individual differences present in 'dyslexic' populations and warn against assuming homogeneity. The authors interpret the figures, too, in terms of a 'realistic target for a child of average ability by the time he reaches secondary school'. They opt for a target reading age of ten years six months and a spelling age of nine years, but should the spelling and reading ages of entrants of average ability to secondary not coincide with average age of entry? Leaving that question aside, the authors point out that from two centres 66 per cent of pupils achieved the reading target and 62 per cent the spelling target; a further 12 per cent achieved a reading age of ten years, and 19 per cent a spelling age of eight years six months. Hornsby and Miles thus claim 'success' rates of 78 per cent for reading and 81 per cent for spelling.

From the information we are given the results are encouraging. But perhaps the report should be taken as an interim one. The tests used are acceptable for research purposes (Clay, 1979a) in the psychometric tradition, but qualitative information would be an invaluable complement. Follow-up data and information on such variables as subsequent success, motivation and interest in reading will be awaited with interest. Could a criticism levelled by Collins at a study by Kellmer Pringle and Sutcliffe (1960) fairly be made of this study?: 'The effectiveness of the remedial work was illustrated by the comparison of the gains made during treatment with the estimated progress made by the same children before treatment. This cannot take practice effects, special coaching effects and regression phenomena into account' (Collins, 1961, p. 129).

The Dyslexia Institute (1975) reported a study of the gains made by 40 children taught at the Institute for longer than six months. Ages of the children ranged from six years to 16 years and IQs from low average to superior. The tests used were the Schonell Graded Word Reading Tests (old norms) and Schonell Graded Word Spelling Tests A & B. The results showed mean gains of three years and three months in reading and two years and five months in spelling for a mean teaching time of one year two months. The study is prey to the usual criticisms: no qualitative evaluation, no follow-up information given, no account of practice effects on the tests used to measure before and after changes.

Summary

The evidence on the efficacy of remedial teaching is not encouraging. That may well mean that attempts to assess gain have been ill-designed. Elkins (1979) suggests that the disappointing research findings may be due to studies not taking account of subgroups of retarded readers within main groups. Applebee (1971), in examining the evidence, observed that if homogeneous subgroups of disabled readers exist, but are ignored when all disabled readers are lumped together, then conclusions which are drawn about distinctions between disabled and normal readers may range from meaningless to misleading. Elkins (op. cit.) used the technique of numerical taxonomy to subdivide a sample of poor readers into more homogeneous subgroups based on ITPA profiles. The discreteness of the subgroups is not proven, and the ITPA itself of suspect validity, but the move towards parcelling out subgroups is welcome both as a way of identifying differences within groups and of assessing the effects of different remedial programmes. Given Naidoo's (1972) findings the likelihood of finding subgroups with clearly differentiated characteristics is not encouraging.

3. Assessment and diagnosis

Assessment, diagnosis and *evaluation* may be seen as necessary stages in helping the child with learning difficulties. Assessment comes first, diagnosis points the way to a programme of teaching and learning, and evaluation is a check on learning. Assessment and diagnosis are sometimes used interchangeably, though logically assessment leads to diagnosis. We are not concerned here with diagnosis in the sense of labelling (unease about the efficacy of that has been discussed earlier) but with its prescriptive value: in what ways does it help the teacher and benefit the child? This section will present research and writing on assessment and diagnosis concerned with the instruments of assessment, what is assessed, when is assessment carried out, and by whom, and to what purpose. Assessment should be functional (what is getting in the way of learning?) and prescriptive (what can be done to further learning?). Carroll (1972) argues for 'more refined diagnostic techniques and more specific reading programmes tailored to meet the individual needs of children with severe reading difficulties'. Cave and Maddison (1978), in their survey of special education research, report on the ways in which categorization (diagnosis) may confuse, mislead or inhibit action. Regardless of the correlation between brain pathology and learning disabilities the reading specialist, or teacher, still has to plan remediation on the basis of behavioural observation. 'General opinion emphasizes the need for an assessment for learning and a descriptive profile for each child' (Cave and Maddison, op. cit.); and further, 'schools which service handicapped children will in the future be less concerned with medical diagnosis as a basis for classifying children and be more concerned with grouping children in terms of specific educational and remedial needs'.

Various writers stress that assessment should lead to workable remedial recommendations. Tarnopol and Tarnopol (1976) see diagnosis leading to a prescription for teaching. Adamson and Adamson (1979) consider that psychological assessment should result in remedial recommendations geared specifically to each child's learning deficits. Sampson (1976) wants attention to be focused on 'behavioural diagnosis and remediation rather than on biological aetiology and the discovery of correlated nervous system deficits'; this is in sympathy with the position reported by Cave and Maddison (op. cit.). Champion (1979a, 1979b) considers that an 'individualized educational programme' and 'prescriptive instructional objectives' should emerge from a good assessment. Sapir and Wilson (1979) advocate a task analysis approach with emphasis on behaviour rather than on test scores: the end goal of diagnosis is a plan that will promote learning in both cognitive and affective areas. Hagger (1970) stresses the importance of prescription, and suggests that the experienced teacher may be the best person to assess learning difficulties. Lerner (1976) wants assessment to lead to a five-step 'clinical teaching cycle' which is self-checking and self-renewing: (i) diagnosis, (ii) planning, (iii) implementation of the teaching plan, (iv) evaluation of student performance and (v) modification of the diagnosis. The importance of prior assessment of the skills involved in reading and writing in planning an effective programme is underscored by Naidoo (1970) who writes as an experienced remedial teacher.

Stott (1978) takes a behaviourist position. Diagnosis (or assessment?) is seen as a developmental process beginning initially with a study of the way a child is failing to use his mental capabilities, followed by an exploration of his ability to respond to a programme of conditioning in good learning and problem-solving strategies. Teachers want practical information from psychologists that will enable them to plan effective programmes. Stott is in agreement with Lerner (op. cit.), if somewhat more dynamic in his advocacy. Diagnosis is an ongoing part of a *diagnostic-remedial* strategy; it is a continuous monitoring of the child's developing capabilities rather than a single occurrence before remediation. In this sense diagnosis has a connotation of evaluation. Other writers (Champion, 1979a) use diagnosis, in its traditional sense, as the identification of a condition, but for Stott it is developmental and is made to fit his concern for a continuous reappraisal of learning strategies. This conception is appropriate for somebody who sees retardation in terms of 'non-use or poor use of capabilities rather than of disabilities or deficits'.

The scope of assessment

There is clear agreement on the need for an assessment which yields usable information. Tyson (1970) draws the distinction between *classification testing* (the assignment of the subject to a group, type or category) and *diagnostic testing* (the detection of specific disabilities for which an educational or remedial programme could be initiated). However, it would be agreed that classification does not necessarily rule out a prescriptive diagnosis as well — say in the instance of a child declared educationally subnormal, but whose abilities and disabilities were documented, and for whom a remedial programme was suggested by the examining psychologist. In the case of children with specific learning difficulties, classification in terms of 'syndromes of presenting symptoms' (e.g. 'dyslexia') is regarded as very unsatisfactory (Wedell, 1973): more to the point is an explanation of learning difficulties which examines the functions underlying impaired performance. Mittler (1970) warns against the over-confident assumptions which classification, with its traditions stemming from the biological sciences and medicine, can engender. But how is functional diagnosis to be achieved? Mittler (op. cit.), writing about some of the common factors in the assessment of handicapped children, would have assessment go beyond the use of intelligence tests to include profile analysis, study of cognitive processes, assessment of personality and non-cognitive variables, and observation of play and behaviour.

The aim of *profile analysis* is to get a plan of a child's cognitive assets and deficits and to break 'intelligence' into constituent processes and skills as a basis for remedial work. The intent is impeccable but, as Mittler points out, the processes are not agreed, the means of analysis are not clearly established and the task of linking teaching methods and processes is formidable. New approaches to the definition and assessment of learning abilities may make profile analysis more feasible (Hegarty and Lucas, 1978), and tests such as the British Ability Scales (Elliott *et al.*, 1978) promise higher validity in the identification of component cognitive abilities than has been possible with the Wechsler and Binet Scales, for example. Other tests which attempt to describe constituent processes include the Illinois Test of Psycholinguistic Abilities (language) and the Marianne Frostig Developmental Test of Visual Perception (perception); both tests are discussed later.

Mittler (op. cit.) suggests using some of the concepts and methods which originated in the psychological laboratory (e.g. Piaget, Bruner) to assess *cognitive processes*; clearly he envisages the psychologist using his or her own insight and skills of assessment rather than depending on orthodox psychometric methods. *Personality and non-cognitive variables* might be assessed using some of the standardized tests available. As well, a careful case study approach would bring together relevant data from family and school sources. The importance of *observation* of the child at work and play is self-evident but not necessarily possible, to the extent thought desirable, by overworked psychologists. Sharing observation among teachers, parents and psychologist, and the use of checklists and schedules, should minimize demands on a single professional and, at the same time, enhance the quality of observations.

Methods of assessment

Assessment of children with specific learning difficulties has two main traditions. The first, involving the use of standardized psychological tests, has as its purpose the assessment of the abilities which underlie educational performance: intelligence, memory and perception are important ones. These abilities are essentially 'constructs' correlating to some extent with learning. Thus the child with faulty visual perception is thought a likely candidate for later learning difficulties or, if he or she is already having difficulties, is thought to be in trouble because of the perceptual deficit. This approach rests, in part, on the belief that improvement in the defective skill will lead to improved learning. It may be thought of as *secondary* or *second-level* assessment because it does not measure the educational deficit but the abilities presumed to underlie it.

The second tradition has as its purpose the assessment of educational achievement. So reading, spelling, writing and mathematics are assessed. For this purpose standardized tests, which give normative scores (reading ages, percentiles, standard scores ...) or qualitative data (level, comprehension skills ...), or a variety of formal and informal procedures which give detailed information usable by a teacher, may be employed. This form of assessment may be styled *primary* or *first-level* assessment because it measures educational achievement.

Secondary assessment, with standardized psychological tests, almost invariably involves a psychologist. Primary assessment may also involve a psychologist but is more often carried out by a teacher as part of his or her day to day evaluation of pupil progress. It is in primary assess-

ment that increasingly valuable insights into children with specific
learning difficulties have been shown by practitioners who have
developed their own assessment procedures (Cotterell, 1970a, 1970c,
1974; Naidoo, 1970). And it is from such practitioners, often in association with psychologists and other professionals, that remedial methods
have evolved. Increasingly, assessment is being regarded as a team affair,
with the contribution of the teacher seen as crucial (Clay, 1966, 1969;
Hagger, 1970; Stott, 1978).

What might be affirmed is that assessment is likely to be most productive when it leads to an analysis of the child's behaviour rather than
to diagnostic classification. Adelman (1979), writing about diagnostic
classification of learning disability (dyslexia), says:

> As used by many practitioners, the classification of a youngster
> as LD not only implies a contemporary problem (which is not too
> surprising, since the youngster usually is referred for diagnosis
> because of a contemporary problem), but also implies (post-
> dictively) that the cause of the problem is related to central
> nervous system dysfunctions and (predictively) that learning
> problems will continue until corrective action related to the CNS
> dysfunction is accomplished.

Unfortunately, as Adelman points out, the available evidence has not
established either relationship. He concludes that until such cause-
effect relationships are established, postdictive and predictive statements (e.g. regarding aetiology, intervention procedures and prognosis
relating to learning problems) are probably based more on theory and
professional biases than on valid assessment data.

Who does the assessing?

Tarnopol and Tarnopol (1976) report that in most countries children are assessed for reading disorders by an individual: usually a
psychologist, educator (teacher), or speech therapist, in that order.
They advocate a diagnostic team comprising physician, psychologist
and speech/hearing/language therapist. There can be no doubt, however, that contemporary thinking is for the teacher to have a central
role especially when assessment is accepted as an ongoing developmental process (Stott, 1978). There is little room for an hierarchy of
assessment personnel when all contributions are necessary but especially
when the interaction between teacher and child is at the heart of the
teaching/learning undertaking. Naidoo (1970) stresses the need for

co-operation between psychologist and teacher in assessment. She considers that ideally a full assessment should be carried out before tuition begins but notes that much can be accomplished within the classroom or remedial group by a teacher who is aware of what to observe and the significance of observations.

The tools and traditions of assessment

Approaches to assessment seem to be similar in various parts of the world. An international survey of children with specific learning difficulties (Tarnopol and Tarnopol, 1976) showed the use of standardized tests to be widespread. The following areas, in order of preference, were those in which standardized tests were most commonly used: reading (unstandardized tests also widely used), intelligence, visual perception, visual-motor co-ordination and auditory perception. Pediatric and neurological examinations were reported as sometimes carried out, and psychiatric examinations less often. The psychological tests most often used were: the Wechsler Intelligence Scales, the Terman-Merrill-Binet scales, the Illinois Test of Psycholinguistic Abilities and the Bender Visual Motor Gestalt (Tarnopol and Tarnopol, op. cit.).

Tarnopol and Tarnopol (1975) observe that prescriptive teaching should follow from the particular test battery used to diagnose specific learning disabilities. The battery should explore: basic sensory modalities including visual, auditory and tactile perception; motor co-ordination and equilibrium; and 'visual–auditory–motor cross modalities'. In each sensory modality measurements may be made of reception, immediate short- and long-term memory, integration and expression. The results of these tests are co-ordinated with the results of tests of language, academic achievement and intelligence. The language evaluation should be of receptive, integrative and expressive functions; should include a thorough evaluation of visual and auditory perception and of speaking and writing processes; and should assess 'ability to receive, understand, remember, sort, organize and retrieve information through visual, motor and auditory channels of communication' (Tarnopol and Tarnopol, 1976). The educational evaluation should be of reading, spelling, writing and arithmetic. As well, a neuropsychiatric examination should identify underlying problems and specify medication.

How well can the available instruments do the job, especially if prescription is the aim? Adelman (1979) advises us not to be too optimistic. Adamson and Adamson (1979), on the other hand, have worked out a scheme of differential diagnosis, based on the Wechsler Intelligence Scale for Children and the Bender Visual-Motor Gestalt, which they claim gives an analysis of learning assets and deficits: language, perception, memory, cognitive style, social skills. . . . Clinical perception appears to be a prime ingredient of the scheme. Although the validity of the approach is not established, there is an attempt to supply a definite remedial programme.

McCarthy and McCarthy (1969) pre-date Adamson and Adamson (1979) with assessment involving intelligence tests and visuo-motor-perception tests; as well as language, personality and educational achievement would be assessed. Blau *et al.* (1969) recommend the following in evaluating dyslexia: visual perceptual screening tests (Marianne Frostig Developmental Test of Visual Perception), laterality, oral reading tests (phonetic sounds, recognizing differences, reversals, directional confusions, substitutions, additions and omissions), handwriting, dictation of numbers, and estimation of distances and heights. Cox (1970) says perception and co-ordination should be looked at carefully in psychological examination.

Champion (1979b) has developed an 'individualized educational programme' (IEP) which attempts to reconcile developmental principles and demands of the task. So an effective IEP will take account of the processing abilities underlying the learning task and the sequence of skills required to master the task itself (Lerner, 1976). Champion (op. cit.) notes the sequence of language development as listening comprehension, oral expression, reading and written expression. This knowledge influences analysis of student performance on diagnostic measures as well as in planning remedial teaching. Similarly, Champion advises, evaluator and teacher (ideally the same person?) need to be aware that visual and auditory discrimination developmentally precede letter and word perception, and acquisition of phonic and structural analysis skills, in reading.

The assessment process, using standardized tests, criterion-referenced tests (which may also be standardized) and informal tests will, in Chapman's approach, take account of the above factors. His IEP assessment is explicit and detailed, combining the primary and secondary traditions discussed earlier. The assessment of language arts includes readiness skills (visual discrimination between letters and words, letter recognition, rhyming, following directions, sequencing); recognizing words as wholes in isolation and in context; word attack skills (use of context, phonic analysis, structural analysis); comprehension from listening and from oral and silent reading; and written expression (printing and writing, spelling, sentence and paragraph construction, capitalization, punctuation and usage). Speech and language assessment is similarly detailed, with comprehensive attention paid to such things as oral expression (vocabulary, syntax, sequence of ideas ...), written expression (sentence development, syntax, vocabulary, visual motor co-ordination ...), auditory reception (accuracy-content, grammar, syntax ...), general language development (age level, conceptual, vocabulary, comprehension, following directions ...), auditory evaluation (acuity, sequential memory, memory for content), speech evaluation.

By contrast with Champion's approach, which may lean towards over-kill, is that proposed by Trevor (1978) where the weight is on teacher assessment in the first instance: 'There is wisdom in attending first to educational factors. If the results of systematic teaching are not up to reasonable expectations, the psychologist or other specialist should then be asked for help.' In Trevor's scheme the following information must be found out.

1. The most difficult material that he can manage: independently with no word or meaning difficulties; with a minimum of help, meeting about one difficulty in 25 words.
2. Difficulty with respect to: understanding what is read; words recognized by sight, that is, without analysis; word attack; spoken language.
3. Interests.
4. Feelings about reading and books.
5. Learning style.
6. Capacity for improvement.

Trevor argues that no more testing should be done than is needed to get the teaching started — that too much time can be spent on testing and investigating difficulties and too little on teaching.

Observation

The place of observation in assessment has substantial support (Stott, 1978; Clay, 1977a; Mittler, 1970). Stott cites Keogh and Becker's (1973) review of research which showed that teachers' observation of children's learning behaviour was more accurate in predicting later school achievement than standardized assessments by psychologists or paediatricians. They advocated the inclusion of systematic observation of classroom behaviour and analysis of children's problem-solving styles as one of the main procedures of assessment. Stott himself has developed such procedures – in particular a *Guide to the Child's Learning Skills* – which, he claims, allow a teacher to arrive at a diagnosis of learning difficulties based on observable behavioural indications (see p. 246): rather than labelling (perceptual problems, hyperactivity, short attention span ...) there is a 'description of how the child copes within a learning situation' (Stott, op. cit.).

Farnham-Diggory (1978) presents the virtues of *protocol analysis*: analysis of an individual's behaviour on a given task (solving a problem, writing a word, 'thinking out loud'). It is a diagnostic system, informal, relying on the diagnostician's sensitivity and intelligence but producing information which will help the design of a remedial programme. It concentrates on what a child is *doing*, and it generates remedial ideas. Farnham-Diggory illustrates with a dozen questions similar to those below as examples:

Jenny is having difficulty in reading.

What is her parsing system?
What are her personal rules for performing the task?
Does she see stable letter patterns?
Does she have a stock of stable letter patterns in memory?
Does she know what these patterns sound like? etc.

Such an approach affirms the importance of informed psychologists working closely with teachers since the method would demand more involvement than a psychologist could allow, and teacher observation would be an important ingredient. Naidoo (1970) endorses the advantages to be had from psychologist/teacher collaboration and teacher involvement through observation. Gulliford (1975) sees teachers' own observations of children learning to read as the foundation for assessment.

Although there might not be general agreement that the following classroom behaviours would confirm a diagnosis of dyslexia, as the authors suggest, there would be acceptance of their importance in assessment and in designing a remedial programme:

1. difficulty in perceiving a word or sequence of words correctly;
2. inability to retain the image of whole words or parts of words for a sufficient length of time in order to recall it accurately for recognition in reading, and reconstruction in spelling;

3. bizarre but sometimes phonetic spelling which usually persists after the child has become an efficient, even an avid reader, because he cannot catch spelling, as many other retarded readers do;

4. keen application to learning after the child's problem has been explained to him (Dyslexia Institute, 1975).

These are all behaviours which a teacher could note from careful observation, perhaps using a checklist as an aid to systematic scanning of behaviour.

An emphasis on prevention

> When a learning problem is thought of as a deficit in the child, researchers often turn to surveys to detect children likely to fail before they enter school ... Such surveys try to predict that an individual child is likely to fail in an experience which he has not yet encountered — but, by and large, predictive correlations are far too small for success in such detection (Clay, 1977a).

Clay suggests that, in any case, it is the severe, rather than the mild, disabilities which will be detected, and these would probably come to notice without a survey anyway. It is in the classroom, Clay argues, that the failure of the child to learn must be detected and there that the impact of any programme designed to reduce reading failure must be felt. Her approach represents a fundamental switch away from both a discrepancy model, based on standardized tests, and the *products* of reading as measured by criterion tests. Clay and others (Lansdown, 1978; Newcomer, 1977) consider standardized tests to be of little value in the first two or three years of schooling. Clay's preference, based on careful research (Clay, 1966, 1977a, 1977b) is for observation of '... the acquisition of strategies in the reading process'. It is the process, not the product, which is important. The strategies to be observed will vary according to the programme which has been decided on; that, in turn, will be related to the description of behaviours considered relevant to progress and written before the programme begins. Having decided what they are looking for, classroom teachers can observe systematically.

One study (Glynn and McNaughton, 1975), in which correct directional behaviours and self-correction behaviour were targets for teacher checking and reinforcement, illustrates the point. Clay (1966) had established that self-correction behaviour seemed to be a reliable indication of a child's response to reading instruction. In this particular study, carried out over a period of one year in a special class for young ESN(M) children, appropriate behaviours were taught; results showed distinct gains in level and stability of on-task behaviour in class during lessons, and substantial gains in reading and writing over base-line levels: gains of one year in reading ages, on the average, and two years for the best of the nine children.

Clay (1977a) comes back to the importance of the class teacher. It is the class teacher who must make sensitive observation of the child's response to the reading process during the first year of instruction. There must be time for recording what children are saying and doing: 'Only from such records can one know, in the early stages, whether the child is moving comfortably through the programme or becoming confused.' Although it is the teacher who has the prime responsibility for monitoring the child's progress, she may need support, and it is here that a 'special educator' or 'teacher consultant' (Newcomer, 1977) to whom the teacher can turn for advice, confirmation, or comment will be needed. Clay's teacher is coping with regular instruction in the classroom. She is responsible for a group of children but, through careful observation, is monitoring their progress as individuals. Some of these individuals will fall behind; they will begin to fail. At this point a special educator will take the children in 'the tutorially more powerful setting of individual instruction' using the same approach as the class teacher to ensure continuity.

A survey of progress, carried out by an experienced teacher, will be desirable at the end of the child's first year at school. This will act as a 'diagnostic net'. Children needing individual help will then get it from an experienced teacher working with a special educator consultant. The special educator will have a teacher-consultant role rather than a diagnostic-remedial one. The emphasis is on co-operative teaching rather than on remediating failure. Clay (op. cit.) notes that such an approach in Sweden prevented more than 80 per cent of the cases identified as potential cases of reading disability at the beginning of the first grade (Malmquist, 1973) from becoming so. The method rests on some fundamental premises: it is preventive rather than remedial; it is posited on a central role for the classroom teacher rather than for the specialist adviser (though the place of experienced consultants is stressed); it is dependent on careful day-to-day observation of children's behaviour — especially language development, directional behaviour and co-ordination – rather than on the use of normative, standardized tests (Clay, 1972); and it places an emphasis on process rather than product.

As Lansdown (1978) notes, the adoption of Clay's approach could have a profound effect in preventing reading disability. It would, he observes, place a great responsibility on the reception class teacher 'who could no longer assume that a remedial net would catch her failures'. The implications for teacher education, both pre- and in-service, are self-evident. As well, the emphasis placed on experienced teacher back-up, and on consultant help, acknowledges the importance of support for the basic teaching role.

The use of standardized tests

The place of standardized tests in the assessment of children with specific learning difficulties was described above as secondary assessment, as it is once removed from assessment of the child's educational achievements. The fact that such tests are widely used in the assessment of specific learning difficulties does not mean that their validity for the purpose has been established, or accepted. In this section the use and validity of standardized psychological tests will be canvassed.

Certain tests come up again and again. In the field of *intelligence* the Wechsler Intelligence Scale for Children (WISC) and the Stanford Binet Intelligence Scale are cited most frequently; others are the Peabody Picture Vocabulary Test, the English Picture Vocabulary Test and Raven's Progressive Matrices. In *language* the Illinois Test of Psycho-linguistic Abilities (ITPA) is a perennial favourite aimed at a range of visual and auditory functions. *Visuo-motor perception* is assessed using the Bender Visual Motor Gestalt Test and the Marianne Frostig Developmental Test of Visual Perception among others. A test popularly used to assess *auditory perception* is the Wepman Auditory Discrimination Test. The Harris Lateral Dominance Test is a frequently used test in the assessment of *laterality*. An overview of tests used in the assessment of children with specific learning disabilities will be found in Ohlson (1978); those cited here, though the tests most often used, are not a comprehensive listing.

Before turning to an examination of individual tests some general comments are in order. Tyson (1970), having argued a case for a clear diagnosis of the child's difficulties, qualifies her position by pointing out that it may not be possible initially to pinpoint disability exactly because of the crudity of some of the psychological tools available.

She says that teaching itself must, in that case, carry 'the burden of diagnosis' but with a general idea of the area of difficulty from the psychological examination. Clay (1977a) attacks the diagnostic-remedial model based on testing as being an obstacle to early intervention: any value any standardized tests do have diminishes rapidly the closer one moves towards the beginning of schooling. She argues that the reliability and validity of tests dwindle when there is little achievement to sample and measure. Wedell (1973) regards the available assessment procedures as fallible. In the first place failure on any of the numerous tests of sensory and motor organization does not indicate which, or how many, underlying functions are deficient. Then, even if the question could be answered affirmatively, it is not clear whether a low level of performance in a given perceptual task constitutes a handicap for the child. Relatively little is known about which particular functions underlie educational performance at a given age; and, even when particular functions are shown to be relevant, little is known about the level of function required to achieve the norms (Wedell, op. cit.).

With so much invested in assessment of various functions, can it be assumed that training of those functions which are defective will lead, through improvement, to improved educational achievement — say in reading? The evidence is equivocal. Wedell reports a variety of training programmes but slight transfer to specific educational skills: 'As far as educational attainments are concerned, the research findings on the effect of sensory and motor organization programmes have not provided support for the claim of generalized positive effect' (Wedell, op. cit.). A review (Hammill and Larsen, 1974) showed that the results of training children in psycholinguistic skills were inconclusive. However, since there is strong research evidence that the skills are necessary for learning, the implication can be drawn that training of the skills should not be in isolation but in specific tasks. Sampson (1976) observed that studies of the Frostig and ITPA programmes seemed to show that, while they bring about improvement in the skills involved there is little carry-over to reading. Hooton (1976), a remedial teacher, advocates teaching the introductory processes involved in reading and writing themselves rather than 'using exercises based on abstractions'.

Does this bring us to the position taken by Smith (1971) as reported by Makins (1977)? Smith's message, deriving from work in psycholinguistics, perception and information-processing theory, is that children cannot be taught rules for reading — they must sort it out for themselves. Reading is not just about books but about making sense of print in all its forms. Children are naturally disposed to learn how to do it. They can be helped along the way by skilful encouragement and relaxed feedback. But they can only learn to read by reading. Attempts to teach 'reading skills' are only likely to interfere with their learning. Thoughtful people would probably agree with Smith's basic propositions that the seeds of learning lie in the learner and that the best way of learning something is to do it. However, it may be a different matter for children with severe learning difficulties: skilled and encouraging adults can help children who have failed by working with them as they attempt to unlock the code. Teaching reading skills in isolation may be counter-productive, but helping children to use effective techniques while reading may be another matter.

The use of psychological tests in identifying incipient learning difficulties has been called into question by Stott (1978), who points out that studies have shown that kindergarten teachers predict first grade reading achievement at least as efficiently as a psychometric battery designed for the purpose (Feshback *et al.*, 1974) and that teachers are surprisingly accurate in early identification of both high-risk and high-potential children (Keogh and Smith, 1970). Stott (op. cit.) also queries the value of attempting to assess visual discrimination, spatial relations, visual memory and auditory-visual integration since a review of 60 studies (Larsen and Hammill, 1975) showed that correlations between these four variables, and attainment in reading and arithmetic, rarely reached 0.35.

Some widely used standardized tests

Following is an examination of some of the more widely used tests. Descriptions and evaluations of these tests and others will be found in such sources as Anastasi (1976), Buros (1978 and earlier editions), Cronbach (1970) and Thorndike and Hagen (1977).

Intelligence tests

Intelligence tests are universally used. *The Wechsler Intelligence Scale for Children (WISC)* is used both for the global estimates of intelligence which it gives (verbal, performance and full-scale IQs can be obtained) and for differential diagnosis based on patterns of sub-test performance. For example Bannatyne (1971) suggests that genetic dyslexic readers score highest in spatial category tests (vocabulary, similarities, comprehension) and lowest in sequential category tests (digit span, coding, picture arrangement). Francis-Williams (1974) postulates that developmental lag and learning problems in school due to brain pathology, and not to 'normal' slow development, may be indicated *inter alia* by ' ... discrepant psychological patterning: for example, in the WPPSI[1] and in the WISC, facility in language, difficulty in block design, object assembly and coding, and frequently poor arithmetic.'

Thomson and Grant (1979) review the literature on 'the WISC sub-test profile of the dyslexic child'. On differences between verbal and performance IQs they conclude that a superior performance IQ *may* be associated with 'dyslexic problems' but that the distinction is by no means conclusive and would not merit diagnostic use in the individual case (Doehring, 1968). This conclusion is no more than expected given the uncertain value which can be placed on the distinction between V (verbal) and P (performance) scales (Cronbach, 1970). Results on sub-test patterning among 'dyslexics' are also reported as inconclusive. Again, this is not a surprising result given the concern with which interpretation of sub-test scores is regarded: 'The design (of the WISC) encourages testers to draw conclusions from zigs and zags in the profile that represent nothing but error of measurement or that lack well-validated meaning' (Cronbach, op. cit.). A study carried out by Thomson and Grant (op. cit.) produced ambiguous findings on sub-test patterns but some agreement with the cluster patterns postulated by Bannatyne (above).

Does the WISC produce useful information on children with specific learning difficulties? The evidence presented by Thomson and Grant (op. cit.) suggests that to persist in the search for sub-test patterns, in the hope that a definitive dyslexic profile will emerge, is to persist in the pursuit of a chimera. Gredler (1978) agrees but suggests that much of the work on differential diagnosis based on standardized tests has increased our understanding of learning disabilities. The research already reviewed intimates that dyslexia is a mythical concept. But upsetting the equation further is the nature of the tool used in the pursuit: the WISC is a primitive tool (Cronbach, op. cit.) whose validity, especially at sub-test level, is equivocal. The saving grace may be that, in the hands of an experienced psychologist, the test is a useful aid to clinical observation.

In summary, the WISC may be used in assessing a child's ability.

---

[1] Wechsler Pre-School and Primary Scale of Intelligence.

If the result is used to decide, on the grounds of full-scale IQ, whether a child is 'dyslexic' — that is if the average IQ, or higher, criterion is met — the charge of irresponsibility may be levelled. It has been argued earlier that children of less than average intelligence may have specific learning difficulties and that they should not be denied remedial teaching on the grounds of low IQ. The WISC may justifiably be used, in the hands of a psychologist, to supplement data already to hand but its use to justify the diminishing or withdrawal of educational stimulus cannot be sustained. Further, the evidence to date for the production of useful prescriptive information, from sub-test profile analysis, which can guide remedial teaching, is not convincing. On balance, it would seem that time spent in analysing profiles would be better spent in assessing achievement and enhancing motivation.

The same general comments may be made about the *Revised Stanford-Binet Intelligence Scale* (Form L-M). This scale is an individual test of intelligence, comprising a mix of verbal, non-verbal and performance items, which must be administered only by a trained tester and which takes up to one hour to administer. It yields a single IQ. There is no tradition of sub-test analysis with the Binet because it is not constructed in a form which lends itself to such analysis. Useful supplementary data can be obtained from the test when it is used by a sensitive clinician as a controlled interview. Care should be exercised in using the results as a justification for withholding remedial treatment.

The *Goodenough–Harris Drawing Test* (formerly called Goodenough Draw-A-Man) is useful as a supplement to an individually administered test of intelligence such as the WISC or the Stanford-Binet. Although this is a long-established test, its validity in its new form has not been well substantiated (Dunn, 1972). Its use as a single indicator of ability should be avoided.

Although styled as a test of listening vocabulary, the *English Picture Vocabulary Test*, like its parent the *Peabody Picture Vocabulary Test*, is sometimes used as a quick substitute for an individual test of intelligence. Although it correlates well (0.76) with WISC Vocabulary and 0.82 with Stanford-Binet Vocabulary it cannot be used as a substitute for either the WISC or the Binet: it is not sufficiently broad or thorough to be used in place of either (Cronbach, 1970).

The British Ability Scales

The British Ability Scales were published in 1978. They were 12 years in the making and represent a distillation of contemporary think-

cannot be assumed, and the child who scores high may also have trouble in the classroom (Kephart, op. cit.). A teacher of children with specific learning difficulties would have to be satisfied that time spent on a Frostig training programme could not be spent more profitably in other ways.

Perceptual-motor assessment

The *Bender-Gestalt Test* (there are various versions of this test) is primarily an ability test (Cronbach, 1970) but occupies ' . . . a unique position among major clinical diagnostic instruments as a brief test that is both projective and non projective'. The test comprises two-dimensional abstract geometrical figures which the subject is asked to copy. From the copies the clinician attempts a 'qualitative integration' (Cronbach, op. cit.) of personality. With children, in addition to giving a 'rough measure of ability', emotional disturbance or brain damage may be suggested by an inferior performance — especially when a child appears normal or superior on conventional ability tests. This last use — assessment of organicity — appears to be a popular one among psychologists (Kitay, 1972). Kitay says: 'The Bender-Gestalt should be included, if possible, in every diagnostic examination of adults or children from age five because of its unique contributions to the evaluation of perceptual-motor functioning, neurological impairment, expressive styles, and maladjustment.' The Bender-Gestalt would appear, then, to have some relevance in the hands of a trained person who is assessing specific learning difficulties. The extent to which it contributes, in a prescriptive way, to specific remedial suggestions will depend on the insights and experience of the examining psychologist both as clinician and educator.

Language functions

The *Illinois Test of Psycholinguistic Abilities*, based on Osgood's model of language acquisition, comprises 12 sub-tests designed to assess receptive and expressive language functions. The sub-tests are auditory reception, visual reception, visual sequential memory, auditory association, auditory sequential memory, visual association, visual closure, verbal expression, grammatic closure, manual expression, auditory closure and sound blending. These read like a checklist for the assessment of specific learning difficulties. The ITPA is a grand conception which, if the promise of the sub-test titles was realized, would put an invaluable tool in the hands of the clinician and eminently usable information in the hands of the teachers.

However, the promise is not realized in practice. Lumsden (1978) claims that the test should not have been published, 'at least in its present form', that the reliabilities of sub-tests are too low for the kind of individual diagnosis recommended (regression effects virtually guarantee marked improvement on retest) and that no direct evidence on the validity of the sub-tests for 'any purpose' is provided. To the pleas of those of his colleagues, who say that in spite of low reliability and unknown (probably low) validity the test is a rich source of hunches for further exploration, he recommends the matchbox test! 'For testers who like to use tests in this way, may I recommend the matchbox test. With a box of matches and some ingenuity, it is possible to give rapid tests of information, motor co-ordination, the Bender-Gestalt, memory for designs, arithmetic, number series, progressive matrices, and even the Rorschach.' Lumsden concludes that the ITPA is inferior to the matchbox test as an intuitive clinical aid and that it is no substitute for the WISC or the Stanford-Binet either. Further, none of these tests could be recommended as a suitable differential aptitude test to guide remedial education.

Wiederholt (1978), after reviewing research on the ITPA, concludes that the test is not an adequate measure of language in children and that the abilities measured by it lack any empirically demonstrated educational significance. And, 'It would be unfortunate if the ITPA were to be used to diagnose or categorize children as having "language", "psycholinguistic", or "learning disability" problems and/or as a basis for planning remedial programmes.' Newcomer and Hammill (1975) surveyed 40 studies on the predictive and diagnostic value of ITPA. They questioned the assumption that the ITPA could identify deficits underlying academic failure, and concluded that neither the visual sequential memory sub-test nor the auditory closure sub-test had predictive or diagnostic value as far as reading attainments were concerned. Lund *et al.* (1978) suggest that Newcomer and Hammill over-generalized from the data reviewed.

Summary

The preceding tests all illustrate secondary testing as discussed earlier: they are designed to assess underlying abilities which are themselves no more than psychological constructs. The efficacy of these tests in the assessment of specific learning difficulties is not spectacular.

That is not to claim that the attempt to assess abilities should be abandoned — merely that there should not be too much optimism that the definitive battery of psychological tests for the assessment and diagnosis of specific learning difficulties is possible. In the meantime psychologists will continue to use such tests and interpret them cautiously in the light of their own experience and insights.

Standardized achievement tests

It is not proposed to examine standardized achievement tests closely. Because they are concerned with primary assessment — with what the child does, rather than with what underlies what he does — they have initially better face validity than the tests examined in the preceding pages. Some tests will give more useful leads than others in devising remedial programmes: examples are the *Standard Test of Reading Skill* (Daniels and Diack, 1958) and the *Neale Analysis of Reading Ability* (Neale, 1966). The Neale, in particular, has world-wide currency. Tests of reading vocabulary, individually administered, remain very useful instruments for giving a quick indication of a child's achievement level, but tell only a small part of the story. Group tests are not discussed but they are useful as a basis for preliminary assessment of a child, although important decisions affecting individuals should not be made on the basis of group tests alone.

The *Standard Test of Reading Skill* (Daniels and Diack, 1958) uses graded sentences as a means of measuring reading accuracy. Reading development is analysed into stages, and diagnostic tests provided for each stage. A useful qualitative instrument.

The *Neale Analysis of Reading Ability* (Neale, 1966) uses a set of graded paragraphs as its measuring instrument. It measures *accuracy, comprehension* and *rate* from a child's reading of one set of paragraphs. It is in three parallel forms and provides a useful scheme of error analysis and diagnostic tests. A paragraph reading test of this kind allows observations of the child's behaviour in a standard situation so that 'a teacher who has thought about the reading process can extract much more information about the chid's system of operating on cues in reading from a running record of the text than is yielded only by the test scores' (Clay, 1972).

The *Schonell Graded Word Reading Test* is an individually administered word recognition test which gives a normative reading age as a quick check of reading level against expectancy and age. The *Burt (Rearranged) Word Reading Test* does a similar job. Both tests give the tester an opportunity to assess word attack skills, and other relevant behaviour, as well as word recognition. It should be kept in mind that a word recognition test is at best a diagnostic tool and not, on its own, a satisfactory way of measuring progress (Trevor, 1978). Clay (1972) points out that reading vocabulary tests will not describe a child's integrated system of reading behaviour. That can be observed only on continuous text.

Two integrated approaches to early assessment

The first recommendation made in the Tizard Report (DES, 1972) was that teachers should, in collaboration with educational psychologists and school medical officers, screen all children for reading backwardness, preferably at the end of the infant stage. In this section two approaches to screening, both carefully integrated, and both designed for use in the first two years of schooling will be examined. The first, the *Aston Index* (Newton *et al.*, 1979), derives from the psychometric, standardized test tradition, and the second, *The Early Detection of Reading Difficulties* (Clay, 1972, 1979a), from an information-processing model of reading behaviour.

The importance of catching children as early as possible is stressed by practitioners (Cotterell, 1970a; Naidoo, 1970). Cotterell wrote that very few children under the age of nine attended the Word Blind Centre in London, when it was functioning (1963 to 1972), but those who did were very easy to teach: 'They had experienced no sense of failure and learning was still fun.' If children are caught early, the gap of retardation is quicker to close (Cotterell, op. cit.). Sampson (1976) noted that 'teachers' thinking is turning more and more to techniques of screening and prevention'.

A normative approach to early assessment

The Aston Index (Newton *et al.*, 1979) has two diagnostic functions: first as a screening instrument to alert teachers to 'at risk' children at the end of the first six months at school, or when problems are suspected; and secondly, for puzzling cases of non-attainment at seven years-plus ('This might include the "slow learning" child who can be equally affected by dyslexic-type confusions in symbolic material as well as lesser all-round intellectual functioning.' Newton *et al.*, op. cit.). The Index is intended for use by teachers, comprises tests which are readily available, requires no lengthy specialist training to administer and is presented as 'easily scorable', with results which can be expressed in profile form. It is assembled in two levels to allow administration at the two ages mentioned above: six-and-a-half- and seven-plus. All of the items of Level I, with two exceptions, are included in Level II, but there are four additional items at Level II to tap the more advanced attainments of the older children.

The Index is made up as follows:

Level I

Level II

General Underlying Ability

1. Picture recognition
2. Vocabulary
3. Goodenough Draw-a-man
4. Copying geometrical designs

General Underlying Ability

1. Vocabulary
2. Goodenough Draw-a-man
3. Copying geometrical designs

Performance Items

1. Write or copy name three times
2. Phoneme/grapheme correspondence
3. Visual sequential memory (symbolic)
4. Visual sequential memory (pictorial)
5. Auditory sequential memory
6. Sound blending
7. Sound discrimination
8. Laterality (including knowledge of left and right, and common sequences)

Performance Items

1. Schonell Graded Word Reading Test
2. Schonell Graded Word Spelling Test
3. Free writing
4. Phoneme/grapheme correspondence
5. Visual sequential memory (symbolic)
6. Visual sequential memory (pictorial)
7. Auditory sequential memory
8. Sound blending
9. Sound discrimination
10. Graphomotor Test
11. Laterality (including knowledge of left and right, and common sequences)

The composition of the Index is at first glance straightforward. At Level I there is an attempt to assess underlying ability (intelligence?) or readiness, perceptuo-motor ability, visual sequential memory, auditory sequential memory, laterality, ability to discriminate and blend sounds, and skill in written language. In addition, Level II taps reading, spelling, 'free' writing and 'graphomotor' skills (Newton *et al.*, 1979, p. 60).

Having administered the Index, what does the teacher then know about a child and what action is indicated? Both questions are essentially validity questions: does the Index tap actual abilities accurately and are the abilities relevant for learning to read, write and spell? The authors present research data to support affirmative answers to these questions but there persists a nagging worry.

In the first place the arguments for the inclusion of the 'general underlying ability' measures are not convincing. We are not given evidence that a composite of items from, or similar to those in, the Stanford-Binet Intelligence Scale, the English Picture Vocabulary Test and the Goodenough Draw-a-man test will prove a valid indicator of a child's 'readiness' level. Cronbach (1970) describes the Peabody Picture Vocabulary Test (the parent of the EPVT) as a substitute for the same two tests. Lovell (1972) questions the validity of the EPVT for the purpose for which it is recommended here. He says: 'At present no evidence exists that it will give an understanding of reading difficulties and other verbal handicaps.' Even if validity for the 'general underlying ability' was high, some present thinking is against using such a measure as an indicator of readiness (Newcomer, 1977). Why not, instead, assess what a child can *do* rather than predict what he is likely to be able to do on the basis of tests once-removed from the actual tasks (Clay, 1977a)? Putting a measure of 'general underlying ability' in the hands of teachers of five-and-a-half-year-olds is questionable at best but to give them one of low validity is doubtful practice indeed.

The performance items in both scales include those which traditionally have been associated with secondary assessment (as discussed earlier) and which are aimed at tapping underlying functions; primary assessment tests of writing (both levels), reading and spelling (Level II only); and tests of other skills associated specifically with reading. The authors report a validity study which shows that the Index does discriminate between groups of retarded and non-retarded readers in laterality, visual sequential memory and auditory sequential memory ($P < 0.001$); vocabulary ($P < 0.01$); and sound discrimination and graphomotor skills ($P < 0.05$). It is suggested that these results provide satisfactory concurrent validity, but does that mean that the tests do identify deficits that are amenable to remedial teaching?

The Index as a screening device

A further study on the validity of the Index as a predictor of written language difficulties was carried out: Index scores at five-and-a-half years of age were correlated with reading (Schonell), spelling (Schonell) and free writing at seven-and-a-half. Low but significant correlations were obtained.

> The aim of the study ... was to see which test items (if any), isolated 'at risk' children. Thus, if a child scored poorly on a particular test item, one would expect him to do poorly at reading and/or spelling two years later if that item was a useful predictor of written language difficulties. Conversely, children performing well on the Index items might be expected to do well in written language (Newton *et al.*, op. cit., p. 75).

The last objective may be attractive at first glance but it conceals hidden hazards. The first is the obvious one that the tests may not be tapping relevant skills (Wedell, 1973); the second is that five-and-a-half may be too young to be attempting identification of difficulties with a test battery of this kind (Clay, 1977a); but the overriding hazard is that teachers may be lulled into believing that this Index is valid for *individuals*, form biased attitudes about particular children and teach them accordingly. To be fair, it should be noted that the authors point out that the validity studies are based on groups and that caution should be shown before confident conclusions are drawn about individuals.

However, Thomson (1979a) claims that the Index may validly be used with individuals to predict success or failure in reading. He writes that the best *predictors* at age five-and-a-half years of success or failure in reading at age seven-and-a-half are: for *success*, total performance, laterality, visual sequential memory, visual sequential memory (symbolic), auditory sequential memory and sound blending; and for *failure*, performance total, free writing, visual sequential memory (symbolic), auditory sequential memory and sound blending. Thomson (op. cit.) establishes probabilities of success or failure by using a Bayesian model of probabilities. This technique is claimed to circumvent regression problems and to yield a more meaningful estimate of likely groups of 'at risk' or 'probable success' children thus enabling appropriate planning for teaching/remediation/intervention. This is an attractive claim but one which must wait further validation before being embraced uncritically. The educational sceptic is likely to be wary of recommending an Index which is based largely on second-order tests rather than on tests of actual achievement. She would also be hesitant about using an Index, at age five-and-a-half, which has yet to be thoroughly validated for predictive purposes and which could incline teachers to incorrect expectancies of children's abilities and achievements.

The Index as a diagnostic instrument

How effective is the Aston Index in the assessment of seven-year-olds with specific learning difficulties? We are not given convincing data on this, but Newton *et al.* do provide an interesting, and detailed, account of how the Index is used as a supplement to an array of traditional tests in an illustrative study of the diagnosis of dyslexia (Thomson, 1979b). The ways in which the Index is used, and the interpretations based on some component tests, may be prone to the same criticisms as cited for the ITPA, WISC and other tests: for example how much confidence can be placed in the validity of *visual sequential memory (pictorial), visual sequential memory (symbolic), auditory sequential memory, sound blending* and *sound discrimination*? Similarly, how much credence can be placed in the *graphomotor test*? The results of these tests, and others, are given for John, the illustrative case by Thomson (1979b), and the results are translated into remedial suggestions which appear to be practical and relevant. What might be questioned is whether the armoury of tests is needed to arrive at the recommended teaching programme. Would a systematic but non-normative attack on the problem be a better alternative? Such a strategy could include many of the same tests used in a descriptive way by an experienced teacher but without reliance on normative assessment: for example, would much be lost if we didn't know that auditory sequential memory and visual sequential memory were at the seven- and eight-year levels respectively?

Summary

The Aston Index represents an attempt to reconcile an expectancy approach to assessment of specific learning difficulty with an analysis of psychological function and educational attainment. The evidence is against the validity and acceptability of the procedure. The component tests are a hotch-potch largely taken, or derived from, existing tests. The attempt to put them into a normative mould is possibly to encourage teachers to pursue spurious precision when the weight of opinion (Lansdown, 1978; Newcomer, 1977; Stott, 1978) is for the systematic development of tools of assessment which will help teachers analyse children's learning strategies, behaviours and educational achievement in such a way that information of direct *educational* relevance is obtained. Some of the tests of the Aston Index do that (reading, writing, spelling) but the majority do not.

A non-normative approach to early assessment

In contrast to the approach of the Aston Index is that adopted by Clay (1972, 1979a). Her procedures for the early detection of reading difficulties, involving a diagnostic survey, are based on the belief that it is desirable:

- to observe precisely what children are doing and saying
- to use tasks that are close to the learning tasks of the classroom (rather than standardized tests)
- to observe what children have been able to learn (not what they have been unable to do)
- to discover what reading behaviours they should now be taught from an analysis of performance in reading, not from pictorial or puzzle material, or from normative scores
- to shift the child's reading behaviour from less adequate to more adequate responding, by training on reading tasks rather than training visual perception or auditory discrimination as separate activities (Clay, 1972).

The emphasis is qualitative, and there is only slight emphasis on scores and quantifying progress, and then mainly as a measure of development in reading. 'The real value of the survey is to uncover what processes and items a particular child controls and what processes and items he could be taught next' (Clay, op. cit.). The survey would appear to meet the concerns of the Bullock Report (DES, 1975) and to satisfy Gulliford's (1975) plea for the development of adequate 'screening' procedures.

The diagnostic survey

The diagnostic survey is carried out with all children who are not making good progress on their sixth birthday. It involves:

1. Accuracy on book reading (five-ten minutes). A *running record* is made of a child reading a sample of 100–200 words from his or her current book. An error rate of more than ten per cent may indicate a problem. The child's *self-correction* behaviour is checked; absence of self-correction is a danger sign. The child's

directional movement is assessed. The child is asked to 'read it with your finger'. Children who have poor motor co-ordination, or who are quick and impulsive, or who are timid and unconfident may have problems of directionality.

2. Analysis of errors. The errors made in the running record are analysed. Information is sought on *oral language skills* (are they good enough to make reading of the text possible?; is language so fluent that it races ahead of the co-ordination of visual perception and motor movement?); *speed of responding* (a child who responds fluently may be a poorer reader than another child who pauses and engages in much self-correction behaviour); *cues* (use of oral language knowledge in unlocking a word, whether responses are grammatical . . .).

3. Integration of skills. Are oral language and visual-search techniques well integrated?

4. Letter identification (five–ten minutes). All letters, upper and lower case, are tested and responses recorded according to the way the letter was identified (alphabetic, sound or beginning similarly to a word). Errors are noted for teaching.

5. Concepts about print (five–ten minutes). An assessment of the child's knowledge about the 'conventions of our written code'. As the examiner reads a book the child is asked such questions as: 'Show me the front of the book', 'Show me where to start', 'Which way do I go?', 'Show me the bottom of the picture.' The test is diagnostic in that it assesses skills which are necessary if the reading of books is to be mastered (Clay, 1974).

6. 'Ready to read' Word Test (two minutes). The test is based on 15 words from the 45 most frequently occurring words in the books of the *Ready to Read* reading series used in the first year of instruction in Auckland (New Zealand) schools. The test is seen as a very good instrument for ranking or grouping children during the first year and for retarded readers in the second year (Clay, 1966). Successive tests indicate whether progress is being made.

7. Writing vocabulary. An assessment of the child's writing behaviour: letter formation, number of letter forms used, availability of a stock of known words? A poor writing vocabulary may indicate faulty visual perception: 'In learning, hand *and* eye support and supplement each other, organizing the first visual discriminations' (Clay, 1972).

8. Dictation test. Simple sentences are used. The *sounds* which the child writes correctly are recorded giving 'some indication of the child's ability to analyse the word he hears or says' (Clay, 1980).

On the basis of the above survey, remedial procedures are proposed. A careful record is kept so that progress is monitored. A child with hard-core problems may be referred to a psychologist if necessary. This method has been employed on a large scale in New Zealand schools, and will be reported on in a later section.

Some specifically 'dyslexic' modes of diagnosis and assessment

The specialists working with dyslexic children (they keep to the term dyslexia) have developed their own diagnostic and assessment habits. Diagnosis is seen as important because it establishes a syndrome which in turn points to a remedial strategy (Hornsby and Miles, 1979). Assessment will frequently call on a battery of tests, and procedures, of the kinds discussed earlier in this section. Thus Hornsby (1973) saw comprehensive assessment as embracing: 1. standardized tests of intelligence, reading, auditory discrimination, lateral dominance and manual dexterity; 2. hearing, vision and neurological tests; 3. case data, family history, personal milestones; and 4. writing of a free composition, writing letters of the alphabet and reciting the days of the week and the months of the year.

Miles (1974) regards the following as 'signs' of dyslexia:

1. Discrepancy between intellectual level and performance in spelling.
2. Bizarre spelling.
3. Confusion of b and d in either reading or writing, or both.
4. Difficulty in distinguishing between left and right.
5. Difficulty in repeating polysyllabic words, such as preliminary, philosophical or statistical.
6. Difficulty in repeating digits in reverse order (and other defects of short-term memory).
7. Inability to do subtractions except with 'concrete' aids.
8. Difficulty in memorizing mathematical tables.
9. Losing the place when reciting tables.
10. A history of clumsiness, late walking or late talking.

These are signs which could be picked up in the classroom and from discussion with parents. Although not indicating a specific remedial/

teaching strategy a knowledgeable teacher would be alerted to incipient (or actual) learning difficulties and could continue assessment as appropriate teaching was being carried out.

Newton *et al.* (1979) adopt behavioural symptoms similar to those of Miles:

 1. Persistent reversal and disordering of letters (e.g. b and d), syllables, words (saw/was) and word order when reading, writing and occasionally speaking.
 2. Mirror-imaging of letters and words.
 3. Inability to perceive, code and subsequently retain a consistent meaningful symbolic image.
 4. The consequent inability to retrieve and express a relevant, meaningful output of linguistic material.
 5. Severe spelling disorder.
 6. Non-resolution of hand, ear and eye dominance.
 7. Late development of spoken language in early childhood.
 8. Difficulties with sequencing, order and direction.
 9. Sometimes motor clumsiness, sometimes hyperactivity and occasionally superior ability in spatial skills in direct contast with the disability in linguistic skills (Newton *et al.*, op. cit., p. 93).

The Dyslexia Institute (1975) regards the following as features characteristic of dyslexic children which are observable in the classroom where the recognition, recall and reproduction of written symbols are expected achievements.

 1. Difficulty in perceiving a word, or sequence of words, correctly.
 2. Inability to retain the image of whole words or parts of words for a sufficient length of time in order to recall it accurately for recognition in reading, and reconstruction in spelling.
 3. Bizarre, but sometimes phonetic, spelling which usually persists after the child has become an efficient, even an avid, reader because he cannot 'catch' spelling, as many other retarded readers do.
 4. Keen application to learning after the problem has been explained to him.

Summary

This section has looked at the nature and scope of diagnosis and assessment, at who does the assessing, at the tools and methods of assessment, at two approaches to early assessment and at some of the assessment practices employed by people who work closely with children with specific learning difficulties. Can any generalizations be drawn from the discussion which will further our understanding of children with these difficulties and inform our remedial practices? If no definitive statements, at least suggestions indicative of trends can be made.

The first is that assessment — whether it leads to diagnosis or not — must be prescriptive; it must yield information about a child's knowledge, learning behaviours, perceptual and cognitive strategies, and motivation which is usable by teachers (and, ideally, parents). Evaluation should be ongoing. Secondly, assessment should engage teachers and parents both in the observation of children and through the supply of information in other ways. Psychologists should continue to be key people in assessment but they should be seen in a partnership role with those who work closely with children and who know them best. Thirdly, an emphasis on prevention of reading failure is an agreed and insistent objective. Thus procedures which assist teachers to identify as early as possible children who are failing — preferably in the first year of schooling — should be developed and fostered. Fourthly, uncritical use of standardized tests — particularly of cognitive and perceptual functions — is to be discouraged but teachers are to be encouraged and helped to monitor pupil progress comprehensively.

Two approaches to the assessment of reading retardation were examined, one based on the use of standardized tests and employing a discrepancy/expectancy model, the other using an approach which analysed learning behaviour and strategies; the first was styled as secondary assessment because it relied heavily on the sampling of functions underlying performance; the second was described as primary assessment because it tapped the components of achievement. The second approach is seen as reflecting trends in current educational thinking and considered to merit encouragement both as a way of picking up problems early and involving teachers in active monitoring.

Examples of assessment procedures adopted by specialists engaged in remedial work with children with specific learning difficulties were cited. These appear to represent careful analysis of behaviour and achievement deriving from long experience and from beliefs about the aetiology and nature of 'dyslexia'. A positive way forward could be the marrying of the skills of the remedialists with the assessment strategies of the early interventionists and the beliefs of those who hold that children with specific learning difficulties are displaying learned behaviours rather than in-built deficits.

4. Remedial methods

This section examines remedial methods. It is interesting that approaches being used are time-honoured ones. They are variations on phonic methods, whole-word methods and mixed methods. These methods have been variously adopted to fit children with characteristic variations of specific learning difficulties. Practitioners are in broad agreement on the methods which work with children with auditory-based problems and those whose problems have a visual base.

The burden of the review is that, to a large extent, methods are rule-of-thumb and experience-based. There is no shortage of affirmation by faith as to which methods are successful with which children but there is a dearth of acceptable research evidence on the efficacy of this or that method with particular difficulties.

An interesting development is the work being done on early intervention, with teacher involvement in the first year of schooling, and a non-psychometric approach to screening (Clay, 1979a). The other provocative theme is that provided by Stott (1978) when he argues that specific reading difficulty is a learned pattern of behaviour rather than an in-built deficiency. Acceptance of that viewpoint – or even of the possibility of its validity – could lead to a change of approach which took the child as carrying the key to his own repair rather than depending on a 'fix-it' model. Motivation (Nicholls, 1976) may ultimately prove the indispensable ingredient for success.

Principles of remediation with specific learning difficulty

Sampson (1976) distilled agreed principles of remediation for dyslexics from authorities publishing since 1965 (Bryant, 1965; Johnson and Myklebust, 1967; Deschaut, 1968; Bannatyne, 1971; Kirk and Kirk, 1971; Jordan, 1972; Newton and Thomson, 1974). In addition to the idiosyncratic points made by each author there was agreement on the following:

1. The need for individualizing the approach.
2. The advantages of multi-sensory stimulation.
3. The adoption of over-learning as a practice, of structured methods with stress on 'rules and regularities', of methods of ensuring pupil success and of 'simple' methods of remediation.
4. Teaching from a child's strengths while remediating deficits was emphasized by two authorities (Johnson and Myklebust, and Kirk and Kirk).

These principles are accepted and followed by the practitioners (Naidoo, 1970; Cotterell, 1970a, 1974b; Pollock, 1976).

Individualizing the approach

Although Sampson (op. cit.) cited the 'individualizing' of the approach as the first principle agreed by various experts, a distinction should perhaps be drawn between developing a programme to meet an individual's needs (individualizing) and implementing that programme in a one-to-one relationship with a teacher. Stott (1978) warns that a one-to-one teaching arrangement may be too threatening for a child. The Dyslexia Institute (1975) adopts a pattern of regular and systematic lessons but not necessarily on an individual basis: the child can be taught with two or three others and, where programmes overlap, consolidation can be carried out in pairs or small groups so that pupils support each other. In these instances the programme may be an individual one but its implementation shared. Gessert (1975) recommends that teaching should be carried out in fairly small groups with at least some opportunity for one-to-one contact.

As corollaries to the import placed on individual teaching are concern for the failing child's emotional adjustment, and active attempts to foster motivation (Vernon, 1971). A child who is interested, and who has a positive view of himself as a learner and as a person, is more likely to learn than one who is demoralized. Perhaps the poet puts it most poignantly?:

THE KEY

My boy sits
Curled over
The book
Holding it
Too tightly
With a thin hand
And
Tense in his uncertainty

My boy looks
Seeing black
Symbols
And
Something close
To loathing
Saps his concentration

> To me
> The words unlock
> A store of vast delight,
> But my boy
> Does not have
> The key

J. Brunskill-Davis (quoted in Hornsby and Shear, 1976).

Gredler (1978), as a former director of a remediation centre for learning-disabled children, testified to the 'overwhelming reluctance and anxiety of the majority of children referred to the center, when first introduced to reading materials and tests'.

Multi-sensory methods

Remedial practitioners are nothing if not realists. Thus they will try anything that works. Multi-sensory methods, based on the use of all available learning channels, fall naturally to their purposes and they use them.

Thomas (1977) advocates a multi-sensory approach with children with remedial problems: the use of audio-visual and mechanical aids — overhead projectors, typewriters, epidiascopes — spelling aloud, sounding out, look-and-say. The aim is to combat failure in the three Rs with training in the three Ss (sight, sound, sequence) and attention to the seven Rs (recognition, reassessment, rapport, reassurance, retraining, repetition and recall).

Hooton (1976) adopts a multi-sensory approach: 'There are few children who cannot be helped by looking at the symbol, saying the sound and feeling the shape simultaneously.' She sees the multi-sensory way as succeeding with any child no matter what his dominant channel for learning. However, she would have the observant teacher giving extra practice in a particular mode when it is seen that there is blockage or under-development.

Hooton stresses the need to teach, right from the beginning, by the multi-sensory method utilizing the advantages of phonic, whole-word and reading experience methods. All the while there must be constant underpinning with plentiful writing experience. If all three channels of learning and memory are stimulated, she claims that a child with perceptual weakness in one area will compensate from the start.

Cotterell (1976) illustrates a multi-sensory approach in working with Nigel, a severe auditory dyslexic:

Systematic step by step teaching was necessary using a multi-sensory approach. The Fernald (1943) and Norrie (1939) techniques were used, the latter being particularly useful for establishing the speech symbol link and for training sequencing skill. Through the building of words in syllable units, learning 'chunks' were naturally provided, and prefixes and suffixes were seen as well as heard. The Fernald Kinaesthetic technique was useful because of its non-phonic approach and its emphasis on learning the whole word through sight, sound and touch.

'If auditory perception is stronger than visual perception and kinaesthetic, the tuition should be based on phonics; the visual recall for words and the hand movements of written symbols should be trained in to support and reinforce what is learned through the auditory channel' (Pollock, 1976). This is the multi-sensory method. Cotterell (1970a) states: 'When writing a word I encourage vocalization, with clear articulation, so that kinaesthetic, visual and auditory pathways to the brain are all engaged to strengthen the memory pattern for recall.' Her method, emphasizing a writing or kinaesthetic approach, is multi-sensory. Sartain (1976) summarizes the treatment given by specialists as providing motivation, re-teaching specific skills, giving practice in consolidating sight words, using multi-sensory methods (auditory-phonetic analysis of words, visual analysis of words, writing of words and phrases), offering kinaesthetic practice and maintaining interest by using tapes and a variety of aids.

Shedd (1969) affirms one-to-one instruction, a multi-sensory approach and highly structured material as the critical ingredients of success. The Alphabetic-Phonetic-Structural-Linguistic (APSL) programme, employing methods similar to those of the UK dyslexia centres, is reported to have achieved a 2.77 grade score increase in nine months with 156 diagnosed dyslexics (grades four to eight) with three periods a week of special instruction, and two of class-based supportive work (Shedd, op. cit.). The use of para-professionals is reported (American Institute for Research, 1970) as successful in an APSL programme.

The Dyslexia Institute (1975) adopts multi-sensory methods at every step of a planned programme of structured language. The individual is helped to acquire the kind of imagery which is possible for him — whether visual, auditory, oral and/or kinaesthetic or a mixture of these. Hickey (1976) has produced a language training course for teachers and learners based on the methods of the Dyslexia Institute. The programme includes a manual, separate reading and spelling packs, a set of materials to be worked through and a tear-off pad for practising handwriting. The method is clearly multi-sensory.

Structure

Hornsby and Shear (1976), in their highly structured programme of teaching reading, writing and spelling, follow a step-by-step sequence which ensures that the pupil is at no point required to 'read or write any spelling pattern or language structure which has not been specifically taught'. The sequence, following the path by which language is acquired, is from the earliest sound patterns, associated with the alphabet, until all the possible combinations of letters required to produce 44 phonemes from the 26 available letters (17 vowel sounds and 27 consonants) are learned. The movement is then to *language structure*: content words first (nouns, verbs, adjectives); function words (prepositions, particles, etc.) last. When the pupil can synthesize sounds into words, and analyse words into their component parts, the words are used in sentences. And so more and more complex sentence structures are taught as basic skills are mastered.

The Dyslexia Institute (1975) advocates building up a child's programme step by step into a complete *structure* of spoken and written language to include reading and spelling. The course adopted is very similar to that followed by Hornsby and Shear (op. cit.) in the Dyslexia Clinic at St Bartholomew's Hospital, London.

> The phonograms are introduced in a certain order. Each one is presented in all its forms: capital, lower-case, printed and written. (The child) is taught how to arrive at the written form over the printed one. He then learns to acquire an accurate image for recall by using all his sensory pathways simultaneously: by looking at its shape, listening to its sound, saying its name and writing it. When the first phonogram is secure and he can recognise it for reading and recall it for spelling, he proceeds to the next one which is learned in the same multi-sensory way and linked to the first. In this way he learns syllables and reacts to the way they are to be read and spelt. From syllables he progresses to words and sentences. As he works through the structure and as the appropriate phonograms are learned, spelling rules and probable ways of spelling sounds are incorporated.

A careful record of progress through the structure is maintained. Nothing is taken for granted, and recall is based only on what has been included in the individual's programme. 'There is no confusion, only certainty and steadily increasing confidence in the pupil's own ability to learn' (Dyslexia Institute, op. cit.).

Hooton (1976) embraces the simplicity (one of Sampson's four points) notion in the teaching of reading and writing. She gives an example:

> Somewhere there must be a simple starting point. It will not always need to be as simple as in the case of one ten-year-old boy brought for help — all he could write was a dot. So we started there. He was praised for his dot and asked for another one. "Now could you do two dots?" "What about three green ones in a row?", and so on, one easy step at a time until within a very few months he was doing very beautiful printing, and reading what he had written.

Writing is begun with the drawing of straight lines and circles: directionality is taught from the beginning.

Teaching from strengths

This may be taken as a basic tenet of the remedialists. It is inherent in their adoption of multi-sensory techniques and it is evident in their practices. These practices will be examined in the succeeding section.

The methods and beliefs of the practitioners

The methods adopted by experienced practitioners are an important source of information. Are the methods used because they are successful, because they are derived from theory, because they have been designed for particular syndromes or because they work for the people who use them? Possibly all of these reasons are true. Whatever the truth, practitioners must be heeded if only because they are the people who are doing the teaching.

It is practitioners who in the end determine the success of remedial work. They adopt methods which have been developed in the past, adapt those methods to suit their own beliefs and circumstances and develop methods of their own. In this section will be summarized their views of specific learning difficulties (they use the term dyslexia), the practices they follow and their experiences in working with children with specific learning difficulties.

Chall (1967) surveyed methods of teaching reading, concluding that people often tended to be emotionally tied to a particular method of teaching reading. Asked why some children failed to learn to read authors of basal readers and proponents of phonics, linguistics, alphabet reform or language experience, all indicated that a return to their method would prevent reading failure! Such a measure of dogmatism does not appear evident in most of the work examined here.

Sampson (1976) suggests that the teacher interprets dyslexia as the total reaction of an individual child to a task which he has so far failed to master, and is therefore guided by her understanding of the actual demands (needs?) of the child. That is, the teacher is less concerned with aetiology than with understanding the immediate needs of the child and with using proven methods to attempt to meet those needs. Not being bemused with aetiology, she can use successfully a well-tried remedial procedure (perhaps with variations) with reading disabilities of disparate causes — possibly because of the confidence, based on professional competence, which she brings to the remedial relationship.

An important commitment by practitioners is to a multi-sensory approach. Advocacy of multi-sensory methods is based on acceptance of deficiencies in associational and perceptual functioning as a basis for learning difficulties. Sampson (op. cit.) notes that teachers subscribe in a general way to the theoretician's view but do not commit themselves as to the origins, or precise character, of the disability. Thus remedial specialists preserve the mystique of the healer (possibly unintentionally) while employing their own systematic and, often scientifically derived, methods. They also differ among themselves: Meredith bans the use of reading primers, Gillingham strictly limits their use, Fernald and Cotterell require the children to make their own reading materials and Newton favours using printed books as soon as possible. At one extreme reading is regarded as a decoding skill; at the other it involves interpreting meanings.

Agreed principles

The emphasis should be one of building on strengths: remedial re-education (Naidoo, 1970). The need for positive motivation and a sympathetic teacher (Naidoo, 1970; Cotterell, 1974) are noted. Methods should be tailor-made, teachers should have a knowledge of diagnostic assessment methods, there should be a minimum of two 20- to 30-minute periods a week, and there should be a conscious effort to reinforce an automatic association between sound (letter or word) and visual symbol (Naidoo, op. cit.). The child should be placed in school according to potential, not attainment.

The nature of the problems

Naidoo (1970) describes dyslexics as having deficits of auditory, vocal, visual and motor modalities in discrimination, perception and recall. Pollock (1976) agrees when she says that dyslexics need training to overcome weakness in auditory perception, visual perception, sequencing and orientation. However, the teacher should distinguish between poor visual perception and poor auditory perception; there is usually an overlap of weakness in both but with one often being stronger than the other. Remedialists report from experience that the degree of improvement is age-related. Vernon (1971) cites research which claimed that 82 per cent of dyslexics diagnosed in the first two grades at school could learn to read normally as the result of remedial teaching, as against 46 per cent in the fourth grade and 10 to 15 per cent in grades five to seven.

Auditory dyslexics

There is agreement that auditory dyslexics are difficult to teach (Cotterell, 1970a). Those with auditory/language deficits tend to make slower progress than those with visuo-perceptual and visual recall problems (Naidoo, 1970). They tend to be slow, indistinct and hesitant in speech, and to twist words in common speech (stelecope: telescope). Other characteristics (Cotterell, op. cit.) include: poor memory for words in common usage; poor auditory discrimination of words and sounds; difficulty in remembering days of the week, months of the year, the alphabet and multiplication tables; poor discrimination of short vowels (big, beg, bag); and inability to recognize rhymes. One teacher said of one boy, a severe auditory dyslexic, 'If Nigel had been a computer, one would have suspected a faulty connection or a crossed wire' (Cotterell, 1976).

Henry (1975) notes the youngster with auditory perceptual difficulties as having poor phonic knowledge or lack of phonic rules (e.g. diphthongs, digraphs). Because of difficulties in auditory perception, memory and integration, children are unable to deal with phonetic analysis. A whole-word approach is therefore chosen. Cotterell (op. cit.) regards the Fernald tracing method, in which tactile kinaesthetic learning is wedded with auditory kinaesthetic learning, as the most effective: 'When writing a word I encourage vocalisation, with clear articulation, so that kinaesthetic, visual and auditory pathways to the brain are all engaged to strengthen the memory pattern for "recall".' Cotterell (1970a) commends the typewriter as an excellent means of kinaesthetic reinforcement but, because it is not a 'whole-word' machine, considers that it should not be used with the Fernald technique.

Cotterell (1976) gives an excellent example of teaching a severe auditory dyslexic. In this case both the Fernald (1943) and Norrie (1939) techniques were used: the Fernald kinaesthetic technique because of its non-phonic approach and its emphasis on learning the whole word through sight, sound and touch; and the Edith Norrie Letter Case because of its value in establishing the speech symbol link and for training sequencing skill. 'Through the building of words in syllable units, learning "chunks" were naturally provided, and prefixes and suffixes were seen as well as heard' (Cotterell, 1976). Vernon (1971) reports no evidence as to the efficacy of whole-word methods for children who suffer from auditory and linguistic deficiencies or of phonic methods for those whose problems are primarily visual, as suggested by Naidoo (1970) and others. The practitioners clearly think otherwise. But is it more that there is uncertainty about which elements in the various methods make for success?

Pollock (1976) advocates teaching children to listen attentively and discriminate between sounds. She writes of initial training done by taping everyday sounds and having children identify them, or rattling objects such as a rubber and a penny in a tin and comparing the different sounds. But she insists that discrimination between letter-sounds follows. Again, although the sound games are likely to make for a pleasant learning environment – and that is important – it cannot be assumed that there is any carry over into learning letters, and words.

Partan (1978) summarizes a wide variety of remediation techniques for overcoming auditory problems. They include suggestions for improving auditory memory for directions (older boys often in need of this), how to cope with auditory distractions, improving auditory memory for letter sounds (see Wendon, 1970; Gillingham and Stillman, 1956), isolation of letter sounds (using multi-sensory methods, games, observing mouth with mirror while sounding), auditory blending and sequencing (kinaesthetic approach) and reading aloud or saying words aloud while spelling (consolidates the feel of words).

An interesting variation on coping with an auditory problem was reported by Dyer (1973) who used an oscilloscope with a bright 11½-year-old boy with a specific learning difficulty who could not differentiate vowel sounds. The oscilloscope enabled him to establish sound patterns visually and then, by practising with the oscilloscope, to learn to enunciate vowels correctly himself (his pronunciation had been awry). Once the feel of sound had been established – finger and thumb on the larynx and lip of his teacher, and then on his own, also helped – the child could be taken off the oscilloscope and work with Gattegno's *Colour Fidels* and *Word Charts* (Gattegno, 1969). His spelling improved 'out of all recognition because he had picked up the art of lip-reading the formation of vowels'. This is an interesting example of the adoption of techniques similar to those used in teaching the hearing-impaired.

Visual dyslexics

'If auditory perception is stronger than visual perception and kin-aesthetic, the tuition should be based on phonics; the visual recall for words and the hand movements of written symbols should be trained in to support and reinforce what is learned through the auditory channel' (Pollock, 1976). This is the multi-sensory method. There seems no disagreement among the practitioners (Cotterell, 1970a; Naidoo, 1970). Cotterell stresses the teaching of letter sounds, then digraphs and then how to blend into meaningful words. The *Stott Programmed Reading Kit* is regarded as a useful collection of games for letter sounds, blending and then recording.

Children with visual perception problems tend to reverse more letters and for longer than other children (b/d, p/b, d/g, u/n, m/w). Those who can perceive rhyme auditorily can proceed quite rapidly (Cotterell, op. cit.). Non-phonetic words are a problem (come, was, done, Mother). For these Cotterell uses mnemonics ('Mother Catches Moths'). Naidoo (1970) regards reinforcement and over-learning of phonically irregular words as necessary. Both Cotterell and Naidoo recommend use of the Edith Norrie Letter Case: Cotterell in begin-ning topic work and Naidoo to reinforce details of word patterns and letter sequence. Spelling problems are persistent even when fluent reading has been acquired.

Naidoo (1970) commends sympathetic, but firm, management and well-ordered short lessons. She recommends use of the typewriter for those children who have visual sequencing difficulties (how would this fit with Clay's (1977b) claim for the place of writing?), who reverse letters frequently when writing and whose penmanship is poor. The Fernald method is also recommended so that kinaesthetic cues can be utilized to assist and reinforce the visual patterns of words. Henry (1975) supports the introduction of phonics as soon as possible, the use of mnemonics and 'variety in presentation and practice'. Cashdan

(1974) cautions of the danger of producing, by phonic methods, a child who is very slow and deliberate and who focuses entirely on making the right noises at the black marks in front of him but who has no comprehension of what he is reading. To avoid that, Cashdan advocates providing a large variety of material, much of it below the child's present level, so he can read it fluently.

Pollock (1976) writes that programmes like the Frostig Programme for Training Visual Perception train a child to look carefully — a necessary accompaniment of successful reading. But, she says, any initial training in visual perception must be continued by discrimination between the shapes of letters and their visual recall. She may be accepting the transferability of Frostig-trained skills to reading, on faith.

Wendon (1970) reports a pictogram method for teaching the letters of the alphabet to dyslexic children. This method goes beyond the teaching of single letters to provide a code for 'interaction of letters in compound phonic units'. There are built-in visual clues for children with poor visual memories, built-in auditory clues for those with poor auditory memories, and familiar directional properties in the visual clues for children with poor left–right discrimination, or poor general ability in spatial orientation.

Mild dyslexics

Cotterell (1970a) offers suggestions. These are the children who have problems mainly with spelling. They may be reading fluently or haltingly at a nine-year level or above. Typically the spelling level is three or four years behind age. A formal approach is used. The emphasis is always on writing with constant reinforcement and over-learning when necessary. Teaching in the first place is through the student's ability to reason, whether or not the weakness is visual or auditory. Word structure, spelling rules and word derivation are studied (seven rules for this work). Cotterell has suggestions for short words, screening words, long words, syllabification, simple prefixes, scrambled meanings, suffixes, reading and mnemonics.

The dyslexic child in the classroom

Cotterell (1974) offers practical suggestions for coping with a dyslexic child in the classroom. Encouragement is desirable: a sympathetic teacher, a seat near the teacher and everything to foster motivation. Pressure must be removed. That includes avoidance of competition with classmates and a limit on homework. O'Bruba (1974) offers useful suggestions for helping children with perception difficulties in the ordinary classroom.

Help with written instructions (for comprehension and mathematics in particular) is advocated. At secondary school level it is better that notes not be required to be taken in class; better to copy a friend's notes later. There should be training in examination techniques – especially on how to précis and take notes. The student should be marked for his oral responses not his written ones (Cotterell, 1970c). Gulliford (1975) emphasizes the importance of the dyslexic child's being placed in the secondary school form appropriate for his ability: he must not be denied access to the curriculum.

Spelling remains a life-long handicap. Cotterell (1974) recommends the following: avoid stress; access to correct spellings is important; an indexed notebook should be used (dictionary too difficult); words should be said as they are spelled; words should be thought of as a collection of sounds or syllables not as alphabetic letters; reduction in the number of spelling words to be learned; mastery of spelling rules; and no demands for good writing.

The dyslexic child at home

Cotterell (1970c) emphasizes the importance of parental co-operation. The child needs the support of his parents. Parents are initially concerned with academic achievement or the vocational limitations which result from school failure; the sense of failure is greater when parents are ambitious. She suggests that working-class parents tend to be less concerned about academic success. Teachers tend to be less concerned when a family is illiterate and 'seldom seek help for such a child'. She advises parents to help a dyslexic child by fostering, and keeping alive, an interest in books.

An interesting point (cited by Sampson, op. cit.) is made by Meredith (1972): 'It is not the special difficulty with words that make the dyslexic's problems so serious. It is the massive, relentless pressure brought to bear on him through the anxiety of parents and the demands of schools.'

Some branch-line approaches

Morgan and Lyon (1978) report a 'paired-reading' technique which could work well for reading-retarded children who have a good working relationship with their parents. Simultaneous reading is carried out when parent and child read in unison. This is 'participant modelling' in which the parent furnishes a model of correct reading simultaneously with the child's attempt to read for himself. The child thus receives both visual and auditory stimuli. There is a further element. The child may signal at any time during paired-reading that he wishes to change to independent reading. If he makes an error which is corrected by the parent, simultaneous reading is reverted to. A pilot study with three boys and a girl showed 'marked' progress in reading ages and comprehension (but not spelling) in a 12- to 13-week period.

Jampolsky and Haight (1975) used a 'suggestive technique' with one boy to help him develop a more effective self-image. They argue that *pictures* people have of themselves determine behaviour far more than an *idea*. They worked with a boy who had basically good phonic skills and good reading and had a passive, restive attitude towards learning to read. By using suggestive techniques ('Close your eyes and imagine yourself with your teacher, enjoying and getting pleasure from reading'), he changed his attitude to reading dramatically, and retrieved his dormant skills to become an effective, interested reader overnight.

Specific reading difficulty: learned behaviour or deficit?

The principles set down by Stott (1978) in his diagnostic-remedial strategy would appear to affirm the importance placed on strengthening student motivation and the boost to self-esteem which success engenders. Having discovered in what ways the child has failed to use his cognitive capabilities, the aim should be to correct faulty learning habits and 'induce the child to bring his capabilities into play'. Rather than seeing the child as having certain deficits Stott sees learned behaviours as the root of the problem. Even if he is wrong, it is an optimistic view which, coupled with systematic teaching, promises success. Any use made of productive strategies on the part of the learner should be rewarded by success – a feeling of effectiveness: 'The main reinforcement should arise from the exercise of competence within the activity itself.' Remedial activities should be so loaded with effectiveness-enhancing opportunities that the child finds them as enjoyable as spontaneous play.

Support for Stott's 'learned behaviour' explanation for specific learning difficulty is provided with a study by Collete-Harris and Minke (1975). Two groups of six children (aged nine and ten years) were given either 'traditional' remedial reading treatment or behavioural therapy: positive reinforcement for correct responses during three phases of instruction (individual word phase, oral reading phase and silent reading phase). Both dyslexic and non-dyslexic subjects receiving the behavioural intervention improved in reading achievement to approximately the same degree, and the dyslexic subjects improved in several perceptual and attentional measures as well. The authors conclude that the results supported the theory that dyslexia can be viewed as a function of deficient learning history. The findings cannot be taken as definitive because of the smallness of the sample and the limited information given.

The Hawthorne effect

An interesting argument on this theme is developed by Parsons (1974). He suggests that inherent in all remediation programmes is the fact that when we work with the reading-disabled child we change what we do to the child. 'We give the child different materials, we make different demands, we place him in a different physical environment and, lo and behold, he begins to learn' (Parsons, op. cit., quoted in Gredler, 1978). Parsons would claim that the child has not been changed in any fundamental way but the adults have changed themselves. Gredler accepts that different demands are being made, that there is a different environment and 'frequently highly motivated and empathetic adults are involved to aid the child in the program'. That is, the Hawthorne Effect cannot be discounted.

Some well-known instructional methods

'Useful as test-related approaches ... may be in righting basic disabilities, direct instructional methods of alphabet-phonic type ... dominate the field in remedial work with dyslexics' (Sampson, 1976). Following are some of the better known package approaches including some which are not of the alphabet-phonic type. Sampson notes that convincing research evidence to guide workers in their choice of particular methods is slight and 'rarely relevant to the dyslexic condition in its severer forms'. Thus remedial specialists develop their own favoured approaches.

Alphabetic-phonic methods

The *Gillingham–Stillman Method* (Gillingham and Stillman, 1956 and later editions), deriving from Orton's (1966) theory, is based on linking letter-combinations of phonemes and digraphs to the appropriate sound. It is phonic but completely multi-sensory, using exercises and games to develop and reinforce auditory, visual, kinaesthetic and vocal abilities (Pollock, 1976). The pupil starts by learning the letters, taken in groups, with naming, feeling and sounding activities, practised in that sequence for each (Sampson, 1976). Familiar three-letter words are built up when consonants and vowels are known. Movement to more complex words and sentences takes place gradually. The demands on the children are rigorous and exacting, yet adaptable (Sampson, op. cit.). Wolf (1970) gives a straightforward description of the method in practice.

The *Edith Norrie Letter Case* (Arkell, 1970) is a well-validated piece of apparatus, highly regarded by practitioners (Cotterell, 1970a; Naidoo, 1970) and particularly useful for teaching children with visual recall and visual sequencing problems but also providing training in auditory perception and sequencing. It was devised by Edith Norrie, a Danish teacher, herself 'word blind', who founded the Word Blind Centre in Copenhagen in 1939. The Letter Case comprises cardboard or wooden letters, variously coloured and grouped phonetically: *vowels* are red (y has a red band to illustrate its vowel connection), and the child learns that every syllable must have a red letter in it; *voiced consonants* are green; and *unvoiced consonants*, black. Consonants are grouped: labials, 'the lip family' (m b v p w f) palatals, 'the tip of the tongue family' (n d t r l s c z j th ch sh) and gutturals, 'the back of the tongue family' (k g q x h y ng). Capitals are found at the bottom of each pile of letters, and there are separate compartments for full stops, commas, question marks and so on. The visual cues help the child learn the structure of words. A mirror provided enables him to 'see' how the sounds are made.

The apparatus is used as follows:

1. The child puts together a dictated sentence from the case of letters.
2. When done, he is asked to read it through. The sentence must be read exactly as written.
3. The teacher goes over what has been written with the child covering necessary points such as: omitted words or letters, syllabification, spelling, reversals, spelling rules.
4. The sentence is corrected.
5. The child copies the sentence into an exercise book.
6. As the child becomes confident, he writes sentences straight into an exercise book and uses the Letter Case as an aid.

Cotterell (1976) gives an example of how the Letter Case was used with a severe auditory dyslexic to establish the speech symbol link and train sequencing skill. Pollock (1976) sees the apparatus as primarily a spelling aid but useful in the early stages of reading.

Phonic Cues (Miles, 1970) is based on the teaching of reading through spelling. The child learns the short vowels in three-letter words, then in four-letter ones and so on. All words are recorded by the child in a personal dictionary. The procedure takes the child through 15 stages, each tested by graduated dictation exercises, until all phoneme combinations and spellings are covered (Sampson, 1976).

The *English Colour-Code Programmed Reading Course* is based on the colour coding of vowels. The approach is phonic. A one-to-one association is established between a single colour and a single sound. There are three stages. In the first, concentration is on letter recognition, initial consonant sounds and short vowel sounds. Stage two emphasizes the serial aspects of words and sentences. In the third stage the pupil concentrates on decoding words of three or four phonemes (Gessert, 1976).

The *Colour Phonic System* (Bannatyne, 1967, 1971) is based on the Edith Norrie Letter Case. This system comprises a set of individual letters and letter combinations colour coded in such a way that once the child has learned the coding system he can identify each sound. Once the child has mastered everything in the box he will be a competent reader. The system is based on the principle that dyslexic children have great difficulty in remembering constantly changing relationships between sounds and symbols and so require simultaneous stimulation of all the sensory modalities to strengthen and reinforce the learning pathways (Hicks, 1978).

Whole-word methods

The *Fernald Method* (Fernald, 1943) is the supreme example of the whole-word approach (Sampson, 1976). The method is basically kinaesthetic and whole-word rather than phonic. The technique is systematic:

1. The teacher writes a word with a crayon or flow-pen on a two-and-a-half-inch by 12-inch card which the child traces, saying the word as he does so. The child repeats the word until able to write it on a scrap of paper without looking at it.

2. After one to eight months the tracing stage is left out and the child learns the word by looking at it, saying it and writing it. In this way tactile-kinaesthetic is reinforced by auditory kinaesthetic.
3. In the next stage the child learns directly from the written word.
4. Finally, the child is able to recognize new words from their similarity to old ones.

Pollock (1976) considered the approach very useful when both auditory and visual perception were weak; when learning through touch and movement was the most effective mode. In such cases a modified method is in order. Letters are moulded in plasticene; the child feels them, tries to recognize them with his eyes shut, draws them in the air, on the table, on the blackboard — using whole arm and shoulder (thus building in physical memory traces?) — and traces over the outline of letters. These children need to write words in order to imprint them in the memory.

Harris (1956) considered the effectiveness of the method to lie in the way the child's attention was drawn to the structure of letters and words, and the order of letters in words. Sampson (1976) considered the procedure slow at first but that it trained the child to observe and retain letter and word detail in a meaningful sequence. Myers (1978), in a review of the literature on the use of Fernald's method with disabled learners, considered that there was no conclusive evidence on which to support or denigrate Fernald. The method worked for some but he thought that the addition of a kinaesthetic element to a visual programme did not result in better learning. Cotterell (1970b) thought the method really a look-say-and-do method rather than kinaesthetic. She considered it useful alongside the Edith Norrie Letter Case.

Vernon (1971) reported success for the method with children whose visual memory was poor. One study showed success with dyslexic children suffering from cortical dysfunction, caused by minimal brain damage, and dyslexic children without brain damage. Is the method successful because it builds in memory traces, or because it focuses the child's attention and appeals to the child's interests because the words learned are ones they choose themselves?

Clay (1977b) believes the reasons for success are complex. She says that to believe the success of the method 'lay in kinaesthetic imagery, the memory for the movement carried out, the feel of the words, or the feel of the letters is (a) myth'. The method of learning involves visual scanning, sounding in sequence, holding a memory for these things and feeling the movement of the sequence. She says that we cannot explain how movement, visual scanning and sound analysis relate to each other in producing a good reader. But she relates the success of this method to her own advocacy of a writing approach to reading.

Breakthrough to Literacy (Schools Council) is a whole-word, look-and-say, experience method based on the proposition that a child will learn more easily if he is able to manipulate printed language directly without the intervention of an adult (Gessert, 1976). The child chooses his own words and builds his own sentences from the materials provided. It is not designed for children with severe visual perception disabilities. The materials include a magnet board and sentence-maker with slots in which word cards can be placed. One of its excellent properties, according to Cashdan (1974), is that it does not penalize the child who may be slow to develop the motor co-ordination needed in writing. Further, he says, it incorporates 'really interesting' reading material, much of it based on children's actual language. Clay (1977b), on the other hand, describes the provision of a compendium of words to save the child the struggle of writing a word as a 'well-intentioned mis-guided myth' because it deprives the children of the opportunity to: trace letters and words; copy letters and words; order or sequence letters in words, or sequence words in sentences; visually scan and analyse letters in words; visually scan and analyse words in sentences; say and analyse words into sounds; and say and analyse sentences into words.

Mixed method

The *Initial Teaching Alphabet* (i.t.a.). The i.t.a. programme is an attempt to establish a direct link between written symbols and language sounds. There are 44 symbols to be learned, each one having only a single correct sound response. Materials include alphabet cards, workbooks and readers in i.t.a. script. Symbols are introduced gradually, beginning with the most frequently used consonants and short vowels. Transition to traditional orthography is usually accomplished towards the end of the second year.

Cashdan (1974) says of i.t.a. that it can be used successfully with either phonic or look-and-say methods. It can also lead to much freer, and earlier, writing on the part of the child. The biggest problem, he suggests, lies in making the transfer to traditional writing and spelling — but probably for a minority of children. It is thought that the switch should not be made to normal spelling until the child is reading well. Cashdan suggests that it is not clear how well children who start on i.t.a. will fare in spelling.

A writing approach to reading

Cotterell (1976) gives an account of a remedial programme with a severe auditory dyslexic boy which illustrates a writing approach to reading. She strongly recommends such an approach for those who do not absorb words by seeing them. Clay (1977b) considers that all children profit enormously from early creative writing, which provides the opportunity to: trace letters and words, copy letters and words, order or sequence letters in words, order or sequence words in sentences, visually scan and analyse letters in words, visually scan and analyse words in sentences, say and analyse words into sounds, and say and analyse sentences into words. 'And when a child writes the simplest message like "Here is Bill" that child has co-ordinated all those behaviours — the movements, the ordering, the visual scanning and the sound analysis. In saving the child effort we may be withholding opportunity.'

Chomsky (1971) suggests that children be introduced to reading through writing as a first activity. Clay (1977b) notes that the ability to analyse words into sounds is a prerequisite to writing and thus a logical sequence in learning to read. She notes that when children write they are forced to carry out an analysis of the words they want to write ' — a first to last segmenting of the sounds in the word. They pay attention to the sounds of words and search for a visual way of representing these' (Clay, op. cit.).

Cotterell (1970a) favours a writing approach to reading. She sees reading, writing and spelling as going alongside one another. She bases her methods of helping dyslexic children to learn the main structures of written language on Spalding's (1957) 'writing road to reading' method. Clay (1977b) endorses that method.

Early intervention: a complement to remediation

An early intervention *Reading Recovery Programme* (Clay, 1979a) which has been developed and trialled in Auckland, New Zealand, has considerable promise as a method of ameliorating early reading failure and thus lessening the incidence of later reading retardation and the need for much diagnostic-remedial intervention. The reading recovery approach derives from an information-processing model of reading behaviour. The child is not taught 'sets of items (letters, words, sounds) but how to carry out different kinds of operations on print, that is how to learn from each encounter with a new text' (Clay, op. cit.): the learner is active rather than passive; the goal is the development in children of self-motivated, self-correcting reading strategies rather than the inert reception of information about reading and how to do it.

The aims are simple and sensible:

- to undercut the reading problem at an early age when recovery is not too difficult
- to get every child started and moving steadily (not to get all children to a particular competence level)
- to keep the distribution of reading ability sufficiently homogeneous for teachers in standard classes who rarely know how to get a child started in reading
- to identify early (by six-and-a-half) the 'hard core' reading cases needing specialist ingenuity (Clay, 1979b).

A reading recovery programme should provide a sequence of opportunities for all children who, by the age of six-and-a-half years, should have had:

1. a chance to move into a reading programme in their own time under a trained new entrant (reception class) teacher
2. a survey of learning needs at six years of age by an experienced teacher, if they are in the bottom third of their age group for reading
3. a second chance to get started with individual teaching using special procedures that begin with their competencies
4. an option of specialist services if needed at six-and-a-half with consistent effort between six-and-a-half and eight years (Clay, 1979b).

The reading recovery approach acknowledges the presence of children with hard-core problems. These are the children who would probably fall into Yule and Rutter's (1976) third category — specific reading retardation — who might be dubbed 'dyslexic' by those who favour that label and who would certainly be the concern of this review: children with specific learning difficulties. 'Clinic tuition from trained experts will still be needed for the latter group but they will also profit from the "Reading Recovery" programme because they would be identified by six-and-a-half years at the latest' (Clay, 1979b). This

approach appears to meet the recommendations of the Tizard Report
(1972) — particularly the first three, which recommend screening of
all children for reading backwardness at the end of the infant stage,
a continuing check on children identified as backward in reading and
the availability of skilled remedial teaching in the ordinary school for
children with specific reading backwardness.

An evaluation of reading recovery

Clay (1979a) reports an evaluative study. In 1978 reading recovery
programmes were introduced into five Auckland suburban schools.
The schools differed in size, organization (two were open-plan), ethnic
composition and socio-economic make-up. Experienced teachers (one
in each school), who had taught for an average of 8.8 years, were
released for full-time teaching on a one-to-one basis. The aim was to
survey all children whose sixth birthdays fell between 1 September,
1977, and 30 September, 1978, and to tutor those who were achieving
in the lowest third in reading in their schools. Children were tested as
near as possible to their birthdays, the mean age of testing being six
years 1.5 months.

The five teachers were trained to administer the tests of the *Diagnostic Survey* (Clay, 1972, 1979a) and to write a *Diagnostic Summary
Report* which analysed the child's useful reading strategies and problem
strategies on *each* of text, words and letters. From the 291 children
who met the age criterion, and who had already been in a reading
instruction programme for one year, a group of 122 children (42 per
cent) were given special help. In the last two months of 1978, 282 of
the original 291 children (nine could not be traced) were retested, by
independent testers, on book level, reading vocabulary and other tests
of reading and writing skills (Clay, 1972, 1980). Two groups of children
were admitted to individual tutoring: the first had learned very little
about reading; the second were reading but had gaps in their reading
behaviours. Children in this second group tended to make rapid
progress and leave the programme after about six weeks.

Programme and methods were regarded as flexible but the underlying rationale was agreed, and approaches had been developed and
modified in an intensive development period, in which six tutor-
teachers with specialist knowledge worked with selected 'very difficult
cases' for two 40-minute lessons each week during four teaching terms
in 1976-7. The goal of teaching was to help the children develop self-

improving error-detecting strategies which would enable them to read text.

Children were seen individually on any timetable that suited the teacher and the school. This could be once a day (30-45 minutes) or twice a day for two sessions of 30 minutes and 10 minutes. Children received daily instruction: that is an essential feature of the programme.

A typical tutoring session was:

- re-reading of two or more familiar books   Text
- letter identification (plastic letters on a magnetic board)   Letters
- writing a story   Text
- sound analysis of words (Elkonin technique)   Sounds
- cut-up story to be rearranged   Text
- new book introduced   Text
- new book attempted   Text

The bias to text was deliberate since children were to return to existing reading groups in their classrooms as soon as possible and they needed the appropriate behaviours in order to fit in and to feel good about themselves (Clay, op. cit.).

The teachers' manual, a draft document, was treated as a resource book rather than as a set of directions. It was substantially modified in the course of the study and a final revision produced at the end. The Research Co-ordinator visited each school fortnightly, and all teachers came together with the researchers for a fortnightly demonstration and discussion session. As the year progressed, the teachers' attention to the reading process seemed to shift 'from teaching for items of knowledge (letters known, words remembered), and from getting the child to habituate a skill or memorise an element, to developing in the child the confidence and willingness to use a variety of strategies' (Clay, 1979a). This, of course, is a fundamental element of the reading recovery approach.

Three groups were differentiated. *Discontinued Group:* those who entered the programme earlier because of date of birth, were given individual tuition, and then returned to their reading groups when judged to be capable of independent progress; this group gained most during the programme, continued to gain after the programme and moved to, or above, the total group mean by the end of the year. *Programme Group:* those who entered the programme later because of birth date, had initial scores much lower than the first group but who gained at a comparable rate; the children in this group were not ready to leave the programme after an average time of 13 weeks in tuition. They appeared to need further time in the programme. *Other Group:* children who did not need special individual tuition.

The results of the study were reported to be encouraging. 'Educationally important gains were made by all children receiving individual tuition.' Significant gains were made by the discontinued children. Children who needed more intensive help were picked up early. The programme was continued in 1979 in 49 Auckland schools, with a class teacher freed for individual teaching for two hours every day. This is a small time-allocation especially when seen against Clay's observation that a small school could use 0.5 of a teacher for reading recovery work, most schools one to 1.5 and a large school (700 children?) two teachers.

The Reading Recovering procedures (Clay, 1979a) have been carefully worked out in the field. They have substantial research backing (Clay, 1977a, 1979b), and are 'in line with a body of theory about the ... reading process that is supported by recognized experts' (Goodman, 1972; Smith, 1977). The approach is an evolving one but with its emphases on the reading process, on the child's ability to learn how to fashion his own learning strategies, on the importance of teacher observation, on the central place of the teacher, and on the necessity for, and effectiveness of, early intervention, it has considerable promise. However, research data on the 1979 programme, and on the effectiveness of 'reading recovery' for children with specific learning difficulties, will be awaited with interest before wholesale adoption of the programme.

Summary of chapter

The practitioners and writers on children with specific learning difficulties are agreed on certain principles of remediation. These include individualizing instruction, over-learning, the importance of structure and teaching from strengths. Some cautionary voices are raised against intensive individual work if it puts undue pressure on the child. A distinction is made between having an individual programme and teaching on a one-to-one basis. Techniques of remediation, and materials for use, with 'dyslexics' who have deficiencies in particular modalities are discussed: visual dyslexics and auditory dyslexics, in particular. The techniques used have roots back to early teachers and theorists but are enhanced by the insights and experiences of sensitive

teachers. To that extent, practice is well established, though not necessarily grounded in contemporary theory on how children master the
intricacies of language.

A particular approach, Reading Recovery, which calls on recent
theory and research is described. It suggests a strategy for discovering
difficulties early and doing something about them. The emphasis is on
intervention in the school but acknowledges a place for remedial
specialists for children with severe difficulties.

Chapter 6

Conclusions and Future Trends

Conclusions
Summaries of the various sections of each chapter have been made throughout the report. This final chapter will bring together the main points.

Terminology
No definition of specific learning difficulties was given in the second chapter. Rather, there was an attempt initially, to reconcile the various definitions in the dyslexia group with the concept of retardation, and then to justify the adoption of specific learning difficulties as a suitable generic term. It was suggested that specific reading retardation, as defined by Yule and Rutter (1976), and dyslexia, were essentially the same thing. Children covered by both labels show similar learning problems and characteristics including average, or better, intelligence, and both are characterized by the severity of the overall learning problem. The main point of departure is that specific reading retardation does not necessarily imply a constitutional element; and as well, it may arise from lack of suitable environmental stimulation.

The term specific learning difficulties extends the ambit of specific reading difficulties to include other subjects such as spelling, writing and mathematics but retains the essential central element of intractable seriousness while not necessarily excluding children of less than average intelligence. There appears to be no ready criterion to hand which justifies excluding children with less than average intelligence from the specific learning difficulties category. Any special provision within schools should include these children. The evidence is clear that there are, as the Warnock Report says, 'children whose disabilities are marked but whose general ability is at least average', but it is difficult to accept the conclusion that there should be 'distinctive arrangements' made for these children without such arrangements being made for all children with specific learning difficulties – including those of below average intelligence.

At this point, a definition of specific learning difficulties is proposed:

> Children with specific learning difficulties are those who, in the absence of sensory defect or overt organic damage, have an intractable learning problem in one or more of reading, writing, spelling and mathematics, and who do not respond to normal teaching. For these children, early identification, sensitive encouragement, special teaching and specific remedial arrangements are necessary.

The definition is deliberately broad to allow inclusion of serious difficulty regardless of aetiology and level of ability. By avoiding an exclusive categorization – which the evidence does not support in any case – the obligation of the education system to all children is affirmed.

Aetiology

During the past few decades, there has been a heavy concentration of research on the aetiology of specific learning difficulties. This shows no sign of abating, but some overall areas of agreement and developing trends can be discerned amongst the welter of information. There is still interest in the question of whether learning disabled children are suffering from actual brain damage but current concern is with 'soft' neurological signs, which tend to be implied rather than measured, and with abnormal EEG findings. Both these aspects of neurological dysfunction present problems of definition and measurement, and although there is some evidence of their association with specific learning difficulties, it is also the case that good readers may show similar patterns of abnormality. It is probably best to view neurological dysfunction as one of the many aetiological correlates of reading disability or as the basis of a separately identifiable group of poor readers.

There has been increasing interest recently in the area of neurological functions, especially those appertaining to cerebral dominance and information-processing. Despite some findings suggesting a relationship between some laterality measures and reading disability for clinic samples, evidence from large-scale surveys has failed to find a similar association. It may be that poor laterality or ill-established cerebral dominance varies with intelligence and age so that only less intelligent and younger children are affected, but more information is needed to clarify this point. Of greater importance, the majority of children with laterality problems have no reading difficulties, and furthermore severe reading disability is not more frequently present in children who are poorly lateralized.

A more promising area of research concerns hemispheric asymmetry and information-processing. Evidence is building up on the functions of the two hemispheres and their interconnections, and investigations in the field of reading disabilities have been related to left hemisphere dysfunction and poor inter-hemispheric processing. There is some indication that poor readers are deficient in left hemisphere functions such as language, speech and analytic sequential processing of information, and even that they may have different patterns of hemispheric function and inter-hemispheric processing from normal or good readers. The blossoming of interest in the information-processing approach has led to the discovery of much useful information. In particular it has been shown that dyslexic children (most of the studies in this area are of dyslexic children) experience delay in the *initial* processing of information, and show deficiencies in the *co-ordination* of both visual and auditory information and in the *retention* and *co-ordination* of information overtime. This has led many researchers to suggest that such children show deficiencies in short-term memory and sequencing ability. Finally, it has also become clear that an additional problem arises when the featural information has to be named or labelled, which is essential during the process of reading.

The information-processing approach has also been used to analyse the successive aspects of the reading process, and, as such, represents one of the few links between theoretical and practical considerations. Increasing attention has been paid recently to the analysis of the skills involved in reading, especially lower-level skills such as grapheme/phoneme correspondence and coding, and higher-level skills such as semantic skills and reading strategies, in which retarded readers have frequently been found lacking. Reading disability models have been developed which attempt to classify some of the evidence collected into meaningful structures. Of these, the sub-skills type of model and in particular the process-oriented type of model look to be the most fruitful.

It has been suggested by some writers that the reading retarded can be classified into various subgroups, of which language disorders could form the basis of one. Others identified in the literature are based on auditory or visual deficiencies or various combinations of these and other deficiencies. Although it seems useful to classify retarded readers according to their primary difficulties, there are serious drawbacks. It is by no means certain that the subgroups isolated are in fact discrete and homogeneous forms. Evidence for different variations of subgroups is conflicting and confusing, and it is not clear whether individuals who are included in one group are also eligible for others. Furthermore eligibility for different groupings may change with age and increasing ability to read. It may, in the long run, be preferable to treat individuals according to the specific reading difficulties they show rather than according to a hypothetical pattern of deficiencies which places them in a limited category.

The question of subgroups has also arisen in connection with perceptual deficiencies, which we have classed as secondary correlates. While there is plentiful evidence of an association of defects in auditory, visual and spatial perception with poor reading, it is not without contradiction. There has been a general shift of interest from perceptual discrimination to memory and sequencing aspects of perception and a recent renewal of concern with auditory and visual acuity. However, it is by no means clear that perceptual defects cause poor reading; rather the reverse is accepted, and further, there is no evidence that perceptual training, whilst it may improve perceptual shortcomings, actually improves reading performance. Other secondary correlates, such as physical, emotional and environmental factors continue to receive attention, but new areas of interest include cognitive style, attentional factors and drug studies, although the findings are as yet inconclusive and of questionable relevance to reading disability.

Throughout the literature on the causes of specific learning difficulties, it has been suggested that a lag in development or maturation may be responsible for at least some of the difficulties faced by retarded readers. Although there is a certain amount of evidence that some early developing aspects associated with reading such as manual preference and visual perception may be affected by maturational lag, there is little evidence that later developing aspects, such as verbal and language skills are similarly affected. There is also no explanation as to why good readers should not be likewise affected. In addition, the long-term prognosis for retarded readers is not good and while this is the case the concept of maturational lag must remain in doubt.

A final point concerns the question of the extent to which the term *specific learning difficulties* is limited to reading or encompasses difficulties with spelling, writing and arithmetic, together with associated speech disorders. It has been the general finding that children with severe and intractable reading problems frequently find difficulty in particular with spelling, and to a lesser extent with writing and arithmetic. They also tend to have a higher than average incidence of speech disorders or delayed speech development. It is our conclusion, then, that *specific learning difficulties* includes these other related difficulties.

Incidence

The general picture regarding the incidence rates for specific learning difficulties is one of confusion. There are problems of definition and measurement, and the variety of different sources makes it difficult to compare figures. Socio-economic and regional variables, plus age and sex differences, all add to the overall complexity of the problem.

Nevertheless some general conclusions can be drawn. Firstly, the estimates tend to cluster around three levels: the highest level, ranging from about 20 per cent upwards, resulting in a very general category, of which reading difficulty is one aspect a middle group clustering around five to 15 per cent, depending on the exact criteria used, but including both backward and retarded readers; and a 'hard core' group of children with severe and specific reading and associated difficulties, amounting to between two and five per cent. Secondly, there is a preponderance of boys with specific reading difficulties, in the order of the ratio three to one for total child populations and four or five to one for clinic samples. Thirdly, there is a higher prevalence rate for urban and economically deprived areas. Fourthly, the figures suggest a fairly even spread of incidence over the entire range of school-age children, although most studies have concentrated on the eight–11 age range. Fifthly, a sizeable proportion of children identified are either receiving no treatment or receiving treatment that is not specifically suited to their needs.

Remediation

Consensus and evidence would appear to concur on the value of analysing *learning characteristics* and behaviours rather than on categorization as such. It is a moot point whether describing a child as having visual perception problems, for example, gives the teacher information which she can use compared with specific information on what a child knows and can do in, say, reading. If a description of learning characteristics leads to a particular diagnosis, that is incidental to the main objective, which is to produce information which will point the way to appropriate teaching, learning and remedial strategies.

The *efficacy of remedial treatment* remains unclear. Studies have frequently not specified remedial methods and have too often employed inadequate methods and tools of evaluation. Individual variations within groups have not been described, being hidden in mean scores and quantitative data: important and significant gains made by individuals may thus have been masked. Studies which have attempted to isolate dyslexic groups give little cause for optimism, there being disagreement on definitions and criteria. Follow-up studies of seriously retarded children after remedial treatment do not reveal substantial results, but more data are needed if the evaluation is to be convincing. On balance the research studies may tell us more about research methodology than about the success of remedial treatment. Approaches discussed under *remedial methods* below give more cause for optimism.

The discussion on *assessment and diagnosis* noted the contemporary quest for prescription — for data and information that could be translated into remedial action. To yield this information the teacher is seen as a vital contributor, with observation, and informal, but systematic, methods assuming importance. The strategies which the child brings to the task are regarded as a prime target for observation and assessment. Support for the teacher from a 'special educator' in the school will be desirable.

It is suggested that the place of standardized tests in assessing children with specific learning difficulties has been overstated. Such tests should not be dismissed in this context, but the criterion of relevance for teaching and learning applied to the results of testing. Nevertheless the place of the psychologist in the assessment process is regarded as important — as much for the insights which he or she draws from the assessment relationship as for the results of standardized tests. The relevance of standardized tests of achievement for assessing progress — especially, perhaps, for research purposes — and for establishing levels of achievement, is accepted, but not uncritically, as tools for assessing learning strategies, behaviours and comprehensive achievement.

Early assessment is seen as one of the most important elements in a concerted attempt to provide for children with specific learning difficulties. The importance of catching children young is agreed, although ways of doing that are in the melting pot. Two integrated approaches were examined, and some doubts cast on the validity of one, which derived from the psychometric tradition. The other approach, which is more avowedly prescriptive, and based on observation of children at work on relevant educational tasks, appears to offer a method of early identification which could circumvent later problems and enable corrective teaching at an age when optimum responsiveness and effectiveness are likely.

The literature on *remedial methods* is a story of patient building up, by dedicated practitioners, of techniques and methods which appear to work with children showing various kinds of problem. In general, practices seem to have long-established roots and to go back to formulations and theories of some years ago. Where remedial teachers use the results of standardized tests of underlying functions it appears to be to complement the information they have already gleaned from their own assessments. The remedial procedures being used are probably sound, but good studies verifying their effectiveness do not appear to be available. One example is the advocacy of a writing approach to reading. This method has substantial expert backing, both on practical and theoretical grounds, and appears to have underpinning from contemporary theory. Research which looked at the approach would be desirable.

A significant innovation in ameliorating reading failure is the Reading Recovery Programme developed by Clay (1979a) in New Zealand. This approach, following on from the early assessment stage discussed above, aims to teach children with reading problems effective learning strategies and to give them confidence and motivation to move ahead independently. The place of the trained expert who would give help to children with hard-core problems is an integral part of this programme. The departure may be that the programme as a whole, including the work of the specialist, is school-based.

Future trends

It is no part of this review to make recommendations on what should be done in the field of specific learning difficulties. But there are some issues which are likely to influence future trends. We think the following to be significant.

1. *Specific learning difficulties*, if adopted as the generic term, is likely to open the way for provision for a greater number of children than if more circumscribed terms are used.
2. If present thinking on school-based provision continues, developments for children with specific learning difficulties will be firmly centred on the school. Early screening or survey procedures will be established practice, teachers will be trained to deal with children with specific learning difficulties, and specialists, whose job will be to support teachers and provide teaching for children with hard-core difficulties, will be permanent members of school staffs.
3. Assessment procedures, if based on present advocacy, will increasingly involve teachers who will be seen to have a key role through observation, and the use of systematic non-normative techniques, in the initial and continuing assessment of children with specific learning difficulties.
4. Assessment techniques and materials are likely to be based on knowledge of how children learn, and on real educational tasks, rather than on standardized tests designed to measure underlying functions. The development of such approaches will be seen as research priorities.
5. If teachers are to be competent to fulfil the roles outlined in 2 and 3 above, initial teacher education and training, in-service training and continuing education will all contribute to improved teacher competence and confidence.
6. With prevailing uncertainty about the effectiveness of remedial methods, research will be initiated which evaluates various methods — particularly those employed by acknowledged experts in specialist clinics and centres. The methods and beliefs of the practitioners are a potentially fruitful source of teaching insights.
7. Long-term follow-up studies of children identified as having specific learning difficulties are likely to be seen as essential if informed judgements are to be made as to their initial and long-term characteristics and prospects.
8. Studies will be required which cover a wider age range than has hitherto been dealt with, for example comparing seven-, nine-, 11-, 13- and 15-year-olds in respect of their specific difficulties according to age and, in particular, investigating the main differences between primary and secondary school-age children in this area.

9. If pleas in the literature are to be heeded, there will be a great need for more detailed information on the incidence of specific learning difficulties, as distinct from backwardness in general. This could be accomplished by comparative studies of several areas, which would overcome the shortcomings of both clinic population and total population studies which are limited to one area.

10. There is likely to be a continuing interest in the skills involved in the reading process, incorporating the information-processing approach to this topic.

Appendix

Current DES sponsored research

1. A follow-up study of a group of children admitted to the Word-Blind Centre some years ago (Professor O. Zangwill, University of Cambridge). The project is to investigate the educational and occupational history of a group of ex-pupils from the Centre and to establish their current attainment level in reading, spelling and related skills. The aim is to facilitate a more adequate assessment of the course and progress of specific educational disabilities, and to throw light on the problem of social adjustment and employment faced by backward readers.

2. Educational testing of CHES (Child Health and Education in the Seventies) cohort to identify children with specific learning disabilities (Professor N. Butler, University of Bristol). This cohort is a nationally representative sample of around 15,000 children born between 5 and 11 April, 1970, which is already the subject of a ten-year study funded by the DHSS and the Joseph Rowntree Memorial Trust. This project will aim to assess their educational progress and to identify and examine the problems of those who are slow learners, poor achievers or have specific reading or learning disabilities. All the children will be screened as they reach ten years of age with a battery of tests of maths, reading, pictorial language, British Ability Scales, and a pupil questionnaire. The results will permit multi-variate examination of the effect on social, school, familial and medical factors on educational performance.

3. A pilot study into the teaching needs of seven-year-old pupils (of near-average ability and above) who display specific difficulties in reading, writing and spelling (Professor T. Miles, University College of North Wales). This involves testing a sample of ten seven-year-olds who display such problems, providing a year's teaching in language skills with specific reference to reading, writing and spelling, and then re-testing after a year. This is to be accompanied by a follow-up study of 90 pupils about one-and-a-half years after their discharge from the University College of North Wales Dyslexia Unit.

4. Assessment and incidence of special educational need: a pilot study for an investigation into the ways in which practising classroom teachers might come to identify children in need of special educational provision (Professor G. Bernbaum, University of Leicester). This involved a study of two classrooms in each of six junior schools in Leicestershire. By means of observation, testing, and extended inter-views with teachers and heads, the study aimed to analyse the aspects of behaviour and performance which lead to children being identified as having special educational needs, and the influence on this process of the teacher's knowledge and perceptions of school and local authority policies and provisions. The results of the pilot study are now with the Department, and it has been agreed in principle that it will be followed up by a much larger project.

5. Prevalence and characteristics of children with specific learning difficulties: a project to determine the incidence of SLD children in the school population of a defined LEA, and to identify variables that discriminate between children with normal abilities, slow learners and children who have specific reading and/or number difficulties (Dr A. Dobbins and Professor D. G. Pritchard, University College of Swansea). This will involve (subject to the agreement of the authority) the screen-ing of all nine- to ten-year-old children in West Glamorgan (probably around 5,500) by testing their general ability, reading ability, spelling and number ability. This will enable the identification of children with specific reading and/or number difficulties who will then be the subject of further in-depth testing. It is hoped that the first phase will provide information that can be utilized by LEAs in planning provision for remedial teaching in reading or numbers for those with specific diffi-culties. The second phase will provide an in-depth data base on the performance profiles of children with specific reading and specific

number difficulties, as well as a test battery, with appropriate weightings, that will concurrently identify children with specific reading and/or number difficulties.

6. Action research project — dyslexic pupils (Mr C. Tyre, University College Cardiff). Three groups of 15 children will be selected from Mid Glamorgan, South Glamorgan, and Gwent. Group A will be 15 pupils diagnosed as dyslexic by recognized independent bodies or specialists. Group B will be 15 pupils selected by LEAs with individual profiles closely matching those of the children in Group A. The third group will be a control group of children, again with similar individual profiles. Intensive precision teaching programmes will be designed to meet the needs of the pupils in Groups A and B, and in-service programmes will be designed for the parents of the children in those groups (the parents' commitment to the project will be a condition of their children taking part) and for teachers. The children in Groups A and B will be treated by structured home tuition by parents who have received in-service training, by support tuition on a regular basis by the teacher/adviser, and by concentrated tuition of three weeks in three sessions at a residential school in school holiday time within a period of one year from teachers who have received the in-service training. The progress made over the year by all 45 pupils will then be evaluated by statistical analysis and individual case studies. At time of writing, details of this project are still being finalized and so the above description may be slightly altered by the time it starts in mid 1981.

7. An integrated diagnostic remediation procedure (Mr G. E. F. Trickey, University College London). The aim of the project is to produce a properly standardized battery of diagnostic tests concerned with reading-related skills, each of which would have specific teaching implications and which would dovetail into a fully integrated component programme system. This will be based on work already done over the past four years by the Barking Schools' Psychological Service (of which Mr Trickey is the Principal Educational Psychologist). The project will use existing data from Barking, and an additional sample of 200 children who will be given a group reading test and all the sub-tests of the diagnostic test battery. The project will allow a thorough review of the existing battery by individual items, for internal consistency, for range of applicability and for efficacy.

Glossary

agnosia:	inability to attach meaning to sensory impressions.
agraphia:	special difficulty in learning to write and spell.
alexia:	inability or unusual difficulty in learning to read.
angular gyrus:	region of the left hemisphere of the brain where triple connections can be made among visual, auditory and kinaesthetic areas.
anoxia:	deficiency of oxygen in body tissues.
aphasia:	loss of speech and inability to comprehend language.
apraxia:	inability to perform tasks requiring intricate muscular co-ordination.
asymbolia:	inability to use or understand language.
ataxia:	imperfect control of voluntary movements.
binocular fusion:	fusion of images perceived by both eyes.
cerebral dominance:	primary control by one hemisphere of the brain of specific function (in this case language).
choreiform movements:	jerky, spasmodic movements.
constructional apraxia:	loss of ability to perform purposeful movements of construction which is not due to any paralysis or sensation loss.
contingent negative variation (CNV):	a direct current (DC) shift in man that occurs in the interval between a signal and the subject's response to it.

corpus callosum: a bridge of fibres connecting the two hemispheres of the brain.

crossed laterality: inconsistent preference for one side of the body in eye, hand, ear and foot usage, e.g. right-handed child using left eye for sighting under binocular conditions.

deep dyslexia: difficulty in reading and writing at later stages in the process of reading, thus typically characterized by output rather than input defects, thought to be associated with partial damage of the left hemisphere which leads to the use of a reading system located in the right hemisphere.

digraph: group of two letters representing one sound. Two letters (vowel or consonant) representing one phoneme.

directionality: ability to determine right and left outside one's body.

dyscalculia: inability to perform the operations of arithmetic.

dysgraphia: extreme difficulty or inability to produce the written form.

dysrhythmia: defective speech rhythm.

electroencephalogram (EEC):   graphic record of electrical discharges from the brain.

eurythmy: harmony of bodily movement.

finger agnosia: loss of awareness as to which finger is which without loss of sensation from the fingers.

Gerstmann Syndrome: a group of symptoms which may result from a lesion in the dominant parietal lobe, characterized by a failure of directionality and forming of conceptions allied with this function, which leads to finger agnosia, right–left confusion, writing disturbances and deficiency in mathematical ability.

grapheme: single letter shape.

haptic: pertaining to sensitivity to pressure or, loosely, touch.

icon: an image, representative or symbolic.

ideognostic (dyscalculia):   disability primarily in understanding mathematical ideas and relations and in doing mental calculation.

kinaesthetic: appertaining to muscle sense and movement, by which weight, motion and position are perceived.

laterality: awareness within the individual of sidedness (left/right), especially of sensory (ear, eye) and motor (hand/foot) mechanisms and the left and right hemispheres of the brain in their involvement with different functions.

morpheme: smallest meaningful unit of form.

nystagmus: rapid oscillation of the eyeballs.

occipital lobe: one of the major divisions of the cerebrum, at the back of the head behind the parietal lobe and above the temporal lobe.

orthography: correct or conventional spelling.

parietal lobe: one of the major divisions of the cerebrum, between the frontal and occipital lobes and above the temporal lobe.

phoneme: smallest unit of sound.

practognostic (dyscalculia):   disturbance of mathematical manipulation.

praxis: the doing or performance of action. Action by command.

protocol: the record of an experiment made during, or immediately after, the experiment.

saccadic movements: the sudden movement of the eyes from one fixation point to another, as in reading.

strephosymbolia: the perception of objects reversed as in mirror images.

symbolia: global identification of word as a whole, as a symbolic entity related to meaning.

tachistoscope: apparatus for rapid presentation of visual stimuli, at controlled time intervals or light intensities.

temporal lobe: that part of the cerebrum just below the fissure of sylvius and in front of the occipital lobe.

References

ABRAMS, J. C. (1968). 'Dyslexia – single or plural'. Paper presented at National Reading Conference, Los Angeles. Available from: 1968 Yearbook of the National Reading Conference.

ABRAMS, J. C. (1970). 'Learning disabilities – a complex phenomenon', *The Reading Teacher*, 23, 4, 299–303 and 367.

ACKERMAN, A. (1974, Revised 1979). *The Importance of Motivation*. London: Helen Arkell Dyslexia Centre.

ADAMS, P. (1968). 'Patterns of intellectual functioning in learning disabled children and their siblings compared with successful students and their siblings', *Bulletin of the Orton Society*, 18, 40–8.

ADAMSON, W. C. and ADAMSON, K. K. (1979). *A Handbook for Specific Learning Disabilities*. New York: Gardner Press.

ADELMAN, H. S. (1979). 'Diagnostic Classification of LD: practical necessity and a procedural problem', *Learning Disability Quarterly*, 2, 2, 56–62.

ALLEN, W. (1971). 'An investigation into the suitability of the use of effort as a teaching method for motor impaired children', *Research Papers in Physical Educ., Carnegie School of Physical Educ.*, 2, 1, 18–23.

ALLINGTON, R. *et al.* (1976). 'Poor and normal readers' achievement on visual tasks involving high frequency, low discriminability words', *J. of Learning Disabilities*, 9, 5, 292–6.

ALWITT, L. F. (1963). 'Decay of immediate memory for visually presented digits among nonreaders and readers', *J. of Educnl. Psychol.*, 54, 3, 144–8.

AMAN, N. G. and SPRAGUE, R. L. (1974). 'The state dependent effect of methylphenidate and dextroamphetamine', *J. of Nerv. Ment. Dis.*, 158, 268–79.

AMERICAN INSTITUTE FOR RESEARCH (1970). *Model Programmes: Childhood Education Perceptual Development Centre Programme*. Washington D.C.: American Institute for Research.

ANASTASI, A. (1976). *Psychological Testing*. New York: Macmillan.

ANDERSON, I. H., BYRON, O. and DIXON, W. R. (1956). 'The relationship between reading achievement and the method of teaching reading', *Univ. Mich. Sch. Educ. Bull.*, 7, 104.

ANNETT, M. (1970). 'Handedness, cerebral dominance and the growth of intelligence'. In: BAKKER, D. J. and SATZ, P. (Eds). *Specific Reading Disability*. Rotterdam: Rotterdam University Press.

ANNETT, M. (1972). 'The distribution of manual asymmetry', *Br. J. of Psychol.*, 63, 343–58.

ANNETT, M. and TURNER, A. (1974). 'Laterality and the growth of intellectual abilities', *Br. J. Educ. Psychol.*, 44, 39–46.

ANTHONY, G. (1968). 'Cerebral dominance as an aetiological factor in dyslexia', unpublished doctoral dissertation, New York University.

APPLEBEE, A. N. (1971). 'Research in reading retardation: two critical problems', *J. Child Psychol. and Psychiat.*, 12, 2, 91–113.

ARKELL, H. (1970). 'The Edith Norrie Letter Case'. In: FRANKLIN, A. and NAIDOO, S. (Eds) *Assessment and Teaching of Dyslexic Children*. London: Invalid Children's Aid Association.

ARNETT, J. L. (1977). Early visual information processing as a function of age and of reading ability. Doctoral dissertation, University of Manitoba.

ASSO, D. and WYKE, M. (1971). 'Discrimination of spatially confusable letters by young children', *J. of Exceptional Child Psychol.*, 11, 1, 11–20.

AVERBACH, E. and CORIELL, A. S. (1961). 'Short-term memory in vision', *Bell System Tech. J.*, 40, 309–28.

BADDELEY, A. D. (1966). 'Short-term memory for word sequences as a function of acoustic, semantic and formal similarity', *Q. J. Exp. Psychol.*, 18, 362–5.

BADDELEY, A. D. (1968). 'How does acoustic similarity influence short-term memory?', *Q. J. Exp. Psychol.*, 20, 249–64.

BADDELEY, A. D. (1970). 'Effects of acoustic and semantic similarity on short-term paired associate learning', *Br. J. Psychol.*, 61, 335–43.

BADDELEY, A. D. (1978). 'Discussion of papers in dyslexia symposium', *Dyslexia Review*, 1, 2, 15.

BAKKER, D. J. (1970). 'Temporal order perception and reading retardation'. In: BAKKER, D. J. and SATZ, P. (Eds). *Specific Reading Disability*. Rotterdam: Rotterdam University Press.

BAKKER, D. J. (1972). *Temporal Order and Disturbed Reading*. Rotterdam: Rotterdam University Press.

BAKKER, D. J. (1973). 'Hemispheric specialisation and stages in the learning-to-read process', *Bull. Orton Society*, 23, 15–27.

BAKKER, D. J. (1974). 'Cortical mechanisms subserving early and fluent reading', Paper presented at International Federation of Learning Disabilities, Amsterdam, Jan. 1974.

BAKKER, D. J., SMINK, T. and REITSMA, P. (1973). 'Ear dominance and reading ability', *Cortex*, 9, 301–12.

BAKKER, D. J., JEUNISSEN, J. and BOSCH, J. (1976). 'Development of laterality – reading patterns'. In: KNIGHTS, R. M. and BAKKER, D. J. *The Neuropsychology of Learning Disorders*. Baltimore: University Park Press.

BALE, P. (1974). Perceptual, motor and language deficits in backward readers of average intelligence and their relationship to developmental history, unpublished PhD thesis, University of Surrey.

BALL, T. S. and OWENS, E. P. (1968). 'Reading disability, perceptual continuity and phi thresholds'. In: *Perceptual and Motor Skills*, 26, 483-9.

BALOW, I. H. (1963). 'Lateral dominance characteristics and reading achievement in the first grade', *J. Psychol.*, 55, 323-8.

BALOW, B. and BLOMQUIST, M. (1965). 'Young adults ten to fifteen years after severe reading disability', *Elementary School J.*, 66, 44-8.

BANNATYNE, A. D. (1966). 'The aetiology of dyslexia', *The Slow Learning Child*, 13, 1, 20-34.

BANNATYNE, A. D. (1966). 'Diagnostic and remedial techniques for use with dyslexic children', *Word Blind Bull. 1*, Numbers 6 and 7.

BANNATYNE, A. D. (1967). 'The colour phonics system'. In: MONEY, J. (Ed.) *The Disabled Reader*. Baltimore: Johns Hopkins University Press, 193-214.

BANNATYNE, A. D. (1971). *Language, Reading and Learning Disabilities*. Springfield, Ill.: Thomas.

BANNATYNE, A. D. (1973). 'Programmes, materials and techniques', *J. of Learning Disabilities*, 6, 3.

BANNATYNE, A. D. and WICHIARAJOTE, P. (1969). 'Relationships between written spelling, motor functioning and sequencing skills', *J. of Learning Disabilities*, II, 1, 4-16.

BARO (1966) quoted in CRITCHLEY, M. (1970). *The Dyslexic Child*. London: Heinemann, p. 86.

BARON, J. (1975). 'Successive stages in word recognition'. In: RABBITT, P. M. A. and DORNIC, S. (Eds) *Attention and Performance V*. London: Academic Press.

BATEMAN, B. D. (1966). 'Learning disorders', *Rev. of Educ. Research*, Chap. V., 36.

BAUER, R. H. (1977). 'Memory processes in children with learning disabilities: Evidence for deficient rehearsal', *J. of Experimental Child Psychol.*, 24, 415-30.

BEAN, W. J. (1967). The isolation of some psychometric indices of severe reading disabilities. Unpublished doctoral dissertation. Texas Technological College.

BEARD, R. M. (1965). 'The structure of perception: a factorial study', *Br. J. of Educ. Psych.*, 35, 210-22.

BEAUMONT, J. G. (1978). 'On testing the maturational left–right gradient hypothesis', *The Behavioural and Brain Sciences*, 1, 2, 280-1.

BEAUMONT, J. G. and RUGG, M. D. (1978). 'Neuropsychological laterality of function and dyslexia', *Dyslexia Review*, 1, 1, 18–21.

BECKER, W. C., MADSEN, C. H., ARNOLD, C. R. and THOMAS, D. R. (1967). 'The contingent use of teacher attention and praise in reducing classroom behaviour problems', *J. of Special Educ.*, 1, 287–307.

BEEZ, W. V. (1968). *Influence of Biased Psychological Reports on Teacher Behaviour and Pupil Performance.* Proceedings, 76th Annual Convention American Psychol. Association, 605–6.

BELMONT, L. and BIRCH, H. G. (1963). 'Lateral dominance and right–left awareness in normal children', *Child Dev.*, 34, 257–70.

BELMONT, L. and BIRCH, H. G. (1965). 'Lateral dominance, lateral awareness and reading disability', *Child Dev.*, 36, 57–71.

BELMONT, L. and BIRCH, H. G. (1966). 'The intellectual profile of retarded readers', *Percept. Motor Skills*, 22, 787.

BENDER, L. (1957). 'Specific reading disability as a maturational lag', *Bull of the Orton Society*, 7, 9–18.

BENDER, L. (1958). 'Problems in conceptualisation and communication in children with developmental alexia'. In: HOCK, P. and LUBIN, J. (Eds) *Psychopathology of Communication.* New York: Grune and Stratton.

BENDER, L. (1968). 'Neuropsychiatric disturbance'. In: KEENEY, A. H. and KEENEY, V. T. (Eds) *Dyslexia.* St Louis, Mosby.

BENDER, L. (1970). 'Use of the visual motor gestalt test in the diagnosis of learning disabilities', *J. of Spec. Educ.*, 4, 1, 29–39.

BENSON, D. F. (1970). 'Graphic orientation disorders of left handed children', *J. of Learning Disabilities*, 3, 3, 126–31.

BENTON, A. I. (1959). *Right–left Discrimination and Finger Location: Development and Pathology.* New York: Hoeber–Harper.

BENTON, A. L. (1962). 'Dyslexia in relation to form perception and directional sense'. In: MONEY, J. (Ed) *Reading Disability.* Baltimore: Johns Hopkins Press.

BENTON, A. L. (1975). 'Developmental Dyslexia: neurological aspects'. In: FRIEDLANDER, W. J. (Ed) *Advances in Neurology Vol. 7.* New York: Raven Press.

BENTON, A. L. and BIRD, J. W. (1963). 'The EEG and reading disability', *American J. Orthopsychiat.*, 33, 529–31.

BENTON, A. L. and SWANSON, R. (1955). 'Some aspects of the genetic development of right–left discrimination', *Child Dev.*, 26, 123–33.

BENTZEN, F. (1963). 'Sex ratios in learning and behaviour', *American J. Orthopsychiat.*, 33, 92–8.

BERGER, M., YULE, W. and RUTTER, M. (1975). 'Attainment and adjustment in two geographical areas. II, The prevalence of specific reading retardation', *Br. J. of Psychiat.*, 126, 510–19.

BERKO, J. (1958). 'The child's learning of English morphology', *Ward*, 14, 150–77.

BERKOWITZ, R. and ROTHMAN, E. (1955). 'Remedial reading for the disturbed child', *Clearing House*, 30, 165-8.

BERLYNE, D. E. (1970). 'Attention as a problem in behaviour theory'. In: MOSTOFSKY, D. I. (Ed) *Attention: Contemporary Theory and Analysis*. New York: Appleton-Century-Crofts.

BIRCH, H. G. (1962). 'Dyslexia and the maturation of visual function'. In: MONEY, J. (Ed) *Reading Disability*. Baltimore: Johns Hopkins Press.

BIRCH, H. G. and BELMONT, L. (1964). 'Auditory-visual integration in normal and retarded readers', *American J. of Orthopsychiatry*, 34, 852-61.

BLACKWELL, J. M. (1976). 'When 2 + ς ain't 4', *Language Arts*, 53, 4, 422-4.

BLANK, M. and BRIDGER, W. H. (1966). 'Deficiencies in verbal labelling in retarded readers', *American J. Orthopsychiat.*, 36, 840.

BLANK, M., WEIDER, S. and BRIDGER, W. (1968). 'Verbal deficiencies in abstract thinking in early reading retardation', *American J. Orthopsychiat.*, 38, 823-4.

BLAU, H., SCHWALB, E., ZANGER, E. and BLAU, H. (1969). 'Developmental dyslexia and its remediation', *The Reading Teacher*, 22, 7, 649-53.

BODER, E. (1970). 'Developmental dyslexia', *J. School Health*, 40, 6, 289-90.

BODER, E. (1971). 'Developmental dyslexia: prevailing diagnostic concepts and a new diagnostic approach', In: MYKLEBUST, H. R. (Ed) *Progress in Learning Disabilities*. Vol. II, 293-321. New York: Grune and Stratton.

BOISE, L. M. (1955). 'Emotional and personality problems of a group of retarded readers', *Elementary English*, 32, 544-8.

BOND, G. L. and TINKER, M. A. (1957). *Reading Difficulties: their Diagnosis and Correction*. New York: Appleton-Century-Crofts.

BOOK, R. M. (1974). 'Predicting reading failure: a screening battery for kindergarten children', *J. Learning Disability*, 7, 1.

BOONE, D. and PRESCOTT, T. (1968). 'Development of left-right discrimination in normal children', *Perceptual and Motor Skills*, 26, 267-74.

BOSHES, B. and MYKLEBUST, H. R. (1964). 'A neurological and behavioural study of children with learning disorders', *Neurology*, 14, 7-12.

BOUMA, H. and LEGEIN, C. H. P. (1977). 'Foveal and parafoveal recognition of letters and words by dyslexics and by average readers', *Neuropsychologia*, 15, 69-80.

BOWLEY, A. (1969). 'Reading difficulty with minor neurological dysfunction. A study of children in junior schools', *Developmental Medicine and Child Neurology*, II, 493-503.

BOWLEY, A. (1970). 'Minimal cerebral dysfunctions', *Forward Trends*, 14, 2, 49-51.

BRADSHAW, J. L., GATES, A. and PATTERSON, K. (1976). 'Hemispherical differences in processing visual patterns', *Q. J. Exp. Psychol.*, 28, 667–81.

BRENNER, M. W., GILLMAN, S., ZANGWILL, O. L. and FARRELL, M. (1967). 'Visuomotor disability in school children', *Br. Med. J.*, 4, 259.

BREWER, W. F. (1967). Paired–associate learning of dyslexic children. Doctoral dissertation, University of Iowa.

BREWER, W. F. (1969). 'Visual memory, verbal encoding and hemispheric localization', *Cortex*, 5, 145–51.

BRITTAN, M. M. (1970). 'Inflectional performance and early reading achievement', *Reading Research Quarterly*, 6, 1, 34–48.

BROADBENT, D. E. and GREGORY, M. (1964). 'Stimulus set and response set: the alternation of attention', *Quarterly J. of Experimental Psychol.*, 16, 309–17.

BROWN, H. D. (1970). 'Categories of spelling difficulty in speakers of English as a first and second language', *J. of Verbal Learning and Verbal Behaviour*, 9, 232–6.

BRUIJEL, R. M. (1967). 'Visuele discriminatie'. Unpublished thesis: University of Leyden.

BRUININKS, R. H. (1968). 'Auditory and visual perceptual skills related to the reading performance of disadvantaged boys', *Perceptual and Motor Skills*, 29, 177–86.

BRYAN, T. (1974). 'An observational analysis of classroom behaviours of children with learning disabilities', *J. Learning Disabilities*, 7, 35–43.

BRYAN, T. and WHEELER, R. (1972). 'Perception of learning disabled children: The eye of the observer', *J. Learning Disabilities*, 5, 484–8.

BRYANT, N. D. (1963). 'Learning disabilities in reading'. Mimeographed. Quoted in WEINER, M. and CROMER, W. (1967). 'Reading and reading difficulty: a conceptual analysis', *Harvard Educational Rev.*, 37, 4, 620–43.

BRYANT, N. D. (1965). 'Some principles of reading instruction for dyslexia', *Reading Teacher*, 43, 567–72.

BRYANT, N. and FRIEDLANDER, W. J. (1975). ' "14 + 6" in boys with specific reading disability', *EEG Clin. Neurophysiol.*, 19, 322.

BRYANT and McLOUGHLIN (1972), as quoted in WALSH, D. (1978). *Project Child: Incidence Survey.* An unpublished report. Wellington, New Zealand: New Zealand Council for Educational Research.

BRYANT and PATERSON, quoted by GOLDBERG, H. K. and SCHIFFMAN, G. B. (1972). In: *Dyslexia. Problems of Reading Disabilities.* New York: Grune and Stratton Inc.

BRYDEN, M. P. (1970). 'Laterality effects in dichotic listening: relations with handedness and reading ability in children', *Neuropsychologia*, 8, 443–50.

BRYDEN, M. P. (1972). 'Auditory-visual and sequential-spatial matching, in relation to reading ability', *Child Dev.*, 43, 824–32.

BUFFERY, A. W. H. and GRAY, J. A. (1972). 'Sex differences in the development of spatial and linguistic skills'. In: OUNSTED, C. and TAYLOR, D. C. (Eds) *Gender Differences: Their Ontogeny and Significance.* 123–57. Churchill Livingstone, Edinburgh and London.

BULLOCK REPORT (1975). See under DEPARTMENT OF EDUCATION AND SCIENCE.

BUROS, O. K. (1978). *The Eighth Mental Measurements Yearbook.* New Jersey: Gryphon Press.

BURT, C. and LEWIS, R. R. (1946). 'Teaching backward readers', *Br. J. of Educnl. Psychol.,* **16**, 116–32.

BUTLER, S. R. (1976). 'Reading problems of Chinese children'. In: TARNOPOL, L. and TARNOPOL, M. *Reading Disabilities: An International Perspective.* Baltimore: University Park Press.

CALNAN, M. and RICHARDSON, K. (1977). 'Speech problems among children in a national survey – associations with reading, general ability, mathematics and syntactic maturity', *Educnl. Studies,* **3**, 1, 55–67.

CANE, B. (1969). *In-Service Training: A Study of Teachers' Views and Preferences.* NFER: Occasional Publication Series No. 22. Slough: NFER.

CARROLL, H. C. M. (1972). 'The remedial teaching of reading: an evaluation', *Remedial Educ.,* **7**, 1, 10–15.

CASEY, T. and ETTLINGER, G. (1960). 'The occasional "independence" of dyslexia and dysgraphia and dysphasia', *J. of Neurology, Neurosurg. and Psychiat.,* **23**, 228–36.

CASHDAN, A. (1970). 'Backward readers-research on auditory-visual integration'. In: GARDNER, W. K. (Ed) *Reading Skills: Theory and Practice.*

CASHDAN, A. (1974). 'Reading schemes: the snags behind each method', *Where,* **98**, 337–9.

CASHDAN, A, PUMFREY, P. D. and LUNZER, E. A. (1971). 'Children receiving remedial treatment in reading', *Educnl. Research,* **13**, 2, 98–105.

CAVE, C. and MADDISON, P. (1978). *A Survey of Recent Research in Special Education.* Slough: NFER.

CAWLEY, N. (1973). 'Feedback (2): Diagnosing difficulties in number', *Remedial Educ.,* **8**, 2, 27–9.

CELDIC (1970). *One Million Children.* Toronto: Commission on Emotional and Learning Disorders in Children.

CENTRAL BUREAU VOOR DE STATISTIEK (1974), as quoted in WALSH, D. (1978). *Project Child: Incidence Survey.* An unpublished report. Wellington, New Zealand: New Zealand Council for Educational Research.

CHALL, J. (1967). *Learning to Read: The Great Debate.* New York: McGraw-Hill.

CHAMPION, B. W. (1979a). 'Educational remediation: from planning to implementation'. In: ADAMSON, M. D. and ADAMSON, K. K.

(Eds) *A Handbook for Specific Learning Disabilities.* New York: Gardner Press.

CHAMPION, B. W. (1979b). 'Educational assessment, diagnosis and evaluation'. In: ADAMSON, M. D. and ADAMSON, K. K. *A Handbook for Specific Learning Disabilities.* New York: Gardner Press.

CHANSKY, N. M. (1958). 'Threat, anxiety, and reading behaviour', *J. of Educnl. Research,* 51, 333–40.

CHANSKY, N. M. (1963). 'Age, I.Q. and improvement of reading', *J. of Educnl. Research,* 56, 439.

CHASEY, W. C. (1972). 'Self-concept, body image, social interaction and perceptual motor changes of learning disability children', *Br. J. of Physical Educ.,* 3, 5, xxxiii–vii.

CHASTY, H. (1979). 'Functional asymmetry of the brain in normal children and dyslexics', *Dyslexia Rev.,* 2, 1, 9–12.

CHASTY, H. J., TURNER, I. and SETH, G. (1976). 'Bilateral asymmetry and behaviour. 2. Bilateral asymmetry and linguistic acquisition in children of school age', *Irish J. of Psychol.,* iii, 2, 137–45.

CHAZAN, M. (1963). 'Maladjustment, attainment and sociometric status', *Univ. Coll. Swansea Ed. J.,* 4–7.

CHAZAN, M. (1967). 'The effects of remedial teaching in reading: a review of research', *Remedial Educ.,* 2, 1, 4–12.

CHILDS, B. (1964). 'Biological basis of human behaviour', *California Inst. of Tech.,* 16 March.

CHILDS, B., FINUCCI, J. M. and PRESTON, M. S. (1978). 'A medical genetics approach to the study of reading disability'. In: BENTON, A. and PEARL, D. (Eds) *Dyslexia: An Appraisal of Current Knowledge.* New York: Oxford University Press.

CHISSOM, B. S. (1972). 'Review of the Marianne Frostig Developmental Test of Visual Perception'. In: BUROS, O. K. (Ed) *The Seventh Mental Measurements Yearbook.* New Jersey: Gryphon Press.

CHOMSKY, C. (1969). *The Acquisition of Syntax in Children from 5 to 10.* Cambridge, Mass.: MIT Press.

CHOMSKY, C. (1971). 'Write first, read later', *Childhood Educ.,* 47, 6, 396–9.

CHOMSKY, C. (1972). 'Stages in language development and reading exposure', *Harvard Educ. Rev.,* 42, 1–33.

Chronically Sick and Disabled Persons Act 1970. London: HMSO.

CIUFFREDA, K. J., BAHILL, A. T., KENYON, R. V. and STARK, L. (1976). 'Eye movements during reading: case reports', *American J. of Optometry and Physiol. Optics,* 53, 389–95.

CLARK, M. M. (1970). *Reading Difficulties in Schools.* Harmondsworth: Penguin Books.

CLARK, M. M. (1971). 'Severe reading difficulty: a community study', *Br. J. of Educ. Psychol.,* 41, 1, 14–18.

CLAY, M. M. (1966). Emergent reading behaviour. Unpublished doctoral dissertation, University of Auckland.

CLAY, M. M. (1972). *The Early Detection of Reading Difficulties: A Diagnostic Survey* (with test booklet, *Sand*). Auckland, New Zealand: Heinemann Educational Books.

CLAY, M. M. (1974). 'Research in brief: orientation to the spatial characteristics of the open book', *Visible Language*, **8**, 3, 275–82.

CLAY, M. M. (1977a). 'An emphasis on prevention', *J. of Special Educ.*, **11**, 183–8.

CLAY, M. M. (1977b). *'Write Now, Read Later', an evaluation.* Opening address to the 1977 International Reading Association Seminar, Auckland, New Zealand International Reading Association.

CLAY, M. M. (1979a). *The Early Detection of Reading Difficulties: A Diagnostic Survey with Recovery Procedures.* Auckland: Heinemann Educational Books.

CLAY, M. M. (1979b). Reading Recovery Project. Seminar paper, 25 July. University of Auckland (mimeographed).

CLAY, M. M. (1980). *Reading: The Patterning of Complex Behaviour.* Auckland: Heinemann Educational Books. (Second edition, in press.)

CLEMENTS, S. D. and PETERS, J. E. (1962). 'Minimal brain dysfunction in the school age child', *Arch. Gen. Psychiat.*, **6**, 185.

CLIFTON-EVEREST, I. M. (1974). 'Immediate recognition of letter sequences by slow learning children', *J. of Genetic Psychol.*, **125**, 1, 13–30.

COHEN, G. (1973). 'Hemispheric differences in serial versus parallel processing', *J. of Experimental Psychol.*, **97**, 349–56.

COHEN, J. (1977). 'Cerebral evoked response asymmetry in dyslexic children', *Psychophysiol.*, **14**, 89.

COHEN, N. J. (1970). Psychophysiological concomitants of attention in hyperactive children. Unpublished doctoral dissertation. McGill University.

COHEN, A. and GLASS, G. C. (1968). 'Lateral dominance and reading ability', *Reading Teacher*, **21**, 343.

COHEN, R. L. and NETLEY, C. (1978). 'Cognitive deficits, learning disabilities and WISC – performance consistency', *Devpl. Psych.*, **14**, 6.

COHN, R. (1961). 'Delayed acquisition of reading and writing abilities in children', *Archives of Neurology*, **4**, 153–64.

COLEMAN, R. I. and DEUTSCH, C. P. (1964). 'Lateral dominance and right–left discrimination: A comparison of normal and retarded readers', *Perceptual and Motor Skills*, **19**, 43–50.

COLLETTE-HARRIS, M. and MINKE, K. A. (1975). A behavioural experimental analysis of dyslexia. Paper presented at the International Federation of Learning Disabilities (Second International Scientific Conference, Brussels, Belgium, 3–7 January 1975).

COLLINS, C. (1975). 'The right to read: some thoughts on dyslexia', *Conference*, **12**, 2, 25–8.

COLLINS, J. E. (1961). *The Effects of Remedial Education.* Birmingham: University of Birmingham Institute of Education. Educational Monographs No. 4.

282 *Children With Specific Learning Difficulties*

COLTHEART, M. (1979). 'Mysteries of reading in brain defects', *New Scientist*, 81, 1141, 368-70.
COMLY, H. H. (1971). 'Cerebral stimulants for children with learning disorders', *J. of Learning Disabilities*, 4, 9, 484-90.
COMMITTEE OF ENQUIRY INTO THE EDUCATION OF HANDI-CAPPED CHILDREN AND YOUNG PEOPLE (1978). *Special Educational Needs* (Warnock Report). London: HMSO.
CONNERS, C. K. (1970). 'Cortical visual evoked response in children with learning disorders', *Psychophysiology*, 7, 418-28.
CONNERS, C. K. (1972). 'I. Symposium: behaviour modification by drugs. II. Psychological effects of stimulant drugs in children with minimal brain dysfunction', *Pediatrics*, 49, 702-8.
CONNERS, C. K. (1974). 'Minimal brain dysfunction and psycho-pathology in children'. In: DAVIDS, A. (Ed) *Child Personality and Psychopathology Current Topics*. New York: Wiley.
CONNERS, C. K. (1976). 'Learning disabilities and stimulant drugs in children: theoretical implications'. In: KNIGHTS, R. M. and BAKKER, D. J. *The Neuropsychology of Learning Disorders*. Baltimore: University Park Press.
CONNERS, C. K. (1978). 'Critical review of "Electroencephalographic and Neurophysiological Studies in Dyslexia"'. In: BENTON, A. L. and PEARL, D. (Eds) *Dyslexia: An Appraisal of Current Knowledge*. New York: Oxford University Press.
CONNOLLY, C. (1971). 'Social and emotional factors in learning disabilities'. In: MYKLEBUST, H. R. (Ed) *Progress in Learning Disabilities*, Vol. II. New York: Grune and Stratton.
CONNOR, J. P. (1966). The relationship of Bender visual motor gestalt test performance to differential reading performance of second grade children. Unpublished doctoral dissertation. Kent State University.
CONRAD, R. (1964). 'Acoustic confusions in immediate memory', *Br. J. of Psychol.*, 55, 75-84.
CONRAD, R. (1965). 'Order error in immediate recall of sequences', *J. of Verb. Learning and Verbal Behaviour*, 4, 161-9.
CONRAD, R. (1972). 'Speech and reading'. In: KAVANAGH, J. F. and MATTINGLY, I. E. (Eds) *Language by Ear and by Eye: The Relationships between Speech and Reading*, Massachusetts: MIT Press.
CORBALLIS, M. and BEALE, I. (1970). 'Bilateral symmetry and behaviour', *Psychol. Rev.*, 77, 451-64.
CORKIN, S. (1974). 'Serial-ordering deficits in inferior readers', *Neuropsychologia*, 12, 347-54.
COTTERELL, G. C. (1970a). 'Teaching procedures', In: FRANKLIN, A. W. and NAIDOO, S. (Eds) *Assessment and Teaching of Dyslexic Children*. London: ICAA.
COTTERELL, G. C. (1970b). 'The Fernald auditory-kinaesthetic technique of teaching reading and spelling'. In: FRANKLIN, A. W. and NAIDOO, S. (Eds) *Assessment and Teaching of Dyslexic Children*. London: ICAA.

COTTERELL, G. C. (1970c). 'The dyslexic child at home and at school'. In: FRANKLIN, A. and NAIDOO, S. (Eds) *Assessment and Teaching of Dyslexic Children*. London: Invalid Children's Aid Association.

COTTERELL, G. C. (1972). 'A case of severe learning disability', *Remedial Educ.*, **7**, 1, 5-9.

COTTERELL, G. C. (1974). 'Suggestions for helping the dyslexic child in the ordinary classroom', *Dyslexia Rev.*, **11**, 15-17.

COTTERELL, G. C. (1976). 'Nigel: a severe auditory dyslexic', *Special Educ.: Forward Trends*, **3**, 4, 19-21.

COX, F. N. (1970). *Psychological Assessment for Remedial Teaching*. Victoria: Specific Learning Disabilities Association of Victoria (Australia).

CRABTREE, T. (1976). 'Dyslexia, goodbye', *New Society*, **35**, 641, 10-11.

CRITCHLEY, M. (1964). *Developmental Dyslexia*. London: Heinemann.

CRITCHLEY, M. (1970). *The Dyslexic Child*. London: Heinemann.

CRITCHLEY, M. (1975). 'The past, present and future of developmental dyslexia', *Dyslexia Rev.*, **13**, 4-7.

CROMER, W. and WIENER, M. (1966). 'Idiosyncratic response patterns among good and poor readers', *J. of Consulting Psychol.*, **30**, 1, 1-10.

CRONBACH, L. J. (1970). *Essentials of Psychological Testing*. New York: Harper (3rd edition).

CROOKES, T. G. and GREENE, M. C. L. (1963). 'Some characteristics of children with two types of speech disorder', *Br. J. of Educ. Psychol.*, **33**, 31.

CROSBY, R. M. N., with LISTON, R. A. (1968). *Reading and the Dyslexic Child*. London: Souvenir Press.

CURR, W. and GOURLAY, N. (1953). 'An experimental evaluation of remedial education', *Br. J. of Educ. Psychol.*, **23**, 45-55.

DANIELS, J. C. and DIACK, H. (1958). *The Standard Reading Tests*. London: Chatto and Windus.

DARBY, R. (1974). Ear asymmetry phenomenon in dyslexic and normal children. Unpublished master's thesis, University of Florida.

DAVIE, R., BUTLER, N. and GOLDSTEIN, H. (1972). *From Birth to Seven*. London: Longmans.

DAVIES, F. (1973). 'Reading theory and instruction: a new approach', *Cambridge J. of Educ.*, **3**, 3, 182-92.

DAVIES, G. (1974). 'Motor development as it influences cognitive development', *Proceedings of the 75th Anniversary Conference of the Physical Education Association of Gt. Britain and Northern Ireland*. April 1974, pp. 143-6.

DAVIDOFF, J., CONE, B. P. and SCULLY, J. P. (1978). 'Developmental changes in hemispheric processing for cognitive skills and the relationship to reading ability'. In: LESGOLD, A. M., PELLEGRINO, J. W. et al. *Cognitive Psychology and Instruction*. New York: Plenum Press.

DAY, J. B. and WEDELL, K. (1972). 'Visual and auditory memory in spelling: an exploratory study', *Br. J. of Educ. Psychol.*, **42**, 1, 33-9.

De HIRSCH, K. (1963). 'Two categories of learning difficulties in adolescents', *American J. Orthopsychiat.*, **33**, 87-91.

De HIRSCH, K., JANSKY, J. J. and LANGFORD, W. C. (1966). *Predicting Reading Failure*. New York: Harper and Row.

DEKABAN, A. (1970). *A Neurology of Early Childhood*. Baltimore: The Williams and Wilkins Co.

DELACATO, C. H. (1959). *The Treatment and the Psychology of Perception*. Nottingham: Peter Skinner Publishing Ltd.

DENCKLA, M. B. and RUDEL, R. G. (1976). 'Rapid automatized naming: dyslexia differentiated from other learning disabilities', *Neuropsychologia*, **14**, 471-9.

DEPARTMENT OF EDUCATION AND SCIENCE (1964). *Slow Learners at School*. London: HMSO (Pamphlet No. 46).

DEPARTMENT OF EDUCATION AND SCIENCE (1972). *Children with Specific Reading Difficulties*. Report of the Advisory Committee on Handicapped Children (Tizard Report). London: HMSO.

DEPARTMENT OF EDUCATION AND SCIENCE (1975). *A Language for Life* (The Bullock Report). London: HMSO.

De RENZI, E. and SPINNLER, H. (1966a). 'Facial recognition in brain damaged patients', *Neurology*, 145-52.

De RENZI, E. and SPINNLER, H. (1966b). 'Visual recognition in patients with the unilateral cerebral disease', *J. Nerv. Ment. Dis.*, **142**, 515-25.

De RENZI, E., FAGIONI, P. and SCOTTI, F. (1970). 'Hemispheric contribution to exploration of space through the visual and tactile modality', *Cortex*, **6**, 191-203.

DESCHAUT, E. (1968). *Diagnosis and Remediation of Reading Disability*. New York: Parker Publishing Co.

DIMOND, S. J. (1976). 'Drugs to improve learning in man: implications and neurological analysis'. In: KNIGHTS, R. M. and BAKKER, D. J. *The Neuropsychology of Learning Disorders*. Baltimore: University Park Press.

DIMOND, S. and BEAUMONT, G. (1974). 'Hemisphere function and paired-associate learning', *Br. J. Psych.*, **65**, 2, 275-8.

DINNAGE, R. (1970). *The Handicapped Child Research Rev.* Vol. 1. London: Longman Group Ltd.

DOEHRING, D. G. (1968). *Patterns of Impairment in Specific Reading Disability*. Bloomington: Indiana University Press.

DOEHRING, D. G. (1976). 'Evaluation of two models of reading disability'. In: KNIGHTS, R. M. and BAKKER, D. J. *The Neuropsychology of Learning Disorders*. Baltimore: University Park Press.

DOEHRING, D. G. and HOSHKO, I. M. (1977). 'Classification of reading problems by the Q-technique of factor analysis', *Cortex*, **13**, 281-94.

DOEHRING, D. G. and LIBMAN, R. A. (1974). 'Signal detection analysis of auditory sequence discrimination by children', *Perceptual and Motor Skills*, 38, 163-9.

DONE, D. J. and MILES, T. R. (1978). 'Learning, memory and dyslexia', *Dyslexia Rev.*, 1, 2, 13-14.

DOSSETOR, D. R. and PAPAIOANNOU, T. C. (1975). 'Dyslexia and eye movements', *Language and Speech*, 18, 312-17.

DOUGLAS, J. W. B. (1964). *The Home and the School*. London: MacGibbon and Kee.

DOUGLAS, J. W. B., ROSS, J. M. and SIMPSON, H. R. (1968). *All our Future*. London: Peter Davies.

DOUGLAS, V. I. (1972). 'Stop, look, listen: The problem of sustained attention and impulse control in hyperactive and normal children', *Can. J. Behav. Sci.*, 4, 259-82.

DOUGLAS, V. I. (1976). 'Perceptual and cognitive factors as determinants of learning disabilities: a review chapter with special emphasis on attentional factors'. In: KNIGHTS, R. M. and BAKKER, D. J. *The Neuropsychology of Learning Disorders*. Baltimore: University Park Press.

DOWNING, J. (1973). 'Causes of reading disability in different languages', *Dyslexia Rev.*, 10, 4-7.

DOWNING, J. and LATHAM, W. (1969). 'A follow-up of children in the first i.t.a. experiment', *Br. J. Educ. Psychol.*, 39, 303-5.

DREW, A. L. (1956). 'A neurological appraisal of familial congenital word-blindness', *Brain*, 79, 440-60.

DUNLAP, W. P. and HOUSE, A. D. (1976). 'Why can't Johnny compute?', *J. of Learning Disabilities*, 9, 4, 210-4.

DUNLOP, D. B., DUNLOP, P. and FENELON, B. (1973). 'Vision laterality analysis in children with reading disability: The results of new techniques of examination', *Cortex*, 9, 227-36.

DYER, C. (1973). 'Use of an oscilloscope to solve a particular reading problem', *Remedial Educ.*, 8, 1, 42-3.

DYKMAN, R. A., ACKERMAN, P. T., CLEMENTS, S. D. and PETERS, J. E. (1971). 'Specific learning disabilities: an attentional deficit syndrome'. In: MYKLEBUST, H. R. (Ed) *Progress in Learning Disabilities* (Vol. 11, pp. 56-93). New York: Grune and Stratton.

DYKMAN, R. A., WALLS, R., SUZUKI, P., ACKERMAN, P. and PETERS, J. (1970). 'Children with learning disabilities. V. Conditioning, differentiation and the effects of distraction', *American J. Orthopsychiat.*, 40, 776-81.

DYKSTRA, R. (1966). 'Auditory discrimination abilities and beginning reading achievement', *Reading Research Quarterly*, 1, 3, 5-34.

DYSLEXIA INSTITUTE (1975). The Identification, Diagnosis, Assessment, and Remedy of Dyslexia or Specific Language Disability. (Submission to the Committee of Enquiry into Special Education.) Staines: Dyslexia Institute (mimeographed).

EARLY, G. H. *et al.* (1976). 'Cursive handwriting, reading and spelling achievement', *Academic Therapy*, 12, 1, 67-74.

EAVES, J. (1978). 'Reading disability and social adjustment in intelligent children', *Educatnl. Studies,* 4, 1, 45–51.

EDUCATION DEPARTMENT OF VICTORIA (1971), quoted in WALSH, D. (1978). *Project Child: Incidence Survey.* An unpublished report. Wellington, New Zealand: New Zealand Council for Educational Research.

EDWARDS, J. J. (1968). 'Lexic-dyslexic diagnostic instruction'. Paper presented at International Reading Association Conference, Boston, Mass. (ERIC document ED 028019).

EISENBERG, L. (1966). 'The epidemiology of reading retardation and a program for preventative intervention'. In: MONEY, J. (Ed) *The Disabled Reader.* Baltimore: Johns Hopkins.

ELKINS, J. (1978). 'Empirical evidence for a model of reading disability research', *Australian J. of Educ.,* 22, 3, 303–9.

ELLIOTT, C. D., MURRAY, D. J. and PEARSON, L. S. (1977). *The British Ability Scales.* Windsor: NFER (pamphlet).

ELLIS, A. J. (1845). *A Plea for Phonotypy and Phonography.* Isaac Pitman Phonographic Institution.

ELLIS, N. C. and MILES, T. R. (1978). 'Visual information processing in dyslexic children', *Dyslexia Rev.,* 2, 10–12.

EPSTEIN, L. C., LASAGNA, L., CONNERS, C. K. *et al.* (1968). 'Correlation of deoxtroamphetamine excretion and drug response in hyperkinetic children', *J. Nerv. Ment. Dis.,* 146, 2, 136–45.

ERIKSEN, C. W. and COLLINS, J. F. (1968). 'Sensory traces versus the psychological moment in the temporal organisation of form', *J. of Experimental Psychology,* 77, 376–82.

ERLENMEYER (1879). 'Die schift, grundzuge ihrer physiologie und ihrer pathologie, Stuttgart'. In: CRITCHLEY, M. (Ed) 1928 *Mirror-writing.* London: Kegan Paul.

ETTLINGER, quoted by GOLDBERG, H. K. and SCHIFFMAN, G. B. (1972). *Dyslexia. Problems of Reading Disabilities.* New York: Grune and Stratton, p. 57.

EVESHAM, M. (1977). 'Teaching language skills to children with language disorders', *Br. J. of Disorders of Communication,* 12, 1, 23–30.

FABIAN, A. A. (1955). 'Reading disability: an index of pathology', *American J. Orthopsychiat.,* 25, 319.

FARNHAM-DIGGORY, S. (1972). 'The development of equivalence system'. In: FARNHAM-DIGGORY, S. (Ed) *Information Processing in Children.* New York: Academic Press.

FARNHAM-DIGGORY, S. (1978). *Learning Disabilities.* London: Fontana/Open Books.

FARNHAM-DIGGORY, S. and GREGG, L. W. (1975). 'Teaching language skills to children with language disorders', *Br. J. Disorders of Communication,* 12, 1, 23–30.

FARNHAM-DIGGORY, S. and GREGG, L. W. (1975b). 'Short-term memory function in young readers', *J. of Experimental Child Psychol.,* 19, 279–98.

FARR, J. E. and LEIGH, J. (1972). 'Factors associated with reading failure', *Social Science and Medicine*, 6, 241–51.

FERNALD, G. M. (1943). *Remedial Techniques in Basic School Subjects*. New York: McGraw-Hill.

FESHBACH, S., ADELMAN, H. and FULLER, W. W. (1974). 'Early identification of children with high risk of reading failure', *J. of Learning Disabilities*, 7, 639–44.

FESTINGER, L. *et al.* (1972). 'Eye movement disorders in dyslexia'. New York: School for Social Research, New York. (ERIC document ED 074 691.)

FILDES, L. G. (1921). 'A psychological inquiry into the nature of the condition known as congenital word blindness', *Brain*, 44, 186–307.

FISH, J. R. (1979). 'Developments in provision for children with specific learning difficulties', *Dyslexia Rev.*, 2, 2, 1–3.

FISHER, D. F. (1976). *Dysfunctions in Reading Disability: There's More than Meets the Eye*. Sponsored by the National Institute of Education (DHEW). Washington D.C.

FISHER, D. F. and FRANKFURTER, A. (1977). 'Normal and disabled readers can locate and identify letters: Where's the perceptual deficit?', *J. of Reading Behaviour*, 9, 1, 31–43.

FITZHUGH, K. B. and FITZHUGH, L. (1966). *The Fitzhugh Plus Program*. Falien, Mich. Allied Education Council.

FLAX, N. (1968). 'Visual function in dyxlexia', *American J. of Optometry and Archives of American Academy of Optometry*, 45, 9, 574–87.

FLETCHER, J. M. and SATZ, P. (1978). 'Developmental changes associated with reading disability: a multivariate test of a theory'. Manuscript submitted for publication.

FLETCHER, J. M. and SATZ, P. (1979). 'Unitary deficit hypotheses of reading disabilities: has Vellutino led us astray?', *J. of Learning Disabilities*, 12, 155–9, 168–71.

FORD, M. (1967). 'Auditory-visual and tactual visual integration in relation to reading ability', *Perceptual and Motor Skills*, 24, 831–41.

FRANCIS-WILLIAMS, J. (1974). *Children with Specific Learning Difficulties*. (2nd ed). Oxford: Pergamon.

FRANKLIN, A. and NAIDOO, S. (Eds) (1970). *Assessment and Teaching of Dyslexic Children*. London: Invalid Children's Aid Association.

FRASER, E. (1959). *Home Environment and the School*. London: University of London Press.

FREDERIKSEN, J. R. (1978). 'Assessment of perceptual, decoding and lexical skills and their relation to reading proficiency'. In: LESGOLD, A. M. and PELLEGRINO, J. W. (*et al.*) *Cognitive Psychology and Instruction*. New York: Plenum Press.

FRIEDMAN, M. P., GUYER-CHRISTIE, B. L. and TYMCHUK, A. (1976). 'Cognitive style and specialized hemispheric processing in learning disability'. In: KNIGHTS, R. M. and BAKKER, D. J. (Eds) *The Neuropsychology of Learning Disorders*. Baltimore: University Park Press.

FRITH, U. (1971). 'Why do children reverse letters?', *B. J. of Psych.*, 62, 4, 451-68.

FRY, M. A., JOHNSON, C. S. and MUEHL, S. (1970). 'Oral language production in relation to reading achievement among select second graders'. In: BAKKER, D. J. and SATZ, P. (Eds) *Specific Reading Disability: Advances in Theory and Method.* Rotterdam: Rotterdam University Press.

GADDES, W. H. (1976). 'Prevalence estimates and the need for a definition of learning disabilities'. In: KNIGHTS, R. M. and BAKKER, D. J. *The Neuropsychology of Learning Disorders: Theoretical Approaches.* Baltimore: University Park Press.

GALPERIN, P. Y. (1957). 'An experimental study in the formation of mental actions'. In: SIMON, B. (Ed) *Psychology in the Soviet Union.* London: Routledge and Kegan Paul.

GALT, R. L. (1973). 'Problem-solving strategies of reflective, impulsive, fast-accurate, and slow-accurate children', *Child Dev.*, 44, 259-66.

GATES, A. I. (1968). 'The role of personality maladjustment in reading disability'. In: NATCHEZ, G. (Ed) *Children with Reading Problems.* New York: Basic Books.

GATTEGNO, C. (1969). *Reading with Words in Colour.* Reading: Educational Explorers Ltd.

GAZZANIGA, M. (1974). 'Cerebral dominance viewed as a decision system'. In: DIMOND, S. and BEAUMONT, J. (Eds) *Hemispheric Functions in the Human Brain.* London: Halstead Press.

GAZZANIGA, M. S. and SPERRY, R. W. (1966). 'Simultaneous double discrimination response following brain bisection', *Psychon. Sci.*, 4, 261-2.

GEFFEN, G., BRADSHAW, J. and NETTLETON, N. (1972). 'Hemisphere asymmetry: verbal and spatial encoding of visual stimuli'. In: COLTHEART, M. (Ed) *Readings in Cognitive Psychology.* Toronto: Holt.

GEHRING, K. (1966). Dyslexia — reading disability with neurological involvement. (ERIC document ED 015 085.)

GESELL, A. *et al.* (1940). *The First Five Years of Life.* New York: Harper.

GESSERT, B. (1976). 'Specific reading difficulties in Gt. Britain'. In: TARNOPOL, L. and TARNOPOL, M. (Eds) *Reading Disabilities: An International Perspective.* Baltimore: University Park Press.

GETMAN, G. N., KANE, E. R., HALGREN, M. R. and McKEE (1964). *The Physiology of Readiness.* Minneapolis, Minn., P.A.S.S., Inc.

GEYER, J. J. (1972). 'Comprehensive and partial models related to the reading process', *Reading Research Quarterly*, 7, 541-87.

GIBSON, E. J. (1966). 'Experimental psychology learning and reading'. In: MONEY, J. (Ed) *The Disabled Reader.* Baltimore: Johns Hopkins Press.

GIBSON, E. (1970). 'The ontogeny of reading', *American Psychologist,* 25, 136-43.

GIBSON, J. J. and GIBSON, E. G. (1955). 'Perceptual learning: differentiation or enrichment', *Psychological Rev.,* 62, 33-40.

GILLINGHAM, A. and STILLMAN, B. (1956). *Remedial Training for Children with Specific Language Disability in Reading, Spelling and Penmanship.* Cambridge, Mass.: Educator's Publishing Service.

GLEITMAN, L. R. and ROZIN, P. (1977). 'The structure and acquisition of reading. I. Relations between orthographies and the structure of language'. In: REBER, A. S. and SCARBOROUGH, D. L. (Eds) *Towards a Psychology of Reading.* Hillsdale, N.J.: Erlbaum.

GLYNN, E. L. and McNAUGHTON, S. S. (1975). 'Trust your own observations: criterion-referenced assessment of reading progress', *The Slow Learning Child* (University of Queensland), 22, 2, 91-107.

GOETZINGER, C. P., DIRKS, D. D. and BAER, C. J. (1960). 'Auditory discrimination and visual perception in good and poor readers', *Annals of Otolaryngology, Rhinology, and Laryngology,* 69, 121-36.

GOINS, J. J. (1958). 'Visual perceptual abilities and early reading progress', *Supplementary Educational Monograph* No. 87. Chicago: University of Chicago Press.

GOLDBERG, H. K. (1968). 'Vision, perception and related factors in dyslexia'. In: KEENEY, A. H. and KEENEY, V. T. *Dyslexia.* St Louis: Mosby.

GOLDBERG, H. K. *et al.* (1960). 'The role of brain damage in congenital dyslexia', *American J. of Ophthal.,* 50, 4.

GOLDBERG, H. K. and SCHIFFMAN, G. B. (1972). *Dyslexia. Problems of Reading Disabilities.* New York: Grune and Stratton Inc.

GOLDMAN, S. R. (1976). 'Reading skill and the minimum distance principle: a comparison of listening and reading comprehension', *J. Exp. Child Psychol.,* 22, 123-42.

GOODACRE, E. J. (1967). *Reading in Infant Classes.* NFER.

GOODACRE, E. (1968). 'Learning to read: differences between girls and boys', *Where,* 40, 23-5.

GOODACRE, E. J. (1971). *Children and Learning to Read.* London: Routledge and Kegan Paul.

GOODACRE, E. (1979). 'The state of reading research in the United Kingdom', *J. of Research in Reading,* 2, 2, 76-9.

GOODMAN, K. S. (1972). 'Reading: the key is in children's language', *The Reading Teacher,* March, 505-8.

GOYEN, J. D. and LYLE, J. (1971a). 'Effects of incentives and age on the visual recognition of retarded readers', *J. of Experimental Child Psychol.,* 11, 266-73.

GOYEN, J. D. and LYLE, J. (1971b). 'Effect of incentives upon retarded and normal readers on a visual-associate learning task', *J. of Experimental Child Psychol.,* 11, 274-80.

GOYEN, J. D. and LYLE, J. (1973). 'Short-term memory and visual discrimination in retarded readers', *Perceptual and Motor Skills,* **36**, 403–8.

GOYEN, J. D. and MARTIN, M. (1977). 'The relation of spelling errors to cognitive variables and word type', *Br. J. of Educ. Psychol.,* **4**, 7, 168–273.

GRANT, R. (1974). 'Laterality and reading difficulty', *The Optician,* 15th February, 8–9.

GREDLER, G. R. (1969). 'A study of factors in childhood dyslexia'. In: ARENA, J. I. (Ed) *Selected Papers on Learning Disabilities.* Pittsburgh Association for Children with Learning Difficulties.

GREDLER, G. R. (1977). 'Severe reading disability – some important correlates'. In: REID, J. F. and DONALDSON, H. (Eds) *Reading: Problems and Practices.* London: Ward Lock Educational.

GREENHILL, N. J. (1973). The relationship between language, categorization, and primary dyslexia. Unpublished PhD dissertation, University of Michigan. (ERIC Document No. ED 084 498.)

GRENN, O. C. and PERLMAN, S. M. (1971). 'Endocrinology and disorders of learning'. In: MYKLEBUST, H. R. (Ed) *Progress in Learning Disabilities,* Vol. 11. New York: Grune and Stratton.

GRODEN, G. (1969). 'Lateral preference in normal children', *Perceptual and Motor Skills,* **28**, 213–14.

GRUBER, E. (1962). 'Reading ability, binocular co-ordination and the ophthalmograph', *Arch. Oph.,* **67**, 280–8.

GRUENBERG, E. (1964). 'Some epidemiological aspects of congenital brain damage'. In: BIRCH, H. G. (Ed) *Brain Damage in Children.* Baltimore: Williams and Wilkins Co.

GUIRGEA, C. (1971). *The Pharmacology of Piracetam (UCB 6215): A Nootrapic Drug.* Report UCB Pharm. Division, Brussels, Belgium.

GUIRGEA, C. (1973). 'The nootrapic approach to the pharmacology of the integrative action of the brain', *Conditional Reflex,* **8**, 108–15.

GULLIFORD, R. (1969). *Backwardness and Educational Failure.* Slough: NFER.

GULLIFORD, R. (1975). 'Remedial aspects', *Reading,* **9**, 2, 51–7.

GUMMERMAN, K. and GRAY, C. R. (1972). 'Iconic storage and visual information processing', *J. Exp. Child Psychol.,* **13**, 165–70.

GUPTA, R., CECI, S. J. and SLATER, A. M. (1978). 'Visual discrimination in good and poor readers', *J. of Special Educ.,* **12**, 4, 409–17.

GUTHRIE, J. T. (1972). 'Visual sequential memory in reading disability', *J. Learn. Dis.,* **5**, 41–8.

GUTHRIE, J. T. (1973). 'Models of reading and reading disability', *J. Educ. Psychol.,* **65**, 9–18.

GUTHRIE, J. T. and SEIFERT, M. (1977). 'Letter–sound complexity in learning to identify words', *J. of Educ. Psychol.,* **69**, 6, 686–96.

GUYER, B. and FRIEDMAN, M. P. (1975). 'Hemispheric processing and cognitive styles in learning-disabled and normal children', *Child Dev.,* **46**, 3, 658–68.

HABER, R. N. and NATHANSON, L. S. (1968). 'Post-retinal storage? Parks' camel as seen through the eye of a needle', *Perception and Psychophysics*, 3, 349-55.

HABER, R. N. and STANDING, L. (1970). 'Direct estimates of apparent duration of a flash followed by visual noise', *Canadian J. of Psychol.*, 24, 216-29.

HAGGARD (1957), quoted by GOODACRE, E. (1968). 'Learning to read: differences between girls and boys', *Where*, 40, 23-5.

HAGGER, T. D. (1970). *The Concept of Specific Learning Difficulties.* Specific Learning Difficulties Association of Australia.

HAGGER, T. D. (1976), quoted by WALSH, D. (1978). *Project Child: Incidence Survey.* An unpublished report. Wellington, New Zealand: New Zealand Council for Educational Research.

HAGIN, R. A. and SILVER, A. A. (1970). 'Learning disability: definition, diagnosis and prevention', *New York University Education Quarterly*, 8, 2, 9-15.

HAITH, M. M. (1971). 'Developmental changes in visual information processing and short-term visual memory', *Human Dev.*, 14, 4, 249-61.

HALLGREN, B. (1950). 'Specific dyslexia', *Acta Psych. Neur.*, Suppl. No. 65, 1-287.

HALSEY, A. H. (1972). *Educational Priority.* Vol. 1, HMSO.

HAMMILL, D. D. and LARSEN, S. C. (1974). 'The effectiveness of psycholinguistic training', *Exceptional Children*, 41, 5-14.

HARDYCK, C. (1977). 'Laterality and intellectual ability: a just not noticeable difference', *Br. J. of Educ. Psych.*, 47, 305-11.

HARDYCK, C., PETRINOVICH, L. F. and GOLDMAN, R. D. (1976). 'Left-handedness and cognitive deficit', *Cortex*, 12, 266-79.

HARRIS, A. J. (1956). *How to Increase Reading Ability.* New York: Longmans Green (3rd ed).

HARRIS, A. J. (1957). 'Lateral dominance, directional confusion and reading disability', *J. of Psychol.*, 44, 283.

HARRIS, A. J. (1976). *Ten Years of Progress in Remedial Reading.* Paper presented at the Annual Meeting of the International Reading Association, May 1976.

HARSHMAN, R. A., CRAWFORD, H., HECHT, E. (1974). Marijuana, cognitive style and cerebral dominance. Progress Report, Dept. of Psychology, University of California, Los Angeles.

HART, L. A. (1976). 'Misconceptions about learning disabilities', *National Elementary Principal*, 56, 1, 54-7.

HART, S. and FAGG, R. (1976). 'Left-handed children', *Where*, 178, 196-9.

HARTSTEIN, J. (Ed) (1971). *Current Concepts in Dyslexia.* St Louis, Mo.: C. V. Mosby.

HAWORTH, M. R. (1970). *The Primary Visual Motor Test.* New York: Grune and Stratton.

HÉCAEN, H. and ANGELERGUES, R. (1963). *La Cécité Psychique.* Paris: Masson.

HEGARTY, S. and LUCAS, D. (1978). *Able to Learn: The Pursuit of Culture – Fair Assessment.* Windsor: NFER.

HENDRY, G. A. (1969). Tests and remediation in the auditory discrimination of backward readers. Diploma of Special Education (ESN). University of Birmingham.

HENRY, A. (1975). 'Specific difficulties in reading', *Remedial Educ.,* 10, 2, 81–5.

HERMANN, K. (1959). *Reading Disability.* Copenhagen: Munksgaard.

HERMANN, K. and NORRIE, E. (1958). 'Is congenital word-blindness a hereditary type of Gerstman's syndrome?', *Psych. Neur.,* 136, 59–73.

HERMANN, K. and VOLDBY, H. (1946). 'The morphology of handwriting in congenital word-blindness', *Acta Psych. Neur.,* 21, 349–63.

HESS, R. D. (1968). Maternal behaviour and the development of reading readiness in urban negro children. Paper prepared for the Claremont Reading Conference, Claremont, California, quoted in: GOLDBERG, H. K. and SCHIFFMAN, G. B. (1972). *Dyslexia: Problems of Reading Disabilities.* New York: Grune and Stratton.

HICKEY, K. (1977). Dyslexia: *A Language Training Course for Teachers and Learners.* 3 Montague Road, London SW19.

HICKS, C. (1978). 'Colour phonic system' (Book review), *Dyslexia Rev.,* 1, 1.

HINES, D. and SATZ, P. (1974). 'Cross-modal asymmetries in perception related to asymmetry in cerebral function', *Neuropsychologia,* 12, 239–47.

HINSHELWOOD, J. (1917). *Congenital Word-Blindness.* London: Lewis.

HINTZMAN, D. L. (1967). 'Articulatory coding in short-term memory', *J. Verb. Learning Verb. Behaviour,* 6, 312–16.

HIRSHOREN, A. (1969). 'A comparison of the predictive validity of the revised Stanford-Binet Intelligence Scale and the Illinois Test of Psycholinguistic Abilities', *Except. Child,* 35, 7.

HITCH, G. and BADDELEY, A. (1977). *Social Sciences: A Third Level Course. Cognitive Psychology Block 3. Unit 15 Working Memory.* Milton Keynes: Open University Press.

HOLMES, J. M., MARSHALL, J. C. and NEWCOMBE, F. (1971). 'Syntactic class as a determinant of word-retrieval in normal and dyslexic subjects', *Nature,* 234, 17th December, 418.

HOOTON, M. B. (1976). *The First Reading and Writing Book.* London: Heinemann.

HORNSBY, B. (1973). 'The dyslexia clinic at Bart's', *Dyslexia Rev.,* 9, 12–14.

HORNSBY, B. and MILES, T. R. (1979). The Effects of a Dyslexia-Centred Teaching Programme (mimeographed).

HORNSBY, B. and SHEAR, F. (1976). *Alpha to Omega.* London: Heinemann (2nd edition).

HUGHES, J. R. (1976). 'Biochemical and electroencephalographic correlates of learning disabilities'. In: KNIGHTS, R. M. and BAKKER, D. J. (Eds) *The Neuropsychology of Learning Disorders.* Baltimore: University Park Press.

HUGHES, J. R. (1978). 'Electroencephalographic and neurophysiological studies in dyslexia'. In: BENTON, A. L. and PEARL, D. (Eds) *Dyslexia: An Appraisal of Current Knowledge.* New York: Oxford University Press.

HUGHES, J. R. and PARK, G. E. (1968). 'The EEG in dyslexia'. In: KELLAWAY, P. and PETERSEN, I. (Eds). *Clinical Electroencephalography of Children.* Stockholm: Almqvist and Wiksell.

HUNT, J. and MacAUSLAN, A. (1979). 'Eurythmy and reading disabilities', *Remedial Educ.,* 14, 1, 12–14.

HUNT, K. W. (1964). Differences in grammatical structures written at three grade levels, the structures to be analyzed by transformational methods. Report to the US Office of Education, Co-operative Research Project No. 1998, Tallahassee, Florida.

HUNT, K. W. (1965). *Grammatical Structures Written at Three Grade Levels.* Champaign; National Council of Teachers of English. (Research Report No. 3).

HUTT, S. J. and HUTT, C. (1964). 'Hyperactivity in a group of epileptic (and some non-epileptic) brain-damaged children', *Epilepsia,* 5, 334–51.

INGRAM, T. T. S. (1964). 'The dyslexic child', *Word Blind Bulletin,* 1, 4, 1.

INGRAM, T. T. S. (1970). 'The nature of dyslexia'. In: YOUNG, F. A. and LINDSLEY, D. B. (Eds) *Early Experience and Visual Information Processing in Perceptual and Reading Disorders.* Washington D.C.: National Academy of Sciences – National Research Council.

INGRAM, T. T. S. (1971). Symposium on reading dyslexia. II. Specific learning difficulties in childhood: a medical point of view', *Br. J. Educ. Psychol.,* 41, 1, 6–13.

INGRAM, T. T. S. and REID, J. F. (1956). 'Developmental aphasia observed in a department of child psychiatry', *Archives of Diseases in Childhood.*

INGRAM, T. T. S., MASON, A. W. and BLACKBURN, I. (1970). 'A retrospective study of 82 children with reading disability', *Developmental Medicine and Child Neurology,* 12, 3, 271–81.

IRWIN, R. and NEWLAND, J. (1977). 'Children's knowledge of left and right', *J. Child Psychol. Psychiat.,* 8, 3, 271–7.

ISOM, J. B. (1969). 'An interpretation of dyslexia: A medical viewpoint'. In: SPACHE, G. D. (Ed) *Reading Disability and Perception.* Newark, Delaware: International Reading Association.

JACKSON, M. S. (1972). *Reading Disability: Experiment, Innovation and Individual Therapy.* Sydney: Angus and Robertson.

JAMPOLSKY, G. G. and HAIGHT, M. E. (1975). 'A special technique for children with reading problems', *Academic Therapy,* 10, 3, 333–7.

JANSEN, M. *et al.* (1976). 'Special education in Denmark'. In: TARNO-
   POL, L. and TARNOPOL, M. *Reading Disabilities: an International
   Perspective.* Baltimore: University Park Press.
JANSKY, J. and de HIRSCH, K. (1972). *Preventing Reading Failure:
   Prediction, Diagnosis, Intervention.* New York: Harper and Row.
JASTAK, J. (1934). 'Interferences in reading', *Psychol. Bull.,* 31, 244–
   72.
JASTAK, J. and JASTAK, S. (1965). *Wide Range Achievement Manual.*
   Wilmington: Delaware Guidance Associates.
JENSEN, A. R. (1973). *Educational Differences.* London: Methuen.
JOHNSON, M. S. (1957). 'Factors related to disability in reading',
   J. of Experimental Educ., 26, 1–26.
JOHNSON, D. J. and MYKLEBUST, H. R. (1967). *Learning Disabilities:
   Educational Principles and Practice.* New York: Grune and Stratton.
JOHNSTON, P. W. (1942). 'The relation of certain anomalies of vision
   in lateral dominance to reading disability', *Monograph for the
   Society for Research and Child Dev.,* 71, 2.
JORDAN, D. R. (1972). *Dyslexia in the Classroom.* Columbus, Ohio:
   Merrill.
JORM, A. F. (1978). 'Reading processes in dyslexia', *Core,* 2, 3.
KAGAN, J. and MOSS, N. (1970). 'Individual variation in cognitive
   processes'. In: MUSSEN, P. H. (Ed.) *Carmichael's Manual of Child
   Psychology.* Vol. 1. Third edition. Ch. 18. 1273–365. New York:
   Wiley.
KAGAN, J., PEARSON, L. and WELSH, L. (1966). 'Conceptual
   impulsivity and inductive reasoning', *Child Dev.,* 37, 583–94.
KÅGÉN, B. (1943). 'Om ordblindhet', *Redagog. skrifter,* 60, 179–80.
KAGEN, J. (1964). 'The child's sex role classification of school objects',
   Child Dev., 35, 151–6.
KAHN, D. (1965). The development of auditory-visual integration and
   reading achievement. Unpublished doctoral dissertation, Columbia
   University.
KAHN, D. and BIRCH, H. G. (1968). 'Development of auditory-visual
   integration and reading achievement', *Perceptual and Motor Skills,*
   27, 459–68.
KAHNEMAN, D. (1968). 'Method, findings and theory in studies of
   visual masking', *Psychol. Bull.,* 70, 404–25.
KALASH, B. D. (1972). The relationship of preferred learning modalities and conceptual tempo to reading readiness of first grade disadvantaged children. Unpublished doctoral dissertation, New York
   University.
KAMIL, M. L. and RUDEGEAIR, R. E. (1972). 'Methodological
   improvements in the assessment of phonological discrimination in
   children', *Child Development,* 43, 1087–91.
KASS, C. L. (1966). 'Psycholinguistic disabilities of children with reading problems', *Exceptional Children,* 32, 8, 533–9.
KATZ, L. and WICKLUND, D. (1971). 'Word scanning rates for good
   and poor readers', *J. of Educnl. Psychol.,* 62, 138–40.

KATZ, L. and WICKLUND, D. (1972). 'Letter scanning rate for good and poor readers in grades two and six', *J. of Educnl. Psychol.*, **63**, 363–7.

KATZ, P. A. and DEUTSCH, M. (1963). 'Relation of auditory-visual shifting to reading achievement', *Perceptual and Motor Skills*, **17**, 327–32.

KAUFMAN, H. S. and BIREN, P. L. (1976/7). 'Persistent reversers: poor readers, writers and spellers?', *Academic Therapy*, **12**, 2, 209–17.

KAUFMANN, A., KALMA, R. and KAUFMAN, N. L. (1978). 'The relationship of hand dominance to the motor co-ordination, mental ability and right–left awareness of young normal children', *Child Dev.*, **49**, 3, 885–9.

KAWI, A. A. and PASAMANICK, B. (1959). 'Prenatal and perinatal factors in the development of childhood reading disorders', *Monog. Soc. Res. Child Dev.*, **24**, 4.

KEEFE, B. (1976). A comparison of laterality between normal and dyslexic readers. Paper presented at the Eastern Psychological Association, April 1976. (ERIC Document No. ED 135 168).

KEENEY, A. H. and KEENEY, V. T. (Eds) (1968). *Dyslexia: Diagnosis and Treatment of Reading Disorders.* St Louis: C. V. Mosby.

KELLMER-PRINGLE, M. L. and SUTCLIFFE, B. (1960). *Remedial Education – An Experiment.* Caldecott Community and Department of Child Study of the University of Birmingham Institute of Education.

KELLMER-PRINGLE, M. L. (Ed.) (1965). *Deprivation and Education.* London: Longmans.

KELLMER-PRINGLE, M. L. and REEVES, J. K. (1968). 'The influence of two junior school regimes upon attainment in reading', *Human Dev.*, **11**, 25.

KELLMER-PRINGLE, M. L., BUTLER, N. R. and DAVIE, R. (1966). *11,000 Seven-year-olds.* London: Longmans.

KEMMLER, L. (1967). *Erfolg und Versagen in der Grundschule.* Götingen: Hogrefe.

KENT, N. and DAVIS, D. R. (1957). 'Discipline in the home and intellectual development', *Br. J. Med. Psychol.*, **30**, 27.

KEOGH, B. K. and BECKER, L. D. (1973). 'Early detection of learning problems: questions, cautions and guidelines', *Exceptional Children*, **40**, 5–11.

KEOGH, B. K. and SMITH, C. E. (1970). 'Early identification of educationally high and potentially high-risk children', *J. of School Psychol.*, **8**, 285–90.

KEPHART, N. C. (1972). 'Review of the Marianne Frostig Developmental Test of Visual Perception'. In: BUROS, O. K. (Ed) *The Seventh Mental Measurements Yearbook.* New Jersey: Gryphon Press.

KERSHNER, J. (1970). 'Children's spatial representation and horizontal directionality', *The J. of Genetic Psychol.*, **116**, 177–89.

KERSHNER, J. (1971). 'Children's acquisition of visuo-spatial dimensionality: A conservation study', *Developmental Psychol.*, 5, 454–62.

KERSHNER, J. (1972). 'Lateral preference and ability to conserve multiple spatial relations by mentally retarded children', *Perceptual and Motor Skills*, 35, 151–2.

KERSHNER, J. R. (1975). 'Reading and laterality revisited', *J. of Special Educ.*, 9, 3, 269–79.

KERSHNER, J. R. (1977). 'Cerebral dominance in disabled readers, good readers, and gifted children: search for a valid model', *Child Dev.*, 48, 61–7.

KERSHNER, J. and BROWN, V. (in preparation). 'Interhemispheric transfer in retarded readers'. Quoted in 'Reading and laterality revisited', *J. of Spec. Educ.*, 9, 3, 269–79.

KERSHNER, J. and JENG, A. (1972). 'Dual functional hemispheric asymmetry in visual perception: Effects of ocular dominance and post-exposural processes', *Neuropsychologia*, 10, 437–45.

KESSLER, J. (1970). 'Contributions of the mentally retarded toward a theory of cognitive development'. In: HELLMUTH, J. (Ed) *Cognitive Studies 1*. New York: Brunner/Mazel.

KIMURA, D. (1963). 'Speech laterlization in young children as determined by an auditory test', *J. of Comparative and Physiological Psychol.*, 56, 899.

KIMURA, D. (1967). 'Functional asymmetry of the brain in dichotic listening', *Cortex*, 3, 163–78.

KIMURA, D. (1971). 'Right hemisphere specialization for depth perception reflected in visual field differences', *Nature*, 231, 344–5.

KIMURA, D. and DURNFORD, M. (1974). 'Normal studies on the function of the right hemisphere in vision'. In: DIMOND, S. J. and BEAUMONT, J. G. (Eds) *Hemisphere Function in the Human Brain*. London: Elek Science.

KINSBOURNE, M. (1967). 'Effect of focal cerebral lesions on perspective and movement reversals', *J. Nerv., Ment., Dis.*, 2, 144.

KINSBOURNE, M. (1970). 'The analysis of learning deficit with special reference to selective attention'. In: BAKKER, D. J. and SATZ, P. (Eds) *Specific Reading Disability*. Rotterdam: Rotterdam University Press.

KINSBOURNE, M. (1975). 'Cerebral dominance, learning and cognition'. In: MYKLEBUST, H. R. (Ed) *Progress in Learning Disabilities*, Vol. 111. New York: Grune and Stratton.

KINSBOURNE, M. (1976). 'The ontogeny of cerebral dominance'. In: RIEBER, R. W. (Ed) *The Neuropsychology of Language*. Plenum Press.

KINSBOURNE, M. and CORBIN, D. 'Simultaneous and successive discrimination of orientation by children', quoted in: BAKKER, D. J. and SATZ, P. (1970). *Specific Reading Disability. Advances in Theory and Method*. Rotterdam.

KINSBOURNE, M. and WARRINGTON, E. K. (1962). 'A variety of reading disability with right hemisphere lesions', *J. Neurol. Neurosurg. Psychiat.*, **25**, 559.

KINSBOURNE, M. and WARRINGTON, E. K. (1963a). 'Developmental factors in reading and writing backwardness', *Br. J. of Psychol.*, **54**, 145-56.

KINSBOURNE, M. and WARRINGTON, E. K. (1963b). 'The developmental Gerstmann syndrome', *Archives of Neurology*, **8**, 490–502.

KINSBOURNE, M. and WARRINGTON, E. K. (1966). 'Developmental factors in reading and writing backwardness'. In: MONEY, J. (Ed) *The Disabled Reader: Education of the Dyslexic Child*. Baltimore: Johns Hopkins Press.

KINTSCH, W. (1977). 'Reading comprehension as a function of text structure'. In: REBER, A. S. and SCARBOROUGH, O. L. (Eds) *Towards a Psychology of Reading*. Hillsdale, N.J.: Erlbaum.

KINTSCH, W. and BUSCHKE, H. (1969). 'Homophones and synonyms in short-term memory', *J. Exp. Psychol.*, **80**, 403-7.

KIRK, S. A. (1968). 'Illinois Test of Psycholinguistic Abilities: its origin and implications'. In: HELLMUTH, J. (Ed) *Learning Disorders*, Vol. 3. Seattle: Special Child Publications.

KIRK, S. A. and KIRK, W. D. (1971). *Psycholinguistic Learning Disabilities: Diagnosis and Remediation*. Urbana: University of Illinois Press.

KIRK (1972), as quoted in WALSH, D. (1978). *Project Child: Incidence Survey*. An unpublished report. Wellington, New Zealand: New Zealand Council for Educational Research.

KITAY, P. M. (1972). 'Review of the Bender–Gestalt Test'. In: BUROS, O. K. (Ed) *The Seventh Mental Measurements Yearbook*. New Jersey: Gryphon Press.

KLASEN, E. (1972). *The Syndrome of Specific Dyslexia*. Baltimore: University Park Press.

KLASEN, E. (1976). 'Learning disabilities: The German perspective'. In: TARNOPOL, L. and TARNOPOL, M. *Reading Disabilities: an International Perspective*. Baltimore: University Park Press.

KLATZKY, R. L. and ATKINSON, R. C. (1971). 'Specialization of the cerebral hemispheres in scanning for information in short-term memory', *Percept. Psychophys.*, **10**, 335-8.

KLEES, M. (1976). 'Learning disabilities in Belgium'. In: TARNOPOL, L. and TARNOPOL, M. *Reading Disabilities: an International Perspective*. Baltimore: University Park Press.

KLEES, M. and LEBURN, A. (1972). 'Analysis of the figurative and operative processes of thought of 40 dyslexic children', *J. of Learning Disabilities*, **5**, 7, 389-96.

KNIGHTS, R. M. and HINTON, G. G. (1969). 'The effects of methylphenidate (Ritalin) on the motor skills and behaviour of children with learning problems', *J. of Nerv. Ment. Dis.*, **148**, 643-53.

KNOTT, J. R., MUEHL, S. and BENTON, A. L. (1965). 'Electro-encephalograms in children with reading disabilities', *Electroenceph. Clin. Neurophysiol.*, 18, 513-33.

KOLERS, P. A. (1975). 'Pattern-analyzing disability in poor readers', *Developmental Psychol.*, 11, 3, 282-90.

KOOS, E. (1964). 'Manifestations of cerebral dominance and reading retardation in primary grade children', *J. of Genetic Psychol.*, 104, 155-65.

KOPPITZ, E. M. (1964). *The Bender Gestalt Test for Young Children.* New York: Grune and Stratton.

KOPPITZ, E. M. (1971). *Children with Learning Disabilities: A Five Year Follow-up Study.* New York: Grune and Stratton.

KOSC, L. (1974). 'Developmental dyscalculia', *J. of Learning Disabilities*, 7, 3, 164-77.

KOWARIK, O. (1976). 'Reading–writing problems in Austria'. In: TARNOPOL, L. and TARNOPOL, M. *Reading Disabilities an International Perspective.* Baltimore: University Park Press.

KUCERA, O., MATEJCEK, Z. and LANGMEIER, J. (1963). 'Some observations on dyslexia in children in Czechoslovakia', *American J. Orthopsychiat.*, 43, 448.

LA BERGE, D. and SAMUELS, S. J. (1974). 'Towards a theory of automatic information processing in reading', *Cognitive Psychol.*, 6, 293-323.

LANE, D. A. (1974). 'A functional approach to persistent reading failure', *Remedial Educ.*, 9, 3, 130-1.

LANSDOWN, R. (1978). 'Retardation in mathematics: a consideration of multi-factorial determination', *J. Child Psychol. and Psychiat.*, 19, 2, 181-5.

LANSDOWN, R. (1978). 'The learning-disabled child: early detection and prevention', *Developmental Medicine and Child Neurology*, 20.

LANSDOWN, R. and DAVIS, V. (1972). 'The language of reading and the E.S.N. child', *Reading*, 6, 2.

LANYON, R. M. (1974). 'An experimental investigation into the relevance of auditory discrimination and articulatory skills for spelling and achievement in children'. In: WADE, B. and WEDELL, K. (Eds) *Spelling – Task and Learner.* Birmingham: University of Birmingham.

LARSEN, S. C. and HAMMILL, D. D. (1975). 'The relationship of selected visual-perceptual abilities to school learning', *J. of Special Educ.*, 9, 281-91.

LEADER, A. B. (1968). 'Relationship of visual perception to word discrimination'. In: ROBINSON, H. M. and SMITH, H. K. (Eds) *Clinical Studies in Reading, 111, Suppl. Educ. Monog.* No. 97.

LEAVELL, V. and BECK, H. (1959). 'Ability of retarded readers to recognise symbols in association with lateral dominance', *Peabody J. of Educ.*, 37, 7-13.

LE BRUN, Y. and VAN DE CRAEN, P. (1975). 'Developmental writing disorders and their prevention', *The J. of Special Educ.*, 9, 2, 201-7.

LECOURS, A. R. (1966). 'Serial order in writing – a study of mis-spelled words in developmental dysgraphia', *Neuropsychol.,* **4,** 221-41.

LEISMAN, G. and SCHWARTZ, J. (1976). 'Ocular-motor variables in reading disorders'. In: KNIGHTS, R. M. and BAKKER, D. J. *The Neuropsychology of Learning Disorders.* Baltimore: University Park Press.

LEONG, C. (1976). 'Lateralization in severely disabled readers in relation to functional cerebral development and synthesis of information'. In: KNIGHTS, R. M. and BAKKER, D. J. (Eds) *The Neuropsychology of Learning Disorders.* Baltimore: University Park Press.

LERNER, J. W. (1971). 'A thorn by any other name: dyslexia or reading disability', *Elementary English,* **48,** 75-80.

LERNER, J. W. (1975). 'Response to critics: reading and learning disabilities', *J. of Special Educ.,* **9,** 2, 179-81.

LERNER, J. W. (1976). (2nd ed) *Children with Learning Disabilities.* Boston: Houghton-Mifflin.

LESÈVRE, N. (1964). 'Les mouvements oculaires d'exploration: étude électro-oculographique comparée d'enfants normaux et d'enfants dyslexiques'. Unpublished doctoral dissertation, University of Paris.

LESTER, M. (1964). 'Graphemic–phonemic correspondences as the basis for teaching spelling'. *Elementary English,* **41,** 748-52.

LETON, O. (1962). 'Visual motor capacities, and ocular efficiency in reading', *Perceptual and Motor Skills,* **15,** 407-32.

LEVINE, M. J. (1976). 'Physiological responses in extrasensory and intersensory integration of auditory and visual signals by normal and deficit readers'. In: KNIGHTS, R. M. and BAKKER, D. J. *The Neuropsychology of Learning Disorders.* Baltimore: University Park Press.

LEVY, B. A. (1978). 'Speech processing during reading'. In: LESGOLD, A. M. and PELLEGRINO, J. W. *et al., Cognitive Psychology and Instruction.* New York: Plenum Press.

LEVY-AGRESTI, J. and SPERRY, R. W. (1968). 'Different perceptual capacities in major and minor hemispheres', *Proc. Natl. Acad. Sci. U.S.A.,* **61,** 1151.

LEVY, J., TREVARTHEN, C. and SPERRY, R. W. (1972). 'Perception of bilateral chimeric figures following hemispheric deconnection', *Brain,* **95,** 61-78.

LIBERMAN, I. Y. and SHANKWEILER, D. (1978). 'Speech, the alphabet and teaching to read'. In: RESNICK, L. and WEAVER, P. (Eds) *Theory and Practice of Early Reading.* New York: Wiley.

LIBERMAN, I. Y., SHANKWEILER, D., FISCHER, F. W. and CARTER, D. (1974). 'Explicit syllable and phoneme segmentation in the young child', *J. Exp. Child Psychol.,* **18,** 201-12.

LISS, P. H. and HAITH, M. M. (1970). 'The speed of visual processing in child and adults – effects of backward and forward masking', *Perception and Psychophysics,* **8,** 396-8.

LITTLE, A., MABEY, C. and RUSSELL, J. (1972). 'Class size, pupil characteristics and reading attainment'. In: SOUTHGATE, V. (Ed) *Literacy at All Levels*. London: Ward Lock Educational.

LOBAN, W. D. (1963). *The Language of Elementary School Children.* Champaign: National Council of Teachers of English. (Research Report No. 1).

LOVELL, K. (1963). 'Informal vs. formal education and reading attainments in the junior school', *Educ. Res.,* 6, 70.

LOVELL, K. (1964). 'A study of some cognitive and other disabilities in backward readers of average intelligence as assessed by a non-verbal test'. *B.J.E.P.,* 34, 58-64.

LOVELL, K. (1972). 'English Picture Vocabulary Test'. In: BUROS, O. K. (Ed). *The Seventh Mental Measurements Yearbook*. Highland Park, New Jersey: Gryphon Press.

LOVELL, K. and GORTON, A. (1968). 'Some differences between backward and normal readers of average intelligence', *The Br. J. of Educnl. Psychol.,* 38, 3, 240-8.

LOVELL, K. and WOOLSEY, M. E. (1964). 'Reading disability, non-verbal reasoning and social class', *Educ. Res.,* 6, 226.

LOWENBERG, E. G. (1979). 'An investigation into a possible relationship between specific learning disabilities and temporo-parietal brain dysfunction in the school-going child', *Humanitas, RSA,* 5, 1, 23-31.

LUCAS, A. R., RODIN, E. A. and SIMPSON, C. B. (1965). 'Neurological assessment of children with early school problems', *Developmental Med. and Child Neurology,* 7, 145-56.

LUMSDEN, J. (1978). 'Review of the Illinois Test of Psycholinguistic Abilities'. In: BUROS, O. K. (Ed) *The Eighth Mental Measurements Yearbook*. New Jersey: Gryphon Press.

LUND, K. A., FOSTER, G. E. and McCALL-PEREZ, F. C. (1978). 'The effectiveness of psycholinguistic training: a re-evaluation', *Exceptional Children,* 44, 5, 310-22.

LUNZER, E. A., DOLAN, T. and WILKINSON, J. E. (1976). 'The effectiveness of measures of operativity, language and short-term memory in the prediction of reading and mathematical understanding', *Br. J. Educ. Psych.,* 46, 295-305.

LURIA, A. R. (1961). *The Role of Speech in the Regulation of Normal and Abnormal Behaviour*. New York: Liveright.

LURIA, A. R. (1966a). *Higher Cortical Functions in Man*. New York: Basic Books.

LURIA, A. R. (1966b). *Human Brain and Psychological Processes*. New York: Harper and Row.

LURIA, A. R. (1970). *Traumatic Aphasia: its Syndromes, Psychology and Treatment*. The Hague: Mouton.

LURIA, A. R. (1973). *The Working Brain: An Introduction to Neuropsychology*. London: Penguin.

LUSTY (1938), as quoted in WALSH, D. (1978). *Project Child: Incidence Survey*. An unpublished report. Wellington, New Zealand: New Zealand Council for Educational Research.

LYLE, J. G. (1969). 'Reading retardation and reversal tendency', *Child Dev.*, **40**, 833.

LYLE, J. G. (1970). 'Certain antenatal, perinatal, and developmental variables and reading retardation in middle class boys', *Child Dev.*, **41**, 481-91.

LYLE, J. G. and GOYEN, J. (1968). 'Visual recognition, developmental lag, and strephosymbolia in reading retardation', *J. of Abnormal Psychol.*, **73**, 25-9.

LYLE, J. G. and GOYEN, J. D. (1975). 'Effect of speed of exposure and difficulty of discrimination on visual recognition of retarded readers', *J. of Abnormal Psychol.*, **8**, 673-6.

LYTTON, H. (1967). 'Follow-up of an experiment in selection for remedial education', *Br. J. of Educnl. Psychol.*, **31**, 79-94.

McBURNEY, A. K. and DUNN, H. G. (1976). 'Handedness, footedness, eyedness: a prospective study with special reference to the development of speech and language skills'. In: KNIGHTS, R. M. and BAKKER, D. J. (Eds) *The Neuropsychology of Learning Disorders: Theoretical Approaches.* Baltimore: University Park Press.

McCARTHY, J. J. and McCARTHY, J. F. (1969). *Learning Disabilities.* Boston: Allyn and Bacon.

McCLEARN, G. E. (1978). Comments on Dr Freya Owen: Dyslexia – Genetic Aspects. Paper presented at the National Institute of Mental Health Conference, Bethesda, Md.

McCLELLAND, J. L. and JACKSON, M. D. (1978). 'Individual differences in reading'. In: LESGOLD, A. M. and PELLEGRINO, J. W. *et al.*, *Cognitive Psychology and Instruction.* New York: Plenum Press.

McGRADY, H. J. (1970). 'Learning disabilities: implications for medicine and education'. Paper presented at ASHA-AMA. Pre-convention session on School Health, Chicago, June 1970.

McGRADY, H. J. and OLSON, D. A. (1970). 'Visual and auditory learning processes in normal children and children with specific learning disabilities', *Exceptional Children*, **36**, 8, 581-91.

McKEEVER, W. F. and HULING, M. D. (1970). 'Lateral dominance in tachistoscopic word recognitions of children at two levels of ability', *Q. J. Exp. Psychol.*, **22**, 600-4.

McKEEVER, W. F. and VAN DEVENTER, A. D. (1975). 'Dyslexic adolescents: evidence of impaired visual and auditory language processing associated with normal lateralisation and visual responsivity', *Cortex*, **11**, 361-78.

MacLEOD, J. (1965). Some psychological and psycholinguistic aspects of severe reading disability in children. Doctoral dissertation, University of Queensland, Australia.

McLEOD, T. M. and CRUMP, W. D. (1978). 'The relationship of visuospatial skills and verbal ability to learning disabilities in mathematics', *J. of Learning Disabilities*, **11**, 4, 237-41.

McLESKY, J. (1977). Learn Set Acquisition by Reading Disabled and Normal Children. Paper presented at the Annual Meeting of the National Reading Conference 27th New Orleans, Louisiana, 1-3 Dec., 1977.

MacMEEKEN, A. M. (1939). *The Intelligence of a Representative Group of Scottish Children*. London: University of London Press.
McNEIL (1964) quoted by GOODACRE, E. (1968) 'Learning to read: differences between girls and boys', *Where*, 40, 23–5.
McNINCH, G. and RICHMOND, M. (1972). 'Auditory perceptual tasks, as predictors of first grade reading success', *Perceptual & Motor Skills*, 35, 7–13.
McNINCH, G., PALMATIER, R. and RICHMOND, M. (1972). 'Auditory perceptual testing of young children', *J. of Reading Behaviour*, 4, 120–8.
MACHEMER, P. (1973). Anslese und verhaltenstherapeutische Behandlung von Legasthenikern. In: VALTIN, R. (Ed) *Einführung in die Legasthenieforschung*. Weinheim: Beltz.
MACIONE, J. R. (1969). Psychological correlates of reading disability as defined by the Illinois Test of Psycholinguistic Abilities. Doctoral dissertation. University of South Dakota.
MAKINS, V. (1977). 'In the real world you can't say cereal when you mean shampoo', *The Times Educational Supplement*, 30, 12, 77.
MAKITA, K. (1968). 'The rarity of reading disability in Japanese children', *American J. Orthopsych.*, 38, 599–614.
MALMQUIST, E. (1958). *Factors Related to Reading Disabilities in the First Grade of Elementary School*. Stockholm: Almqvist and Wiksell.
MALMQUIST, E. (1961), as quoted in WALSH, D. (1978). *Project Child: Incidence Survey*. An unpublished report. Wellington, New Zealand: New Zealand Council for Educational Research.
MALMQUIST, E. (1973). 'Perspectives on reading research'. In: KARLIN, R. (Ed) *Reading for All*. Newark, Del.: International Reading Association.
MANN, H. P. (1957). 'Some hypotheses on perceptual and learning processes with their applications to the process of reading', *J. Genet. Psychol.*, 90, 167.
MARCEL (1978) quoted by MILES, T. R. and ELLIS, N. C. (1980). 'A lexical encoding deficiency II: clinical observations'. In: PAVLIDIS, G. and MILES, J. R. (Eds) *Dyslexia Research and its Application to Education*. Chichester: John Wiley and Sons.
MANZO, A. V. (1977). 'Dyslexia as specific psychoneurosis', *J. of Reading Behaviour*, 9, 3, 305–8.
MARCEL, T. and RAJAN, P. (1975). 'Lateral specialisation for recognition of words and faces in good and poor readers', *Neuropsychologia*, 13, 489–97.
MARCEL, T., KATZ, L. and SMITH, M. (1974). 'Laterality and reading proficiency', *Neuropsychologia*, 12, 131–9.
MARSHALL, W. and FERGUSON, J. H. (1939). 'Hereditary word-blindness as a defect of selective association', *J. Nerv. Ment. Dis.*, 89, 164–73.
MARTIN, C. (1955). 'Developmental inter-relationships among language variables in children of the first grade', *Elem. School J.*, 32, 167.

MARTINIUS, J. W. and HOOVEY, Z. B. (1972). 'Bilateral synchrony of occipital alpha waves, oculomotor activity and "attention" in children', *Electroencephalography and Clinical Neurophysiology*, 32, 349–56.
MATTIS, S., FRENCH, J. H. and RAPIN, I. (1975). 'Dyslexia in children and adults: three independent neuropsychological syndromes', *Developmental Medicine and Child Neurology*, 17, 150–63.
MEICHENBAUM, D. (1976). 'Cognitive–functional approach to cognitive factors as determinants of learning disabilities'. In: KNIGHTS, R. M. and BAKKER, D. J. *The Neuropsychology of Learning Disorders*. Baltimore: University Park Press.
MENYUK, P. (1961). A descriptive study of the syntactic structures in the language of children. Unpublished doctoral dissertation, Boston University.
MENYUK, P. (1963). 'Syntactic structures in the language of children', *Child Development*, 34, 407–22.
MENYUK, P. (1964). 'Syntactic rules used by children from pre-school through first grade', *Child Development*, 35, 533–46.
MERCER, C. D., ALGOZZINE, B. and TRIFILETTI, J. (1979). 'Early identification: an analysis of the research', *Learning Disability Quarterly*, 2, 2, 12–24.
MEREDITH, P. (1972). *Dyslexia and the Individual*. London: Hamish Hamilton.
MERRITT, J. (1972). 'Reading failure: a re-examination'. In: SOUTHGATE, V. (Ed) *Literacy at All Levels*. London: Ward Lock Educational.
MILES, J. S. (1973). General and Specific Spelling Disability. Unpublished M. Phil. Dissertation, University of Nottingham.
MILES, T. R. (1961). 'Two cases of developmental aphasia., *J. Child Psychol. Psychiat.*, 2, 47.
MILES, T. R. (1970). *On Helping the Dyslexic Child*. London: Methuen.
MILES, T. R. (1971). 'More on dyslexia', *Br. J. of Educnl. Psychol.*, 41, 1, 1–22.
MILES, T. R. (1974). *The Dyslexic Child*. London: Priory Press.
MILES, T. R. (1978). *Understanding Dyslexia*. London: Hodder and Stoughton.
MILES, T. R. and ELLIS, N. C. (1980). (in press). 'A lexical encoding deficiency II: clinical observations'. In: PAVLIDIS, G. and MILES, T. R. (Eds) *Dyslexia Research and its Application to Education*. Chichester: John Wiley and Sons.
MILES, T. R. and WHEELER, T. J. (1974). 'Towards a new theory of dyslexia', *Dyslexia Rev.*, 11, 9–11.
MILNER, B. (1974). 'Hemispheric specialization: scope and limits'. In: SCHMITT, F. O. and WARDEN, F. G. (Eds) *The Neurosciences: Third Study Programme*. Cambridge, Mass: MIT Press.
MILNER, E. (1971). 'Handedness and the pattern of human ability', *Br. J. Psych.*, 62, 111–12.

MYKLEBUST, H. R. (1967). *Progress in Learning Disabilities,* Vol. 1. New York: Grune and Stratton.

MYKLEBUST, H. R. and BOSHES, B. (1969). *Final Report, Minimal Brain Damage in Children.* Washington, D.C.: Dept. of Health, Education and Welfare.

MYKLEBUST, H., BANNOCHIE, M. and KILLEN, J. (1971). 'Learning disabilities and cognitive processes'. In: MYKLEBUST, H. (Ed) *Progress in Learning Disabilities,* Vol. 11. New York: Grune and Stratton.

MYKLEBUST, H. R. and JOHNSON, D. (1962). 'Dyslexia in children', *Exceptional Children,* **29**, 14–25.

NAIDOO, S. (1961). An investigation into some aspects of ambiguous handedness. Unpublished M.A. Thesis, University of London.

NAIDOO, S. (1970). 'The assessment of dyslexic children'. In: FRANK-LIN, A. W. and NAIDOO, S. *Assessment and Teaching of Dyslexic Children.* London: Invalid Children's Aid Association.

NAIDOO, S. (1971). 'Specific developmental dyslexia', *Br. J. of Educnl. Psychol.,* **41**, 1, 19–22.

NAIDOO, S. (1972). *Specific Dyslexia.* London: Pitman.

NAIDOO, S. (1973). 'The Dyslexia Institute', *Dyslexia Rev.,* **9**, 14–16.

NEALE, M. D. (1966). *The Neale Analysis of Reading Ability* (1st Ed). London: Macmillan.

NELSON, H. E. (1974). 'The aetiology of specific spelling disabilities – a neuropsychologist's approach'. In: WADE, B. and WEDELL, K. (Eds) *Spelling: Task and Learner.* Birmingham: University of Birmingham. (Educational Review Occasional Publications No. 5).

NELSON, H. E. and WARRINGTON, E. K. (1974). 'Developmental spelling retardation and its relation to other cognitive abilities', *Br. J. of Psychol.,* **65**, 2, 265–74.

NELSON, H. E. and WARRINGTON, E. K. (1976). 'Developmental spelling retardation'. In: KNIGHTS, R. M. and BAKKER, D. J. (Eds) *The Neuropsychology of Learning Disorders.* Baltimore: University Park Press.

NEWBOLD, S. C. (1978). An investigation into lateral differences in the tachistoscopic recognition of familiar and unfamiliar words in normal, backward and dyslexic children. Unpublished M.Sc. dissertation.

NEWCOMER, P. and HAMMILL, D. (1975). 'The I.T.P.A. and academic achievement: a survey of the literature', *The Reading Teacher,* **28**, 8, 731–41.

NEWCOMER, P. L. (1977). 'Special education services for the mildly handicapped. Beyond a diagnostic and remedial model', *J. of Special Educ.,* **11**, 153–65.

NEWSON, J. H. (1963). *Half Our Future.* London: H.M.S.O.

NEWTON, M. (1970). 'A neuro-psychological investigation into dyslexia'. In: FRANKLIN, A. W. and NAIDOO, S. (Eds) *Assessment and Teaching of Dyslexic Children.* London: Invalid Children's Aid Association.

NEWTON, M. and THOMSON, M. (1974). *Dyslexia: A Guide to Teaching*. Birmingham: University of Aston.

NEWTON, M. and THOMSON, M. (1975). *Dyslexia: A Guide for Teachers and Parents*. University of London Press.

NEWTON, M. J., THOMSON, M. E. and RICHARDS, I. L. (1979). *Readings in Dyslexia*. Wisbech: Learning Development Aids.

NICHOLLS, J. G. (1976). 'At last, a test to tell if pupils are working to potential', *Education*, (New Zealand), 25, 2, 21–2.

NICHOLLS, J. G. (In Press). 'Quality and equality in intellectual development: the role of motivation in education'. *American Psychologist*.

NIELSON, H. H. and RINGE, K. (1969). 'Visuo-perceptive and visuomotor performance of children with reading disabilities', *Scand. J. Psychol.*, 10, 225.

NOBLE, J. (1966). 'Mirror-images and the forebrain commissures of the monkey', *Nature*, 211, 1263–5.

NOBLE, J. (1968). 'Paradoxical interocular transfer of mirror-image discrimination in the optic chiasm sectioned monkey', *Brain Research*, 10, 127–51.

NODINE, C. F. and LANG, N. J. (1971). 'Development of visual scanning strategies for differentiating words', *Dev. Psychol.*, 5, 221–32.

NORRIE, E. (1939). Edith Norrie Letter Case. Copenhagen. (Available from Helen Arkell Dyslexia Centre, 14 Crondace Road, London SW6, with instruction manual).

OAKEN, R., WIENER, M. and CROMER, W. (1971). 'Identification, organization, and reading comprehension for good and poor readers', *J. of Educ. Psychol.*, 62, 1, 71–8.

O'BRUBA, W. (1974). 'Remedial activities for children with perception difficulties', 9, 3, 140–1.

O'DONNEL, R. C. GRIFFIN, W. T. and NORRIS, R. C. (1967). *Syntax of Kindergarten and Elementary School Children: A Transformational Analysis*. Champaign: National Council of Teachers of English. (Research Report No. 8).

O'DONNELL, P. (1970). 'A re-evaluation of research on lateral expression', *J. of Learning Disabilities*, 3, 344–50.

OETTINGER, L. Jnr. (1964). 'Cerebral dysrhythmia induced by reading', *Subclinical Reading Epilepsy, Internat. Copenhagen Congr. Sci. Study. Ment. Retard.*, 58, 460–5.

OETTINGER, L. Jnr., NEKONISHI, H. and GILL, I. G. (1967). 'Cerebral dysrhythmia induced by reading (subclinical reading epilepsy)', *Dec. Med. Child Neur.*, 9, 191–201.

OHLSON, E. L. (1978). *Identification of Specific Learning Disabilities*. Champaign, Ill.: Research Press.

OLSON, A. V. and JOHNSON, C. I. (1970). 'Structure and predictive value of the Frostig Developmental Test of visual perception in grades 1 and 3', *J. of Spec. Ed.*, 41, 1, 49.

OLSON, M. E. (1973). 'Laterality differences in tachistoscopic word recognition in normal and delayed readers in elementary school', *Neuropsychologia*, 11, 343–50.

ORTON, S. T. (1925). 'Word-blindness in school children', *Archives of Neurology and Psychiat.*, **14**, 582–615.

ORTON, S. T. (1937). *Reading, Writing, and Speech Problems in Children.* New York: Norton.

ORTON, J. L. (1966). 'The Orton–Gillingham approach'. In: MONEY, J. (Ed) *The Disabled Reader.* Baltimore: Johns Hopkins University Press. 119–46.

OWEN, F. W. (1978). 'Dyslexia: genetic aspects'. In: BENTON, A. L. and PEARL, D. (Eds) *Dyslexia: An Appraisal of Current Knowledge.* New York: Oxford University Press.

OWEN, F. W., ADAMS, P. A., FORREST, T., STOLZ, L. M. and FISHER, S. (1971). *Learning Disorders in Children: Sibling Studies.* Monographs of the Society for Research in Child Development, Serial No. 144.

PARK, G. E. (1959). 'Reading failure in children', *Archives of Pediatrics,* **76**, 401.

PARK, G. E. and SCHNEIDER, K. A. (1975). 'Thyroid function in relation to dyslexia (reading failures)'. (In press). Quoted by HUGHES, J. R. in: KNIGHTS, R. M. and BAKKER, D. J. (Eds) *The Neuropsychology of Learning Disorders.* Baltimore: University Park Press.

PARK, G. E., BIEBER, M. and ZELLER, E. A. (1975). 'Functional dyslexia: abnormal pattern in platelet monoamine oxidase'. (In press). Quoted by HUGHES, J. R. in: KNIGHTS, R. M. and BAKKER, D. J. (Eds) *The Neuropsychology of Learning Disorders.* Baltimore: University Park Press.

PARRY, P. (1973). The effect of reward on the performance of hyperactive children. Unpublished doctoral dissertation. Montreal: McGill University.

PARSONS, R. A. (1974). 'Behavioural approach to the diagnosis and remediation of learning disabilities'. Temple University. (Unpublished paper).

PARTAN, D. (1978). 'Auditory problems and remediation', *Remedial Education,* **8**, 2, 7–10.

PAVLIDIS, G. Th. (1978). 'Eye movements and dyslexia'. Paper presented at the symposium on 'Dyslexia: its diagnosis and treatment', held at Manchester University, 15–17 February.

PAVLIDIS, G. Th. (1978). 'The dyslexics' erratic eye movements', *Dyslexia Rev.,* **1**, 1, 22–8.

PAVLIDIS, G. Th. and ROBINSON, A. (1978). 'Differences in simple and choice RT between dyslexics and matched normal controls'. (Unpublished study).

PERFETTI, C. A. and GOLDMAN, S. R. (1976). 'Discourse memory and reading comprehension skill', *J. of Verbal Learning and Verbal Behaviour',* **14**, 33–42.

PERFETTI, C. A. and HOGABOAM, T. W. (1975). 'The relationship between single word decoding and reading comprehension skill', *J. of Educnl. Psychol.,* **67**, 461–9.

PERFETTI, C. and LESGOLD, A. (1978). 'Discourse comprehension and sources of individual differences'. In: JUST, M. and CARPENTER, P. (Eds) *Cognitive Processes in Comprehension*, Hillsdale, N.J.: Lawrence Erlbaum.

PERFETTI, C. A., BELL, L. C., HOGABOAM, T. W. and GOLDMAN, S. R. (1977). 'Verbal processing speed and reading skill'. Paper presented at the Psychonomics Society, Washington, D.C.

PERFETTI, C. A., FINGER, E. and HOGABOAM, T. W. (1978). 'Sources of vocalization latency differences between skilled and less-skilled readers', *J. of Educnl. Psych.*, **70**, 5, 730–9.

PETERS (1976), quoted by DOUGLAS, V. I. 'Perceptual and cognitive factors as determinants of learning disabilities: A review chapter with special emphasis on attentional factors'. In: KNIGHTS, R. M. and BAKKER, D. J. *The Neuropsychology of Learning Disorders.* Baltimore: University Park Press.

PIAGET, J. (1926). *Judgment and Reasoning in the Child.* New York: Harcourt and Brace.

PICK, A. D., CHRISTY, M. D. and FRANKEL, G. W. (1972). 'A developmental study of visual selective attention', *J. of Exper. Child Psychol.*, **14**, 165–75.

PIDGEON, D. A. and YATES, A. (1957). 'Abilities and attainments', *Bulletin*, NFER, 10.

PILLINER, A. E. G. and REID, J. F. (1977). 'The definition and measurement of reading problems'. In: REID, J. F. and DONALDSON, H. (Eds) *Reading Problems and Practices.* London: Ward Lock.

PIROZZOLO, F. J. and RAYNER, K. (1978). 'The neural control of eye movements in acquired and developmental reading disorders'. In: AVAKIAM-WHITAKER, H. and WHITAKER, H. A. (Eds) *Advances in Neurolinguistics and Psycholinguistics.* New York: Academic Press.

PIZZAMIGLIO, L. (1976). 'Cognitive approach to hemispheric dominance'. In: KNIGHTS, R. M. and BAKKER, D. J. (Eds) *The Neuropsychology of Learning Disorders.* Baltimore: University Park Press.

PLATE, E. (1909). 'Vier Fälle von Kongenitaler wortblindheit in einer Familie, *Münch. med. Woch.*, **56**, 1793.

POLLACK, R. H., PTASHNE, R. I. and CARTER, D. J. (1969). 'The effects of age and intelligence on the dark-interval threshold', *Percept. Psychophys.*, **6**, 50–2.

POLLOCK, J. (1975). *Dyslexia. The Problem of Spelling.* London: Helen Arkell Dyslexia Centre.

POLLOCK, J. (1976). 'More about dyslexia', *Preparatory Schools Review*, 25, 2, 9–12.

POLLOCK, J. and WALLER, E. (1978). *The Problems of Sequencing and Orientation.* London: Helen Arkell Dyslexic Centre.

POPHAM, W. J. (1967). *Educational Statistics: Use and Interpretation.* New York: Harper and Row.

PUMFREY, P. D. and NAYLOR, J. (1978). 'The alleviation of psycho-linguistic deficits and some effects on the reading attainments of poor readers', *J. of Research in Reading*, 1, 2, 87–107.

RABINOVITCH, R. D. (1959). 'Reading and learning disabilities'. In: ARIETI, S. (Ed) *American Handbook of Psychiatry*. New York: Basic Books.

RABINOVITCH, R. D. (1968). 'Reading problems in children: definitions and classifications'. In: KEENEY, A. H. and KEENEY, V. T. (Eds) *Dyslexia: Diagnosis and Treatment of Reading Disorders*. St Louis: Mosby & Co.

RABINOVITCH, R. D., DREW, A. L., De JOHN, R., INGRAM, W. and WITHEY, L. A. (1954). 'A research approach to reading retardation', *Assoc. Res. Nerv. Ment. Dis.*, 34, 363–96.

RAGLAND, G. G. (1964). The performance of educable mentally handicapped students of differing reading ability on the ITPA. Doctoral dissertation, University of Virginia.

RANKIN, J. and BARBER, P. (1978). 'Peripheral visual cues during reading', *B.P.S. Bull.*, 31, 196–7.

RAVENETTE, A. T. (1979). 'Specific reading difficulties: appearance and reality', *AEP J.*, 4, 10, 1–12.

RAVENETTE, R. D. (1968). *Dimensions of Reading Difficulties*. Oxford: Pergamon.

RAWSON, M. B. (1968). *Developmental Language Disability*. Baltimore: Johns Hopkins Press.

REBERT and WEXLER (1977) quoted in BEAUMONT, J. G. and RUGG, M. D. (1978). 'Neuropsychological laterality of function and dyslexia: a new hypothesis', *Dyslexia Review*, 1, 1, 18–21.

REED, J. C. (1967). 'Reading achievement as related to differences between WISC verbal and performance IQs', *Child Dev.*, 38, 835–40.

REED, J. C. (1968a). 'The ability deficits of good and poor readers', *J. Learning Disabilities*, 1, 44–9.

REED, J. C. (1968b). 'The ability deficits of good and poor readers', *J. Learning Disabilities*, 2, 134–9.

REED, J. C. (1970). 'The deficits of retarded readers – fact or artifact', *The Reading Teacher*, 23, 347–52.

REHAB (1974). *People with Dyslexia*: Report of a working party. London: British Council for Rehabilitation of the Disabled (under the chairmanship of Dr John Kershaw).

REID, J. F. (1969). 'Dyslexia: a problem of communication', *Educational Research*, 10, 2, 126–33. Reprinted in REID, J. F. and DONALDSON, H. (1977). *Reading: Problems and Practices*. London: Ward Lock Educational.

REID, J. F. (1977). 'The scope of the reading problem'. In: REID, J. F. and DONALDSON, H. *Reading: Problems and Practices*. London: Ward Lock Educational.

REID, J. F. and DONALDSON, H. (1977). *Reading: Problems and Practices*. London: Ward Lock Educational.

REILLY, O. H. (1971). 'Auditory visual integration, sex and reading achievement', *Amer. J. Educ. Psychol.*, **62**, 482–86.

REITAN, R. M. (1964a). In: WARREN, J. R. and AKERT, K. A. (Eds) *Frontal Granular Cortex and Behaviour*. New York: McGraw-Hill.

REITAN, R. M. (1964b). 'Relationships between neurological and psychological variables and their implications for reading instruction'. In: ROBINSON, H. A. (Ed) *Meeting Individual Differences in Reading*. Chicago: University of Chicago Press.

REYNELL, J. (1970). 'Specific learning disorders in pre-school children', *Forward Trends*, **14**, 2, 52–5.

RICHARDSON, G. (1974). 'The Cartesian frame of reference: a structure unifying the description of dyslexia', *J. of Psycholinguistic Research*, **3**, 1, 15–63.

RICHARDSON, J. and BROWN, J. (1978). 'A study of three methods of helping children with reading difficulties', *Reading*, **12**, 2, 10–21.

RICHIE, D. J. and ATHEN, J. L. (1976). 'Auditory retention of non-verbal and verbal sequential stimuli in children with reading disabilities', *J. of Learning Disabilities*, **9**, 5, 321–8.

RIDING, R. J. and PUGH, J. C. (1977). 'Iconic memory and reading performance in nine-year-old children', *Br. J. of Educnl. Psychol.*, **47**, 132–7.

RIZZO, N. D. (1939). 'Studies of visual and auditory memory span with special reference to reading disability', *J. of Exp. Educ.*, **8**, 208–44.

ROBINSON, H. M. and SMITH, H. K. (1962). 'Reading clinic – ten years after', *The Elementary School J.*, **63**, 22–7.

RØNNE, H. (1936). 'Congenital word-blindness in school-children', *Tr. Oph. Soc. U.K.*, **56**, 185–92.

ROSENTHAL, J. H. (1973). 'Recent advances in the neurophysiology of some specific cognitive functions', *Academic Therapy*, **8**, 4, 423–8.

ROSNER, J. (1973). 'Language arts and arithmetic achievement and specifically related perceptual skills', *American Educ. Res. J.*, **10**, 1, 59–68.

ROSNER, J. and SIMON, D. P. (1971). 'The Auditory Analysis Test – an initial report', *J. of Learning Disabilities*, **4**, 384–92.

ROSS, A. O. (1976). *Psychological Aspects of Learning Disabilities and Reading Disorders*. New York: McGraw-Hill.

ROSS, A. O. (1977). 'Learning disability: the unrealized potential', *Book Reviews*, **80**, 4, 805–7.

ROURKE, B. (1974). Brain-behaviour relationships in children with learning disabilities: A research programme. Presented at the Annual Meeting of the American Psychological Association, New Orleans.

ROURKE, B. P. (1976). 'Reading retardation in children: developmental lag or deficit?' In: KNIGHTS, R. M. and BAKKER, D. J. *The Neuropsychology of Learning Disorders*. Baltimore: University Park Press.

ROURKE, B. P. and CZUDNER, G. (1972). 'Age differences in auditory reaction time of "brain-damaged" and normal children under regular and irregular preparatory interval conditions', *J. Exp. Child Psychol.*, 14, 372-9.

ROURKE, B. P. and FINLAYSON, M. A. J. (in press). 'Neurophysiological significance of variations in patterns of academic performance: verbal and visual-spatial abilities', *J. Abnorm. Child Psychol.*

ROURKE, B. P., ORR, R. R. and RIDGLEY, B. A. (1974). 'Neuropsychological abilities of normal and retarded readers', A three-year follow-up. Presented at the meeting of the Canadian Psychological Association, Windsor.

ROZENBERGER, P. B. (1970). 'Visual matching and clinical findings among good and poor readers', *American J. Diseases of Child*, 119, 103-10.

ROZIN, P. and GLEITMAN, L. R. (1977). 'The structure and acquisition of reading, 11. The reading process and the acquisition of the alphabetic principle'. In: REBER, A. S. and SCARBOROUGH, D. L. (Eds) *Towards a Psychology of Reading*. Hillsdale, N.J.: Erlbaum.

RUBIN, R. and BALOW, B. (1971). 'Learning and behaviour disorders: a longitudinal study', *Exceptional Children*, 38, 293-9.

RUBINO, C. A. and MINDEN, H. A. (1971). 'Visual-field restrictions in cases of reading disability', *Perceptual and Motor Skills*, 33, 3 (Part 2), 1215-17.

RUDEL, R. G., DENCKLA, M. A. and SPALTEN, E. (1976). 'Paired associate learning of morse code and braille letter names by dyslexic and normal children', *Cortex*, 12, 61-70.

RUGEL, R. (1974). 'WISC subtest scores of disabled readers: a review with respect to Bannantyne's recategorization', *J. of Learning Disabilities*, 7, 48-55.

RUTTER, M. (1967). 'Psychiatric aspects of multiple handicap: some epidemiological findings'. Paper read at Study Group on Neuropsychiatry, Alfriston.

RUTTER, M., GRAHAM, P. and BIRCH, H. G. (1966). 'Interrelations between choreiform syndrome, reading disability and psychiatric disorder in children of 8 to 11 years', *Developmental Medicine and Child Neurology*, 8, 2, 149-59.

RUTTER, M., TIZARD, J. and WHITMORE, K. (1970). *Education, Health and Behaviour*. London: Longman.

RUTTER, M., YULE, W., TIZARD, J. and GRAHAM, P. (1966). 'Severe reading retardation: its relationship to maladjustment, epilepsy and neurological disorders', in *What is Special Education?* Association for Special Education, pp. 280-94.

RUTTER, M. and YULE, W. (1973). 'Specific reading retardation'. In: MANN, L. and SABATINO, D. (Eds) *The First Review of Special Education*. Buttonwood Farms: JSE Press.

SABATINO, D. A. and HAYDEN, D. L. (1970). 'Information processing behaviours related to learning disabilities and educational mental retardation', *Except. Child*, 37, 21-8.

SAKITT, B. (1976). 'Iconic memory', *Psychol. Rev.*, **83**, 257–76.

SALMON, S. (1978). 'Music against dyslexia', *Music in Education,* **42**, 39, 210–11.

SAMPSON, O. C. (1966). 'Reading and adjustment', *Educ. Res.,* **8**, 184–90.

SAMPSON, O. C. (1975). 'Fifty years of dyslexia. A review of the literature, 1925–1975. I Theory', *Research in Educ.* **14**, 15–32.

SAMPSON, O. C. (1976). 'Fifty years of dyslexia. A review of the literature, 1925–1975. II Practice', *Research in Educ.,* **15**, 39–53.

SAPIR, S. G. and WILSON, B. (1979). *A Professional's Guide to Working with the Learning Disabled Child.* New York: Brunner/Mazel.

SARTAIN, H. W. (1976). 'Instructions for disabled readers', *J. of Learning Disabilities,* **9**, 8.

SATZ, P. (1975). 'Developmental parameters in the lateralization of brain functions'. Presented at the *Boerhaave Conference on Lateralization of Brain Functions,* Leiden, The Netherlands.

SATZ, P. (1976). 'Cerebral dominance and reading disability: an old problem revisited'. In: KNIGHTS, R. M. and BAKKER, D. J. *The Neuropsychology of Learning Disorders.* Baltimore: University Park Press.

SATZ, P. and FRIEL, J. (1974). 'Some predictive antecedents of specific reading disability: a preliminary two year follow up', *J. of Learning Disabilities,* **7**, 7, 437–44.

SATZ, P. and SPARROW, S. (1970). 'Specific developmental dyslexia: a theoretical formulation'. In: BAKKER, D. J. and SATZ, P. (Eds) *Specific Reading Disability: Advances in Theory and Method.* Rotterdam: Rotterdam University Press.

SATZ, P. and VAN NOSTRAND, G. K. (1973). 'Developmental dyslexia: An evaluation of a theory'. In: SATZ, P. and ROSS, J. J. (Eds) *The Disabled Learner: Early Detection and Intervention.* Rotterdam: Rotterdam University Press.

SATZ, P., RARDIN, D. and ROSS, J. (1971). 'An evaluation of a theory of specific developmental dyslexia', *Child Development,* **42**, 2009–21.

SAVIN, H. B. (1972). 'What the child knows about speech when he starts to learn to read'. In: KAVANAGH, J. F. and MATTINGLEY, I. G. (Eds) *Language by Ear and Eye.* Cambridge, Mass: MIT Press.

SAWYER, C. E. and BROWN, B. J. (1977). 'Laterality and intelligence in relation to reading ability', *Educ. Review,* **29**, 81–6.

SAWYER, C. E., LORD, B. and BROWN, B. J. (1979). 'Laterality and intelligence in relation to reading ability: a replication', *Educnl. Rev.,* **31**, 1.

SCHEERER-NEUMANN, G. (1977a). 'Prozessanalyse von Lesestörungen'. In: VOLKER EBEL (Ed) *Legasthenie.* Koblenz: Bundesverband Legasthenie, 63–83.

SCHEERER-NEUMANN, G. (1977b). 'Funktionanalyse des Lesens', *Psychologie in Erziehung und Unterricht,* **24**, 125–35.

SCHEERER-NEUMANN, G. (1978a). 'A functional analysis of reading disability: the utilization of intraword redundancy by good and poor readers'. In: LESGOLD, A. M. and PELLEGRINO, J. W. *Cognitive Psychology and Instruction*. New York: Plenum Press.

SCHEERER-NEUMANN, G. (1978b). Die Ausnutzung der sprachlichen Redundanz bei leseschwachen kindern: I. Nachweis des spezifischen Defizits, zeitschrift für Entwicklungs-psychologie und Pädagogische Psychologie 1, 35–48, **10** (1), 35–48.

SCHILDER, P. (1944). 'Congenital alexia and its relation to optic perception', *J. Genet. Psychol.*, **65**, 67–88.

SCHONELL, F. J. (1942). *Backwardness in Basic Subjects*. Edinburgh: Oliver and Boyd.

SCHUBENZ, S. and BOHMIG, S. (1964). 'Untersuchungen zur Legasthenie: 11' (Research on Dyslexia: 11), *Zeitschrift für Experimentale und Angewandte Psychologie*, **11**, 3, 515–23.

SCHUBENZ, S. and BUCHWALD, R. (1964). 'Untersuchungen zur Legasthenie: 1' (Research on Dyslexia: 1), *Zeitschrift für Experimentale und Angewandte Psychologie*, **11**, 155–68.

SCOTT, S. (1976). 'Dyslexia: a review of the literature', *Dyslexia Rev.*, **15**, 9–13.

SEMMES, J. (1968). 'Hemispheric speculation: a possible clue to mechanisms', *Neuropsychologia*, **6**, 11–26.

SENF, G. M. and FREUNDL, P. C. (1972). 'Sequential auditory and visual memory in learning disabled children'. *Proceedings of the Annual Convention of the American Psychological Association*, **7**, 511–12.

SETH, G. (1973). 'Eye–hand co-ordination and handedness: a developmental study of visuo-motor behaviour in infancy', *Br. J. Educ. Psych.*, **43**, 35–9.

SETH, G. (1975). 'Bilateral asymmetry and behaviour. Introduction', *Irish Journal of Psychol.*, iii, 1, 54–62.

SEYMOUR, P. H. K. and PORPODAS, C. D. (1978). 'Coding of spelling in normal and dyslexic subjects', *Dyslexia Rev.*, **1**, 2,14–15.

SHANKWEILER, D. (1964). 'A study of developmental dyslexia', *Neuropsychol.*, **1**, 267.

SHANKWEILER, D. and LIBERMAN, I. Y. (1972). 'Misreading: a search for causes'. In: KAVANAGH, J. F. and MATTINGLY, I. G. *Language by Ear and by Eye*. Cambridge: MIT Press.

SHANKWEILER, D. and LIBERMAN, I. Y. (1976). 'Exploring the relations between reading and speech'. In: KNIGHTS, R. M. and BAKKER, D. J. (Eds) *The Neuropsychology of Learning Disorders*. Baltimore: University Park Press.

SHAPIRO, D. (1965). *Neurotic Styles*. New York: Basic Books.

SHEARER, E. (1967). 'The long-term effects of remedial education', *Educatnl. Research*, **9**, 3, 219–22.

SHEARER, E. (1968). 'Physical skills and reading backwardness', *Educatnl. Research*, **10**, 3, 197–206.

SHEDD, C. L. (1969). Some exploratory studies on the clinical management of dyslexia. Paper presented at Association for Children with
Learning Difficulties Conference, 1969.

SHEER, D. E. (1976). 'Focused arousal and 40-Hz EEG'. In: KNIGHTS,
R. M. and BAKKER, D. J. (Eds) *The Neuropsychology of Learning
Disorders*. Baltimore: University Park Press.

SHERIDAN, M. D. and PECKHAM, C. S. (1978). 'Follow-up to 16
years of school children who had marked special defects at 7 years',
Child: care, health and development, 4, 145–57.

SHIELDS, D. T. (1973). 'Brain responses to stimuli in disorders of
information processing', *J. of Learning Disabilities*, 6, 7, 501–5.

SILVER, A. A. (1968). 'Diagnostic considerations in children with
reading disability'. In: NATCHEZ, G. (Ed) *Children with Reading
Problems*. New York: Basic Books.

SILVER, A. A. and HAGIN, R. (1960). 'Specific reading disability:
Delineation of the syndrome and relationship to cerebral dominance', *Comparative Psychiat.*, 1, 2, 126–34.

SILVER, A. A. and HAGIN, R. A. (1964). 'Specific reading disability:
follow-up studies', *American J. of Orthopsychiat.*, 34, 95.

SILVER, A. A. and HAGIN, R. A. (1966). 'Maturation of perceptual
functions in children with specific reading disability', *The Reading
Teacher*, 19, 253–9.

SILVER, A. A. and HAGIN, R. A. (1967). 'Specific reading disability:
an approach to diagnosis and treatment', *J. of Spec. Educ.*, 1,
109–18.

SILVER, A. A. and HAGIN, R. A. (1970). 'Visual perception in children
with reading disabilities'. In: YOUNG, F. A. and LINDSLEY, D. B.
(Eds). *Early Experience and Visual Information Processing in Perceptual and Reading Disorders*. Washington, D.C.: National
Academy of Sciences.

SILVER, L. B. (1971). 'Familiar patterns in children with neurologically based learning disabilities', *J. of Learning Disabilities*, 4
(7), 349–58.

SILVERMAN, L. J. and METZ, A. S. (1973). 'Number of pupils with
specific learning disabilities in local public schools in the United
States: Spring 1970', *Ann. N.Y. Acad. Sci.*, 205, 146–57.

SILVERMAN, J. S., FITE, M. and MOSHER, M. M. (1959). 'Clinical
findings in reading disability children', *American J. Orthopsychiat.*,
29, 298.

SIMON, A. and WARD, L. (1978). 'Further doubts about the Frostig
Test of Visual Perception', *Remedial Educ.*, 13 (4), 200–3.

SINGLETON, C. H. (1975). 'The myth of specific developmental
dyslexia. Part 1. History, incidence and diagnosis of the syndrome',
Remedial Educ., 10, 3, 109–13.

SINGLETON, C. H. (1976). 'The myth of specific developmental
dyslexia. Part 2. Aetiology', *Remedial Educ.*, 11, 13–17.

SKLAR, J. H. and SIMMONS, W. W. (1972). 'An EEG experiment
aimed toward identifying dyslexic children', *Nature*, 240, 15
December, pp. 414–16.

SMITH, C. E. and KEOGH, B. K. (1962). 'The group Bender–Gestalt as a reading readiness screening instrument', *Percept. Motor Skills*, 15, 639.

SMITH, D. D. (1978). The influence of modelling on children's oral reading performance. Paper presented at World Congress on Future Special Education: July 1978.

SMITH, D. E. P. and CARRIGAN, P. M. (1959). *The Nature of Reading Disability*. New York: Harcourt Brace.

SMITH, F. (1971). *Understanding Reading: A Psycholinguistic Analysis of Reading and Learning to Read*. New York: Holt, Rinehart and Winston.

SMITH, F. (1973). *Psycholinguistics and Reading*. New York: Holt, Rinehart and Winston.

SMITH, F. (1977). *Understanding Reading: A Psycholinguistic Analysis of Reading and Learning to Read* (2nd ed). New York: Holt, Rinehart and Winston.

SMITH, L. (1950). 'A study of laterality characteristics of retarded readers and reading achievers', *J. Exp. Res.*, 18, 321–9.

SOBOTKA, R. and MAY, J. G. (1977). 'Visual evoked potentials and reaction time in normal and dyslexic children', *Psychophysiology*, 14, 18–24.

SOMMERS, R. and TAYLOR, M. (1972). 'Cerebral speech dominance in language-disordered and normal children', *Cortex*, 8, 224–32.

SPACHE, G. O. (1957). 'Personality patterns of retarded readers', *J. Educ. Res.*, 50, 461.

SPALDING, R. B. and W. T. (1957). *The Writing Road to Reading*. New York: Whiteside and Morrow.

SPARROW, S. S. (1968). Reading disability: a neurological investigation. Unpublished doctoral dissertation, University of Florida.

SPARROW, S. and SATZ, P. (1970). 'Dyslexia, laterality and neuropsychological development'. In: BAKKER, D. J. and SATZ, P. (Eds) *Specific Reading Disability: Advances in Theory and Method*. Rotterdam: Rotterdam University Press.

SPERLING, G. (1960). 'The information available in brief visual presentations', *Psychological Monographs*, 74, 11, entire issue.

SPERLING, S. (1963). 'A model for visual memory tasks', *Hum. Fact.*, 5, 19–31.

SPREEN, O. (1976). 'Neuropsychology of learning disorders: post-conference review'. In: KNIGHTS, R. M. and BAKKER, D. J. *The Neuropsychology of Learning Disorders*. Baltimore: University Park Press.

SPRING, C. (1976). 'Encoding speed and memory span in dyslexic children', *J. of Spec. Educ.*, 10, 1, 35–40.

SPRING, C. and CAPPS, C. (1974). 'Encoding speed, rehearsal, and probed recall of dyslexic boys', *J. of Educnl. Psychol.*, 66, 780–6.

SPRAGUE, R. L. and SLEATOR, E. K. (1976). 'Drugs and dosages: implications for learning disabilities'. In: KNIGHTS, R. M. and BAKKER, D. J. *The Neuropsychology of Learning Disorders*. Baltimore: University Park Press.

SROUFE, L. A., SONIES, B. C., WEST, W. D. and WRIGHT, F. S. (1973). 'Anticipatory heart rate deceleration and reaction time in children with and without referral for learning disability', *Child Dev.*, 44, 267–75.

STANGVIK, G. (1978). 'Learning disabilities in Norway', *Rem. Educ.*, 13, 1, 26–37.

STANLEY, G. (1975). 'Visual memory processes in dyslexia'. In: DEUTSCH, D. and DEUTSCH, S. (Eds) *Short-Term Memory*. London: Academic Press.

STANLEY, G. (1975). 'Two part stimulus integration and specific reading disability', *Perceptual and Motor Skills*, 41, 873–4.

STANLEY, G. (1976). 'The processing of digits by children with specific reading disability (dyslexia)', *Br. J. of Educ. Psych.*, 46, 81–4.

STANLEY, G. and HALL, R. (1973). 'A comparison of dyslexics and normals in recalling letter arrays after brief presentation', *Br. J. of Educ. Psych.*, 43, 301–4.

STANLEY, G. and MALLOY, M. (1975). 'Retinal and visual information storage', *Acta Psychologia*, 39, 283–8.

STEINER, R., WIENER, M. and CROMER, W. (1971). 'Comprehension training and identification for poor and good readers', *J. Educ. Psychol.*, 62, 506–13.

STEINHEISER, R. and GUTHRIE, J. T. (1977). 'Perceptual and linguistic processing of letters and words by normal and disabled readers', *J. of Reading Behaviour*, 9, 3, 217–25.

STEPHENS, W. E., CUNNINGHAM, E. S. and STIGLER, B. J. (1967). 'Reading readiness and eye/hand preference patterns in first grade children', *Except. Children*, 33, 7, 481–90.

STEVENS, H. A. and HEBER, R. (1965). *Mental Retardation: A Review of Research*. Chicago: University of Chicago Press.

STEVENS, J. R., SACHDEV, K. and MILSTEIN, V. (1968). 'Behaviour disorders of childhood and the electroencephalogram', *Arch. Neurol.*, 18, 160–77.

STEWART, M. (1971). 'Use of drugs to help children with learning problems'. In: HARSTEIN, J. *Current Concepts in Dyslexia*. St Louis: C. V. Mosby and Co.

STEWART, R. S. (1950). 'Personality maladjustment and reading achievement', *American J. Orthopsychiat.*, 20, 410.

STOTT, D. (1971). *Behavioural Aspects of Learning Disabilities: Assessment and Remediation*. Washington: American Psychological Association, Experimental Publication System, 11, 1–44.

STOTT, D. H. (1978). *Helping Children with Learning Difficulties*. London: Ward Lock Education.

STRANG, R. (1964). *Diagnostic Teaching of Reading*. New York: McGraw-Hill.

STRANG, R. (1969). *Diagnostic Teaching of Reading* (2nd edn). New York: McGraw-Hill.

STRAUS, E. W. *et al.* (1971). 'A phenomenological approach to dyslexia', *J. of Phenomenogical Psychol.*, 1, 2, 225–35.

STREET, J. (1977). 'Report on the one day conference on the medical aspects of dyslexia', *Dyslexia Rev.*, No. 17, unnumbered.

STRICKLAND, R. C. (1962). 'The language of elementary school children: its relationship to the language of reading textbooks and the quality of reading of selected children', *Bull. of the School of Educ.*, Indiana University, 38, 4.

SWANSON, H. L. (1977). 'Non-verbal visual short-term memory as a function of age and dimensionality in learning disabled children', *Child Dev.*, 48, 51–5.

SYKES, D. H. (1969). Sustained attention in hyperactive children. Unpublished doctoral dissertation. McGill University.

SYKES, D. H., DOUGLAS, V. I. and MORGENSTERN, G. (1973). 'Sustained attention in hyperactive children', *J. Child Psychol. Psychiatry*, 14, 213–20.

SYVÄLAHTI, R. (1976). 'Reading–writing disabilities in Finland'. In: TARNOPOL, L. and TARNOPOL, M. *Reading Disabilities: an International Perspective*. Baltimore: University Park Press.

TALLAL, P. (1976). 'Auditory perceptual factors in language and learning disabilities'. In: KNIGHTS, R. M. and BAKKER, D. J. *The Neuropsychology of Learning Disorders*. Baltimore: University Park Press.

TALLAL, P. (in press). 'Implications of speech perceptual research for clinical populations'. In: KAVANAUGH, J. and JENKINS, J. (Eds) *Language Research in the Laboratory, Clinic and Classroom*.

TAMKIN, A. S. (1960). 'Survey of educational disability in emotionally disturbed children', *J. of Educnl. Res.*, 54, 67–9.

TANSLEY, A. E. (1967). *Reading and Remedial Reading*. London: Routledge and Kegan Paul.

TARNOPOL, L. and TARNOPOL, M. (1975). 'Program for educationally handicapped children in California', *Danish J. School Psychol.*

TARNOPOL, L. and TARNOPOL, M. (1976a). *Reading Disabilities: An International Perspective*. Baltimore: University Park Press.

TARNOPOL, L. and TARNOPOL, M. (1976b). 'Reading and learning problems worldwide'. In: TARNOPOL, L. and TARNOPOL, M. *Reading Disabilities: an International Perspective*. Baltimore: University Park Press.

TARVER, S. and HALLAHAN, D. (1974). 'Attention to deficits in children with learning disabilities: A review', *J. Learning Disabilities*, 7, 36–45.

TAYLOR, D. C. (1969). 'Differential rates of cerebral maturation between sexes and between hemispheres', *The Lancet*, 2, 140–2.

TAYLOR STRATTEN (1953). Quoted by GOLDBERG, H. K. and SCHIFFMAN, G. B. (1972). *Dyslexia: Problems of Reading Disabilities*. New York: Grune and Stratton, p. 57.

THACKRAY, D. V. (1965). 'The relationship between reading readiness and reading progress', *Br. J. of Educ. Psychol.*, 35, 252–4.

THOMAS, H. B. G. (1973). 'Genetic and psychodynamic aspects of developmental dyslexia: a cybernetic approach', *Journal of Learning Disabilities*, 6, 1, 30–40.

THOMAS, M. M. (1977). 'Two schools', *Dyslexia Rev.*, 18, 20–2.

THOMPSON, A. (1979). 'A new look at adolescent learning problems', *School Psychol. International*, 1, 1, 22–4.

THOMSON, M. (1975). 'Laterality and reading attainment', *Br. J. Educ. Psych.*, 45, 3, 317–21.

THOMSON, M. E. (1976). 'A comparison of laterality effects in dyslexics and controls using verbal dichotic listening tasks', *Neuropsychologia*, 14, 243–6.

THOMSON, M. E. (1978). 'A psycholinguistic analysis of reading errors made by dyslexics and normal readers', *J. of Research in Reading*, 1, 1, 7–20.

THOMSON, M. E. (1979a). 'A Bayesian model for the identification of the disabled reader'. In: NEWTON, M. J., THOMSON, M. E. and RICHARDS, I. L. (Eds) *Readings in Dyslexia*. Wisbech: Learning Development Aids.

THOMSON, M. E. (1979b). 'Diagnosing dyslexia in the clinic: an illustrative study'. In: NEWTON, M. J., THOMSON, M. E. and RICHARDS, I. L. (Eds) *Readings in Dyslexia*. Wisbech: Learning Development Aids.

THOMSON, M. E. (1979c). 'Use of sequential redundancy in the visual identification of words in dyslexics and controls'. In: NEWTON, M. J., THOMSON, M. E., RICHARDS, I. L. *Readings in Dyslexia*. Wisbech: Learning Development Aids.

THOMSON, M. E. and GRANT, S. E. (1979). 'The WISC subtest profile of the dyslexic child'. In: NEWTON, M. J., THOMSON, M. E. and RICHARDS, I. L. (Eds) *Readings in Dyslexia*. Wisbech: Learning Development Aids.

THOMSON, M. E. and NEWTON, M. J. (1979). 'A concurrent validity study on the Aston Index'. In: NEWTON, M. J., THOMSON, M. E. and RICHARDS, I. L. *Readings in Dyslexia*. Wisbech: Learning Development Aids.

THOMSON, M. E. and WILSHER, C. W. (1978). 'Some aspects of memory in dyslexics and controls', *Dyslexia Rev.*, 1, 2, 8–10.

THORNDIKE, R. L. (1963). *The Concepts of Over- and Underachievement*. New York: Teachers College.

THORNDIKE, R. L. (1973). 'Reading comprehension education in fifteen countries', *International Studies in Evaluation*. III. Almqvist and Wiksell.

THORNDIKE, R. L. and HAGEN, E. P. (1977). *Measurement and Evaluation in Psychology and Education*. New York: Wiley (4th ed.).

TINKER, K. J. (1965). 'The role of laterality in reading disability'. In: FIGUREL, J. A. (Ed) *Reading and Enquiry*. Newark, Delaware: International Reading Association.

TIZARD REPORT (1972) GREAT BRITAIN. See under DEPARTMENT OF EDUCATION AND SCIENCE.

TOPPING, K. J. (1977). 'An evaluation of the long-term effects of remedial reading', *Remedial Education*, 12, 2, 84–6.

TORGESEN, J. and GOLDMAN, T. (1977). 'Verbal rehearsal and short-term memory in reading disabled children', *Child Dev.*, **48**, 56–60.

TREISMAN, A., RUSSELL, R. and GREEN, J. (1975). 'Brief visual storage of shape and movement'. In: RABBITT, P. M. A. and DORNIC, S. (Eds) *Attention and Performance V*. London: Academic Press.

TREVARTHEN, C. B. (1962). 'Double visual learning in split-brain monkeys', *Science, N.Y.*, **136**, 258–9.

TREVOR, R. (1978). *Reading: Suggestions for Teaching Children with Reading Difficulties in Primary and Secondary Schools*. Wellington: Department of Education.

TRIESCHMAN, R. B. (1966). The relationship of undifferentiated handedness and perceptual development in children with reading problems. Unpublished doctoral dissertation, University of Minnesota.

TRIESCHMAN, R. B. (1968). 'Undifferentiated handedness and perceptual development in children with reading problems', *Perceptual and Motor Skills*, **27**, 1123–34.

TRITES, R. L. and FIEDOROWICZ, C. (1976). 'Follow-up study of children with specific (or primary) reading disability'. In: KNIGHTS, R. M. and BAKKER, D. J. (Eds) *The Neuropsychology of Learning Disorders*. Baltimore: University Park Press.

TRUSSELL, E. M. (1969). 'The relation of performance of selected physical skills to perceptual aspects of reading readiness in elementary school children', *Res. Quarterly*, **40**, 2, 383–90.

ULLMAN, C. A. (1969). 'Prevalence of reading disability as a function of the measure used', *J. of Learning Disabilities*, **2**, 11, 556–8.

UPSON, P. G. (1968). 'The psychodynamics of reading disability', *Br. J. Project. Psychol.*, **13**, 15.

VALTIN, R. (1970). *Legasthenie – Theorien und Untersuchungen*. Weinheim: Beltz, 3rd ed. 1974.

VALTIN, R. (1972). *Empirische Untersuchungen zur Legasthenie*. Hanover: Schroedel.

VALTIN, R. (1973). 'Report of research on dyslexia in children'. Paper presented at the Annual Convention of the International Reading Association, Denver. (ERIC Document Reproduction Service.)

VALTIN, R. (1978). 'Reading disabilities and the problem of subtypes'. Paper presented at the World Congress of the International Reading Association, Hamburg.

VALTIN, R. (1978/9). 'Dyslexia: deficit in reading or deficit in research', *Reading Res. Quarterly*, **2**, XIV, 201–21.

VANDE VOORT, L., SENF, G. M. and BENTON, A. L. (1972). 'Development of audiovisual integration in normal and retarded readers', *Child Dev.*, **44**, 1260–72.

VANDE VOORT, L. and SENF, G. M. (1973). 'Audiovisual integration in retarded readers', *J. of Learning Disabilities*, **6**, 3, 170–9.

320   *Children With Specific Learning Difficulties*

VAN MEEL, J. M., VLEK, C. A. J. and BRUIJEL, R. M. (1970). 'Some characteristics of visual information-processing in children with learning difficulties'. In: BAKKER, D. J. and SATZ, P. (Eds) *Specific Reading Disability*. Rotterdam: Rotterdam University Press.

VELLUTINO, F. R. (1979a). 'The validity of perceptual deficit explanations of reading disability: a reply to Fletcher and Satz', *J. of Learning Disabilities*, 12, 3, 160-7.

VELLUTINO, F. R. (1979b). *Dyslexia: Theory and Research*. Massachusetts Inst. of Technology.

VELLUTINO, F. R. and CONNOLLY, C. (1971). 'The training of paraprofessionals as remedial reading assistants in an inner-city school', *The Reading Teacher*, 24, 506-12.

VELLUTINO, F. R., BENTLEY, W. and PHILLIPS, F. (1978). 'Inter- versus intra-hemispheric learning in disabled and normal readers', *Developmental Medicine and Child Neurology*, 20, 71-80.

VELLUTINO, F. R., HARDING, C. J., PHILLIPS, F. and STEGER, J. A. (1975). 'Differential transfer in poor and normal readers', *J. of Genetic Psychology*, 126, 3-18.

VELLUTINO, F. R., PRUZEK, R., STEGER, J. A. and MESHOULAM, U. (1973). 'Immediate visual recall in poor and normal readers as a function of orthographic-linguistic familiarity', *Cortex*, 9, 368-84.

VELLUTINO, F. R., SMITH, H., STEGER, J. A. and KAMAN, M. (1975). 'Reading disability: Age differences and the perceptual deficit hypothesis', *Child Dev.*, 46, 487-93.

VELLUTINO, F. R., STEGER, J. A., KAMAN, M. and De SETTO, L. (1975). 'Visual form perception in deficient and normal readers as a function of age and orthographic linguistic familiarity', *Cortex*, 11, 22-30.

VELLUTINO, F. R., STEGER, J. A., De SETTO, L. and PHILLIPS, F. (1975). 'Immediate and delayed recognition of visual stimuli in poor and normal readers', *J. of Exp. Child Psychol.*, 19, 2, 223-32.

VELLUTINO, F. R., STEGER, J. A., MOYER, S. C., HARDING, C. J. and NILES, J. A. (1977). 'Has the perceptual deficit hypothesis led us astray?', *J. Learning Disabilities*, 10, 6, 375-85.

VERNON, M. D. (1957). *Backwardness in Reading*. London: Cambridge University Press.

VERNON, M. D. (1971). *Reading and its Difficulties*. Cambridge: Cambridge University Press.

VERNON, M. D. (1975). 'Comments on "Towards a new theory of dyslexia" ', *Dyslexia Rev.*, 14, 21-2.

VERNON, M. D. (1977). 'Deficiencies in dyslexia', *Dyslexia Rev.*, No. 17, unnumbered.

VERNON, M. D. (1978). 'A note on hemispheric lateralization and dyslexia', *Dyslexia Rev.*, 1, 2, 15-16.

VERNON, M. D. (1979). 'Variability in reading retardation', *Br. J. of Psychol.*, 70, 1, 7-16.

VERNON, P. E. (1965). 'Environmental handicaps and intellectual development', *Br. J. Educ. Psychol.*, 35, 9, 117.
VERNON, P. E. (1969). *Intelligence and the Cultural Environment.* London: Methuen.
VERNON, P. E. (1979). 'Effects of perinatal and other constitutional factors on intelligence', *Ed. Rev.*, 31, 2, 141-8.
VIK, G. H. (1976). 'Reading disabilities in Norwegian elementary grades'. In: TARNOPOL, L. and TARNOPOL, M. *Reading Disabilities: an International Perspective.* Baltimore: University Park Press.
VOGEL, S. A. (1974). 'Syntactic abilities in normal and dyslexic children', *J. of Learning Disabilities*, 7, 2, 103-9.
VOGEL, S. A. (1976). 'Assessment of morphological ability in good and poor readers'. Paper presented at the Annual International Convention, The Council for Exceptional Children, Chicago, Illinois, 4-9th April. (ERIC Document No. ED 122 501.)
WADE, B. and WEDELL, K. (Eds) (1974). *Spelling: Task and Learner.* Birmingham: University of Birmingham.
WALLBROWN, F. H., HUELSMAN, C. B., BLAHA, J. and WALL-BROWN, J. D. (1975). 'A further test of Myklebust's cognitive structure hypotheses for reading disabled children', *Psychology in the Schools*, XII, 2, 176-81.
WALLER, E. (1978). *Dyslexia: the Problem of Handwriting.* Helen Arkell Dyslexia Centre.
WALMSLEY, S. (1970). 'Training programmes for related difficulties'. In: FRANKLIN, A. and NAIDOO, S. (Eds) *Assessment and Teaching of Dyslexic Children.* London: Invalid Children's Aid Association.
WALSH, D. (1978). 'Specific learning disability: problems'. *Set 78*, 2, Item 14. (New Zealand Council for Education Research.)
WALSH (1976), quoted by WALSH, D. F. (1978). *Project Child: Incidence Survey.* An unpublished report. Wellington: New Zealand Council for Educational Research.
WALSH, D. F. (1978). *Project Child: Incidence Survey.* Wellington: New Zealand Council for Educational Research.
WALTON, D. (1975). 'The relationship between short-term memory capacity and intermediate reading skills', *Cambridge J. of Educ.*, 5, 3, 125-30.
WARNOCK REPORT (1978). See under COMMITTEE OF ENQUIRY INTO THE EDUCATION OF HANDICAPPED CHILDREN AND YOUNG PEOPLE.
WARRINGTON, E. K. (1967). 'The incidence of verbal disability associated with retardation in reading', *Neuropsychologia*, 5, 175-9.
WAUGH, N. C. and NORMAN, D. A. (1965). 'Primary memory', *Psychol. Rev.*, 72, 89-104.
WEDELL, K. (1968). 'Perceptual-motor difficulties', *Special Educ.*, 57, 4, 25-30.

WEDELL, K. (1973). *Learning and Perceptuo-Motor Disabilities in Children*. London: Wiley.

WEDELL, K. (1977). 'Perceptual deficiency and specific reading retardation', *J. of Child Psychology and Psychiatry*, 18, 191–4.

WEINER, M. and CROMER, W. (1967). 'Reading and reading difficulty: a conceptual analysis', *Harvard Educational Rev.*, 37, 4, 620–43.

WEISS, G., MINDE, K., WERRY, J. S., DOUGLAS, V. I. and NEMETH, E. (1971). 'Studies on the hyperactive child; a five-year follow-up', *Arch. Gen. Psychiat.*, 24, 409–14.

WELSANDT, R. F. and MEYER, P. A. (1974). 'Visual masking, mental age, and retardation', *J. of Experimental Child Psychol.*, 18, 512–19.

WELSANDT, R. F., ZUPNICK, J. J. and MEYER, P. A. (1973). 'Age effects in backward visual masking', *J. of Experimental Child Psychol.*, 15, 454–61.

WENDON, L. (1970). 'Decoding for dyslexia', *Remedial Educ.*, 5, 2, 95–8.

WEPMAN, J. M. (1960). 'Auditory discrimination, speech and reading', *The Elementary School J.*, 9, 325–33.

WEPMAN, J. M. (1962). 'Dyslexia: its relationship to language acquisition and concept formation'. In: MONEY, J. (Ed) *Reading Disability*. Baltimore: Johns Hopkins Press.

WESCHLER, D. and HAGIN, R. A. (1964). 'The problem of axial rotation in reading disability', *Perceptual and Motor Skills*, 19, 319–26.

WESTWOOD, P. (1972). 'Auditory skills and remedial progress', *Remedial Education*, 7, 1.

WHEELER, T. J., WATKINS, E. J. and McLAUGHLIN, S. P. (1977). 'Reading retardation and cross-laterality in relation to short-term information processing tasks', *Br. J. Educ. Psych.*, 47, 126–31.

WHIPPLE, C. I. (1965). Discrimination and perceptual learning in the retarded reader. Unpublished doctoral dissertation, University of Kentucky.

WHIPPLE, C. I. and KODMAN, F. Jr (1969). 'A study of discrimination and perceptual learning with retarded readers', *J. of Educnl. Psychol.*, 60, 1, 1–5.

WHITE, R. W. (1959). 'Motivation reconsidered: the concept of competence', *Psychological Rev.*, 66, 297–333.

WHITTEY, P. A. and KOPEL, D. D. (1936). 'Factors associated with the etiology of reading disability', *J. Educ. Res.*, 29, 449–59.

WIEDERHOLT, J. L. (1978). 'Review of the Illinois Test of Psycholinguistic Abilities'. In: BUROS, O. K. (Ed) *The Eighth Mental Measurements Yearbook*. New Jersey: Gryphon Press.

WIENER, J., BARNSLEY, R. H. and RABINOVITCH, M. S. (1970). 'Serial order ability in good and poor readers', *Canadian J. of Behavioural Science*, 2, 116, 123.

WIIG, E. H. and SEMEL, E. M. (1976). 'Productive language abilities in learning disabled adolescents', *J. of Learning Disabilities,* **8,** 578-86.

WIIG, E. H., SEMEL, M. S. and CROUSE, M. B. (1973). 'The use of English morphology by high-risk and learning disabled children', *J. of Learning Disabilities,* **6,** 454-65.

WISBEY, A. (1977). 'Can music help children to read and write?', *Psychol. Today,* **3,** 34-7.

WISEMAN, S. (1964). *Education and Environment.* Manchester: Manchester University Press.

WISSINK (1972), as quoted in WALSH, D. (1978). *Project Child: Incidence Survey.* An unpublished report. Wellington, New Zealand: New Zealand Council for Educational Research.

WITELSON, S. (1976). 'Sex and the single hemisphere: specialization of the right hemisphere for spatial processing', *Science,* **193,** 425-7.

WITELSON, S. (1977a). 'Neural and cognitive correlates of developmental dyslexia: age and sex differences'. In: SHAGASS, C., GERSHON, S. and FRIEDHOFF, A. (Eds) *Psychopathology and Brain Dysfunction.* New York: Raven Press.

WITELSON, S. F. (1977b). 'Developmental dyslexia: two right hemispheres and none left', *Science,* **195,** 309-11.

WITELSON, S. F. (1977c). 'Dyslexia: A hemispheric explanation', *Science News,* **3,** 4.

WITELSON, S. and RABINOVITCH, M. (1972). 'Hemispheric speech lateralization in children with auditory-linguistic deficits', *Cortex,* **8,** 412-26.

WITKIN, H. A. (1965). 'Psychological differentiation and forms of pathology', *J. of Abnorm. Psychol.,* **70,** 5.

WITKIN, H. A., DYK, R. B., FATERSON, H. F., GOODENOUGH, D. R. and KARP, S. A. (1962). *Psychological Differentiation: Studies of Development.* New York: Wiley.

WITKIN, H. A., GOODENOUGH, D. and KARP, S. (1967). 'Stability of cognitive style from childhood to young adulthood', *J. Personal-Soc. Psychol.,* **7,** 291-300.

WOLF, A. G. (1970). 'The Gillingham–Stillman Programme'. In: FRANKLIN, A. W. and NAIDOO, S. *Assessment and Teaching of Dyslexic Children.* London: Invalid Children's Aid Association, 82-96.

WRIGHT, L. S. (1974). 'Conduct problem or learning disability', *J. of Spec. Educ.,* **8,** 4, 331-6.

YENI-KOMSHIAN, G. H., ISENBERG, S. and GOLDBERG, H. (1975). 'Cerebral dominance and reading disability: Left visual field deficit in poor readers', *Neuropsychologia,* **13,** 83-94.

YULE, W. (1973). 'Differential prognosis of reading backwardness and specific reading retardation', *Br. J. of Educ. Psychol.,* **43,** 244-8.

YULE, W. (1976). 'Dyslexia', *Psychol. Medicine,* **6,** 2, 165-7.

YULE, W. and RUTTER, M. (1976). 'Epidemiology and social implications of specific reading retardation'. In: KNIGHTS, R. M. and BAKKER, D. J. (Eds) *The Neuropsychology of Learning Disorders*. Baltimore: University Park Press.

YULE, W., RUTTER, M., BERGER, M. and THOMPSON, J. (1974). 'Over- and under-achievement in reading: distribution in the general population', *Br. J. of Educnl. Psychol.*, 44, 1, 1–12.

ZAIDEL, E. (1977). 'Unilateral auditory comprehension in The Token Test following cerebral, commisurotomy and hemispherectomy', *Neuropsychologia*, 15, 1–16.

ZANGWILL, O. L. (1960). *Cerebral Dominance and its Relation to Psychological Function*. Edinburgh: Oliver and Boyd.

ZANGWILL, O. L. (1962). 'Dyslexia in relation to cerebral dominance'. In: MONEY, J. (Ed) *Reading Disability*. Baltimore: Johns Hopkins Press.

ZANGWILL, O. L. (1976). 'Thought and Brain', *Br. J. Psych.*, 67, 3, 301–14.

ZANGWILL, O. L. and BLAKEMORE, C. (1972). 'Dyslexic: reversal of eye-movements during reading', *Neuropsychologia*, 10, 371–3.

ZIMMERMAN, I. L. and ALLEBRAND, G. N. (1965). 'Personality characteristics and attitudes towards achievement of good and poor readers', *J. Educ. Res.*, 59, 28.

ZURIF, E. and CARSON, G. (1970). 'Dyslexia in relation to cerebral dominance and temporal analysis', *Neuropsychologia*, 8, 351–61.

Index

Index of Researchers